S0-ANE-195

THE SECRET POW DIARY OF WALTER J. HINKLE

The Secret POW Diary of Walter J. Hinkle

Life in Japanese Captivity during WWII

Researched and Edited by
J. Forrest Pollard

SCHIFFER MILITARY
4880 Lower Valley Road   Atglen, PA 19310

Designed by J. Forrest Pollard
Type set in Minion Pro

ISBN: 978-0-7643-6350-4
Printed in Serbia

Published by Schiffer Publishing, Ltd.
4880 Lower Valley Road
Atglen, PA 19310
Phone: (610) 593-1777; Fax: (610) 593-2002
Email: Info@schifferbooks.com
Web: www.schifferbooks.com

For our complete selection of fine books on this and related subjects, please visit our website at www.schifferbooks.com. You may also write for a free catalog.

Schiffer Publishing's titles are available at special discounts for bulk purchases for sales promotions or premiums. Special editions, including personalized covers, corporate imprints, and excerpts, can be created in large quantities for special needs. For more information, contact the publisher.

We are always looking for people to write books on new and related subjects. If you have an idea for a book, please contact us at proposals@schifferbooks.com.

For my sons, Ross and Dean

CONTENTS

INTRODUCTION

This book preserves the diary of Lieutenant Walter J. Hinkle along with firsthand accounts from others who are mentioned in his writing. The diary begins in 1941 as he prepared for duty in the Philippines. The University of Michigan ROTC graduate was one of many military men sent to reinforce the former US territory when relations with Japan soured.

After Japan attacked the Philippines on December 8, 1941, Hinkle was wounded on a night mission and taken to a hospital for surgery.

When the Philippines fell in May 1942, Hinkle became a prisoner of war at the Davao Penal Colony, where his wound refused to heal and his right leg was amputated below the knee.

As a bedridden invalid, Hinkle suffered from scurvy, malaria, beri-beri, and starvation. Despite these afflictions, he wrote about his life as a prisoner of the Japanese.

After filling two bound volumes, paper grew scarce, and he wrote upon whatever scraps that he could find. To prevent the ever-growing diary from being confiscated by camp guards, he concealed it within a false compartment in his wooden leg.

The diary ends in February 1945 after 1,061 days—making Hinkle one of the longest-held prisoners of the Pacific War.

Historical Setting
MacArthur Prepares

When Japan invaded French Indochina in 1940, the defense of the Philippines became a US military priority. Japan might seize the Philippines as a base from which to target the Netherlands East Indies for its wartime assets: oil, rubber, and tin.

The commonwealth of the Philippines, however, had a weak and poorly trained army. To strengthen militarily, they merged with US armed forces stationed in the Philippines to create the United States Armed Forces in the Far East (USAFFE), with General Douglas MacArthur as commander.

In November, when diplomatic negotiations crumbled with Japan, MacArthur's headquarters organized these USAFFE tactical commands: the North Luzon, South Luzon, and Visayan-Mindanao Force—and prepared them for the coming war.

The Pacific War Begins

Japanese planes attacked the American Fleet anchored at Pearl Harbor at 2:30 a.m., December 8, 1941, Philippine standard time. Ten hours later, Japanese aircraft attacked the Philippines and the Imperial 14th Army, under the Command of General Masaharu Homma, prepared to invade Luzon by sea from Formosa.

Homma put his 14th Army ashore at Lingayen Gulf on December 22, followed by a smaller force landing at Lamon Bay. When the successful landings dashed hopes for an American-Filipino victory, MacArthur notified his subordinate commanders that War Plan Orange-3 was being activated.[1]

War Plan Orange-3

In this contingency, USAFFE on Luzon would retreat to the Bataan Peninsula and Corregidor Island and hold out until the US Pacific Fleet could bring relief. Their mission was to defend the entrance to Manila Bay, the finest harbor in the Far East, and deny its use to the Japanese navy.

To make a long-term defense possible, Bataan warehouses had to be stocked with supplies to sustain 43,000 men for up to six months. MacArthur, however, had already scattered supplies to support active combat troops on Luzon, making it impossible for sufficient stores of food, equipment, supplies, and quinine to be brought to the peninsula in time. As a result, the plan was doomed to failure.

Battle for Bataan

The withdrawal to Bataan proceeded quickly, and a battle line was organized across the peninsula between the municipalities of Mabatang and Mauban in January 1942, beginning the most intense phase of the Japanese invasion.

When USAFFE's defense began crumbling in March, President Roosevelt grew concerned for MacArthur's safety; he would not have his highest-ranking military expert on Asia be taken prisoner. Roosevelt ordered MacArthur to leave for Australia, where he would assume command of the South West Pacific Area.

MacArthur's second in command, General Jonathan Wainwright, resumed the Bataan defense, which appeared hopeless unless help arrived soon.

By the first of April, after months of combat and living on half rations, fewer than half of his men on Bataan were "combat effective" or able, by definition, to walk 100 yards without staggering and still have the strength to fire his weapon.

With supplies exhausted and men suffering from hunger, disease, and fatigue, Wainwright's frontline commander, General Edward P. King, took it upon himself to surrender Bataan on April 9, rather than see his men slaughtered.

---

1 A color-coded prewar scenario identifying Japan as an opponent in a future conflict. Leading up to the invasion, MacArthur rejected the Orange-3 defensive strategy and asserted his aggressive plan to hold the entire archipelago, harass Japanese communications, mount air raids against nearby enemy bases on Formosa, and work with the Netherlands and Great Britain to fend off the Japanese. It was a dubious plan that underestimated the strength of the Japanese and overestimated his own situation. His force was undertrained and poorly supplied. His air force consisted of a few dozen Boeing B-17 Bombers, one hundred Curtiss P-40 Tomahawk fighters, and scores of outdated planes.

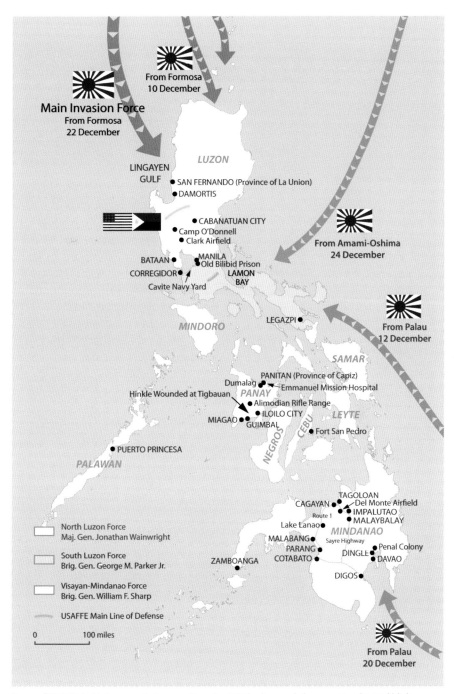

A map of USAFFE tactical commands, Japanese December 1941 landings, and places mentioned in Hinkle's diary

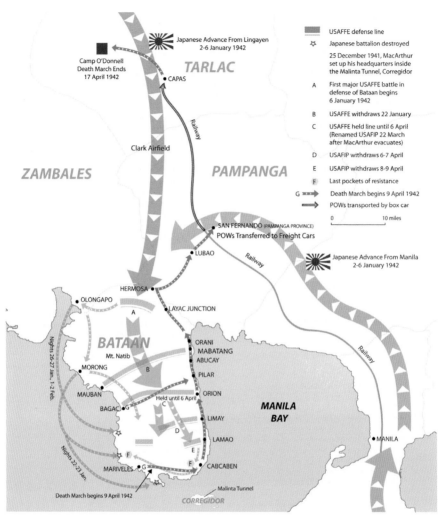

The Bataan Peninsula.

Bataan Death March

General Homma was now free to focus on Corregidor, and the removal of prisoners from Bataan became the responsibility of his transportation officer, Major General Yoshikata Kawane. His plan called for prison-ers to be marched 65 miles to San Fernando, packed into freight cars, and taken by rail to Camp O'Donnell, a prewar American training area. The plan, however, had fatal flaws: it failed to provide for 80,000 prison-ers instead of 25,000 as expected. The plan also relied on guards who fought and suffered in the Battle for

Bataan—they had nothing but disgust and hatred for these captives.

When the march began, it was under a blistering sun. Those who fell behind or attempted to obtain food or drink along the way were brutalized or killed by their guards. Prisoners with malaria or dysentery were denied medical treatment. Anyone caught with Japanese money in their pockets was shot on the presumption that it had been looted from the corpses of Japanese soldiers.

Of the 66,000 Filipino and 10,000 American soldiers who began the march, approximately 9,000 Filipinos and 650 Americans perished before reaching Camp O'Donnell. The death rate at O'Donnell was also high; approximately 26,000 Filipinos and 1,500 Americans died before the Americans were moved to a new camp near Cabanatuan City in June.

In November, when 1,000 Cabanatuan prisoners arrived by sea at the Davao Penal Colony on Mindanao, Hinkle, who was already there, witnessed their pitiful arrival in his diary.

Homma's Southern Campaign and Hinkle's Place in the Puzzle

While the men from Cabanatuan had been fighting on Bataan, Hinkle remained relatively unaffected by the war. As long as the battle for the Philippines was fought on Luzon, the Visayas[2] and Mindanao remained safe from invasion.

Homma had insufficient troops to conduct operations in the North and South Philippines simultaneously, except for a foothold at Davao City on Mindanao. The Miura Detachment[3] arrived at Davao City in late December to conduct limited operations until the Bataan campaign drew to a close. Only then would Homma deploy the Kawaguchi and Kawamura Detachments to conquer the Visayas, and together all three detachments would take the island of Mindanao.

Opposition in the South was led by General William F. Sharp, the Visayan-Mindanao Force commander. His orders were to defend the Philippines south of Luzon. If organized resistance proved impossible, he would split his force into guerrilla groups and fight from bases hidden within the interior of each island.

Sharp's ability to defend the South was marred by a shortage of weapons, supplies, and enough Filipino recruits who were trained to fight effectively. For this reason, in August, Lieutenant Hinkle, fifty other officers, and a number of NCOs from the 31st Infantry on Luzon were detached to the 63rd Infantry as instructors with the Philippine army on Panay.

In mid-December, as the fighting on Luzon raged, Panay got its first bombing raid, which set the islanders on edge. Then a rumor circulated that 3,000 Japanese troops were landing near Iloilo City, and the garrison commander called for a US officer to authenticate the claim. Hinkle spoke

---

2   Cebu, Panay, Negros, Leyte, and Samar islands.

3   Japanese units were identified by their commander's name. In this case, Lt. Colonel Toshio Miura.

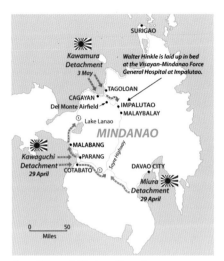

General Homma's Mindanao Campaign.

up and said, "I'd go," and traveled at night to his destination. At a checkpoint he was mysteriously shot in the ankle by someone lurking in the shadows. Despite the searing pain, Hinkle carried out his orders and discovered the rumor to be false.

After dispatching the news to headquarters, he received medical treatment at the IloIlo Mission hospital. During his recuperation, Hinkle kept abreast of the latest news. On April 9 he wrote in his diary with alarm, "Bataan has fallen! Jeez — I gotta get out of here, quick, or I'll never see the folks again."

Days later, Hinkle traveled to Del Monte airfield on Mindanao with orders to catch a plane for Australia. General Sharp angrily denied the orders and sent Hinkle packing to Force General Hospital at Impalutao.

Meanwhile, Homma began the Visayan campaign. One of the landings took place at Iloilo City, where Hinkle had been a hospital patient days earlier. When strategic points on Cebu and Panay were in Japanese hands, the Kawaguchi and Kawamura Detachments boarded ships and sailed for Mindanao island.

On April 29, the Kawaguchi Detachment landed at Cotabato and Parang, and a smaller contingent headed east to rendezvous with Colonel Miura's troops.

On May 3, the Kawamura Detachment came ashore at Cagayan and Tagoloan on Mindanao's northern coast.

General Sharp tried to halt their advance by ordering bridges destroyed, and sent troops to defend the Sayre Highway.

Minutes away lay Walter Hinkle in an Impalutao Hospital bed, writing anxiously in his diary:

> Japanese planes bombed and MG'd motor pool a few kilometers from here, and it was a terrifying experience. Seemed as if the bombs were dropping only fifty feet away. The planes maneuvered right over hospital with MGs going. MGs were most frightful. Was very nervous, weak, and unable to move. Pain aggravated. During bombing we had two mattresses over us, as though that would help!!

At the same time, from his headquarters on Bataan, General Homma stepped up attacks against Corregidor—the last obstacle to securing Manila Bay. Japanese pilots had already flown 600 missions and dropped 1,700 bombs that amounted to 365 tons of explosives since December. They were now joined by artillery pieces that pounded Corregidor day and night.

When Japanese landing craft made their assault on May 5, Wainwright committed his last reserves, and on the following day Homma received news of a white flag raised over Corregidor. Prior to his surrender, Wainwright sent a coded message to Sharp naming him as commander of all remaining forces in the Philippines, and directed him to report to MacArthur for orders.

Wainwright was escorted to Bataan by a senior Japanese officer. When he sat at the conference table, Homma nodded in his direction, expecting him to begin, and Wainwright put forth a proposal. He was hoping to limit the surrender of troops to Corregidor and three other islands in Manila Bay. Homma replied that all troops in the Philippines must be unconditionally surrendered, and implied that Wainwright's men would be held hostage until this occurred.

Wainwright broadcast a message to Sharp informing him that if he did not surrender, the Japanese would resume their attack on Corregidor and exact reprisals on the American prisoners on Luzon. Sharp relayed the message to General MacArthur's headquarters in Australia and requested clarification. There came a prompt reply: "Orders emanating from General Wainwright have no validity. If possible separate your force into small elements and initiate guerrilla operations."[4]

As Sharp deliberated his next move, Japanese troops on Mindanao tightened their noose. On May 9, Sharp sent MacArthur a final message: "North front in full retreat. Enemy comes through right flank. Nothing further could be done. May sign off any time now."[5]

Sharp met with a colonel from Wainwright's staff to discuss the situation on Corregidor, while commanders in the Visayas communicated their eagerness to fight on as guerrillas. Sharp's mind was torn. Should he obey Wainwright's request to surrender or follow MacArthur's instructions to conduct guerrilla operations and risk a massacre at Corregidor?

Sharp concluded that the only way to prevent a massacre was to capitulate, and from his hospital bed, Walter Hinkle made a single entry: "Sunday, May 10, 1942—P. I. surrendered."

1944
Retaking the Philippines

Many POWs felt abandoned by the United States during their long captivity, but in September 1944 Hinkle wrote about a renewed optimism among the men:

> In the last few days we've had two air raid "alerts." The sirens blew this morning at about 10:30. Thru a reliable source, we hear that the alert of two days ago was the "real McCoy" and that the Americans were close. We hope

---

4 Louis Morton, *The Fall of the Philippines* (Washing-

ton, DC: Department of the Army, 1953), 575.
5 Ibid., 519.

they get closer and closer. Whereas we once dreaded and feared the sound of and destructive power of bombs, we are now all anxiously awaiting the advent of a bombing raid!!

The prisoners were experiencing the first fruits of Operation Musketeer, a plan outlined in the summer of 1944 to retake the Philippines.

Such a massive undertaking required preliminary operations to establish air, naval, and supply bases on nearby islands. However, when Admiral Halsey's Third Fleet hit the Philippines to support impending operations against the nearby islands of Morotai and the Palau, his carrier pilots experienced an unexpected weakness in the enemy's air defenses.

Halsey surmised that the Japanese had few serviceable airplanes left in the Philippines due to their support of operations in New Guinea. In his report to Nimitz, Halsey stated that "there was no shipping left to sink," "the enemy's non-aggressive attitude was unbelievable and fantastic," and "the area is wide open."[6] With the Japanese air shield depleted, Halsey advised Nimitz to cancel preliminary operations and immediately and cheaply seize Leyte instead.

Nimitz concurred but directed that the Palau and Ulithi island operations be carried out as scheduled because the former was needed as an air base, and the latter as a fleet anchorage.

Nimitz relayed the recommendations to the Joint Chiefs of Staff, who

were participating in the Quebec Conference with President Roosevelt and Prime Minister Churchill. The Joint Chiefs of Staff authorized the date of the Leyte operation be moved forward by two months.

General MacArthur's view was also requested, as was his opinion on the proposed new invasion date for Leyte. MacArthur replied, "I am prepared to move immediately to execution of King II with a target date of 20 October 44."[7]

Other decisions were made in quick succession while the Third Fleet repeatedly attacked Mindanao, the Visayas, and other locations—with the first raid near Manila recorded by Hinkle in his diary.

They're here!! And the boys are really doing some snappy dive bombing. Man! When Hell breaks loose it's really bedlam. One peeled off and dove down near us — apparently at the RR station. His motor sounded like a symphony; so smooth and well-pitched. As he came down, the engine seemed to scream and we thought he'd never make it, then we heard him pull out after which we waited breathlessly. Then came the "ka-woomph!"

Hinkle and his fellow POWs were not alone in their eagerness for the American military to arrive. Torture, humiliation, and summary executions were a day-to-day reality for the Filipino people. Out of their mistreatment grew a fierce guerrilla resistance supplied by United States Navy subma-

---

6   E. Potter, *Nimitz* (Annapolis, MD: Naval Institute Press, 1976), 323.

7   CINCSWPA Radio No. C-17744 to JCS, CINCPOA, 14 Sep 44, G-3, GHQ, Admin 385 (TS).

In February 1945, as American pilots bombed and strafed Manila, Hinkle watched from Old Bilibid Prison and worried about the safety of his civilian friends interned in Santo Tomas. "Bow to Sentry" says the sign on the barbed-wire fence at the gate to the largest such wartime facility in the Philippines. The Santo Tomas campus housed a diverse group of internees that included business executives, bankers, plantation owners, writers, beachcombers, prostitutes, and mothers with their children. German nationals such as Hinkle's friend Max Klinger, however, were allowed to live freely in the Philippines, as can be seen in his diary entry for July 6, 1944: "Had a surprise yesterday. Vernon Booth, from Iloilo is here in camp — on the work detail. He looks well, and cause I knew him well in Iloilo, hence he'll probably do all he can for me. Millie is in Santo Thomas. Jackie and Max Klinger are free, on the 'outside.'" *Hinkle Archive*

rines. When the American invasion began, they pledged to strike openly against the Japanese, conduct surveillance operations, and fight beside the advancing American divisions.

The Japanese, meanwhile, were reluctant to release their hold on the archipelago. A loss of the Philippine Islands would tear the empire in two and deprive the Japanese war machine of much-needed oil.

The Japanese steadily strengthened their ground defenses to meet the anticipated Allied attack. This meant that every day the Americans cut from their timetable translated into a reduction in the cost of their campaign. The Leyte operation would be Operation Musketeer's crucial first battle. On its outcome rested the fate of the Philippines, and freedom for Walter J. Hinkle, one of the longest-held prisoners of the Pacific War.

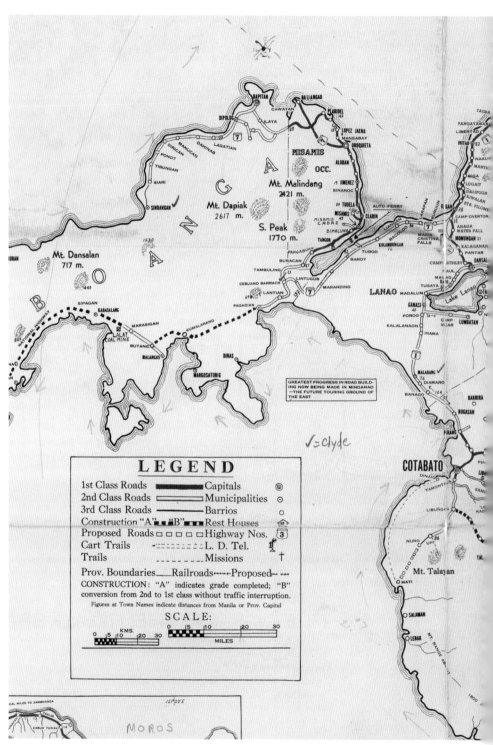

Hinkle hid this map with his diary. The pencil-drawn arrows mark his 1944 hell ship journey to Manila. *Hinkle Archive*

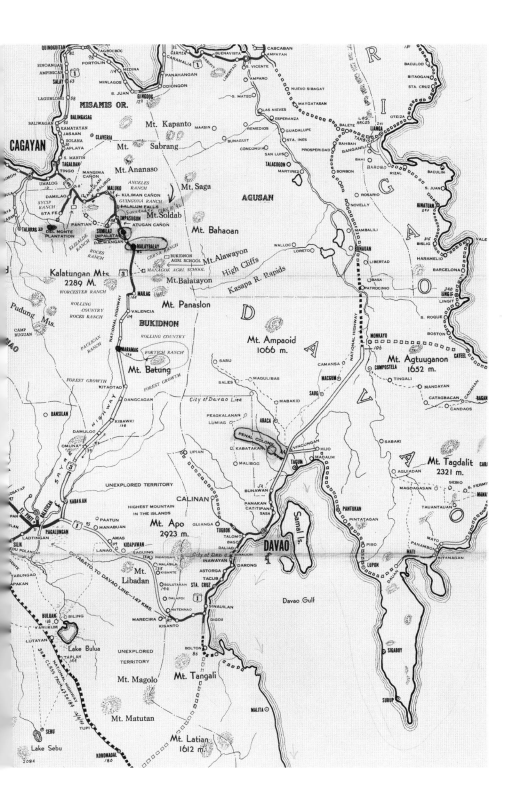

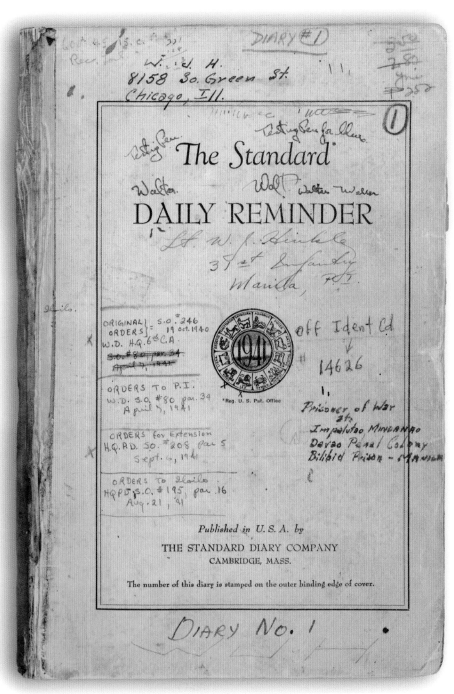

Volume (Diary) No. 1, the first of eight volumes that make up Hinkle's diary. *Hinkle Archive*

The Secret POW Diary of Walter J. Hinkle[8]

Life as a Prisoner of the Japanese

In case of death or disaster of some kind, send these notebooks to:

Miss Eileen K. Mathewson
2040 Mission Ridge Road
Santa Barbara, California
U.S.A.

Fort Sheridan
Wednesday, April 16, 1941
This is the day! I leave on my first lap on the road to the Philippines. Boarded TWA Stratoliner in Chicago at 12:20 A.M. It was hard to say good bye to everyone, so when the time came I just waved and ran to the plane. I'm going to miss'em all. Mom and Dad trying to keep their chins up. I tried to, but it didn't work. Must look ahead, keep the future bright. It's tough to leave the folks and home, but what an adventure ahead! Best of all — Pete![9] I've waited five and one half years to see her. During those years, deep down I know I've been in love with her, but who would believe me? They'd all say it was crazy, impossible! We'll see.

Had a grand trip, slept very little; too much to think about; home, Pete, Philippines, orders, ships, plane, how long will I be gone? Some say two-

and-one-half years! I pray not. Maybe never! (get back).

Dawn at 4:30 and getting closer to Los Angeles. Beautiful scenery from plane. Will Pete feel the same about me as I do about her??

Los Angeles
Thursday, April 17, 1941
Landed Los Angeles at 10:15 and saw Pete smiling and walking toward me! I wanted to drop my brief case, grab her up in my arms and hold her tight and close to me. Oh, she's so lonely — golly, I felt like a — well, I was weak and tingling all over. I knew definitely then that I loved her and the thought that we'd have to say "adieu" so soon hurt me deeply. We were ready to leave the airport when I got a wire from Mom and Ada. Gee, they think of the swellest things!

Pete and I drove to Aunt Emma's but she wasn't in, so we left a note. Went to the Padre Hotel and got a room, then drove Pete to work. She gave me her car and I was to pick her up at 9 p.m. Tried to sleep in afternoon but couldn't. Reserved plane space to Frisco. Got Pete at 9 p.m. and we went to Aunt Emma's and had cake and coffee, and left at about 11:00 p.m. — Aunt Emma's swell. Pete and I drove around, stopped at the hotel for awhile, talked, and before we knew it, it was 5:30 a.m.!! Drove her home and then shaved and got her at 9:00 a.m. out to airport, and with a broken heart told Pete so long and kissed her,

---

8   This book is a literal presentation of Walter Hinkle's diary with original phrasing, spelling, entry dates and abbreviations.

9   Pete was Eileen Mathewson's nickname.

telling her I loved her. Ringing in my ears were her words, "God Bless you. I'll pray for you." I'm not ashamed — I cried all night.

San Francisco
Friday, April 18, 1941
The plane got me in Frisco at 1:10 p.m. and I checked in at the Mark Twain Hotel. Got out to Ft. Mason and straightened out several things. Was very tired — had gone sixty-five hours without sleep! Went to bed at 7:00 p.m. and awake at 7:00 a.m. Sunday!!

Saturday, April 19, 1941
Made final arrangements for boarding ship on Monday. Found mail waiting for me from folks and it cheered me up a lot. Took sightseeing trip around Frisco. Very interesting city, but don't care to live there. Have been thinking of Pete constantly and looking thru plane schedules. Called up Pete and surprised her. Pete's sick! I've got to catch a plane for Los Angeles at 2:05 a.m. Packed, went to show and wrote letters, got plane, and once again was happy. Gee — it feels wonderful to be going to Pete instead of away.

Met a war vet in hotel bar named Mike Burke, who had some severe scars. If Mike Burke can take it, so can I!

Los Angeles
Sunday, April 20, 1941
Got in at Los Angeles at 5:30 a.m. Told Pete not to meet me, but there she was! What a somersault the ole heart made! This time I got off the plane and we were in each others arms before we said a word! We got in the car and headed for Santa Barbara to see Mr. and Mrs. Mathewson. It was a swell trip up, but Pete was having a hard time with her cough and I felt so helpless; I couldn't help her. In Santa Barbara at 8:15 and after calling up her folks, we drove to her house and were greeted by Mrs. Mathewson. She looks fine and is a swell person — I like her alot. After breakfast, like a dope, lack of sleep again caught me and I went to bed while Pete and her mother went to church. Mr. Mathewson came home in the afternoon and he is looking fine — says he'd know me on the street. We talked about the SS *I'le de France*,[10] and of Pete and myself. Had dinner, then Pete and I headed back for the Los Angeles airport. On the way, stopped for a few minutes when Pete asked me to kiss her. At the airport Pete and I felt very close to each other. I hated to say good-bye — I knew I would be away a long time. Would she wait? Will she? Just before I got in the plane Pete tried to tell me something. She only got as far as "I think it's something you want to know . . ." Then, "G'bye—darling."

San Francisco
Monday, April 21, 1941
I've left my heart with Pete. It's like leaving the breath of life behind me,

---

10   The first ocean liner to be decorated in the art deco style. Walter Hinkle was introduced to Eileen Mathewson while traveling aboard the ship in 1931 (Walter and Eileen were fourteen years old at the time). Walter and his mother, Sophie, were traveling to visit relatives in Warsaw, Poland. Afterward, Walter and Eileen kept in touch by writing letters.

and now I must go on alone. My three loved ones will be with me in spirit. Mom, Dad and Pete. I hope Pete loves me as much as I love her. If she does I know she'll wait for me. I'll never be worth anything without her. Boarded the U.S. Army Transport *Washington* and assigned to cabin B-2 with Lieutenant Howe (AC),[11] Little, (AC), and Holmes, (QMC).[12] Good group. Also assigned to duty on ship with "8th Ships Co." Our troops were quartered in the swimming pool!

Sailing time delayed till Tuesday a.m., about 3:00 o'clock. No one allowed on pier to see us off. Good-bye U.S. — so long Pete, wait for me, and so long Mom and Dad, the best in the world. On to the Blue Pacific.

At Sea
Tuesday, April 22, 1941
Nothing exciting on board ship. Have 2,300 troops and about 300 officers and passengers on board. Duty with troops more or less a farce! Yet, I have to be at the Co. at 7:30 every a.m. Found mail for me on board ship from the folks and friends. It was good to hear from home.

Wednesday, April 23, 1941
Blue Pacific is very peaceful. Ship has a gentle roll to it, causing some sea-sickness among the more delicate. Had fire and boat drill today — damned confused if you ask me!

Thursday, April 24, 1941
Water and more water! A deep, royal blue — it's beautiful. Played penny-ante. I do lots of reading and sleeping. After the show in the evening I have a favorite spot on the Prom Deck where I gaze into the pitch black night and inky sea. The stars shape themselves into images of Pete, Mom and Dad. Lord — fighting homesickness and love-sickness and loneliness is a real man's job! Can I take it?

Friday, April 25, 1941
Honolulu passengers getting things packed. We get there tomorrow a.m. Wonder what Hawaii is like? I played piano for my "Night Serenade," and "Red" sang the words tonite. We did this for the officers and passengers at dinner tonite. I think they liked it. I never played it better, for as I played, I realized that my dormant love for Pete seemed to be in the words and music both.

Honolulu
Saturday, April 26, 1941
Beautiful Hawaii! From a distance the island of Oahu, where Honolulu is located, has huge mountains and volcanic craters on it. There's a blue haze that seems to shroud the island and the vegetation, and the colors are very beautiful. Honolulu itself is very much like any other city. It is quite modern in all respects. Traffic is very polite to pedestrians, which is quite unusual. Sailors overrun the city — in the bars, on streets, in shows; sailors everywhere! Went to Waikiki Beach to

---

11   Army Corps.
12   Quartermaster Corps.

see it at night. Guess it was too dark! Forgot — Army planes greeted us as did an Army band. A thrilling and exciting welcome.

Sunday, April 27, 1941
Went swimming at Waikiki beach and was rather disappointed. It's like any other beach, and furthermore, there are coral heads on the bottom which cut you feet if you aren't very careful. The breakers are beautiful to see, however, and the surf board riders are quite amazing. We rented a paddle board, and after practically exhausting myself in trying to manipulate the board, we all gave up and returned to the ship. We unloaded 1,700 troops and about half the passengers. Scheduled to sail from Honolulu at 5 p.m., we weighed anchor at 3:30 a.m.! Same old Army game!!

At Sea
Monday, April 28, 1941
Was supposed to be relieved from duty today but got the run-around from the adjutant. Ship is much lighter and rolls nicer! Am getting sunburned and should be getting tan pretty soon. From now on, I think my diary will find I have little to say till I get to Manila! Nothing happens on this ship!

Wednesday, May 7, 1941
Sighted my first Philippine Island today! There are many of them and most of them quite large and mountainlike. Army planes around us all day, welcoming us as we went on thru the

wide San Bernadino Straits. Saw Mt. Mayon — one of the most perfectly volcanic cones in the world. Baggage all packed. Chin up! We'll know tomorrow where I'll be assigned.

Manila, Philippine Islands
Thursday, May 8, 1941
Dropped anchor in Manila Bay at 3:10 a.m. Got up at 5:30 and had my first view of Manila as a grey haze began to drop over the city. By 6:30 a.m. the city was screened from our view. Boarding party came on at 8:00 a.m. Received orders assigning me to Post of Manila Cuartel del Espania, 31st Infantry. Lieutenant Ryan, our host from 31st Infantry took five of us to HQ.[13] Met the Colonel and then was measured for uniforms and white suits. From there to Army and Navy Club for our "bien vendida" welcoming reception. Drinks and food on the house. Went to Leonard Wood Hotel — roomed with Hooker and Mathews. Impressions: Manila is the most unusual city I have ever been in. All traffic drives on left side of street. Most cars and all cabs are right-hand drive. Hundreds of "Caramedas": two-wheeled buggies powered by ponies. The drivers here are nuts! All horn and no brains. They drive 40 to 50 m.p.h. in the city and are reckless. Residential district quite beautiful — palm trees, flowers, flower trees are everywhere. Felt like royalty when I first clapped my hands and had a servant appeared! Temperature today was 94.6 degrees. Quite hot

---

13 Headquarters.

and sticky but did not bother my appetite. Went to show in evening.

Friday, May 9, 1941

Rat race started at 8:00 a.m. Went to tailor to get fitting, also to QM[14] to get credit card and campaign hat. At HQ meeting was assigned to "G" Company, 2nd Battalion, 31st Infantry stationed at Estado Major at Manila. Went apartment hunting with Bush, Hooker, Mathews and self and got located in apt. #26 of "Elena Apartments" on Romero Sallas Street in the Ermita district. Three bedrooms, two tile baths, combined living room and dining room, outside porch, kitchen, refrigerator, maids room, gas and light for 200 pesos a month (furnished with rattan furniture). We figure that with all expenses including cook and house boy and lavandera, it'll be from $40 to $50 per month apiece — swell place. Called on Colonel Jones in evening, Co. 31st, then went to show and came back "home." Cabs are very cheap. Drove around Tondo district where a fire last week did 5,000,000 pesos damage and it cost us $.25 apiece (3 of us). Quite a sight — must have been terrible. Four of us can go most anywhere in town for not more than 20 centavos apiece (ten cents). Found a Filipina curio shop and bought a kris (dagger). Will return there later. City is rather fascinating and think I'll like it well enough to stand my tour of duty. This driving will wreck my nerves!

Saturday, May 10, 1941

In a.m., hired Alfonso Villagonzalo

The Elena Apartments were located on Romero Salas Street, in the Ermita district. *Hinkle Archive*

as combination cook and houseboy. Former cook for Lt. Commander Parker. Seems very clean and good worker. Also hired Angela as lavandera. We are paying 35 pesos to Alfonso and 25 to Angela, who has been working on the apartment all day. We won't have any food till Monday. Went to finance office and arranged to be paid next week. Then to HQ and received swell letter from Mom and Dad, which brought sudden realization of how homesick I could get if I let myself go. Gee — I bet my room at home looks swell, and I can just see my Pontiac outside the window! No letter from Pete, and my heart is longing so much to hear from her. She's such a grand girl — all I've ever wanted in a girl I'd choose for a wife, Pete has. If she waits, I'm going to ask her to marry me when I return. But why doesn't she write?

Did some shopping. Got photo album and bought "For whom the Bell Tolls," autographed this a.m. by Ernest Hemingway who was in the store. Also got a Spanish book (!?). Spent afternoon figuring food supplies,

14 Quartermaster.

Elena Apartments, built in 1936 and designed by architect Juan Nakpil. *Hinkle Archive*

Written on the back side of this photo, "Looking down Romero Salas Street." *Hinkle Archive*

etc. — some housewife!! Expect white uniform in few minutes — going to "Despedida" tonight at A&N Club for 31st Infantry. Wonder what it'll be? Probably a drunken brawl! Expect films tonight too.

Sunday, May 11, 1941

Mother's Day and I'm so far from home. I'm with you in heart Mom, and hope you're having a happy day. Some party last night. Met my Co. Commander, Capt. Pahl and his wife. Both are swell people and made us feel as though I'd known them for years. He is about 36, getting bald, of my build and quite humorous. Also, likes Scotch. Mrs. Pahl asked me over today and she gave me various tips about servants, shopping, etc. She is going to pick me up tomorrow a.m. at the Company and take me shopping! It's too bad she's leaving on Wednesday for the U.S. If she'd stay, we'd be sure to get our apartment rolling smoothly! She and the Capt. are willingly going out of the way to get us started right. We appreciate it. She says that if Pete loves me, she'll wait. Mrs. Pahl waited two years for Capt. while he served in the Philippines!!

It's been very hot today and we went to a show to cool off. Saw "The Invisible Woman." We saw her — but she wasn't there!! G'nite Mother.

Monday, May 12, 1941

Reported for duty at 6:45 a.m. to Co. G, 31st Infantry at Estado Mayor. Read certain bulletins, alert plans, etc. Major Nelson lectured on Bn.[15] alert plans. Went shopping with Capt. Mrs. Pahl. We got enough to get started with today. She sure helped us out a lot.

So — we went to another show, and while inside we forgot our troubles. Walking out of the show it was a jolt

---
15   Battalion.

to realize we were in the Philippines! Later, Alfonso cooked our first meal and did a fine job: pork chops, washed potatoes, cut beans, onions, slaw, and iced tea. Not bad for a starter. Decided to get two lavanderias — too much work for one.

Tuesday, May 13, 1941
Woof! It was hot last night! Woke up at 1:00 a.m. and thought my throat was on fire. After a cool drink of water I dropped off to sleep — a hot, sweaty sleep. It seems no matter how much sleep I get, I wake up exhausted: my eyes are heavy and it takes about twenty minutes to partially awaken! We have to get up at 5:50 a.m.

Hooker, Alfonso and I went to the commissary and did most of our shopping. We plowed through a list a mile long and it took us about two hours! Also went to finance office and got paid. Decided to put money in bank, so deposited $450. Was vaccinated against smallpox. Went shopping for glasses, pitcher and kitchen utensils: Mathews broke a glass already! Have put deposit on electric steel guitar (cost 140 pesos), but have decided not to take it. I want it, but with half that money I can call Mom and Pete, both! Their voices will be sweeter to my ears than any music.

Played baseball 4 to 5:30, as requested — better yet, as required! Am very tired!! Staying "home" tonight. When will I hear from Pete?

"Side view of apartment #26." *Hinkle Archive.*

Wednesday, May 14, 1941
Got a letter each from Mom and Dad and am thanking science for clipper planes.[16] But clippers aren't worth much without word from Pete; why doesn't she write?? Went down to see the USAT *Washington* sail for the United States today, carrying mostly women and children (officer's families). It was like seeing the last hope of going home floating out to sea. The birds flying about in my stomach are not caused by indigestion! Lord — I wish I could have gone back — I miss everyone so. I long so to be with Pete. This place would be like a dream island if she were here.

Was at the Yanks market today and it's worse than Zelazna Brama in Warsaw.[17] All kinds of shapes there, from shoes to monkeys. The odor is terrific! Dead fish would be quite aromatic compared to the market smell! Must go again and take pictures next time.

16   The Boeing 314 Clipper was a long-range flying boat and was the largest aircraft of its time. It was used for flights across the Pacific Ocean.
17   The central Warsaw district of Osiedie Za Zelazna Brama (meaning Behind the Iron Gate) was a mainly Jewish area before the Second World War.

Hinkle Archive.

Preparing tonight for two and one half day reconnaissance trip down to Lucena, to look over our particular defense area. Have to get up at 4:30 tomorrow morning.

Wednesday, May 15, 1941
Left Estado Mayor at 6:15 a.m. Three "recon" cars, ten officers, and mess equipment. We set out on a reconnaissance trip to our defensive sector in the southern section of Luzon. As we left Manila and we got into the provinces the natives became more friendly. As we'd drive through a barrio, the natives, young and old, would line the streets and yell, "Hi ya Joe!" and cheer and laugh. They all render the salute from two to eighty. The kids are cute when they salute. The country is beautiful — vast coco-

nut groves, palm trees, banana trees, and various vegetation, the names of which I don't know. We managed to get some of the coconuts down and cut them open. Drank the somewhat sweet coconut milk, and ate the tough meat — it was good!

We rode for two hours today, covering about 180 miles, and my back is sore and bruised from bouncing around in that damned car! We're camped under coconut trees and it's very comfortable. It's cooler than Manila. Took quinine tablet at chow-time. Slept under mosquito bar.[18]

Friday, May 16, 1941
I can't remember the names of all the

18 A net or curtain for excluding mosquitoes that was designed to go over a cot or sleeping bag

Hinkle Archive.

places we have been to. They include Lucena, Tayabas, Lucban, Pagbilao, and others. We'd get to a sector, then get out and walk and look over the terrain. Personally I feel that if we have to fight here, it'll be a suicide stand. We don't have enough men or equipment to save off landing parties, and with our present equipment, I don't think we could delay them very long either. I'm speaking of the Japs, of course. I also think they are too smart to seek war with the U.S. I wish Roosevelt would take it easy though. I want to be able to go back to Pete.

The natives live in grass shacks which are built on stilts. They are very curious, and no matter what we do, we have an audience, whether it be dress, eat, or just talk!

We rode for ten hours today, but I've toughened up some — no backache today!

Sunday, May 17, 1941
Well — back to Manila at four o'clock this afternoon. Didn't get much sleep last night. Was thinking so much of Pete and what she means to me. It

"Recon car." Hinkle Archive.

makes no difference what I do, her face is ever before me. She hasn't written though and it worries me — worries me terribly much. I find myself counting back hours on my watch, figuring out what time it is in Los Angeles. Sometimes I get very mad when I picture her out driving with someone else, or dancing with some smooth devils' arms around her, some guy who's spilling out honeyed words which he doesn't mean but is using for a purpose — God, I get so mad.

Monday, May 18, 1941
Wrote Mom and Dad this morning and hope that letter and the one to Pete get on the next clipper. Went to a show this afternoon — felt as though I needed a laugh. Saw "Buck Private." It was funny, but when the Andrews Sisters sang "Sweetheart, I wish you were here," I was right back alongside Pete and found myself singing the words to her.

Was notified that I've to go to Fort McKinley tomorrow to relieve one of the officers in the Recruit Camp. Bush and Mathews are going too. I don't know whether I'll be there a day, or for three weeks — I'll find out tomorrow. Am still somewhat unsettled. Don't have my white suits or new Khaki uniforms. Can't get a haircut tomorrow — or get my films down to the developer or get a present and mail it to Mom.

Monday, May 19, 1941
Sent to 31st Infantry Recruit Camp,

near Fort McKinley today. Some hellspot! Dusty, no shade, and plenty hot. Was assigned a tent and informed that I would be here for about three weeks, instead of just "today!"

My battalion was on the range today, so I went out and got acquainted to the tune of ten hours on the range! Spent four and one half hours as "Pit Officer," with the sun shining in the pits all afternoon.[19] Was dog-tired and went to bed at 8:30 — found myself unable to sleep all night. Lay awake and at 4:20 a.m. we had to get up. Out to the range again was the schedule. Came into Manila Monday night to get some clothes. This place will do me no good!

Tuesday, May 20, 1941
Up at 4:20 a.m. and marched one-and one-half miles on a trail, up and down hills to range. Was wringing wet and panting like a race horse when we got there. Acted as range officer in morning, and it was very hot. The continual racket of .30 cal. shells gave me a headache. Was in the pits in the afternoon. Hot and grimy in the pits — no place to sit down. At 3:00 p.m. I felt as though I'd never make the march back to camp — felt like I had a fever. Was informed that after we got back to camp, the officers were

---

19 Soldiers assigned to pit duty on a rifle range spent hour after hour pulling down targets and hunting for a bullet hole. The hole was patched and the target frame was pushed back up. The soldier on pit duty then held a stick with black disc at one end over the patch to show the shooter where he had hit, or missed. The officer in charge of the pit used a PA or microphone system for communicating with the pit detail.

to go to Manila to play baseball!! Of all the damned things! From 6:30 a.m. to 3:20 p.m. on the range, and a long march thrown in — then baseball. I swore a blue streak, made the march, and got on the truck for Manila. I got off at some street in Manila, told the advocates of baseball to go to hell, and came to the apartment. Sent Alfonso out for thermometer and some medicine. Went to bed with fever of 102°. Here we go!

Wednesday, May 21, 1941

Major Kerr, AMC[20] came to see me, and said I had the flu. Gave me some medicine and told me to stay in bed, which I certainly hated to do. (Like hell — after that camp — a bed and clean sheets was heaven!)

Began coughing — dry cough, and was sweating buckets! Kept reading to occupy my mind and also slept. Continually thinking of Pete and why I've had no word from her. Gee — I'm no iron-willed fellow. I've got to hear from her soon. Nothing else — just sleep.

Thursday, May 22, 1941

Fever 101° today, cough seems worse. Have been "jumpy" all morning and very restless. Took some dope and slept for awhile. About 2:00 p.m. — I was reading. Suddenly something inside told me to call up Pete — something was wrong! I grabbed the phone without thinking any further. The operator called Los Angeles and

I was told that Pete could be reached in Santa Barbara at the hospital or at home. Miserable thoughts and agonizing moments, and then contact with Santa Barbara. Mrs. Mathewson answered and said Pete was in the hospital and had been ever since I left. She's seriously ill, and the Doctor says she'll be a long time recovering from bronchial Pneumonia. She said Pete thought she'd be able to write to me tomorrow. Everything inside me froze. I tried to ask Mrs. Mathewson to tell Pete I love her, but I couldn't get it out. I hung up. I cried then — I cried and swore. Pete sick, and me thousands of miles away — helpless. Why didn't I realize sooner that something was wrong? Oh, Pete — I'll try to come back — I'll do all I can. It hurts me terribly to think of you in the hospital.

Friday, May 23, 1941

At midnight I called up Mother. I was so comforted to hear her voice. I told her what had happened and asked them to help get me back. She said she'd try. I called Capt. Pahl and asked him to help. Was nervous and angry and worried all day today. Why won't they let me go to Pete? The recruit camp took all the glory out of the Army for me anyway, and if I can't get sent back to the States — well, the Army still has no glory. Major Kerr didn't think I could do anything about it. Pete — my thoughts have been with you a thousand times more than usual today. I'm pretty well shot to pieces thinking about the whole

---

20 Army Medical Corps.

business, but I'm with you and praying for you. God — what a fool I was to ask for this assignment! I'll go crazy over here, Pete. I _____what's the use — I can't write anymore.

Saturday, May 24, 1941
My fever is down some, but my blood pressure isn't. My face is beginning to break out from the emotional stain. Lord, how it hurts to be unhappy and continually worrying about someone you love!!

The Dr. had me come to his office today — am still marked Quartered. From his office I went to Major Lewis, 31st Adjutant. Told him I wanted to be sent home. Was willing to help, but he could do nothing and sent me to see the Adj. General at HQ Phil. Dept. I went and talked to Colonel Torrey — rather I listened mostly. For the first time in my life I talked back to a full colonel and told him I thought he was warping the picture and dishing out the old lecture on "Duty, Honor, Country." Sure — it was crazy but what would you have done? He was understanding though, and is my friend, I know — but I can't go home! Dad sent me a wire saying they could do nothing either. There's my problem; the women I love, seriously ill, thousands of miles away — me stuck here for how long? What will I do, weaken or face the facts?

Sunday, May 25, 1941
Pete — there's nothing left for me to do but put my chin out and take it.

I can't get back without losing my commission and being disgraced and of course that's out of the question. I want you and the folks to be proud of me. You too — have to face the future with a brave chin and heart. My love for you is strong and true enough to make this possible, I'm sure. I want to be with you and at your side, but there's a thing called our country that says they need me here — worthless as I claim I am now, and I must stay. As soon as this emergency is over we'll be together again. If I can't get back soon enough, we'll try and have you come over here. I'll write often and send notes and pray for your quick and complete recovery. You're with me every minute, Pete, and I love you.

Monday, May 26, 1941
I'm now convalescing, and will do so until Saturday. Col. Jones, CO[21] of the 31st Inf. called on me last nite and asked how Pete was, and if I had heard from home. He was here about ¾ of an hour, which is unusually long for a social call on the part of a Lt. Col. I've no ambition to do anything — just read and sleep — and think all the time — still looking for that loophole that will send me home. I've not weakened, but I've not given up hope, either. Clipper comes in today — hope there's mail.

Tuesday, May 27, 1941
Got my mail OK. Letters from Mom and Dad, Eleanor, and from Carroll Brown. Am feeling better physically,

21 Commanding officer.

but coughing like a fog horn! God, that cough will rip my inside apart. It's the kind of cough Pete had when I saw her in Los Angeles, and I kick myself for keeping her out so much, and yet, who would blame us? Never realized that I was capable of worrying so much. I never have worried about anything — usually let it come as it chooses. Pete, however, has me worrying, suffering with her and praying for her. My heart feels sore and inside my chest is an ache — what better proof of my love?

Wednesday, May 28, 1941

I now have "walking privileges," though marked "quarters." Packed my $\Theta\Delta X$[22] pin and sent it via clipper to Pete. If I can't be with her, my most valued possession will have to take my place. I hope she'll wear it and that it will keep me close and warm in her heart. Nothing else new. Went to a show (on the sly) to try and forget and relax. Half-way thru the picture, one of two white girls in the row behind me pops up with, "Let's sit over here Eileen!" That was the spark that brought me out of my temporary state of forgetting and sent the world of worry crashing back down on my head.

Capt. Pahl called tonite, and he was anxious to know if I'd heard from my fiancee. I've told them all that you're my fiancee, Pete, do you mind?

Thursday, May 29, 1941

Went to the Cuartel[23] today to see about some tailoring. Major Lewis asked about Pete, and the Chaplain and the Col. did likewise. I had no news to give them — another factor which has me worrying. I've sent 2 or 3 wires, can't remember — but no answer. Is there anything further wrong? If there's no letter on the next clipper (June 2nd), I'll wire "RCA reply."

Friday, May 30, 1941

"Holiday." I go back to the Camp tomorrow, but am not looking forward to it. Went to two shows today. Nothing else to do, except worry and think and I'm beginning to feel the strains of that. If I'm to return to Pete with all my faculties, I must put up a better fight and try to occupy my mind more with other things.

P.S. Got my hair cut short today! You ought to see me, hah!!

Saturday, May 31, 1941

Took a car for camp at 1:30 a.m. Damned thing broke down two miles from camp and I hiked over field and up and down hills for two miles! Was all wet of course when I got there. Inspected rifles and tents, and at 9:30 a.m. went on one hour HIKE!! Cripes! I dragged it back into Camp at 10:30, hopped a recon car and came into Manila. Was downtown, got a second red filter for my camera, and met Lt. Murray Sneddon, AC, and went curio hunting with him at night. Am to play

---

22 Theta Delta Chi, a social fraternity founded in 1847. The pin was from Hinkle's days as a student at the University of Michigan.

23 Barracks.

baseball tomorrow morning rather than go on picnic at the Camp, with a three mile hike thrown in!

Sunday, June 1, 1941
Was at the baseball field, but didn't play. 31st Inf. beat Nichols Field 13-6.[24] Spent afternoon in apt. taking it easy. Am to go with Lt. Strong, Ass't. Provost Marshal on his "run" tonite. Every pay day, there are pay-day patrols of MPs, and they try to keep order in the various nite clubs, red-lite districts and dance halls. Strong has to inspect these places, and I can't think of a better way to see Manila than by virtue of having to do so in an "official capacity." So, I'm going tonite.

It was very interesting, but not too exciting. Saw nothing unusual — left for Camp at midnite.

Monday, June 2, 1941
Back at the recruit camp and up at 4:30 a.m. — believe me, that's tough going! Then went out on an attack problem in the morning, and it was hot and sticky. Up and over the hills, and the sweat was heavy. Returned to Camp and found out I was Charge of Camp and Officer of the Guard (OG). In the afternoon, a defense problem, and when we returned to camp, it started to rain. Boy, did it pour! And we had a nite problem scheduled!
The rain slacked up, and out into the night we went. After half an hour the

rain came down again and it took me one hour to assemble my platoon. By that time we were soaked to the skin and didn't give a damn if it rained or not. We returned to camp and the OD[25] told me to go to bed and he'd make my inspections for me — damned nice of him. Got to my tent and found my bunk rather damp — there was a leak in the tent, right over it! Peeled off my wet clothes and, wet or not, I went to bed and slept very good!

Tuesday, June 3, 1941
Woke up to find it was still raining. So this is why they call it the rainy season! At 10:15 a.m. asked to go to Manila to get a dry uniform. Had to put wet clothes on this a.m. — had no extras! Grabbed a motorcycle driver and climbed in the sidecar. Half way to Manila the rain again got my number and I was soon again a drowned rat! My dry uniform was dry for about twenty minutes, 'cause when I put it on, I spent some time in the apartment — I had a letter from Pete — my Eileen! Oh, it was like a tonic, a new lease on life to know she was getting better and would come out of it alright, and best of all, that she wants to learn to love me! That field of clover they talk about is mine! Hah! Let it rain, snow, sleet or typhoon — I'm happier today than I've been in ages — somebody does care!

We broke camp today and returned

---

24   Soldiers from a US military airfield located 10 miles south of Manila. It was home to several US Air Corps pursuit squadrons.

25   Officer of the Day.

to Manila, thank God. A wet sloppy mess —we did it all in the rain!

Wednesday, June 4, 1941
Luxury — didn't have to raise until six a.m. Reported over to G. Co. Estado Mayor, and did nothing much. It's a half day anyway. Returned home to find a radio-gram[26] from Eileen. What a fight one has to put up against homesickness and loneliness for the ones you love. The false front that one puts on — the veneer of gaiety and happy-go-lucky, which, after one finds himself in the solitude of his room at night turns into a bleak, miserable feeling. The ache in the heart grows daily, and yet you dare not show it. Torture? What else?

Thursday, June 5, 1941
Mom's birthday — I hope she gets my wire in time. If it doesn't get there on time, she'll think I've forgotten; but she should know better, I've never forgotten. I wish we were together, and here's hoping she's thinking of me today. Spent the day with my nose in books, trying to learn company administration — morning reports, duty rosters, mess arrangements (I'm mess officer), and company fraud. I've a heckuvalot to learn. Wonder if I'll make it?

Friday, June 6, 1941
No news — it's just been raining and raining. It is a little cooler, but that's all we can say for it.

Sunday, June 8, 1941
"Anniversary" — damned one month anniversary! Just one month since we landed here. Four weeks and a couple days. Spent the morning idly.

Monday, June 9, 1941
Nothing new today. Clipper gets in, and I'll be looking for my mail as usual. I'm sure there'll be one from Pete.

Tuesday, June 10, 1941
X?Δ![27] Regimental alert at 3:00 a.m. and we were up in the middle of the night and down to our companies, packed and ready to go to the field by 4:00 a.m. I was to have the advance guard — sure enuff, I'd draw the gang that would meet the enemy first! As it turned out, our battalion didn't move out — the third did. I had to march the advance guard however, to Cuartel de España, and then march back, at 5:30 a.m.! The day sure was long, and I was pretty sleepy. So was everyone else. Things were so disorganized and no sleep for tomorrow since "G" Co. goes on guard today at 12:30 p.m.!

Mounted guard and I was Officer of the Guard. Made inspection at 8:30 p.m., and midnite. Letter from home, but not from Pete! Cripes, no letter from her is going to make this a long, miserable week — I had counted on one so much. I certainly hope she realizes how much I love her, and how much word from her means. Two

---

26   A written message transmitted by radio. It is printed out at the receiving destination and delivered to the intended recipient. Also known as a radio telegram.

27   Hinkle often used a grawlix in his writing to represent an obscenity.

years ago today I was commissioned and the Army seemed a glorious institution — honor, duty, country, and all that. Today, I've learned too much about the Army — disorganization, snobbishness, sacrifice with no returns, jealousness, and bales of red tape. Amen!

Thursday, June 12, 1941
Dopey and slept today, and very happy to get off guard. Was transferred to Co. "E" today, and am fairly happy about it. Am the senior Lieutenant in the Co., and may be able to get my silver bars shortly. Capt. Christensen is a fine chap, and after I learn the ropes, I will have a free hand in executing the duties he assigns me. At present, I am executive, mess, and supply officer with a helluva lot to learn.

Friday, June 13, 1941
Lucky Day! Well — nothing happened to prove otherwise. Won 6.50 pesos shooting craps!! Seem to get along fine with my CO and men. Keep thinking back a year ago — of senior prom at Michigan, and my Ford — the big wonderment in my life, my own car!

Saturday, June 14, 1941
Just had to stand inspection this morning. Nothing new, except that we may be alerted again on Monday, about 2:00 a.m. I wish they'd cut it out — that's too damned early! Went to meet Countess Potocka, but she wasn't in, so I went to jai-alai and won a couple of pesos.

Sunday, June 15, 1941
I suddenly realized it's Father's Day and I think I can get a wire to Pop in time. He sure deserves a lot of thought and gratitude on this day — more than the usual day brings him. There's none finer in the world, and I hope and pray I'll be able to get back with him and Mom (and Pete) so we can celebrate next Father's Day together.

Clipper came in today, and I went down to the city post office to get my air mail a day ahead of time. There was no mail, however, either from Pete or home — and it made the whole week totally not worthwhile. Two weeks now, and no word from Eileen. Something must be wrong — she wouldn't make me wait this long. If I don't hear from her tomorrow, I'll call up again.

Met Countess Potocka today and went out with some of her friends. The Countess is — well, let's see — a live wire, domineering, rather ah — fleshy, reddish blonde-hair, sort of good-looking (no prize winner), and she swims in whisky and water. She travels around in the best of company — Mr. Duckworth, Mgr. of International Harvester — Mrs. Pennington, owner or manager of a Duco outfit that exports to China — and well, what the hell — I was there, too! Had a good time in a miserable sort of way — hearing music, watching people dance — all the while thinking of Pete, and wishing we were together.

Thursday, June 17, 1941

No word from Pete, so I called up at 4 p.m. I explained to the operator that I wanted to speak to Miss Eileen only — no one else. She stunned me when she called back to report and said, "Miss Mathewson is in the hospital and cannot speak to you, sir!" I tried to see if I could get a phone connection in the hospital, but no soap. Mrs. Mathewson told the operator that she would receive the call, but I felt so terrible that I just mumbled "No" a couple of times and hung up. Lord, why doesn't she let me know when things aren't going as expected? It's a shock to have such information handed you by a phone operator. There I had begun to feel more at ease because I thought Eileen was out of the hospital — and instead, *this*!

Wednesday, June 18, 1941

Happy birthday Dad. I wrote a letter home to you today, and I hope my package doesn't arrive too late! Yessir, my Pop gets a year younger every birthday. I know, 'cause he can still whip me at every game! Wonder what you two will be up to today? The club? Show? Lucky you — think of where I'll spend my birthday! Under a coconut tree with pineapple in one hand and papaya in the other!

Friday, June 19, 1941

Went on reconnaissance trip to "E" Co.s defense sector today. Traveled directly east of Manila, over mountains and beautiful country, toward Infanta. Nice trip. Nothing more to say.

Saturday, June 20, 1941

More reconnaissance; this time in south Luzon, down to Tagaytay Ridge, and to Batangas. Sure is cool up on Tagaytay Ridge — even shivered up there!

Sunday, June 21, 1941

Inspection as usual — nothing exciting. Mr. Duckworth asked me to tag along with the Countess and himself tonite, so I went, to the movies and then to jai-alai. It was OK, riding in a big private car with a chauffeur — all checks taken care of! Wearing a small orchid in my buttonhole that cost me .025 pesos!! (2½¢). I hope he doesn't expect me to traipse along every week. I don't care about sitting around half the nite over drinks and jabbering about nothing.

Sunday, June 22, 1941

I'm taking it easy today — lots of sleep. The 2nd Bn. will probably move out for maneuvers about 3:00 a.m. tomorrow, and "E" Co. will follow on Tuesday. We'll be gone ten days and there's a sixty mile march to go thru on the way back!

Monday, June 23, 1941

Second Bn. moved out at 3:00 a.m. today. We (E. Co.) follows tomorrow. Clipper isn't due till tomorrow. It's late, so I won't get any mail for a long time — ten days. Went to bed early but didn't sleep well, wondering when the phone was going to ring for alert.

"Setting up tents." *Hinkle Archive*

Tuesday, June 24, 1941

E. Co. alerted at 6:00 a.m. Convoy of twelve trucks moved out at 8:20 a.m. and started for Tignuan. After fifteen minutes, half the trucks were missing. I took one truck and went to look for Lt. Lawhon and rest of convoy. Found "lost patrol" and started out again, with me in command, since the Capt. went on. Consulted map and used hunches. Roads poorly marked. Traveled over mountains. Reached Tignuan sector at 2 p.m. and set up bivouac and began to dig in position. My platoon had area including high hill, road, bridge, and river. Placed guns in position, then ready for chow. Tents were set up and mosquito bars in place. Plenty of bugs and all kinds of crickets, bats, frogs, and lizards, plus other stranger animals are mak-ing peculiar noises. We are in a valley, a deep valley, completely surrounded by jungle-covered mountains.

Wednesday, June 25, 1941

Had lots of company in bed last nite! Crickets, ants, mosquitoes and little gnats almost drove me nuts! They kept me busy for about two hours before I fell asleep. Slept under a sheet for a change — it was fairly cool. This morning took truck and drove to Infanta and beyond, to point opposite Polillio Island. Road terrible, and it was a mere trail in many spots. Continued fixing positions. Walked about one mile up road to points where road and mountain-side will be blown up "in case." It's damned hot in this valley during the day. Man! How the sweat does pour out! Clipper mail should be

"Peeling potatoes." *Hinkle Archive*

due today. Wonder if there'll be any for me? Pete, did you write?

Back in camp. We went and swam in the river — water very warm.

Thursday, June 26, 1941

Lt. Lawhon and 2nd platoon started "attack" against my position. We spotted "enemy" quite easily and the defense was well executed. Our positions here are good — we could hold out for quite awhile. Picked out a beach on the ocean and took the men swimming during P.M. Rained most of the afternoon, and raining hard now (3:15 p.m.). Radio from P of M orders Lawhon and I return Manila on Sunday to attend training school of some sort. Another radio assigned Lts. Fitzgerald and Ramsey to E. Co.

Hinkle's musette bag hangs from a post in front of his cot. *Hinkle Archive*

Friday, June 27, 1941

Strong winds and heavy rains caused HQ to order us back to Manila today — maneuvers cancelled, and we didn't have to take our "walk." High Commissioner's dance tonite and will probably go. Got letter from Pete, folks, Aunt Bess, Harriet, and Uncle Jack. It was especially swell to here from Eileen, in spite of her silly demand that I not love her so much. How can I help it? I'll always love her, and more every day.

Went to Commissioner's dance for newly arrived single officers. A good number (*not* a "number of good!") white girls were there. I did my share of dancing, and met a couple of pretty nice girls. It was almost a new experience to sit down and talk to a white girl. Sort of felt bashful. Wonder if that tendency increases?

Saturday, June 28, 1941
Nothing new at P of M. Got a wire from folks which made me feel pretty good. They're sure tops.

Three of us went to jai alai and proceeded to win some money for a change. I cleared about 22 pesos. Met the Countess, Mr. Duckworth, Mrs. Pennington, and Noa Nolant there, and almost spent the evening at their table — they wouldn't let me go. Hope that doesn't happen ever time I meet them someplace.

Sunday, June 29, 1941
Hah! Slept most of day. Sunday is a good day for that. As a result there's no more news.

Monday, June 30, 1941
This "Philippine Army" school started today. A number of officers and NCOs are attending the school for purpose of being qualified to instruct the Philippine Army when that outfit is

organized. Each officer will probably have a Bn. of "gooks"[28] and will handle the Bn. with the aid of two NCOs. He'll be *on his own*, too. I hope I am not detailed for such a job if this ever comes about. Lord knows where they'll send these officers — how they'll live — rice and fish to eat!! But the school goes on — main purpose to teach us to be adept at instructing. This is not too interesting a school — it's quite dry.

Tuesday, July 1, 1941
School — and rain. Oh yes — its been doing some fancy raining of late. Typhoon signal is down. Clipper is overdue — supposed to arrive tomorrow.

Wednesday, July 2, 1941
Rain — school — rain. Morning and afternoon school. Try to get your bills paid; odds and ends attended to. Yeah, *try* it. Clipper held over in Guam. Now due tomorrow. Saw *I Wanted Wings* tonite, and when the navigator said, "Estimate we're directly over Santa Barbara," well, I was too and that's where I bailed out! Even shows can't get my mind away from Eileen.

---

28   A slur that has its origins in the Philippine War of 1899–1902. It was directed toward the Philippine people and appears once in Hinkle's diary. An 1893 citation from *Slang and Its Analogies* defines gooks as tarts, particularly camp-following prostitutes catering to the Army. Another explanation is that gook developed from goo-goo, which may have been a mocking imitation of Tagalog, a language spoken in the Philippines. This version of the word's origin squares with the contemporaneous "spik," the derivation of which, H. L. Mencken held, came from Spanish speakers' alleged attempts to say they did not "spik" (speak) English.

Friday, July 4, 1941
No parade. Heavy rains.

[*No entries for July 5–11.*]

Saturday, July 12, 1941
School for PA[29] ended today after we fired on the range. Made a perfect score with the revolver. If it had been in war, I would have murdered six men called "enemies." What is the good of war? I'm being taught how to kill to preserve peace?!

Sunday, July 13, 1941
Slept, and slept.

Monday, July 14, 1941
Regular duty with Co. again. Usual rat-race right from start! First Sergeant has been AWOL[30] five days and everything is a mess! I've got to make a supply inventory, begin work on company fund, map out a BAR[31] course, etc.!

Tuesday, July 15, 1941
Happy day! Mail, of course. Got a wonderful letter from Pete, and it made me feel so very lonely and homesick. Gee, it was swell, and it's so good to know she is getting better, even if it is a slow go. I think she's realizing how much I really care for her. Letters from the folks too. Sure glad my letters make Mom feel better. I don't want to worry her. Why did I ever come here? [*In the margin is written, "Yeah, why? 8/20/43."*]

29 Philippine army.
30 A person who holds "absent without leave" status is absent from one's post but without intent to desert.
31 Browning Automatic Rifle.

Wednesday, July 16, 1941
Forgot this day, somehow.

Thursday, July 17, 1941
Had a fifteen mile night march tonite and I stood it much better than I had expected to. We tramped all around Manila, starting at 6:30 p.m. and returning at 11:30 p.m. Didn't drink any water during entire march, but sure made up for it when I got in!

Friday, July 18, 1941
Kind of a holiday today after last night. Didn't have to go to work, so I slept till 11:00 a.m. Was pretty stiff in the joints today (of my body!).

Saturday, July 19, 1941
2nd Bn. went to see several training films today and that's all there was to today's work. Went to McKinley and sent a wire to Eleanor, since it is her birthday, and I've never forgotten it. Had a date tonite with Betty Gardiner, an American girl who was born here and has never been to the U.S., but is going next year. Met her at the Commissioner's dance. She's very wholesome and a lot of fun — clean cut. A rarity in Manila as far as girls are concerned. I thought I'd rather have a date with her than let myself get drawn to associating with native girls, or with fellows who had dates with those girls. I don't go for it, and I'm sure Pete will understand and approve. I wanted to talk and dance with a white girl — just have fun — no playing around, or passes. Something on the "brother and sis-

ter" idea is what I want, and I think Betty will qualify.

Sunday, July 20, 1941
Sunday and sleep — same story!

Monday, July 21, 1941
Usual duties at P. of M.

Tuesday, July 22, 1941
Mail day, and two very important letters arrived from Mom and Dad, and one from Pete. Pete's letter this week proves further to me that she is the one girl in this world who is meant for me. She gave me a tongue lashing in her letter in such a nice way that at the same time gave me the extra spark of fight I needed. "The brave will laugh to still the pain."

Wednesday, July 23, 1941
"E" Co. went on "para-guard" today. We are fully dressed, fully equipped and will be on the alert for twenty-four hours, never leaving the barracks. We are to be prepared to fight dropping parachute troops! Who's gonna drop 'em? Japs don't use 'em.

Thursday, July 24, 1941
Off guard at 1 p.m. — school till 2, then started on another fifteen mile hike at 6:30 p.m. We walked too damned fast, and in the first hour covered three+ miles; only supposed to cover two! Made hike easily this time, in spite of fast cadence. Actually, we covered thirteen miles.

Friday, July 25, 1941
Holiday today, so I slept most of the way. Was quite tired from the guard and hike. Hah! I'm OD tomorrow. Went to Army and Navy Club and chewed over ole times with Howie Martin.

Saturday, July 26, 1941
Officer of the Day today, so I spend a hectic nite. Also put in five hours on the Co. collection sheet, besides my other duties. Inspected guard at 11 p.m. and 4:30 a.m. Got about four hours sleep.

Sunday, July 27, 1941
Off guard at 11:45 a.m. and came to apt. and caught up on some sleep. Wrote letters to Eileen and Mom and Dad. Sunday is usually pretty inactive for me. I really try to make it a day of rest. Hmmm — a year ago I was in Three Rivers at the Mains, with the folks. We celebrated Dad's birthday and mine together. One year ago! Seems ages.

Monday, July 28, 1941
During morning orders came out rescinding all furloughs, so that takes care of my birthday celebration!!

Went on a fifteen mile hike tonight, and returned to the post. This was the first lap of our sixty miles. Felt pretty tired but made it fairly well. Wore out my shoes! Now I'll have to buy a new pair and break 'em in tomorrow nite! Got my letters from my honey and from Mom and Dad. Pete's card was swell too. Was a little disappointed in it though.

Tuesday, July 29, 1941

At midnite we started on the rest of our sixty miles, and it was terribly hot. We walked and walked, and those damned new shoes began to have me sweating extra about the tenth mile. We went over pavement and gravel roads, and the loose rocks were very hard on the feet. At 7:00 a.m. we finally rounded a curve to see where our camp would be. We were fifteen miles out of Manila. Chow was late and the Major had us get all tents lined up. Tried to sleep, but sweat so much I couldn't. At 6:30 we started on approximately fifteen miles more (7.7 out — 7.7 in). This was a killer of a march — up and down long grades — rocks. I used my benzedine inhaler as a stimulant and was making OK. Also had on garrison shoes instead of field shoes. (Remember this march is actually on Wednesday nite). On the way back at about the ninth mile, one of Ramsey's men fell out, and just as my platoon got near him, he passed out. I went to help him and my outfit went on. Poured my canteen of water in and over him. Used artificial respiration 'cause he was breathing way too fast from exhaustion and heat. He came to, and finally the ambulance came and got him. They gave me a ride to the tail of my column, but my Co. was about five-hundred to six-hundred yards ahead, and physically I couldn't overtake 'em. So I marched about three-hundred yards behind the tail of the column, and during the

home stretch found others along the road to help with first aid — mostly cramps and sore feet. Three men started marching back with me. Then it started to rain, and we had about two or three hours to go yet. I was out of water and my throat was dry. I sucked water out of my sleeve as soon as it began raining, but it was salty from sweat! Finally dragged in and I doused my insides with four cups of cocoa and five cups of water!! God — I was pooped! thirty miles in twenty-four hours!

Thursday, July 31, 1941

Got some sleep last nite alright, and then just lay on my bunk the rest of the day. Broke camp at 4 p.m. and started marching back to Manila at 6:30 p.m. Made it first seven miles fine, and then began getting headache. Had blisters on both big toes, and got dizzy now and then. Didn't dare fall out since none of my men had weakened, and I wasn't going to be the first. Steps became harder to take. Every little stone could be felt through the sole of the shoe, and when it started to rain, we were ninety minutes out of Manila! Boy, did it rain. We sloshed in to the post at 12:15 a.m. — damned tired, aching, still trying to laugh — some feeling sick and nauseated, but thankful that it was finally over!

Friday, Aug. 1, 1941

Got records (home recordings) from the folks, and sure got a kick out of 'em. Bought a radio-vic so's I can hear their voices anytime. Sure was a swell idea. Most everyone sounds natural and it made me pretty homesick to hear them talking to me. Thanks.

Saturday, Aug. 2, 1941
Whee! Got another birthday gift — six rolls of film. That's great. Sure hope I get some good shots for you Dad. Guess I'm in the doghouse with the Army. I thought the Capt. said we wouldn't have to come to work till Monday, but guess we had a mis-understanding. Lawhon and I both are in for it come Monday. What the devil — if they don't like it, they can send me home!

Sunday, Aug. 3, 1941
Did nothing in the morning. Got to thinking about folks and their anni-versary number twenty-five. If they're going to New Orleans for another honeymoon, I'd better call 'em up to-day, instead of Aug. 12th as planned.

The call is in now, has been for 1½ hours, but no soap yet.

Boy oh boy! Just finished talking to Dad and Mom and it put lots of zip and pep in me. Sure was great to hear them talking directly to me. They sounded OK, but somewhat worried. So long folks, see you . . . ?

Monday, Aug. 4, 1941
Humph! Got the hell bawled out of me 'cause I wasn't at the Co. on Saturday! Just a lot of blah, blah, and that was all. Clipper was supposed to

be in today, but has been delayed till Thursday. Damn it! Had a date with Betty last nite, and we doubled with Dick Anderson. A date over here is just something to do. I can work up no more enthusiasm about going out with a girl than I can about taking a sixty-mile hike! I know of one good reason for this — Eileen. Golly, if she only knew the terrific grasp she has on my heart!

Tuesday, Aug. 5, 1941
No excitement or interesting events today. Just hot, humid and raining.

Wednesday, Aug. 6, 1941
Captain Christensen was transferred from E. Co. to HQ 2nd Bn, so now Ramsey will be CO X?Δ! I can't stand the man. He drives me wild with all his silly mannerisms and sarcastic smirks. I've always been able to get along with people in gen-eral, but Ramsey has me up a tree. There'll be trouble along the line in the future — just wait and I'll be right in the middle of it! Damn his supervisor attitude.

Am spending the week learning all about, and compiling the vouchers and figures for the company fund, and it's quite a job. Guess I should have taken some bookkeeping in school.

Thursday, Aug. 7, 1941
Usual slow day, plus the regular fifteen-mile hike at 6:30 p.m. We hiked out Dewey Boulevard, and Doc Hibbs walked along with me at

the tail of the column. I got to talking with him about Eileen's illness, and from him I learned that the result could be tuberculosis, but that it depended on the condition of her lung, and on other case factors. He said she'd be alright though, and with proper rest and time she'll be herself. Golly, and she thinks her illness makes a difference in the way I feel about her! Why, kitten, I just can't stop loving you merely because a couple of bugs got the best of a battle with you! This is a fight, and fights from now on are to be *ours*, not just yours or mine.

Made the hike easily. Also, made a recording today for Mom and Dad's anniversary, and sent it air express. I hope they enjoy it.

Friday, Aug. 8, 1941
Day off. After effects of hike not so bad this time — got up at 7:30, though I didn't have to. Went to a show — wrote a letter to Pete. Boy, I got a *wonderful* letter from her on the clipper. She's feeling better, temperature down, and she's getting to sit up a little. Thank God. She's so grand, and I love her. And two swell letters from Mom and Dad — now the week is complete.

Saturday, Aug. 9, 1941
Wrote to Mom and Dad in the afternoon and rested till dinner. Then went to show with Fitz and Hooker and later to jai-ali, where I ran into Mr. Duckworth and Noa Nolant, so

we sat at their table, and as usual, I had a lot of fun just kidding with 'em. The Countess was supposed to be there, but she didn't show up.

An order came out today stating that all officers would provide themselves with white mess jackets! Of all the *?Δ! things at a time like this, and it'll be at least 50 pesos, with all the gold braid and crap that goes on one. What an Army!

Sunday, Aug. 10, 1941
Ah, yes — Sunday, and another week closer to going home! I like these days of rest, and make the most of them — *in bed*! So, that's what I'm doing today — sleeping!

Monday, Aug. 11, 1941
Silver wedding anniversary of Mom and Dad tomorrow.

Tuesday, Aug. 12, 1941
Mom and Dad — twenty-five years together. God bless them, and may they have a happier twenty-five years to come.

Wednesday, Aug. 13, 1941
This is an organization day for the 31st Infantry. In fact it's the twenty-fifth anniversary of the 31st! Course, E Co. would get paraguard, so we didn't get in on any of the celebration, except a turkey dinner.

Thursday, Aug. 14, 1941
Ramsey went to the hospital today with dengue fever — so that puts me

in command of E Co. till he gets out. There are hundreds of things I have to take care of, it seems, and I'm learning, doing, and deciding all in one sweep. Being a CO is quite a task, and there are lot of new angles that crop up and disturb the mental alertness of a still-learning 2nd Lieutenant!!

Friday, Aug. 15, 1941
Uh-huh! It happened this morning!! I'm to be assigned to duty with the Philippine Army! About fifty officers and a number of NCOs[32] from our Regiment are going. Lts. Mathews, Hansen, Mallet, Brokaw and myself are going from the 2nd Bn. We don't know exactly when or where we're going or any details about it. It may happen next week. I wonder where I'll end up? Gee — mail will probably be very slow in reaching me — now I won't be able to call Pete on her birthday — I can't call now, 'cause I haven't enough money. One thing about this assignment — I'll be able to save money, and I've got to save money so Pete and I will *have* something on which to start. Oh, Pete didn't you really know? I'm going to ask you to be my wife, if I come out of this alive and enough like myself to be recognized. You will say "yes," won't you? You must.

Saturday, Aug. 16, 1941
Second Bn. is going out for a two day

field exercise next week, and I went a Co. Commanders meeting to learn the plans. I'm scared — hope I do O.K.! Guess I'd best pray for rain on Thursday.

Hah! Had a date with Diana Hill, *cousin* of Betty Gardiner, and you should have seen the fuss between them when the three of us bumped into one another at the Army and Navy Club!! I sure had a good laugh — it's all so silly — they know I'm deeply in love with Pete and that any dates I have over here are merely for a break in the monotony of continuous male companionship. And yet, they got all flustered 'cause I was out with both of them and they were cousins! What they don't know is that my good time is put on, and that my every thought is with Eileen when I have a date — that when I slip into a stare it's because I'm dreaming of Eileen and burning up inside with longing, yearning and fiery love.

Sunday, Aug. 17, 1941
Rain and plenty of it today. It certainly drops in sheets over here. The clipper is finally due in today and I'm way over-anxious and impatient for its arrival. Will write to the folks and Pete this afternoon and then I guess I'd better start getting a trunk ready with miscellaneous stuff to be sent home.

Monday, Aug. 18, 1941
Wonderful day today 'cause I got letters from folks and from Pete. Expected to have some word on Philippine Army, but not info. as yet.

---

32 Noncommissioned officers are appointed by a commissioned officer, generally to supervise enlisted soldiers and aid the commissioned officer corps. NCOs typically function at the rank of sergeant but can also serve as corporals.

Tuesday, Aug. 19, 1941

Having quite a time as CO! More worries to this job than meets the eye, but I am learning a lot and I think I'll profit, even from this short experience. Understand that we leave for the Philippine Army on the 25th.

Wednesday, Aug. 20, 1941

Usual grind today. Another clipper is due tonite. The field maneuvers have been put off till next Tuesday and Wednesday, and I'll probably be gone by then. Had a lot of trouble juggling the dull schedule around!

Thursday, Aug. 21, 1941

Darling Pete — you came thru for me again with your letter on the clipper, and it was grand to know you were, and are, able to sit up and type letters to me. It was such a warm letter too. I love you more than ever.

There's a meeting for the PA officers tomorrow — probably find out where we're going.

Friday, Aug. 22, 1941

Ramsey came back to duty. Found out I'm to go to the Island of Panay, to Iloilo City, about 350 miles from here (south). I'll be away about three months. Go by boat and we leave Tuesday, Aug. 25th. There's a helluva lot to do before then — wonder if I've enough to pay up everything and still keep enuff in for a checking account. Wish Holmes would pay me my 55 pesos. Bought a footlocker — guess I'll take my wardrobe trunk with me and my dress uniforms.

Saturday, Aug. 23, 1941

Gen. Wainwright in his address to officers going to PA said,

> You will have to use your ingenuity and pioneering spirit . . . we want results and we want them as soon as possible. Troops must be able to march and shoot. Prepare the PA for combat as soon as possible . . . your word is law, for you represent the next higher American CO.

Did a lot of running around today trying to arrange for my boat transportation. Bought stiff shirt white dress hat, and other incidentals. Had to go to a Red, White, and Blue tea dance that the Filipino debutantes gave for bachelor officers. I was so damned tired too — but if I hadn't gone, the Old Man would've jumped me. It was a party I could have missed and never known the difference.

Sunday, Aug. 24, 1941

Wrote to folks and Pete in the morning. Started packing, and was wishing I was packing for the United States! Jeez, I sure throw stuff in — I *should know* how to pack by now! Mom, I miss your experienced hand. You'd probably get all this stuff in one trunk whereas I'll be taking one wardrobe and two footlockers!

Guess I'll stay home tonight — don't feel like doing anything.

Monday, Aug. 25, 1941
Completed last minute pick-ups for trip to Iloilo.

Tuesday, Aug. 26, 1941
Sailed at 3:00 p.m. aboard S.S. *Corregidor* and it was quite loaded. Many Filipino officers, women and children and U.S. officers. Most of the Lieutenants had to sleep in the salon, on cots with a sheet for a mattress. We felt like a bunch of refugees instead of Army officers! It seemed good to be aboard a ship and to watch the wake foam up — if *only* this ship were going home — to Eileen! Felt very blue during the trip 'cause I daydreamed all the way; *almost* had myself believing I *was* going home — there'll come a day!!

Iloilo, Panay Island
Wednesday, Aug. 27, 1941
We were up at 5:30 a.m. — hell, the sun was so bright you couldn't sleep! Getting into the southern islands and the scenery is beautiful — mountainous islands with white sandy beaches decorated with high reaching green palm trees, and a blue haze covering the whole picture.

Arrived in the colorful port of Iloilo during the heat of day — 1:00 p.m., and after the boat was turned around in the channel, Capts. McLish, Forte, Jones, Hill, Lieuts. Katz, Weiland, Childers, Hinkle, and Bickerton got off. Considerable delay and confusion reigned for five hours as we tried to get transportation to Miagao,[33] 40 kilometers away. At last thru Don Paco Lopez, "Ward Boss" of half the Philippine Islands, we got to Miagao after dark. Our quarters we made in a house and we're quite comfortable. There are lots of ants and flies to keep us going too! The Army camp is on a nice site, and in the background are mountains and palm trees all around.

Miagao, Panay
Thursday, Aug. 28, 1941
Well, we started in checking property today and what a job. The 3rd Lieuts. of the PA had everything ready for us and things went quite smoothly. I checked clothing and equipment for F Co. of the 2nd Battalion. Jeepers, counted more stuff — today checked it all against memo — receipts. Hundreds of undershirts, pants, guns, towels, etc. I'm seeing an army going thru its growing pains and history in the making.

Friday, Aug. 29, 1941
Completed actual physical check of property today and helped officers of the PA with their paper work. Everything is going along quite smoothly. We eight officers are fairly well pleased with this place, though the ants are a terrific nuisance! There's always a breeze around our little knoll, but during the day it is very hot. Col. McClannan will probably come out to inspect the place and talk things over with us tomorrow.

---

33 Officially known as the municipality of Miagao, in the province of Iloilo, on the Philippine island of Panay.

Saturday, Aug. 30, 1941

Hallelujah! Col. McClannan came out and brought some mail for us! Way out here — I got a letter from Eileen and two from the folks. Gee, it was wonderful to get word from them. I needed a good tonic after feeling so homesick from the boat trip to here. Pete, I'm so happy you are finally getting up and doing a little walking; thank God for bringing you your health. But, *growing*!! Jeepers, don't grow anymore — I'm not too tall myself!!

Three of us went down to the market in Miagao this morning and what a sight! We had a mob of about 75 to 100 following us everywhere we went! It was very colorful, and many sights were repulsive — such as the complete hogs head; the bulls tail, testicles and penis, *intact*, hanging bloodily from a nail!! Everything is sold at these markets; cloth, meats, vegetables, hardware, etc.! Each of us bought a bolo knife and I think they're very beautifully made. Sent a wire to Pete — hope she gets it!

Sunday, Aug. 31, 1941

Lazy day, and read and slept from 6 a.m. to 11:00 a.m. Then Don Paco and two of his friends paid us a visit. He's some character alright. At times, he is quite ribald, and then impresses you with his authority and apparent power in the islands. Yes, Don Paco, (Francisco Lopez) is quite a man; shrewd, learned, traveled and very sociable. He wants to have us call on

him for anything we need. It'd be a beautiful setup, but as Army officers we must be careful to incur no obligations on our part. Tomorrow we induct the PA into the U.S. Army, check property again, and then Lt. Childers will go to Dingle; Capt. McLish will stay here, and Capt. Forte, Lieuts. Weiland, Bickerton, Katz, Layton, and myself will go back to Iloilo City.

Iloilo City
Monday, Sept. 1, 1941

At 7:30 a.m. today, we U.S. officers inducted the 61st Filipino Infantry into the U.S. Army. The ceremony was brief and to the point. Following that, there were hectic hours of checking equipment. Ye gads — how things did get messed up! We had a terrific time. The Filipinos couldn't quite grasp the idea and that made our work that much harder. Finally, at 8:15 p.m., we left Miagao mid a pouring rain and returned to Iloilo and took up residence at Heise's, an American who married a fine Filipina, and who operates a very nice boarding house hotel. My room and board will be 120 pesos a month.

Tuesday, Sept. 2, 1941

Now we are situated, and I have been detailed as rifle instructor for the cadres we are to train. Our location is Camp Delgado,[34] formerly barracks of an engineer cadre. We have cadres from the 62nd and 63rd Infantry, and more officers than men. Practically

---

34   Located on the waterfront in Iloilo City.

"Major Thayer instructing PA (USAFFE) officers at Camp Delgado. Iloilo, 1941." *Hinkle Archive*

on the same ground as the camp is an airfield and the planes will probably prove a hazard to our training program. I like Iloilo — it's much cleaner than Manila and the people are so hospitable and friendly. The only thing I am not going to like is the heat! God! How the sun does beat down on this island!

Wednesday, Sept. 3, 1941

Boy oh boy — I wish this rat race would come to a finish! Hell, no one seems to know what's going on and there are one hundred questions to be answered. We're *really* going to have to work to bring these parade ground Johnnies around to the point where they can be called officers! All they know is "yessir," and it makes you so goddamned mad when they say "yessir" and then go ahead and follow your orders in just the opposite manner, or in such a round about way that you feel like shooting the lot, and calling it a bad job.

There's not a heckuvalot to do here in Iloilo — there's the Swiss Club, which will probably be our hangout 'cause there's a bar, two good bowling alleys and a swimming pool. Happily, there are no dateable girls around and that makes it much easier to keep our gang together!

Thursday, Sept. 4, 1941

I've been working so damned hard and long that I'm beginning to wonder how long this can go on! Jeepers — after the day's work is done, we have to study up and prepare for our next day's work. At the present, we U.S. officers are actually conducting the classes and putting the initial screws on the men. My classes are mostly with the officers, and though they seem ready and willing, the able element has yet to be proven. Sometimes I feel that they're just plain dumb — then I figure that they don't understand everything — then I go back to the dumb theory! They love close order drill, but cripes, they've got to learn to become leaders of soldiers. I'll be damned if *I'll* fight *their* war!!

Friday, Sept. 5, 1941

This is quite a grind, and I'll be glad when Sunday comes around so I can get some sleep. We have to get up at 5:45 a.m. — drill starts at 7. Usually we get about 1¼ hours for lunch, and then back to work from 1:30 to 5 p.m. In this heat such a schedule is really quite an ordeal. Wait till the *afternoon* hikes start — ohh-boy!!! Hmmm — an added attraction — I had to teach officers school tonite from 7 to 9. What will they think of next???

Saturday, Sept. 6, 1941

Pete's birthday tomorrow. Believe it or not, didn't have to work this afternoon! Four of us took a "banco" with a sail and outriggers on it and went to Guimaras island, across the way. It was a fine little ship and the island was just like a Hollywood version of a tropical scene. Bamboo huts on stilts dotted the waters edge, and palm trees formed a protective canopy over the village. Certainly was colorful. Went to a party tonite — having been invited by Major Fran (PA). It was nothing to brag about and though there seemed to be life in this party, it was unattractive to us.

Sunday, Sept. 7, 1941

Pete — I love you. Yes I do, and I've put in a call to you and will expect to talk to you at 10 p.m., which will be 7 a.m. on your birthday at home. The manager of the telephone company gave me special permission to use a private phone at the Co. so I'd have no disturbance. [*On this page is a pressed orchid blossom and a written note, "Orchids to you kitten. What more can I say?"*]

Played nine holes of golf today on a very beautiful little course at Santa Barbara!! What could be more appropriate?? Made 57 on the nine.

Oh Pete, you're still unable to answer the phone! I'd counted so much on talking with you and hearing you say "Hello Wally" when the operator gave me the same dismal news. Oh darling, you *must* get well soon. I *must* talk with you! I've been thinking extra muchly of you today, and hoping you'd have as pleasant a day as you could. God bless you kitten, and make you well. I pray that we can spend our birthdays together from now on.

Monday, Sept. 8, 1941

Well, back with the rat race. Boy, I got mad at the officers today and really gave 'em a lacing. Oh, how I boiled! Why the damned dodoes — they pay no more attention to what you say than they do to the number of blades of grass in a field!! They go off and do something on their own and jazz things up just as you think you have things organized. Sooo — I let 'em have both barrels and then stood 'em at strict attention for a while. Hope it did some good!

Hah! Got four packages from home! Two records (fishing trip and birthday), talc, and Luckies. Thanks Mom — you're a peach. Decided that playing golf would do me some good over here, and after all, have to be able to keep up with Pop!

So, I sunk 54 pesos into five clubs and a bag. I'll have to add to the clubs as the months go on.

Tuesday, Sept. 9, 1941

It's getting to be regular routine now — this hard work and long hours. The hot sun certainly saps my energy — makes me feel weak and

"Typical Filipina in native dress — very colorful — blouse made of pina & hemp cloth. Sept. '41." *Hinkle Archive*

"Typical jungle. Panay '41." *Hinkle Archive*

"Native hearse." *Hinkle Archive*

"Church in Iloilo City, September '41." *Hinkle Archive*

"Bank of channel, Iloilo City. Left to Right: Layton, Weiland, Bickerton, Harding." *Hinkle Archive*

most disinterested in many things. Went and got tight last nite and now regret it! Felt pretty blue, though not having been able to talk to Pete. Am all worried again.

Wednesday, Sept. 10, 1941
Now we're having rain to contend with, and I hate to take my groups inside for lectures!

Thursday, Sept. 11, 1941
Same grind today. Captain Forte and I went to a war relief bazaar and had a fair time — something to do.

Friday, Sept. 12, 1941
Diary, my friend, you are going to suffer while I'm in Iloilo 'cause there is very little doing outside of Army duties! There was a despadida ball for Major Sevilla, and I wore my mess jacket for the 1st time!

Saturday, Sept. 13, 1941
Hah! Got some more records from home and really did enjoy them. Just about like being with the folks. Glad beyond words that they bought that recorder. Eventful Saturday nite — stayed in bed and read a book!

Sunday, Sept. 14, 1941
Hired Juan, a 13 year-old Filipino to look after my room and put my clothes away, take off my shoes, etc.!! He saw Pete's photo and asked, "Sir, is this your sweetheart? She is pretty as an artiste." Hence, Juan is undeniably an excellent houseboy!

Played 18 holes this morning with the amazing score of 110!! Boy, did I have an odor in my playing!! Got the exercise and some healthy swearing out of it, though!!

Monday, Sept. 15, 1941
Hot and tired today. At the start of a week here, it feels as though Sunday will never come! We're really putting out the work here, and the ignorance and stupidity of these Filipinos becomes more apparent everyday!

Tuesday, Sept. 16, 1941
Received a grand letter from Pete today, which will make the week so much easier. Doggone — wish the months would hurry by! Got my orders, extending my active duty. Orders read that I'm to be back in Chicago by October 27, 1942, but can't tell that to Pete or the folks. Will save it for about May or June, then the couple of more months won't seem so long — I hope!

Wednesday, Sept. 17, 1941
Drive, drive, yell, holler and sweat! Gave a short exam in rifle marksmanship today to my 173 Filipino officers, and the regimental commander got an "E!!" for effort. What a dope! What an uncontestable, irresponsible, impenetrable, naive, contemptuous dope! Lieutenant Almacen — nuts!!

Thursday, Sept. 18, 1941
Seems to me that just a year ago I was on my way to Utica, New York, in my new V-8, and proudly rolling along the highways. Hope those days aren't

gone forever! Hope Roosevelt takes it easy. I don't mind dying for my country, but I also believe in being cautious and not letting propaganda, emotions and headlines sweep the people off their senses. I see Japan has moved in the direction I predicted.

Friday, Sept. 19, 1941

Say, this is great. Got another wonderful letter from Pete, and she wrote the grandest words ever! I'm so glad the Chinese robe fit her. Hope she's not kidding me. God, how I love that little lady! Also got a letter from Eleanor. A letter from her has always proven stimulating and interesting. She's one of my fondest friends and I wish I had more like her, but then, there's only one Eleanor.

Saturday, Sept. 20, 1941

Had to take the whole camp out on a three and one half hour hike this morning. I had charge and Harding went with me.

Sunday, Sept. 21, 1941

Mr. Saul and Don invited us to Guimaras Island for the day. We took one of the outrigger sailboats and sailed the short distance over. Garcia has a cottage over there and liquor and food furnished. Its very beautiful. There's a small bay, and the shores have tall palm trees sticking up, and on either side are hills of about 500 feet in height. The hills are all green — palm trees, banana trees, nipa palm, etc., etc. The water in the bay is fairly calm and we

"Don Garcia's cottage on Guimaras Island — September 21, 1941." *Hinkle Archive*

went swimming at one of the sandy beaches. Before I went in, I was very thorough in my questioning about sharks. Swimming was undisturbed, however. Very peaceful over there. I can honestly say I liked the spot — enjoyed its serenity and beauty.

Monday, Sept. 22, 1941

Usual work today, and after 5:p.m. Capt. Paul Meng pilot of INAC, invited me for a flight over Iloilo in the Sikorsky S-43, which naturally I took! [*Written in the margin: "Later shot and killed while trying to burn his car in Iloilo sometime in April, during the invasion."*] It was the first time I'd seen the tropics from the air, and it was quite interesting to see the palm groves and the maize of water patties. Iloilo seems spread out all over the place! What really was beautiful was the very crimson sunset, with the mountains in the foreground — it was really a sight.

Tuesday, Sept. 23, 1941

Got my mail from home — that is, a "puzzle" compliments of Pabst Blue

Ribbon! and the Tribune! Sure enjoy reading about home; and get homesick as the devil.

Wednesday, Sept. 24, 1941
These Filipinos are getting to be a greater headache every day! They just can't seem to grasp things quickly, and about the time they do be learning, they do the stuff backwards! Tomorrow, Major Thayer and I take the riflemen out on the range, AMEN!

Thursday, Sept. 25, 1941
Off to Alimodian, the rifle range — a roar of three old buses and a crummy station wagon and two Army trucks. The range has ten targets, and the pits are across the river from the firing point! The firing point is full of rocks and mud, and the entire area is muddy. Surrounding the range are some mountains, and plenty of palm trees. Had them put up our fly tent in a sheltered spot. The Caribao[35] had apparently been using the spot as a "dump!!" Cripes — it smelled like a rabbit farm! The targets weren't ready for us, and then when we were ready to fire, it poured rain! After the rain we again attempted firing and this time found that we had the wrong ammo. So — the Lieutenant "O" goes back to Iloilo to find Bickerton and ask him what the Hell? Returned to camp at 8 p.m., amidst a swarm of moths, crickets, mosquitoes and ants. I crawled in my bunk and slept very soundly.

---

35   Carabao are swamp-dwelling, domestic water buffalo native to the Philippines.

Friday, Sept. 26, 1941
Oh, what a mess these "soldiers" are! They're scared of the rifle and they haven't gained a damned thing from three and one half weeks of labor I've spent on them! It makes me so damned mad! They can't remember a thing! Left and right elbows all in the wrong position — jerking the trigger, flinching — X?!!?

Saturday, Sept. 27, 1941
Had quite a time today with rapid fire! Lt. Romana irked me to the Nth degree, since he was in charge of the pits and jazzed up all orders and directions I gave him! I swear I could have killed him — all the time he wasted for us. We were supposed to be there by noon, but didn't finish until 4 p.m. Even then, we didn't have the men fire the BAR. Instead, I fired it in demonstration for them. I don't know what's the matter with these men. Perhaps they get nervous when all the shooting takes place. If that's so, they're no damned good as soldiers!! I'm sure my instruction has been good, and that an American group of recruits would have known how to go about firing a rifle properly on the range. These men don't seem to be too interested however, and I guess they don't like the hard work. By the way — it rained all morning but we had to keep firing!

Sunday, Sept. 28, 1941
Oh boy — slept till 7:55 this morning, got up, and went down to get a haircut at a Japanese barbershop.

It was quite a ritual. A male cut my hair, and next, I was handled by a Jap gal who gave me a neck shave that continually threatened to involve my back! This "shave" was followed by hot towels and a Listerine rub-down. Then I was placed in the "horizontal" position and my face, neck and ears were steamed and washed, and again the Listerine! Sitting up again my hair was combed and then my arms, from the biceps to fingers, were washed off with hot towels and that was the end!! All of this for .40 pesos.

Capt. Forte, myself and Lts. Harding and Leyton were invited to dinner at Mrs. McCreary's today. Before a swell turkey dinner we had a real mint julep that was really a mint julep!! After dinner came the cordial. Yessir, we really did things up today!

Monday, Sept. 29, 1941
Range "season" started out with a bang today, and as usual we were two hours late in getting started. Got out to the range with the officers, set up camp, and began firing.

Tuesday, Sept. 30, 1941
Up at 4:30 and very tired. It rained hard all day, but we continued firing because of the limited time we have. The officers show little improvement over the enlisted men when it comes to shooting. Came into Iloilo for supper and then at 8 p.m. drove back to Alimodian, where our camp is, and slept on my bedding roll.

"Our rifle range at Alimodian." *Hinkle Archive.*

"Lt. Amor calls the pits on the rifle range. One of the best PA officers." *Hinkle Archive*

"The rifle range at Alimodian." *Hinkle Archive.*

Wednesday, Oct. 1, 1941

This is getting tiresome already. We yell our heads off, striving for correct position, good shooting and discipline, but these people just can't seem to catch on. Almost ready to give up! Rain again.

Thursday, Oct. 2, 1941

Rain, rain! It's cool this way, but it sure raises hell with the morale and with the guns!

Friday, Oct. 3, 1941

Last of this! At 4:30 six of the seven buses arrived to take us back to Iloilo. Major Thayer took the six busses in, and I waited with the last twenty-one men for the last bus. At 6:30 p.m. it finally came, and we loaded up, glad we were finally on the way! At 6:40 we had a flat tire!! Three-quarters of an hour later we again were on our way — made it this time!

Saturday, Oct. 4, 1941

Inspection as usual on Saturday. Mail day, and how! Clipper finally made it! Two letters from Pete, three from the folks, one from Eleanor, and one from Dink. Feel much, much happier now. Life's worth living and more so as long as I can live for Eileen.

Golf today: gave me a 64 and a 46 — same difference, eh?

Sunday, Oct. 5, 1941

Catching up on my letter writing, bill paying, filing and studying. Otherwise no new events.

Monday, Oct. 6, 1941

Started work on technique of fire of rifle and tactics of squad. Gotta do lots of studying for this. Finally got one of my ideas incorporated into our methods of training, and now we have "assistant instructors" who are responsible for teaching! Had to get into position to show these men just what was required — words mean nothing to them.

Tuesday, Oct. 7, 1941

Jeepers, my face breaking out a little bit — must be from shaving too close. Doesn't itch, more like a couple of cold-sores on my chin.

Wednesday, Oct. 8, 1941

Well, my face is a mess now, and it itches like a bushel of mosquito bites! Went to the hospital and the Dr. said it was a rash caused by some grass pollen. Hence, it was incurred "in line of duty" when I was showing the men how to get into a firing position. Got marked "Quarters" and came back to Jackie Heise's and slapped mercurochrome and boric acid powder on my face! Juan said I looked like a clown. Golly, how it does itch. Am supposed to stay out of the sun, so I unexpectedly get a day of rest. Five months ago I landed at Manila. I pray that twelve months from now I can set sail from Manila and return home.

Thursday, Oct. 9, 1941

Face all plastered with two new kinds of salve, and I'm staying in Quarters this morning. Golly, I can't stay in all day — gotta do my part of the work around here.

Friday, Oct. 10, 1941
Forgot to fill in.

Saturday, Oct. 11, 1941
Woof! What a day!! Fiesta at the Army camp, and Jakie Heise's wedding. She was married at 7:30, we had our first drink at the Swiss Club, as we sat around enjoying "breakfast." A good number of people were there and Jackie looked very lovely in her wedding gown, and we didn't look so bad in our "whites" either. The drinks kept coming and then we saw them off on the boat for Manila. Katz and Harding "did up" the wrong cabin, and some Filipino congressman found rice and whatnot in his bed!! Next came the fiesta, and changed into mess jacket. Stayed at the dance for about two hours, but didn't enjoy it. Kept thinking how wonderful it will be to go out someplace and dance with Eileen — to go someplace where we won't be stared at — where I won't be expected to be setting examples and shaking scores of hands! Met Father Casey during the day and told him my problem of church, Eileen and myself and he said he'd teach me about the church, since it's never too late. Given the time, I'll let him teach and see how much I can accept.

Saturday, Sunday, & Monday
Oct. 12-13-14, 1941
Slept till seven, then up for a game

"Oct. 11, 1941. Jackie Heise and Fritz Loring having a laugh. Walter Saul, Buck Layton and Murry Katz on left." *Hinkle Archive*

of golf. At 3:00 p.m. Capt. Meng said he'd take us up "dead-head" for a flight over Panay in the Sikorsky 43, an amphibian. So, at 3:30, seven of us climbed aboard, and took off for what we thought was to be a twenty minute test flight. As we winged our way over Panay, Capt. Meng told us we'd be up three hours, which made us happy indeed. Over Panay we went over high mountains, coconut groves and rice patties. Came back along the coast, over Guimeras, across Negros toward Cebu. At Cebu we began to turn back, and as we did, the right motor began sputtering and Meng was shutting off and turning it on. We thought he was testing it so didn't worry at all. Then we were told to fasten our belts, and saw Meng starting to work the fuel pump. Capt. Van Nostrand and I began talking about how swell it'd be to land on the water, and as we kept losing altitude, that's exactly what happened, and with *both* motors dead, and the right one smoking a little, we glided to a landing on the smooth water at 5:00

p.m. We had landed at San Carlos, Negros — about 50 minutes by plane from Iloilo! Meng told us we'd have to stay over-night and that there was a sugar plantation in San Carlos run by Mr. Robinson, and also that an Australian, Mr. Philips would put us up for the night. There were about 5,000 people on the pier and coast watching our actions, and a banca, hollowed from a log, came out and took us to land. It smelled of fish and was rocky and unstable. Quite nerve racking thrill to ride in it, and quite uncomfortable. Layton and I bought some flashlights and batteries and took them back to the plane, and then we went to Philips, met him, had a beer and then ate supper. He, in turn, introduced us to Mr. Robinson of the Sugar Plantation, and we went to the latter's house for the night. He has a beautiful place — wonderful wood carvings, beautiful furniture, brass works, swell bedrooms with beds plus real springs and mattresses, and tile baths! For the first time in seven weeks I slept without being confined under a mosquito bar! At 5:30 a.m. we went to the plane — they had repaired the damage and we took off at 6:15 and arrived in Iloilo safely at 7:05. Got back to find that everyone was worried about us and hadn't received word about our whereabouts till 8:30 p.m. Sunday. Grabbed breakfast, washed, changed into a uniform and off to work by 7:45. So ended our adventure! The folks'll never know of this until I read it from here personally, 'cause they'd just worry.

Tuesday, Oct. 14, 1941
Off we go to Guimbal, 30 kilometers away and there we'll camp for two weeks so we'll have terrain for our tactical problems. On the way out, my gang and I had to march ten kilometers in the hot sun, and after we arrived in Guimbal, we pitched tents in a coconut grove. Our afternoon training was rained out, and it really rained! We're working it so only two U.S. officers have to stay at the camp at night, and the rest of us can come in for a good meal. Food is really a problem, 'cause we can't eat the stuff Filipinos do, so we have to exist on bananas and sandwiches! Say!! Johnny Stevens of U. of M. arrived here in Iloilo yesterday, and I was never more surprised and pleasantly so, in my life! Golly, and I initiated Johnny into Scabbard and Blade, and now we're almost together over here! He's going to Negros to the same kind of work I'm doing. We had a lot of fun talking over old times, and both of us got pretty homesick at the same time. He arrived in P.I.[36] Sept. 26. Good luck "Junior."

Wednesday, Oct. 15, 1941
Am conducting field problems for the squad, giving them simple problems for patrols, defense, outposts, etc. They're doing fair — nothing fiery. I don't want to have to fight with them, ever!!

Thursday, Oct. 16, 1941
This week is dragging; its so damned hot under this sun, and its such a

---

36 Philippine Islands.

"Maneuvers, Guimbal, Iloilo." *Hinkle Archive*

job to get these men to do what you want them to do. Harding and I stay in camp tonite. The rest of the officers are invited to a dinner for General Grunert, and of course the 2nd Lieutenants get the dirty end of the deal. They did leave us a fifth of scotch though, which we massacred!!

Friday, Oct. 17, 1941

The general came out to the camp, turned on the hot air for awhile, and between the lines we American officers kept hearing, "This is a paper army." I wonder if we're not right?

Saturday, Oct. 18, 1941

The week is over, and seven weeks of training are finished, which theoreti-

cally leaves only six more weeks to go. Happy day!

Sunday, Oct. 19, 1941

At 9 a.m. Major Thayer, "Pop" Heise and I went to a show!! Saw "Underground," some propaganda. Wonder how true it is?

Well! Of all the damnable things. Here I'm just getting over that doggoned itch, and now I discover I have a dose of crabs!! Apparently picked them up in the banca in San Carlos. Nuts! And, I've also a cold and running a fever. What more can a fellow ask?

Monday, Oct. 20, 1941

Walked Quarters today and have been

rubbing salve into the crabs, showering, taking laxatives, nose drops, and
reading. I'm picking up everything
around here. Father Monte and Father
Carr came to see me in the afternoon
and brought some books that give
some of the history of the church, and
I'm glad to read them so that Pete and I
can discuss this very important subject.

Tuesday, Oct. 21, 1941
Still on quarters. Getting lots of rest
but have a headache and am moody
and blue. Have too much time just
to think of home and of Eileen, and
though I love my memories, they
make the time crawl slowly.

Wednesday, Oct. 22, 1941
Well, it looks like a week on quarters.
Am still "chasing crabs," and my cold
is no better. It's a touch of the flu, I
know, 'cause I feel about the way I
did last May.

Thursday, Oct. 23, 1941
Thought I'd go to work today, but
Captain Forte said there was no need
for me to do so, and "Whyn't you
just stay in all week?!" 'Course I said,
"Ok," why not?

Friday, Oct. 24, 1941
Hmmm — the days are dragging because of being idle, though I've read
six books, almost completed a photo
album, wrote letters — slept. Where
the hell's the clipper?!!

Saturday, Oct. 25, 1941
Off quarters today, return duty on

Monday. There's a barn dance party
at the Iloilo Club tonite, and we're all
going. (Suckers!)

Some party! Some barn-dance, too,
where they had a twelve piece orchestra and played tangos, rhumbas,
waltzes, etc.! Maybe it was a Spanish
barn! At least we couldn't teach the
English, Swiss, and Spanish how to
square dance, and they couldn't do
much with us when it came to their
folk dances. Met Manolita Lanhorra,
a rather pretty Spanish girl and danced
with her quite a bit. Couldn't take
her home, of course. That is not one
of the "old Spanish customs!" Drank
surprisingly little — two drinks, and
it was really a wet party. Captain Forte
put on a despicable demonstration
of how drunk and obnoxious a U.S.
Army officer can get, and I'm afraid it
didn't help our cause any. Am rapidly
losing my respect for the egoist.

Sunday, Oct. 26, 1941
No mail all week, and that makes it a
dreary weekend no matter what goes
on. Hope Michigan won yesterday.
Bet the folks had a swell time at the
game. Lucky people. Boy, wait'll
I can take Eileen to an Ann Arbor
football game!

Dingle[37]
Monday, Oct. 27, 1941
Layton and I took a convoy of eight
trucks full of reservists to Dingle
this morning, and we'll stay there all
week. The officers will be out tomor-

---

37   A municipality northeast of Iloilo City, Panay.

row. Dingle is fourty-two kilometers out. The Army post there is well situated, what with lots of coconut trees around and mountains in the near background. Buck and I put our cots up in Capt. Van Nostrand's quarter. We'll get to go in tomorrow nite to get our mail.

Tuesday, Oct. 28, 1941
Well, here it is — one years service, and if I hadn't come over here, I might've stopped playing soldier and gone to work like a good civilian! And a year form now I'll probably still be on duty.

Took a trip up to Banate to see terrain for beach defenses. I think this island is really beautiful. The beach looked so picturesque and peaceful — native bancas with their sails, on the green blue water, and the shacks on the beach. After haranguing to get transportation we got back to Iloilo to find no mail! Jeez — this is getting irksome and nerve-wracking.

Wednesday, Oct. 29, 1941
The training at Dingle is going along O.K. I've put most of the responsibility in the hands of the Filipinos, to let them know how it feels — 'cause I'm certainly not going to be here to lead them forever! As a result, I've found several nice bamboo clumps that produce shade, and I've parked under them for hours, and instead of thinking of the tactical problems on hand, I'd find myself right in Santa Barbara with you, Pete, wondering how you

are now, praying that everything is alright, and finally I'd get all in a stew about the clipper not getting here.

Thursday, Oct. 30, 1941
Every day, we ride the 42 kilometers in to get our mail, but there isn't any to get!

Iloilo City
Friday, Oct. 31, 1941
We got back to Iloilo this afternoon at 3 p.m., so Harding and I went to a show to kill time.

I knew it was going to happen one of these days, but I was wondering how long I would hold out. Captain Forte, Layton and myself had it out, Forte vs us. Forte has shown himself to be of a very over-bearing nature, and is as egotistical as can be. All that's done should be Forte's way, 'cause Forte "went to the Point and to Benning." He has been getting on our nerves with his continual bitching and verbal worrying, and at last when Layton and I saw the work laid out for the two of us for next week, we blew up. So of course, Forte had first say, during which time *I* was raked over coals, and told wherein I was a "disappointment." Among the childish things (always found as excuses in ego-arguments) came incidents on the golf course and at a party! After Forte seemed well exhausted, I worked my way into talking steadily for about 15 or 20 minutes and really told Forte what I thought of him, and that if he took inventory of himself, he would find more to blame in Forte than anyone else. After me, Layton got in and pitched. Result = we're all more relaxed and understand each other, and all shall go smooth now.

Saturday, Nov. 1, 1941
Guess the clippers have ceased operations. Two weeks now, and no mail. Had an easy morning. Played golf in afternoon, did rottenly — 111. Went to Halloween party (mixed races, of course). Fair time, nothing worth writing about. Forte and Katz flew to Manila just for the week-end. Dopes! Think of *Forte* leaving his men for such a period of time! *What a disappointment!*

Sunday, Nov. 2, 1941
Mrs. Heise took some of us to Arevalo where the natives weave piña into beautiful things. They use very primitive hand looms and the work is most tedious. Working from dawn to dusk, everyday, a woman can finish only four yards in a week. The piña fiber is gained from the pineapple, and each fiber is only about thirteen or fourteen inches long, very fine and strong. These fibers must be *hand-tied* together to make them longer. Their work is beautiful. I bought 25 pesos worth of piña goods, and I wouldn't be too far off if I guessed that it would cost me $75 in the States!

Monday, Nov. 3, 1941
Uppermost in my mind is the arrival of mail, and as yet such has not been

the case! Tomorrow the gang is supposed to go back out to Dingle.

Tuesday, Nov. 4, 1941
Regular drill in the morning. At 1:30 p.m., the crew moved out for Dingle. Three of us had the afternoon off, and stayed in Iloilo. Received two letters from Mom and Dad today, but none from Pete. At least the clipper has arrived.

Wednesday, Nov. 5, 1941
Went to Dingle in the morning, and since I wasn't scheduled for any afternoon classes, Harding and I came into Iloilo via hitch-hiking! It was great. All we had to do was stand in the middle of the road, a hand on the gun while ordering trucks to stop. After they stopped we'd order people out of the most comfortable seats, and move in!! AND — I got my letter from Pete today, and it was wonderful. Every letter she writes is bringing her closer to me, and she's becoming more dear to me.

Dingle
Thursday, Nov. 6, 1941
Back out at Dingle and to sweat away in the hot sun. Just six months ago today since I landed in the Philippine Islands. Eleven more months and twenty-one days! (I hope!)

Friday, Nov. 7, 1941
Damn! I broke one of the supports in my cot last nite, and now I have to sleep in a young counterpart of the Rocky Mts.! It's bad enough eating

fried chicken for lunch and dinner, with tomato juice and pork and beans for breakfast!!

Iloilo City
Saturday, Nov. 8, 1941
Hah! At 4 a.m., we called the men out for an alert, and it was sad — very sad! By 5 a.m. they were still puttering around, so we gave up and weren't back to bed for one hour. Then inspection, and at 8:30 we boarded busses and headed for Iloilo. Our jitney broke down, and luckily, the Major and I were able to hail an Army truck to bring us back in! Got in my room and Juan handed me a fist-full of mail which made me extremely happy. A g-r-e-a-t letter from Eileen, telling me she was sitting up and walking more! Wonderful — thank God! A swell letter from Eleanor, another from Mom and Dad, one from Mabel Heise and some bills. In the p.m. — went shooting color pictures in the market, then went to play golf and shot the best game ever. Made 97! If it hadn't been for a "10" and an "8": it might (might!) have been 90!

Sunday, Nov. 9, 1941
Slept till luxurious hour of 7:30! Then had breakfast. Read some more, and then completed writing up diary. Will write Pete and folks today as usual. Went banca sailing, and then we put in a lot of exercise at Villa Beach — high jumping, touch football, coconut tree climbing and swimming. Plenty tired.

[No entry for November 10.]

Tuesday, Nov. 11, 1941
Holiday today — Harding, Layton and I had the official car and drove up to Calinog to take in the scenery and take pictures. Once you see this part of this island, you've seen everything.

Wednesday, Nov. 12, 1941
Am seriously thinking, in fact have almost fully decided to open up a delicatessen when I get home. Will try and get a counter job in one for a couple of months to learn the business, then will branch out on my own. Thought I'd open around 79th or over East. I hope Eileen finds this agreeable. Otherwise its Eleanor, Shirl or a bachelor life. Will probably change my mind tho! Plan on a large Frigidaire, stainless steel fittings, water sprinklers for the vegetables and small tobacco and magazine stand. Will seek to cater to upper classes with German foods, and Kosher style meats and bread, as well as pickled herring. Should go for around $10,000 or 15.

[No entries for November 13–14.]

Saturday, Nov. 15, 1941
I remember this was a Holiday — Commonwealth Day. (I'm writing this on Nov. 23rd, seemed to have neglected my diary writing — since most everything has been usual stuff.)

Sunday, Nov. 16, 1941
Think I loafed all day!

Monday, Nov. 17, 1941
Found out the 31st has moved 65 miles north of Manila to Tarlac. The Estado Mayor is to be a hospital (happy preparation!) and the Cuartel is to house an AA[38] outfit. Wonder what Tarlac is like? Think I'd rather stay here.

[No entry for November 18.]

Wednesday, Nov. 19, 1941
Some new officers arrived today. They're going out to Dingle to take over a unit of field artillery there. A Lt. Col., Maj. and 3 Lieuts.

Thursday, Nov. 20, 1941
Thanksgiving Day, at the Heise's, and I had to mix Barcardi cocktails, which baffled me at first, 'cause I'd never before mixed cocktails. But, I made OK, and now I *do* know how to mix! Had a California turkey and all the trimmings, plus a long sleep in the afternoon. It wasn't like last year though, or the years before. I sure missed the ole smell of turkey roasting at 8201 S. Peoria, and Mom fussing around the kitchen with whipped cream, potatoes, salad, etc. I missed home very muchly today and kept thinking of you, Mom and Dad, and of you Eileen, because you gave me something for which I'm thankful.

Friday, Nov. 21, 1941
Captain Forte, Lt. Katz, and Van Nostrand, Childers, McLish and their gang all left for Negros today, and

that leaves the Col., Maj., and four of us here with the 63rd Cadre, and not a helluva lot to do, and no orders! Wonder what will happen to us?

Saturday, Nov. 22, 1941
Piddled around in the morning. Went to a show in the afternoon, then slept.

Had a date with Alice Schmid tonite, and Fritz went along as chaperon. It helps me to talk to Alice about Eileen, and all my worries and troubles. She, (just as I tell myself) says not to worry. If Eileen is in love with me, she'll wait. Will you darling?

Sunday, Nov. 23, 1941
Slept late. Wrote to folks and Eileen.

Monday, Nov. 24, 1941
No airmail as had been expected. Can't understand why not. Notified today that the 63rd Inf. Cadre would be divided, and groups plus one U.S. officer would be sent to difficult camps for training with the 62nd. I'm going to Panitan, Capiz, one-hundred-and-two kilometers north of here, and taking the First Battalion, which amounts to fourty-five men! Cripes — now I gotta pack, buy food, etc., and don't know how long I'll be gone! Juan is going with me — hope he doesn't get too homesick!

Had a date with Alice tonight and told her more about the wiles of American men, and warned her on what to beware of. She's too nice to be made a sucker of!

---

38   Antiaircraft.

"View of Cadre at Panitan, province of Capiz, Panay." *Hinkle Archive*

"Officers 63rd Infantry PA enroute to Panitan, Province of Capiz, Panay. December, 1941." *Hinkle Archive*

"My battalion HQ." *Hinkle Archive*

Tuesday, Nov. 25, 1941

All set to go. Said "Adios" and got on the motor train at 2:20 p.m. It stopped about every five or ten minutes, and finally at 6:30 p.m. we arrived. Lieutenant Montag and Weiland met us, and after a lot of horsing around, we put the baggage and men on the two trucks and went two kilometers to camp. Got the men quartered, and then me. I'm with Montag and Weiland, in the upstairs of one of the barracks. It's cool, but there are 1000s of ANTS! Let the problems be forgotten and went to sleep.

Panitan, Province of Capiz, Panay
Wednesday, Nov. 26, 1941
Well, this is almost going to be a rest camp for me for a few days at least! My group is attached to the 62nd for training, so that puts them on the 62nd morning reports, and relieves our paper work. There are many, many Scout[39] instructors and besides, too many of the newly inducted do not know English. So, as an assistant instructor there isn't a helluva lot for me to do! This is Camp del Castillo, and it's the most scenic of all the camps I've been to. We're in a small valley here and completely surrounded by rolling hills, and a few peaks. Palm trees stud the horizon and sky lines, and the breeze is fairly perpetual since we are near the sea. Water is the greatest problem, and we have a rain water receptacle, plus a well, pump and motor, and 45,000 gallon capacity tank. It takes three days to fill the tank, hence it is never full. Food! I'm sure I shall lose some weight. Canned foods present such a fine diet! Our "cook" was ambitious and we had banana soup for breakfast this morning!! Almost tossed my cookies for a touchdown!!

Thursday, Nov. 27, 1941
Stewed tomatoes, a fried egg, coffee, bread and peanut butter for breakfast. Not so bad, really.

I'm doing nothing, and I don't like it. My interest in this work has been dropping, and now its really going down. This wasn't a good idea — splitting up the 63rd, 'cause my officers and men don't have any special duties or authorities and we all feel like bastards!

Friday, Nov. 28, 1941
Weiland and I took a truck and headed for Iloilo. I'll stay the weekend — Weiland will return tomorrow. Ordered some food, silverware, etc. Then went to Heise's and got a room. Had a date with Alice, and we went to a show. Sure felt good to sleep in a bed!

Saturday, Nov. 29, 1941
Found out today that the 63rd Infantry will be mobilized on December 15th, and I will induct the First Battalion at Banga.[40] Headaches ahead! Lost more money at craps, and have finally sworn off!

Sunday, Nov. 30, 1941
Having caught cold, I overdosed on benzedrine yesterday, and didn't sleep last nite. Plenty dopey — like today, yet I tried to write the folks and Eileen, but I'm sure they won't enjoy the letters — maybe shouldn't have sent them. Layton dragged me along with Alice and we went out to Fritz

39   The Philippine Scouts were a military organization of the US Army from 1901 until 1948. These troops were generally Filipinos and Filipino Americans assigned to the United States Army Philippine Department, under the command of American commissioned officers. Walter Hinkle was one of these officers.

40   Banga is located approximately 30 miles west of Panitan, in the northwest portion of Panay. However, it is possible that Hinkle is referring to Banga-an, a barangay in the municipality of Panitan, in the province of Capiz. Panitan is politically subdivided into twenty-six barangays, the Filipino term for a district or ward.

"Ferrying my car at New Washington, Capiz. Dec. '41." *Hinkle Archive*

Loring's beach house and just "lolled" around all afternoon. Another show at night to make me sleepy — and at that I slept. Looks like the Japs are getting out of hand.

Monday, Dec. 1, 1941
Slept late — It's a Philippine holiday. Bowled a few games of duck-pins, had lunch, and at 2:30 p.m. again boarded "train" for Panitan.

Hot at Panitan, and had a meal of corned beef, spaghetti, and chocolate late (which I brought from Iloilo, courtesy of Mr. Heise).

[*No entries for December 2–4.*]

Friday, Dec. 5, 1941
Went to Iloilo to get supplies and prepare for 15th.

Sunday, Dec. 6, 1941
Letters from folks, Eileen, George Karpers and Tribune.

Sunday, Dec. 7, 1941
Slept late – then was ordered to remain till tomorrow a.m. when the Colonel is going to have a meeting of officers. Wrote Eileen and folks. Gee, Xmas is less than three weeks away, and then I can call up Eileen, and Mom and Dad; it'll be swell to hear their voices again. Hope Pete can get to the phone.

Monday, Dec. 8, 1941
WAR!
WAR!
WAR!
U.S. declared WAR on Japan! At 6:30 a.m. we got the report that the Japs had bombed Pearl Harbor, in Hawaii. Then reports that Davao, Baguio, Fort Stotsenburg had been bombed. This is war — I have mixed feelings. My stomach has butterflies in it and I feel empty and suddenly totally lonely. My first thought was of Eileen and Mom and Dad — they are probably worrying about me, and I wish they wouldn't — it'll just wear them out. Had our meeting — everyone suddenly serious and hard, at the same time not believing the reports. Our defense plan was discussed, and we realized how poorly equipped we were and at what disadvantage we are.

On the train to Panitan — people are evacuating Iloilo and the train was packed! Everywhere was the stir of excitement. Arrived in camp and found out that my battalion had received orders to go to Banga at once, and we made preparations. All men issued ammo — from now on we shoot first and then ask questions.

Tuesday, Dec. 9, 1941
It's a new experience to lie awake part of the night and listen for airplanes and bombs — I don't like it! Dined in Banga and immediately had 1,001 things to do such as; post my MGs; arrange for food; pick a camp site; form an alert system; place outposts;

visit the mayor and chief of constabulary to arrange for obtaining information about Japs, clearing roads and blackouts; arrange for telephone to be installed; talk to officers concerning our job, its seriousness, etc.; arrange for digging latrines; give orders to interior guards, outpost guards, Bn. Ex. Off; Start S-3 on schedule-mailing; teach officers new kind of tactics for defense. Mailed radiograms to be sent by KAIHR to Pete and folks. Hope they get them. Clipper mail will probably stop, and they won't get word for a long time. Finally I got to bed, only to be awakened by three shots, but it was a U.S. plane so we were at ease again.

Wednesday, Dec. 10, 1941
Have been steadily busy all day. Checking clothing, rifles, MGs, etc. for over 400 men. They should have assigned at least two of us here. It's a hard job trying to prepare to mobilize a Bn., such as defend your camp, start training men and get your own required work done. Report today that Jap planes were over 'Frisco! God grant we are strong enough to protect Eileen and all the other American citizens on our coasts. Am not particularly worried about the safety of Chicago, it is inland sufficiently. Report Japs landed at Aparri on north Luzon. Also that Tarlac (31st. Infantry) and Nichols Field were bombed. Am personally prepared to shoot down anyone who gets in my way. I want to return to Eileen, so that we can fulfill our lives and be together as

"I swear in some of my Bn. Bunga, Capiz." *Hinkle Archive*

we should have been all these years. I will come back Pete — never fear, and I'll be carrying my dog tags, not wearing them!

Thursday, Dec. 11, 1941

I go to bed nites, but I'm not sure whether or not I'll wake up alive! Wonderful feeling!

Report — MANILA BOMBED. No reports on U.S. activity. What the Hell? Are we pulling an England? We ought to land a force in [*censored by Hinkle with heavy black india ink*] all the way back to their first ancestors. I'm itching to get into action now that we're in it. Trouble is, I have no men. I have to induct my Bn. — then train them!! We've been alerted sev-

eral times by our guards, but all have been U.S. planes.

Friday, Dec. 12, 1941

I am getting worn out! All the damn things to think of! Telegrams and orders keep coming in and they have to be deciphered 'cause they're all mixed up. Was ordered to send what men I have and all property to Lambunao, in Iloilo Province. Have never been there, but believe it is in mountains. Luckily, I saw a motorcycle and sidecar, and had the owner teach me how to drive it. After ten minutes I was on my way to Kalibo (12 kms.) to get transportation for my men and equipment. Finally, at 12:15 noon, a convoy of five buses and five trucks pulled out for Lambunao. Had

"Mobilization of my BN at Banga, Capiz." *Hinkle Archive*

to do most of directing and ordering myself. These Filipino officers just can't seem to catch on to the word action. In the afternoon, volunteers and uncalled reservists began pouring in and I began sending telegrams to find out what the hell to do with them. I've a headache bigger than this building and my brain is becoming weary of all the small questions that are asked — things that a little initiative would take care of.

Report — Manila bombed last nite.

Saturday, Dec. 13, 1941
Now I've orders to "induct everyone I can handle," whatever the hell that means. I'm sending men all over, it seems, and I don't know where they

are going. I get no news or info other than my orders and instructions via telegram. I send telegrams to HQ but never know whether to send them to Iloilo, Santa Barbara (Iloilo!), or Lambunao!! Report — one-hundred-and thirteen planes (Jap) flew over Batangas yesterday, but no bombs.

Sunday, Dec. 14, 1941
Received orders to move my Bn. to Lambunao tomorrow — lock, stock and barrel. What a job trying to round up the transportation!

Monday, Dec. 15, 1941
After a lot of cursin' and screamin' around, got my convoy of some ten busses and trucks headed toward Lambunao. We got there and I im-

mediately had to reconnoiter and pick a campsite and then gave orders to pitch camp. Was told I was acting Bn. CO and all it's worries were mine!

Tuesday, Dec. 16, 1941
Have our HQ in the house of a Filipino Padre — eating fairly well. My Bn. is spread out down a hillside nearby. Will be here for one day or so, and then move on. Fitzpatrick, Greathouse, Horney and self here. Juan is with me, of course. Woke up about 3:00 a.m. and realized that I was feeling my first earth quake!! Boy! My cot was really catching hell! Just as though someone was standing at the foot of it and shaking it vigorously. For a few seconds I was seized with fear. Then I heard Greathouse wake up and say, "What the hell?!!" Accordingly, I burst out laughing so loudly that I awakened the rest of the gang, so we all had a cigarette, talked of the quake, and back to sleep.

Wednesday, Dec. 17, 1941
Tomorrow to move my Bn. to Pavia, near Sta. Barbara, about ten or twelve kilometers from Iloilo.

Thursday, Dec. 18, 1941
Iloilo bombed 1:30 p.m. I was in Pavia and kilometers away at our new camp when I saw forty-two Japanese planes. Went to Iloilo just as last planes dropped bombs and another strafed. Terrorizing sensation. Saw many wounded — torn apart — bodies ripped and shredded. Many killed by concussion, fragments and MGs.

Japanese used MG about 50 or 60mm, explosive shell — very damaging, brutal, and Bn. firing at planes when I sighted them.

Started on motorcycle, broke down, got car. I was shot in right ankle at 8:15 p.m. while on mission. Sgt. Ludublau hit by same bullet. Completed mission first, then we were taken to hospital at 9:30 p.m. and doctor operated on me. Was on table two-and-one-half hours! All doctors and head nurses in attendance. Guinea pig!

Friday, Dec. 19, 1941
In Iloilo Mission Hospital. Ok. Will keep foot. Major Deter,[41] MC, did operation; help of Dr. Waters. I've been wounded pretty badly, it's true, but at least I've proven something to myself... during a crisis, in a period of excitement, I'm able to keep my head and think coolly. Pain or not, I didn't get over-excited, but went ahead and finished my job first. I wasn't wounded in battle, nor wounded by the enemy, but I was on (what was firmly believed at the time), an important mission, by command of my general. This mission I accomplished, and I'm damned proud of that fact.

Facts about my getting wounded.
(Dec. 18, 1941)

During day, Iloilo got its first bombing by Nip planes. Result, natives all quite jittery. That nite, about 7:30, I returned

---

41   Dwight M. Deter was later promoted to lieutenant colonel, US Army Force Headquarters, Medical Corps.

to HQ 63rd Infantry (P.A.) and was told that the General Chynoweth had received a report that 3,000 Nips were landing at Guimbal, Iloilo and he wanted U.S. officer to authenticate the report. No one else volunteered for what seemed likely to be a dangerous mission, so I spoke up, and said "I'd go." Took motorcycle and Scout Sgt. Ludublau. Had to travel about thirty-five kilometers, going first to Iloilo. In Iloilo, motorcycle broke down. Commandeered Ford coupe and went on. Near Tigbauan, Iloilo, volunteer guards slowed car to almost a stop. Identified self, speaking to guards on right side of car — no one on my side (left). As we prepared to go on, a shot sounded from the pitch black coconut grove on left, severely wounding me in right foot and Sgt. in the left foot. Nevertheless, went on to finish mission. Didn't know who had shot me. Nips, Filipino, or Yank. After having necessary information telegrammed into HQ I got a car, two men and a doctor for the Sgt. and self, and went back to Iloilo to have Mission doctor Dwight Deter USMC, operate on foot. Lost lot of blood. State of shock. Found out later that man who shot me was a "guard" from 61st Division Philippine Army. Apparently mistook me for Nip. Actually never found out exactly *why* he *did* shoot me. No longer am I an active participant in the daily details and confusion of combat preparation. My name on the roster was marked, "Permanently Disabled." This fact, however, will not keep me from engaging in the war news. My

hospital room is a rendezvous for officers, and we discuss the problems on hand in our area, and then we launch into the general picture of the Philippine Islands. The most pressing questions on everyone's mind is, "Will our forces be able to hold out till help gets here?" Never did the question of surrender arise. That is, of *our* surrender.

[Entries become irregular.]

Tuesday, Dec. 30, 1941
Iloilo raided twice. 11:30 a.m and 1:40 p.m. No casualties, but scared the hell out of us. Foot in cast, was raised off bed about 3" by the concussion of each bomb.

Emmanuel Mission Hospital, Capiz
Sunday, Jan. 4, 1942
Transferred to Emmanuel Mission Hospital of Capiz, now a USA field Hospital at Dumalag, about ninety kilometers from Iloilo. Ambulance was like a truck. Had Dr. and nurse go with me, plus two shots of morphine. Terribly bumpy causing very painful trip. Took us 5½ hours. Arrived at 12:30 a.m. Dr. Myers in charge — very nice. Jolly and competent.

Thursday, Feb. 5, 1942
I downed a half glass of Canadian Club, straight, before they removed cast this morning. Wasn't supposed to be painful but it hurt like Hell! Jeez, what a fine looking foot — discolored, swollen like a balloon, a hole on the right side yet, and very painful.

Friday, Feb. 6, 1942
Took my first crack at crutches. Went a total of about sixty yards and got pooped out. Great day — "baby's first step!"

Monday, Feb. 9, 1942
Doctor Myers promised me another month of pain, and I'm just about washed out. Hope I've the guts to keep taking it. It's so *steady* a pain — 24 hours a day, EVERY day. Sometimes I feel I'll go crazy, but the thought of returning to Mom, Dad, and Eileen keeps me going. I'll be back, if ever that hospital ship gets here. Got the radiogram today from Mom and Dad — place of sending is Los Angeles. Good to hear from you — it's been so long. I'll try to send more messages, but I haven't a cent to my name. We haven't been paid.

"Room #10, Emmanuel Mission Hosp." *Hinkle Archive.*

"The view from the porch of my room." *Hinkle Archive.*

Tuesday, Feb. 10, 1942
Received copies of orders promoting to temporary 1st Lieutenant. Signed MacArthur. Wish I could send some greetings for Valentines day — but no money! Damn!

Iloilo Mission Hospital
Sunday, Feb. 15, 1942
Transferred to Iloilo Mission Hospital again, now located in Calinog. Foot still hurt like hell. Lieutenant Gordon Benson, AC pilot, here too. He had to bail out of his P-40 when his motor conked. He fractured his right shoulder, and will probably be here for several weeks.[42]

Tuesday, Feb. 24, 1942
I was told something today that made me feel good all over. It was said so sincerely and simply and I never thought I'd hear it. One of the Filipino Captains from the 63rd Inf. was in to see another patient and then he saw me. After some talk he said, "Well, the 63rd certainly lost a brave man when you got shot. The officers and men in your battalion have always admired you for your

42   During the fighting on Bataan, Colonel Hal George, commander of the Bataan air force, called for air support from P-40s based in Mindanao. After drawing cards to decide who would go, four pilots set out from Del Monte Airfield on January 18, 1942. Lieutenant Benson's aircraft was lost when his rough-running engine quit over water. Benson bailed out and was later interned with Hinkle a the Davao Penal Colony.

courage!" Jeez, what a helluva nice thing to be told! That courage is ebbing now — this foot is too powerful.

Wednesday, Feb. 25, 1942
They're bringing some wounded soldiers from Bataan down here. Quezon is now in Iloilo, came down in a submarine. Got a hunch that Panay is going to see WAR pretty soon. Arrangements have been made to get me up in the hills if the Japs invade. Christ — why don't the States hurry and send us help?? We need planes, ammo, food, medicines, and fewer Roosevelt "fireside chats!" Sent a radio message to the folks last week. Pray God they get it OK. Ever dreaming of that ship that will come in and take me to a U.S. hospital and get me out of this hell-torn country, and back to those I love!

Thursday, Feb. 26, 1942
Ten weeks today — seventy days of continuous pain! God, how I've suffered. Now, my right knee is stiff with arthritis and fibrosis from being in one position so long, and I can't straighten the damn leg and that means more pain and work. I'm trying my crutches a little every day and the blood rushes down into my foot till it feels like it's going to burst. I manage one or two hours a day in the wheel chair but it's a helluva painful job. Sleep is something to be desired — if I get no sedative, I'm lucky to get four or five hours of sleep.

Friday, Feb. 27, 1942
If I'm killed by the Japanese, remember to have the government send my back pay to my folks.

Saturday, Feb. 28, 1942
The longer I lie in bed, the greater is my realization of the total inhumanness of war. It's brutal, uncivilized, unmerciful, born of hate and so unquestionably unnecessary. Oh, God, what a fool is man. Why can't he see his folly? Why must men kill and maim one another? It's not for peace, or democracy, or principle — I'm convinced its a blood lust from pre-historic days. Damn war and all its advocates — ignorant, cowardly bastards!

Sunday, March 1, 1942
Colonel Deter told me today that he's trying to get authority to send me to Australia, then to USA, or directly to USA. General MacArthur has to OK it, and then I'll be sent to Cebu and get the first boat that comes along. God, how I pray that this may come true! To get home again! Wonder when and if?? Colonel Deter also told me that my wound is a "permanent disability" and hence, I'll be drawing a pension. Jeez, it hurts so damned much.

Monday, March 2, 1942
General MacArthur disapproved my being transferred out of this country. Now I don't know how long I'll be stuck in this hole. Colonel Deter says they'll probably do some bone grafting in my ankle if, and after, I get back

to the States. Otherwise I won't have a solid underpinning. Oh Damn.

Wednesday, April 8, 1942

Pain still quite strong, though wound is now closing up rapidly. Foot still swollen to a ghastly size. Unable to straighten out my leg, and trying to do it is a painful job. Praying more fervently than ever for the chance to get the hell out of here. The last three nights have seen planes from Australia flying to Bataan with medicines. Today, two of them were on their way back. Seems as though I ought to be able to get a ride out of here! Damn! No word from home in ages — hope everyone is OK. God — how I long to see Mom and Dad.

Thursday, April 9, 1942

Bataan has fallen! Jeez — I gotta get out of here, quick, or I'll never see the folks again.

Friday, April 10, 1942

11,000 Japs in Cebu! We're getting hemmed in and I'm getting more and more worried. Wrote a letter to Col. Fitzpatrick asking him to try to get me out via plane to Australia.

Sunday, April 12, 1942

Went for a ride with Mr. and Mrs. Aboitez, and asked them to take me to see Fitzpatrick and Greathouse. I saw them and started rehashing my getting out of here. I sweat it out and wrote a letter to Col. Christy and begged him to get me out by plane to Mindanao and thence to Australia.

Maybe something will come of it. Just have a hunch I'd better get out of here if I possibly can. I've taken the bull by the horns — hope something comes of it.

Monday, April 13, 1942

Got an order this morning from Colonel Christy to catch plane to go to Australia! Went to house (Santa Barbara, Iloilo) near airfield, and at 5:20 p.m. a B-25 came in, and I was rushed out to it. Got in and sat in radio man's place. On board were two Hawaiian born Japs, a Chinese Colonel, a Navy fellow and a newspaperman, all from Corrregidor. The flight to Mindanao was excitement to the Nth degree. Over land, Capt. Gunn flew about ten feet above the ground, and about five feet above treetops! Over water we were always about four to seven feet high!! Never over mountains but between them in sharp banks! After one-and-one-half hours flight we suddenly zoomed and I got a deep feeling of death being near, but the plane diving at us was a P-40. Landed at Del Monte — saw remains of B-17, destroyed by MGs only one hour before.

Should have stayed in plane and waited for take off to Australia, but was scared and kept with group to report to General Sharp. Met General Royce (Scott's father) at Sharp's HQ. Everything was OK until I showed Sharp my orders, and he realized I was from General Cheynoweth's gang. Then he blew up and asked me, "What do you think this is? A general exodus? You can't leave here. You've no authority!" *He could have given me the authority,* but he wouldn't and he said, "I've got the best hospital, best food, and best surgeon you could ask for. You'll stay here!" When I asked him what good a permanently disabled officer could do here, he paid no attention. Then he called up a medic and said, "There's some lieutenant here with a sprained ankle or something!" The sonofabitch wouldn't even listen to me when I tried to explain the nature of the wound! Then he sent me across the road to the Del Monte Club House, and a very badly arranged swayback army cot and two blankets!!! And my foot was paining to beat hell — I had fallen on it out on the airfield. No one paid any attention. The American general was too busy with a Chinese Colonel, a newspaperman and two Japs to bother about one of his own officers!!! God, how did he stay in the Army so long? At 10:30 p.m. an ambulance came (it wasn't to come for me till 7 a.m.). Sergeant Campbell had broken his leg, so we both got a shot of morph. and a five agonizing hour ride to the hospital. (The next morning the club house I was staying in was bombed off the earth's surface!!) Thanks General Sharp. I'll always remember this dirty deal of yours. I'll carry hatred in my heart for you as long as I live, and if I ever get a chance to "hang" you, I'll do it.

Impalutao, Mindanao
Force General Hospital
Thursday, April 16, 1942
So — this is General Sharp's "fine"

hospital! Jeez, it's the dirtiest, damned place I've been in for a long time. Chow is terrible, not fit for pigs, and the nurses and attendants appear to be utterly useless. Met Dr. Davis. Had x-ray of foot and he says the foot is infected, and I need an operation, but we'll wait for awhile to see if I can get on to Australia. He says I'd be much better off there — that I need a real hospital and lots of rest. But then, General Sharp is a better Doctor than Doctor Davis! Iloilo invaded today! Just made it! God guide the lads and their poor equipment. They haven't a chance in the world — better take to guerrilla warfare if they're going to fight.

Monday, May 4, 1942
Early this morning a Japanese plane dropped two bombs in a barrio about one kilometer from hospital. It scared the daylights out of us.

Tuesday, May 5, 1942
Dr. Davis performed sequestrectomy on my foot. Operation performed under ether, and leg was partially straightened at same time. Woke up to much pain. Morphine every four hours. Terribly painful — leg in cast above knee. Dr. says I'll be in cast three or four MONTHS!! Jesus — what a future!

Wed., May 6, 1942
Japanese planes bombed and MG'd motor pool a few kilometers from here, and it was a terrifying experience. Seemed as if the bombs were dropping only fifty feet away. The

planes maneuvered right over hospital with MGs going. MGs were most frightful. Was very nervous, weak, and unable to move. Pain aggravated. During bombing we had two mattresses over us, as though that would help!! But it helped morale. I jammed my fingers in my ears and prayed. I hate the sound of the machine guns. Dropped about fifty to seventy bombs today. Full of morphine.

Thursday, May 7, 1942
More bombing, MGs, fear, and nerves.

Saturday, May 9, 1942
Order to get plane for Australia! Went to airfield in ambulance and waited for four-and-one-half hours but plane never came in!

Sunday, May 10, 1942
P.I. surrendered.

May 29, 1942
For three days now we have been besieged by thousands of grasshoppers! They're all over the place, inside the hospital, and outside — continuously on the march, night and day. They're eating the green foliage that comes in their path. They attack and eat each other. We had to use our mosquito nets day and night to keep the damned things out of our beds. Their continual marching could be distinctly heard — like the rush of leaves in a strong wind. The natives and some Americans had feasts of fried grasshoppers. I almost tried some, but backed out. They say they're delicious.

Friday, June 5, 1942
I pray God that your birthday may bring you much happiness as possible, dear Mom, and let us hope that we may be together again very soon. I've been so homesick, lonesome, and wondering how you and Dad are. Please take care of yourself. *Why* doesn't the U.S. realize that we HAVE surrendered??! God bless you Mom. Don't worry — someday I'll be back; someday.

June 10, 1942
Became godfather of Lieutenant Charles Callahan, who was baptized by Father Houseman. Other sponsor was Miss M. Estrada, RN. Charles desired to become Catholic, after he saw the courageous work of the priests during the war. A fine lad.

June 18, 1942
Doctor Davis said it would take about 3 or 4 months for my wound to granulate and heal. The pain has been considerably cut down, except for "electric shock" on the sole and in my toes. Am getting around on crutches now. Fell down yesterday! Rainy season makes it hard to get outdoor exercise.

There is talk of sending us to Manila and concentrating us there. Dad — Happy Birthday. Can we count on being together for the next and rest of them?? May God grant it.

[*Continued on page 82.*]

The Fall of Panay & Mindanao
A Japanese Soldier's Diary
Translated by Kazunori Tanoue

This war-damaged diary was penned by an unnamed Japanese soldier serving with the Kawamura Detachment. He describes events leading up to and during operations on Panay and Mindanao, as Hinkle prepared for war.

Shōwa 17, April 1 (1942)
We boarded the escort transport ship *Italy Maru* on the 16th of March and departed Singapore at noon on the 18th. Right now I'm taking a break in the cabin, lying down, with my forehead covered in sweat. After morning we did gymnastics. In the afternoon all the crew participated in the on-board drill. After that I spent time reading and sleeping. The waves were high today.

April 2
Some are seasick because of the high waves driven by strong winds. Therefore there was no training today, which is annoying. No sign of land, and there is a warning that an enemy submarine is approaching. At night, light control was implemented. Hence, we stayed in the cabin and not on deck.

April 3
I am on watch duty and the waves are high. Here on the bow of the ship I feel the cool wind against my face. However, this is duty! and not just a chance to rest and enjoy the breeze — this is my responsibility.

April 4
Finished antiaircraft surveillance at 10 a.m. and then took the drill of climbing up and down the rope ladder. According to the plan, we should have arrived in the Philippines today. However, arrival has been delayed until tomorrow, because of our slow speed. No sign of land all day. Light control was ordered at night in anticipation of approaching enemy vessels.

April 5
At noon we set anchor at the port of Lingayen in the Philippines. As in Malaysia, there is a dense forest of trees, and it is hot as expected, and the people here have brown skin just like in South China. We bathe throughout the day and took outside training. After roll call, we sang the military song!

April 6
The troop captain and others went ashore to pick up additional men for the landing. No training or exercises today; instead, we unloaded cargo onto the deck. Afterward, I and others took a small

boat ashore, standing by until 5 p.m. to receive Second Lieutenant Ito and thirteen other men newly assigned to the ship. Thus, the cabin is now very cramped. Several of us had to move to a corner because the new men were second-time call-up soldiers.[1] I cannot bear the miserable heat.

April 7

The cabin below deck was so hot that even the fan was useless, and soon I was covered in sweat. I did clerical work, creating "The Table of Organization" and "The Deployment and Reorganization Order." At night there was sake and extra rations. We are anchored off shore at a place called Damortis, but no one is allowed to go ashore.

April 8

The squads were reorganized and there was much shuffling between cabins. I was beginning to wonder if I would remain an artillery specialist, when I suddenly received my transfer to the battalion's artillery squad! The supplemental troops that came aboard are from the Second Sino-Japanese War. Rookie soldiers like myself feel depressed because these cocky combat vets only cause us misery.

April 9

Fine weather. Organized the documents, such as the payments and receipts for April and May. Although the only food service aboard ship was *kori-dofu*,[2] we have begun to eat more vegetables since entering the bay. Normally we do not receive word from home, but since it is now possible to send a postcard, I decided to write a brief note and mailed it when I had the chance.

April 10

This afternoon we practiced the transfer exercise to landing craft using the rope ladders. I am plagued by the extreme heat and humidity aboard ship, and now we cannot wash due to water-conservation measures! Needless to say, we cannot wash our clothes, and everyone, and everything, is filthy.

April 11

I went ashore with Corporal Nishimoto to deposit the troop savings at 8:30 a.m. The Damortis bus then dropped us off at Post Office No. 23, where I concluded my work for the day. We then reboarded the ship at 2:30 p.m., and the fleet departed at 4:00 p.m. At 9:50 there was a comprehensive training. Even the transfer exercise was conducted in complete darkness!

---

1 Soldiers in the Japanese army completed military service in two years (three years for navy) and remained eligible for recall in the reserves until the age of forty.

2 Frozen tofu.

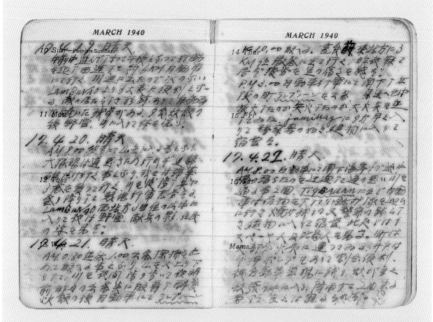

Sweat-soaked pages—evidence of the extreme heat that the soldier referred to in his diary. *Hinkle Archive*

April 12

At 9:10 a.m. Captain Date, under imperial decree, revealed the details of our upcoming mission: "The conquering of Panay Island would begin one week from today."

Exercises such as gymnastics were performed before departing Lingayen Gulf at noon, on a heading southwest. There was a party for the men aboard ship at 2:00 p.m., but I didn't bother to go.

April 13

Fine weather. We spent the day aboard ship as it steamed to the southwest. From the port side of our ship I could see the Philippine Islands. There were landing exercises, and the alarm training after roll call. In the afternoon we passed Manila Bay with our three escort destroyers. At night the wind picked up, and the ship began to roll. Corporal Miyazawa's seasickness is getting worse.

April 14

Fine weather. Islands could be seen on every side of the *Italy Maru* as we continued our journey south. As I stood antiaircraft watch, the wind began to blow, and by evening it was raining and the waves became high again.

April 15

Fine weather. Preparations have begun for tomorrow's early-morning surprise landing on Panay Island. At night I loaded my mess kit and all was done.

10:00 p.m.—anchored.

April 16

Unloaded the boats from the ship at midnight; it was a bloodless landing. I was in the second wave, which landed at 4:00 a.m. We came ashore on a sandy beach just east of Oton.[3] The road from there was asphalt, and when we entered Iloilo City there was no sign of the enemy, but several of the Japanese shops had been torched by employees who were *Futei-Jin*.[4] I then served as security guard for the town and treated myself to melon, banana, watermelon, and even ice cream, which I have not eaten in a long time. Later in the day we marched, and judging by the looks of things it was the dry season because there were big cracks in the nearby paddy—even the road has cracks. We passed through the ruins of a bridge that had been blown up, and in a nearby field there were remnants of sugar cane, which we picked up and ate happily as we advanced. Made camp in the evening and my legs ache from marching all day—the pain was unbearable and there were plenty of mosquitoes too. This place where we made camp is called Jaro.[5] The residents evacuated earlier—the houses there are all empty.

April 17

At 8:00 a.m. we assembled into formation and then boarded our trucks, which arrived last night. We headed north as the second echelon, waiting for a while after going ahead a little to let the *Jitensha-butai*[6] catch up. After that, we entered Dueñas and camped. It is an inconvenient site due to the lack of water. Still no sign of the enemy.

April 18

Fine weather. We departed by truck at 8:30 on a road that has grown narrow and is covered with gravel. We then came to a collapsed bridge with a few abandoned defensive positions made from fallen palm trees. At 3:00 p.m. we entered Lambunao,[7]

---

3   Located just west of Iloilo City.

4   A Japanese pejorative for "rebellious Koreans." During the first half of the twentieth century, Korea existed as a colony of Japan. Today *Futei-Jin* is a word unknown to most Japanese and is used primarily by *Netto-Uyooko* (Japanese extreme nationalists).

5   One of the seven districts of Iloilo City.

6   Bicycle troops. They lessened the demands on the Japanese war machine since they needed no fuel, vehicles, or maintenance and could carry more equipment and travel greater distances than foot soldiers.

7   A municipality in the province of Iloilo, near the center of the island, north of Iloilo City.

which was abandoned and without water because they put poison and heavy oil into the wells. This is very inconvenient.

10:00 p.m.—Everyone fell asleep after getting drunk on beer and whiskey. Gear is scattered everywhere.

April 19

I took it easy this morning. Here on the river it is much nicer, compared to Lambuano, where there isn't any water. Went toward the west about 6 kilometers by truck in the afternoon, where I saw signs of the enemy, and a burned-out automobile. After dinner I took a bath in the river.

April 20

Left camp at 8:00 a.m. to pursue the enemy in the mountains. Because of the bad road we did not carry the battalion gun.[8] Instead we carried mortars. I shouldered three mortar rounds as we crossed the river and climbed up and down hills, struggling under the heavy load. Upon entering the mountainous area 3 ri[9] northwest of Lambuano, we camped for the night. There was no sign of the local residents or the enemy.

April 21

Woke up at 12:30 a.m. and departed camp by 1:00, but we soon ended our search and turned back, arriving before dawn at yesterday's starting point. Just before lunch, I went 3 kilometers northeast for requisitioning. At 3 p.m. we left Lambuano and passed through a town in the hills. Looking back in the direction of the town I could plainly see the destruction caused by arson, or by *Yabi*.[10] We arrived in Janiuay[11] in the early evening and occupied the local police station.

April 22

We left by truck at 8 a.m., crossing the river twice along the rough road in order to bypass the fallen bridge. At Tigbuan [*where Hinkle was wounded months earlier in December*] we unloaded the baggage and went to pick up troops assigned to cutting trees in the forest. After that, we saw Spanish and Filipinos, and a large part of the town that was burnt down. We then entered a building that looked like the remains of a fire-damaged police station, and camped. It was a convenient campsite because the well had a hand pump. At night I remained near the transports and shared

---

8 The Type 92 battalion gun was a light howitzer, and each infantry battalion had a pair. The Type 92 designation referred to the year the gun was accepted for use by the Imperial Army: the year 2592 in the Japanese calendar, or 1932 in the Gregorian calendar.
9 7.32 miles.

---

10 Rocket artillery.
11 A municipality in the province of Iloilo, northwest of Iloilo City and south of Lambuano.

my tent with a squadron of mosquitoes that attacked me without mercy, having entered through a hole in my net—I couldn't sleep.

April 23
Woke up at 6 and departed at 7 a.m., traveling east, passing through Oton, where we landed last week. A printing shop was selected for our shelter, and I went out to requisition in the afternoon, finding nothing of interest except an old pair of pants.

April 24
We cleaned up in the morning, and the truck went out for service. Went to requisition in a nearby hamlet and returned after liberating 1 kilogram of sugar. Roll call in the evening.

April 25
I did weapons maintenance work, and at 11 a.m. the platoon had a weapons inspection. Everyone then went to the nearby hamlet, but I didn't go, preferring instead to nap. Dinner was *Ohagi*.[12]

April 2
This morning, when the mortar platoon went to exercise, the battalion artillery took a rest—so I went to Jaro with Funaki to explore. In the afternoon I went to

headquarters for clerical work, and after entrusting Lance Corporal Mitani to finish the job, I returned to this miserable hovel of a printing shop in Mandurraio. We sang military songs in the evening.

April 27
We have been prohibited by the military police from entering the homes of civilians. After dinner, a few of us in the platoon went to a seaside beach on the west coast of Iloilo for a swim in the evening ocean. I swam for the first time in a while and indulged in many memories from the past. The day of boarding for our next landing is fast approaching, and it is rumored that the day will be tomorrow or the day after tomorrow, and that we are headed to Mindanao. How I long for the day when my military service is completed!

April 28
Our work here on Panay was finished yesterday, and I thought for sure that we would depart today, but didn't. All day there were interrogations related to the murder of a *Dojin*,[13] and I trembled with fear as I loaded gear onto the truck.

12   Rice ball coated with sweetened red beans.

13   A native.

April 29

Got up at 5:30 a.m. and prepared for departure. But first, *Hohai-Shiki*[14] was held because today was *Tencho-setsu*.[15] Departed by truck at 7:40 and arrived at the west pier of Iloilo City thirty minutes later. I boarded the *Italy Maru* and after dinner took it easy. *Hohai-Shiki* of the battalion was held in the evening. Aboard ship I had a good view of the fire-damaged portions of the city.

April 30

After loading, we left the quay, went 1,000 meters into the bay, and set anchor. At 10:00 a.m., we divided the cargo, setting a portion aside for the landing. We loaded our boats this afternoon, and beer and cigarettes were supplied. We did this until nightfall, and then there were transfer exercises. I couldn't sleep topside. Below deck it is hot and humid—I cannot bear it!

May 1

Fine day. Departed Iloilo Bay. Nothing today except physical exercises and roll call. There are islands to the right and left as the ship traveled at a moderate pace, escorted by two destroyers. At night there was a preinvasion party in the second hold. There was a performance by men selected from each squad, and I found it to be most enjoyable!

My Enlisted Man's Song

We are here in Hamada-shi,[16] Shimane, Hotei-21-rentai.[17]
Bullied by hated second-time call-up soldiers.
Night falls with my tears.

I am very far from home, when a visitor came to me disguised as a letter.
How happy I am to receive it.
With a lovely girl's handwriting.

There is no time to bite the *Anpan*.[18]
Lights-out and trumpets blare.
A soft straw berth with a view of the night sky—this is our dreaming bed.

Awakened from my dreams still sleepy.
Tough work for a nightlong vigil.
If I doze, I face hard time in the stockade.

Examinations for the first, second, and third periods served.[19]
After finishing the Autumn exercise, the disagreeable second-time soldiers make their military service complete.
How will we feel when seeing them off?

---

14 The ceremony of saluting the emperor from afar.
15 Birthday of the emperor.
16 A city in Japan's Shimane Prefecture.
17 Hotei = Infantry; 21–rentai = 21st Regiment. The 21st Infantry Regiment was transferred to the control of the Southern Expeditionary Army Group and participated in the landing at Lingayen Gulf on February 26, 1941.
18 Sweet roll with bean jam.
19 There were six periods in a soldier's two years of service. An examination was taken after each period.

May 2
There was a squall last night that continued through early morning, as Kusaka, Corporal Yamaji, Higami, Lance Corporal Kimura, Corporal Okano, myself, and five others in the artillery service loaded gear into the truck, because today is a day of preparation for tomorrow's landing! At 9:00 a.m. we formed into lines on the front deck, and the ceremony for instructions from the commander was held.

24:00—received breakfast aboard ship and got ready.

May 3
Woke up at 1:00 a.m.—transferred to our landing craft at 3:00 a.m.—and the landing began at 3:40, directly in front of the enemy between Cagayan and Tagoloan on the north side of Mindanao Island.

In the surf there were wire fences, and the first wave was in continuous battle as flares lit up the night sky around the landing spot.

Now it is our turn to go in!
When we entered the bay and traveled toward the shore, there were flashes of light from enemy positions all along the beach. Cagayan City was on fire, and I saw one wooden bridge after another either burning or being set ablaze!

We landed at Tagoloan and fought bitterly with the enemy, and as the cannon fired, the muzzle flash illuminated the dead and wounded lying all around me.

Shortly after dawn I was taken by surprise when enemy aircraft attacked. Then we moved out, and although we brought our truck, I had to march in the hot weather and soon became exhausted. After entering Cagayan City, we made preparations for a night departure into enemy territory but camped instead because the bridge ahead had been destroyed.

May 4
I awoke at 3:00, even though our departure was for 5:00 a.m. In town I found some potatoes in front of a church and made a meal of them. We then boarded the truck and, after advancing just 1 kilometer, encountered yet another blown-up bridge and had to stop. After preparing the riverbank to receive the *daihatsu*,[20] we put the roof on the truck and loaded it with some difficulty aboard the craft. We transported the truck across the river, and it took many hours to get everyone across. We then pressed southwest before arriving at a second bridge that had been destroyed. To our

---

20 Landing craft with a bow ramp that lowered to disembark cargo and men onto a beach.

right was an airfield,[21] and on the nearby riverbank I spread a net in an area beneath many palm trees. I camped there for the night, listening to the sounds of rippling water. I did not hear the sound of enemy gunfire all day

May 5

Progress on repairing the bridge was slow—a delay that allowed time for me to swim, paddle a canoe, and cook. Later on, personnel from the battalion artillery alternately went by truck across the river through the gate bridge, where I stood as sentry in the evening. Since today is *Sekku,*[22] everyone is no doubt making *chimaki.*[23] Looking up at the North Star from behind the palm tree, I am reminded that it has been one year and four months passing since I first put out to sea.

May 6

After sentry duty I went to sleep on the net. Something bit me as I slept, and now I have a rash, and my private parts are swollen! At 7:00 everyone awoke to help rebuild the bridge, and my groin ached as I walked. Later it was decided that we go back to Cagayan via the battalion headquarters truck to move cargo, which we loaded and

unloaded many times, crossing the river to and fro. Other troops then crossed the river in their trucks and camped in Cagayan. Only surveillance troops remained camped on the opposite riverside.

May 7

At around midnight, Second Lieutenant Ogawa woke me up and ordered me to help load cargo for tomorrow's action. We entered the river, and I was in water up to my waist as we loaded the cannon and ammunition onto the *Daihatsu.* Work was completed by 2:00 a.m. I spent the evening in Cagayan, woke up at 6:30, cooked breakfast, boarded the second battalion's truck, and joined in the march.

[*Pages for May 8, 9, and 10 are missing from the diary—a time when Sharp deliberated surrender. It resumes a day after his surrender, as the diarist marched toward Impasugong, a settlement just north of Impalutao, where Walter Hinkle was hospitalized.*]

May 11

The greeting ceremony for our regimental commander and *Hohai-Shiki* was held at the square in front of the church—a collecting site for enemy arms. The confiscated weapons were loaded and carried away by truck. We then departed by foot to Impasugong, where we stopped

---

21 Del Monte Airfield.
22 *Tango no Sekku*—Boy's Day in Japan.
23 A sweet rice paste wrapped in bamboo leaf.

at a small hamlet that passes for a town on this island; each squad was assigned a filthy house, and each camped separately.

May 12
Woke up at 6:00 a.m. and traveled by truck to work at the battalion accounting office. On the way to Malaybalay I saw a group of enemy soldiers surrendering one after another.[24] Moreover, in Malaybalay, many Americans surrendered and left a considerable number of trucks filled with supplies. I picked up a pair of sunglasses from inside one of the trucks and looked through them out to the horizon, where I saw animals grazing and felt the vastness of the Bukidnon plateau. Later I spent the day dwelling on a variety of rumors—that prisoners came to Cagayan, or we received them in Davao, or that some of our own have reached the maturity date of their service. Like those who have reached the end of their term of service, I too would like to return home—not because I have come too far or that so much time has passed, but because I am fed up with this military life!

[Last entry]

---

24 Soldiers surrendered on Mindanao were interned at Camp Casisang, a Philippine army cantonment at Malaybalay. In late June or early July 1942, the Japanese screened Filipino and American prisoners for war criminals. After arranging the prisoners into a single line, Japanese civilian and military personnel moved slowly down the line, pointing out several men to be interrogated by the Kempetai in Davao City. Literally translated "Law Soldiers Regiment," Kempeitai were secret police— the "Gestapo" of Imperial Japan. They were responsible for rear-area security with the power to arrest, interrogate, condemn, and execute Filipinos and escaped POWs. In August 1942 many POW officers from Camp Casisang were shipped to Formosa in the hold of a filthy ship, several dying along the way. In September, technicians and other prisoners were shipped to Japan. In October the remaining prisoners were moved to the Davao Penal Colony, just prior to Hinkle's arrival there in November.

June 19, 1942

A number of Japanese officers have visited the hospital and all have been friendly and very courteous; all of which is contrary to our propaganda. They are real soldiers, and I hesitate to believe much about the stories of their "atrocities." We're all praying that the U.S. and Japan will make some agreement for exchange of prisoners so we can go home. It is logical to conclude that the Japanese officials desire to have the American influences removed from the islands which they have now captured; therefore, "exchange" negotiations would be possible, providing the U.S. doesn't get pig-headed and over-demanding.

June 29, 1942

Major Davis said today that there is no more plaster, so I won't get a new cast this week. Instead, this one stays on. In the meantime, bacteria are causing the odor of the wound to be quite "ripe!" I don't know how long I'll remain in a cast — another month? I'd give anything to be rid of this uncomfortable cast. The foot is less painful and I think the swelling is going down. The food situation is becoming critical. We have run out of lard, and this cuts out bread and hot cakes. It's rice three times a day, with beef or sardines, and flour gravy. Day in and day out, the chow is the same with no immediate hope of having the situation alleviated. There is continual rumor of our going to Manila, and yet no one knows. Talk is also rampant about prisoner exchanges, and every

time we hear it, our hearts beat faster and our spirits rise, only to fall again lower than before when no official statement is forthcoming. We wait and WAIT for news of the U.S. doing something, but everything seems at a standstill. WHEN will we get home? Will we be exchanged? God only knows and we pray he will be kind and merciful.

Saturday, July 4, 1942

Great Day! Dr. Davis and the pharmacist fixed up twenty gallons of rectified alcohol, pineapple juice, banana and lemon flavoring for the American soldiers who are working here at the hospital. They really had quite a time. A couple of my friends brought me some of the "punch," and after three glasses I went fast asleep (out) while someone was talking to me!! For the first time in six and one half months, I slept ALL night without pain. But I had a helluva hangover in the morning, yet it was very much worth it.

Wednesday, July 9, 1942

I don't believe I have ever written about the tobacco situation. The last "tailor made" cigarette I had was about a month ago — and the ones I bought then were 20 pesos for a pack of ten! Since then we've been buying tobacco leaves by the "hand" (one hundred leaves) for three to six pesos. We wash the tobacco and soak it in sugar, cut it up, and then smoke it — real "roll your own" stuff. Strong?! Holy hell — it'd knock a debutante on her tail, and a he-man wouldn't take a second drag! But we're smoking it. There's nothing else to smoke. If ever the Red Cross ship comes in maybe we'll get some cigarettes. But the Red Cross is off my list — I'm sorry Mom is working so hard in that organization. The Japanese have said that the Red Cross has–made no mention of coming here — no attempt. Mom, all your efforts are for British interests, not we Americans in the Philippine Islands — if you only knew. The Red Cross will NEVER get another cent out of me!

Friday, July 10, 1942

You ought to hear our grandstand quarterbacks fight this war! One is a civilian from Masbate. The other is the AGO.[43] They're blabbing about blowing the hell out of Japan, etc., etc. Where is the sense in that? Why should we kill and kill — kill helpless women and children?? Those who have seen the great bloodshed and suffering can't uphold this view. We are soldiers — the Japanese army is made up of soldiers — at some time *we* EXPECTED to fight for our countries, but civilians, women and children should be kept out of the picture. At least that's how I feel.

Saturday, July 11, 1942

There has been considerable unrest today because the word has come through that the Japanese Army is tightening up, and that barbed-wire has been put up around Malaybalay.

In 1940 William Russell "Doc" Davis (1904-1944) and his wife, Mary Hamilton Davis, lived on Negros Island, where he was head surgeon at a sugar company hospital. At the outbreak of hostilities, Davis, who was in the Army reserves, joined the US Army Medical Corps. The 1934 graduate of Tulane Medical School was posthumously awarded the Legion of Merit for treating POWs at Davao and Bilibid. His wife was interned during the war years at Santo Tomas in Manila and did not learn of her husband's death until after liberation in 1945. *Photograph (ca. 1940) courtesy of the Bunn family and obtained with help from Millard Greer*

A contingent of Americans was forced to march from Lanao to Malaybalay, and they were told that stragglers would be shot. The report is that Lt. Navin (31st) was shot and killed, and also Major Vesey (31st). Doctor Davis is quite worried. Seven damned Filipinos have escaped from the hospital area, and the Japanese authorities said that henceforth, Major Davis will be held personally responsible for any

---

43 Army general officer; an officer of high military rank.

future escapees. The penalty, we presume — death. How can he possibly control these Filipinos? They don't realize that their actions may cost the Major his life.

Sunday, July 12, 1942
Doctor Davis says that I will get a new cast tomorrow. My foot has been giving me considerable pain during the last four days, and I've been worrying again about the outcome of these months in the hospital. God, how terrible it would be to have to have my foot amputated after all this suffering! I fervently pray that it doesn't come to that.

July 15, 1942
Changed cast again today and it was finally done under Evipal.[44] Have another month in cast. Feel very discouraged and low. It has been quite painful and my fight is just about gone.

Sunday, July 19, 1942
And again — "Happy birthday," Eleanor Lee, on your 24th year! July 19 is always a strong reminder of pleasant hours and days spent with you, and I hope you are having a gay ole time this year. Someone must.

Monday, July 20, 1942
The screws were really put on last Saturday. We had no sugar for our coffee or for our bowl of soft rice. Thursday and Friday we had no meat — just fish. There are 80,000 head of cattle on this island, and

there is no call for the Japanese to cut the beef supply. The Japanese prisoners in the States or Australia and Hawaii are undoubtedly getting good food and plenty. When the U.S. moves in and takes over again, and this group is taken as prisoners, they'll have a hard time. I don't know how long we can exist on this chow. I know our resistance will be lowered — a bout with pneumonia would ring your bell and life would be over! We're continually hungry: rice and sardines have become sickening. No fruit — no vegetables. We're becoming discouraged — asking "why should we try to fight for life?" The U.S. remains as inactive, as Britain and Russia continuing to hold the bag. What a bull shit country we turned out to be!

Tuesday, July 21, 1942
Growing hunger! Yes, we're getting fed three times a day but none of it satisfies the craving for food. Today the cooks were able to put out two pancakes and some rice per person for breakfast. At noon the patients in the ward, at last, got liver (fried) and so help me, I was so hungry I ate it right up without stopping to taste it. The rest of the meal was the usual crap — rice and flour gravy. God what I'd give for a real meal, or just a can of pork and beans! We get around and talk of food — of steaks and french fries — of breaded veal cutlets and mashed potatoes and gravy — of head lettuce and 1,000 island dressing — of lemon cream and banana

---

44   A rapid-acting barbiturate.

cream pies, and good coffee with fresh cream — and fresh milk!!!! Oh God I'm so hungry as I lay here and write this. Just thinking of it all has brought tears to my eyes. Think of the supper in store for each of us tonite — a bowl of unclean rice and a few mashed up, overgrown sardines! Thanks Mr. Roosevelt for sending the Red Cross ships over here — or haven't you heard of our surrender yet?

Wed., July 22, 1942

I'm finding out how vicious an enemy hunger can be. It makes you wish you were dead. It drives you to stealing and sneaking ways. I stole a can of milk and a can of tomatoes out of a Lieutenant's bag yesterday — God forgive me. The future is dismal — a damned cripple. Will we even get home?? If I don't talk fast, the gov't and War Dept. will try to beat me out of my pension. Brown and Bigelow[45] probably won't want me — a cripple. If the U.S. ever does land here, I'll probably be killed by one of our own bombs, an ironical end. And the hot burning coal continues in the pit of my stomach.

Sunday, July 26, 1942

The Imperial Japanese High Command from Manila visited the hospital today. What the purpose, or what the outcome I don't know. It'd be wonderful to hear that we were going to be traded, but that's almost a lost hope. I wish they'd do something about the

food — let us have fruits or something. On this island there are 50,000 pineapples rotting every day (according to the Del Monte manager), and we do not ever get a pineapple! Food is uppermost in our minds. This low ration of poor food makes the suffering twice as great, and the healing twice as slow.

Monday, July 28, 1942

Had two teeth filled — temporary fillings.

Thursday, July 30, 1942

Well, I did get to celebrate my birthday this evening, and it was one of the most appreciated and desirable celebrations ever! Managed to get two chickens, courtesy Al Layton, USN,[46] and I got eight eggs. Mess Sgt. Walter Haddock and one of the cooks, "Chief" Blanche,[47] did the rest! At 7:30 p.m., seven of us went down to a "private" room in the mess hall, me in the wheel chair; and festivities began!

---

46   Radioman Third Class Albert E. Layton (not to be confused with US Army lieutenant Layton mentioned earlier in Hinkle's diary) is believed by many to be the first American casualty in the Far East. Layton was sitting on the wing of his PBY seaplane patrol bomber, which was anchored in Davao Gulf, when suddenly and without warning the seaplane was strafed by Japanese aircraft at approximately 0600 on December 8, 1941, Philippine time. Layton's right leg bone was shattered by a bullet in the attack. He made shore and was passed from one local hospital to another until arriving at the Force General Hospital at Impalutao, Mindanao, where he was operated on by Dr. Davis. Layton recovered but walked with a slight limp. He later died aboard *Shinyō Maru*. This information was provided by Brigadier General John H. McGee in his book, *Rice and Salt: A History of the Defense and Occupation of Mindanao during World War II* (San Antonio, TX: Naylor, 1962). McGee was a colonel when he appears in Hinkle's diary entry for June 15, 1944.

47   Pvt. "Chief" Osborne Blanche died September 7, 1944, aboard *Shinyō Maru*.

---

45   A promotional products distributor based in St. Paul, Minnesota.

We had wonderful fried chicken with southern gravy, rice, a loaf of bread, skewed apricots, coffee, sugar and a can of milk!! And the cake — oh, boy! Swell frosting and raisins, god it was good. In between we had pineapple juice and rectified alcohol (180 proof!!!) and we *really* felt jovial. I gorged myself with three plates of chicken, fruit, rice, coffee and all of us gave our stomachs a violent shock by suddenly filling them! The chicken was so tasty and tender it almost melted in your mouth. All day, people were giving me little things that were so deeply appreciated — but those back home would scoff at them; coconut candy from Sgt. Callahan; half of a sweet potato from Capt. Cruz; extra hotcakes and flowers from the dietitian; a banana from one of the ward boys; a bunch of bananas from my favorite nurse (Cres); a medal of the Sacred Heart of Jesus from Father Housman; a towel, and a bar of Lifeboy soap from Capt. Gray. I thank God for these real friends and for making my birthday as pleasant as it was. And Mom and Dad — I thought of you so much during the day, and surely next year we'll be together on July 30th. God bless you.

Friday, July 31, 1942
Getting a few things from the outside, but very expensive. Coconuts for 50¢, oranges and bananas for 90¢, eggs (little ones) for 25¢! But while money lasts, I'm buying!!

Saturday, Aug. 1, 1942
The civilians here have received notice to be able to be ready to leave at very short notice for a "boat ride," which means they will probably be exchanged and sent HOME! Lucky people — when will WE get to go?? I hope Father Ewing sends words to my folks.

Thursday, Aug. 6, 1942
The civilians are still here, though the information is authentic that they and the American Nurses are going to be taken to Luzon to Cabanatuan, one hundred and fifty kilometers North of Manila. We don't quite know whether they are to be exchanged and sent to the U.S. or not, but they, of course, hope so. Whether it's rumor or what I don't know, but there's also been talk of the patients and non-combatants being sent "out" of the islands soon. We don't know what to believe, but we know what we'd like to believe. Will soon be out of money, and then no more eggs, bananas, etc.! Wonder if the Red Cross is sending a ship? That will be my hope of escape.

Tuesday, Aug. 11, 1942
Now there's a rumor that a Red Cross Ship is in Cagayan, with food, sugar and medicines! We don't believe it, and if it *is* there, will the six of us permanently disabled get to go?? We'll see what the next day or so brings.

The civilians now have to do their own cooking and have their own mess. All the American soldiers were sent back (?) to Malaybalay, including our cooks. The only American staff left are Major Davis, Father Houseman, and Capt. Speck. Things are becoming more and more available from the outside, but at outlandish prices. I now have six kilos of native sugar, at 3 pesos per kilo! This is just sugar and juice, pressed and dried — has lumps and tastes like molasses. Got two kilos Irish potatoes at 1.50 pesos per kilo! Eggs are up to 30¢ ea. Now that things are available, they're trying to keep us from buying. Hah! — if we didn't buy something, we'd really hurry the "skinnying up" process!!!!

Wednesday, Aug. 12, 1942
Another year for you (26), Mom and Dad, and my thoughts are with you more than ever. Wish I could have arranged another party this year, but maybe next year — maybe. God grant you are both well and happy, and I'm praying that you are not doing an overly amount of worrying.

We've heard that quite a naval battle is going on near the Solomon Islands.[48] Radios are being confiscated hereabouts. The Japanese, I hear, are camouflaging their trucks here — apparently expecting something to break. I hope war does not come again to these islands — we've had enough — we want to go home. The people here

Written on the back: "To Walter. In heartfelt appreciation and esteem for your kindness and for being a good patient of mine — thanks for your picture too. God bless you, Walter! — Cres." *Hinkle Archive*

have had enough; they're tired, too. These islands can be regained without further fighting here.

Thursday, Aug. 13, 1942
I don't believe I've mentioned the rainy season we have been having. Since about the 3rd week in May, it has rained practically every day. Up until about two weeks ago, one could say that the rain would begin falling between 3:30 p.m. and 4:30 p.m. It would then continue raining until early morning. Now, we still have rain at some time during the 24 hour period, but most of it is falling at nite. Most noticeable now are the terrify-

---

48   The Allies counterattacked the Japanese in the Solomon Islands with landings at Tulagi, Gavutu, and Guadalcanal on August 7, 1942. The Imperial Japanese Navy, in response to the landings, mobilized a task force that resulted in the August 8–9 Battle of Savao Island, the first major naval engagement of the Guadalcanal Campaign.

Hinkle kept these stamps tucked inside his billfold. They were a gift from Tadao Iwamoto on August 28, 1942. *Hinkle Archive*

ing thunder storms — and believe me they are loud!! Several sharp, and very loud claps of thunder have really scared the daylites out of us — sounds like a nearby cannon report. Usually, though, the thunder is very long, and rumbling. Lightning has struck quite close at times.

Monday, Aug. 17, 1942

Well, at 10:15 a.m. today the civilians, padres, and our American Army Nurses left Impalutao, presumably to go to Cagayan, then by boat to Davao. Perhaps they'll get home. We'll sure miss them here — the nurses and padres especially. God grant them safety. Helen Gardner, Rita Palmer, and Rosemary Hogan and Sally Blaine — four swell gals. See you someday, maybe?!

Thursday, Aug. 20, 1942

It's been very quiet and monotonous since the civilians and nurses left, and life is exceedingly dull. Cast should have been changed last week but there is no more good plaster. Cast now on

five weeks, and Doc. says he's going to leave it on as long as possible! Guess it won't make much difference to me — I've been so uncomfortable for so long that a few more weeks won't matter. I'm going to get my hair cut short, may as well. I shaved Sgt. Campbell's head today — "shore looks purty!"

Monday, Aug. 24, 1942

Well, the new rumor, brought up by Dr. Matsui is not very clear. It runs as follows; the American medical force will be sent home next month! Doctor Davis is not certain, but he thinks Dr. Matsui meant all of us. At any rate, our belief in it is nil. It's a good rumor though!! The Japanese are training the PA to fight the Americans!

Friday, Aug. 28, 1942

We have a Japanese soldier as a patient, and he has another Japanese soldier as an orderly. Both are very jolly and pleasant. The orderly is very good at sketching and we have had lots of fun watching him draw. He speaks some English and is well informed on books, movies, art, and travel. He dislikes war and wants to be back in Japan for the cherry blossoms. I gave him a photo of myself and he was quite pleased. Next, we exchanged some postage stamps, in which he is interested in as a hobby. Also learned a little of Japanese language. He apparently likes me enough to give me cigarettes, and sugar and these are things I heartily accept.

Saturday, Aug. 29, 1942
Doggone! I genuinely like this little Japanese soldier, named Tadao Iwamoto, and we've spent quite a bit of time talking to each other. He's been kind and generous, and we share with everything the two of us have — candy, pineapple, cigarettes, and milk. He enjoys my telling him all about Chicago, and is continually amazed when I tell him, e.g., how far it is between large cities; or that men and women are on equal status, whereas in Japan, the woman is considered very low — the wife classed with the servants. When man and wife go someplace, the wife follows him at two meters. Men do not marry until they are thirty — no sweethearts — families arrange marriage. He promises to send me a Japanese Kimono after the war, if he doesn't commit "hari-kari" before he gets home!

Tuesday, Sept. 1, 1942
Found out today (tonite) that starting today I'm supposed to get milk twice a day. Naturally, *was* to get it. Quite by accident I found out about it, and if I handn't found out, I probably NEVER would have gotten any. God, how these people do try to rook you at every opportunity.

Wednesday, Sept. 2, 1942
Hmph? Capt. Piang again gets a basket of stuff from his Filipino and Moro[49] cohorts. Gets about ten packs of Piedmonts and some Tobacalera

---

49 A Muslim Filipino man is called a Moro, and a woman is called a Mora.

cigarettes!! Christ! And the Americans wonder where everything went! Besides that, he gets a tin of Swift's Corned Beef and some other stuff. I got one cigarette, thank you!

Had my hair cut extremely short. Even thought of having it shaved — but only thought!

Monday, Sept. 7, 1942
God bless you Pete, and keep well and happy and unmarried. Perhaps you shouldn't wait for me. I'll not blame you. Always love you, come what may. Dreaming of you, and you and I, darling.

Thursday, Sept. 10, 1942
Am getting my "Alpine" milk twice a day, now, after much hounding of people. Perhaps I'll pick up some of that lost weight, but more important, that hole in my ankle may finally heal up. Nine months already!!!! In this cast eight weeks, one day today! Should come off this week or next Monday. Wonder if I'll have one more? If not, wonder what my leg and foot will look like and how soon I can put weight on it? Colonels and generals left Malaybalay Sunday — given fourteen days rations. Destination? Probably Manila, perhaps Tokyo. Feeling is that all of us will be leaving here soon. Expect Philippine Army to be disbanded here this month. Tadao gave me a pack of cigarettes today — he sure has a good heart. And the people back home are gobbling up all that false propaganda! Gave Tadao

my Eversharp[50] — he sure appreciated it, and gets a kick out of it like a little boy with a new toy. He likes to draw, so it'll come in handy for him. It's the least I could do.

Friday, Sept. 11, 1942
Listened to a lot of crap from KGEI[51] concerning Labor Day, and the workers "sacrificing" so much by agreeing to work, instead of taking a holiday. Jeez — they should be working *every day*, Sundays included, twenty four hours a day. You don't take Sundays or holidays off in the front lines, why should workers? They have a home to return to after work, good food, peaceful sleep, money and places to spend it — happy hours with their families. Sacrifice!! Hah! They don't know the meaning of the word. They probably got pay-and-a-half for working on Labor Day too!! What a load of fertilizer!!

Walked last nite without aid of ANYTHING!!!! Hard to navigate with cast, but I made it around my bed twice!! First step in nine months! No pain.

Cast changed. No anesthesia, some pain. The wound is one-and-one-half

inches deep. Leg very thin — looks like infantile paralysis!

Saturday, Sept. 12, 1942
New rumor (never a dull moment!). U.S. officers to be taken out of islands between Sept. 21 and Oct. 1. Where? Why? You believe it, diary. I don't know if it's to Japan — I hope it is not true. Japanese pursuit plane swooped low over hospital today. Scared the hell out of us.

Monday, Sept. 15, 1942
This cast isn't any too damned comfortable, and besides, I can't bend my knee very much. When I try to it hurts to beat hell. Doctor Davis grabbed me this morning and gave the knee a quick bend, and I damned near hit the ceiling.

Tadao sent us some cigs today; good boy. There's one who keeps a promise anyway. Got a can of beef and beans — $.75!! Got a can of pork and beans — $.60!! Bought some more brown sugar, and green onions.

Tuesday, Sept. 16, 1942
Dr. Matsui "interviewed" me along with four other Americans, questioning disabilities, home address, etc. and occupation. He told Dr. Davis that he thinks we will be sent *home*! *Please* God, *let* it be true this time!

Thursday, Sept. 18, 1942
Nine months ago tonite I got shot! Tried to bend my knee too much tonite and only brought on severe

---

50 A mechanical pencil.
51 A privately held shortwave radio station based in Redwood City, California; the only voice from home for GIs fighting in the Pacific. Their shortwave news broadcasts reflected the philosophy of William Randolph Hearst, who tended toward nonintervention. Nearly all international stations at that time were operated by governments, and foreign listeners assumed that KGEI reflected official US foreign policy. As Japan continued its territorial expansion in Asia, America's Asian allies were dismayed by these broadcasts, which often sympathized with Japanese propaganda.

pain. Given phenobarbital, and finally a quarter shot of morphine! Long time since last one! Slept about two hours. Hurts like hell.

Rumor — Davao was shelled and that Japanese declared it an open city!

Wednesday, Sept. 23, 1942
Tadao sent me ten packs of cigarettes today — quite a pleasant surprise. He's certainly proving to be an amazingly fine chap! Had quite an argument with Dr. Davis today. A nurse gave me the wrong medicine and I chided her about. She seriously began to lie to me about it, and I got damned mad and told her I'd get the damned stuff analyzed and prove she was a liar. She cried to Dr. Davis and he, as usual, without listening to an American, took her side, and ate my tail bone out for giving the nurse hell! Even I can see that a medicine mix-up could prove fatal to some patients. What a goddam set-up.

Chow has not been good lately. I've passed up about three out of seven meals lately. Just can't eat all of this hog feed; for a poor breed of hogs at that.

Thursday, Sept. 24, 1942
Good God! Where is all of this going to lead to?? I'm sick at heart — it's hell to be a hated "Americano," more hated, I honestly believe, by Filipinos than Japanese. To have a Filipino nurse stand at your bed, talking to you, smiling, and yet in her eyes the fierce glare of a burning hate. More

friendship, more sincere friendliness has been shown by the Japanese with whom we've come in contact. And when do I get home? What then? Another hospital siege, no doubt. I expect the rebreaking of bones and more casts. A cripple — a damned limpy — an object for flowery sympathy — a person to be pitied. What will I do? Music? Write? Will Eileen look at me — or anyone else? A burden on the folks for how long? Questions by the score, leaving my brain weary. Would death solve all?

Tuesday, Sept. 29, 1942
Dr. Matsui was up today and gave each of us two cigarettes. Every one in hospital in on this. He still says we wounded are to be sent home, but he doesn't know or won't say when.

Wednesday, Sept. 30, 1942
Two-hundred-and-eighty Americans left Malaybalay today. They were air mechanics, technicians and engineers. Suspect they are being taken to Japan. Good luck fellows — God keep you safe.

Friday, Oct. 2, 1942
Wish these goddamn rumors would stop flowing or come true. They're very trying on the nerves. I don't want to believe them, and yet there's that ever glowing spark of hope — that continual "maybe this time." The rumors stack up as follows.
1. All Americans will be out of here by Oct. 12.
2. We're going to Davao, and all

Americans in the Islands will be concentrated there.

3. We're going to Manila.
4. Patients are going home.
5. Patients are going to Wake Island.
6. Doctor Davis is going to Davao.

Which if any, will turn into fact?? God grant #4 come thru for us.

Saturday, Oct. 3, 1942
MICH. = 20
MICH. STATE = 0

Tuesday, October 6, 1942
Four Japanese wounded and one killed today by a group that ambushed a truck near Carmen Ferry. Group first reported as Moros — then as Filipinos led by an American. Whoever they are, they're doing no good to anyone and ought to realize this. The wounded were brought to the hospital, here, and Tadao is back again as a "companion." One shot thru thigh, one in arm, and one above knee. None serious. Lieutenant Minamaya grazed on right arm.

Friday, October 9, 1942
Now what? I've been having some sharp pains around my kidney and groin. Urine exam was negative. Doctor Davis says it might be a kidney stone — threatens to cystoscope me, which consists of giving a spinal and then running a sort of periscope affair up the penis to the kidney and looking around. Says he is going to do it, but I don't know whether he's kidding or not. At least there's no order for it tomorrow.

Later — Dr. says I don't have to be cystoscoped, it's just an inflammation. Dr. Matsui said a radiogram came in today, and that all Americans are to leave for Manila on Oct. 18. Nothing about patients going home. We'll see!

October 12, 1942
Today, the ambulance came up from camp, and with it this news that Dr. Davis is to be relieved from duty here tomorrow! Where he's to go is in question. Also, this hospital is to be taken over by Filipino doctors from Mindanao. However, Dr. Matsui has not mentioned this, nor has Dr. Davis received any direct orders. So — we class it as rumor. Another rumor from camp is that Dr. Davis is to take us patients back to the states. Doctor Matsui may come up today. Maybe we can find out from him.

Thursday, Oct. 15, 1942
Say diary, have I let you in on the fact that it now takes only very little chow to keep me alive? Well, for example, yesterday's total amount of food consumed by me was:
4 glasses of coffee.
1 bowl of boiled rice (lugao).[52]
1 cup condensed milk.
2 small pieces fried liver.
2 pieces unbaked bread.
About 10 spoonfuls of rice.
This is *usual*, and entirely unexaggerated. Great stuff, eh?!

---

52 Also spelled "lugaw," a universal term for various recipes of Philippine rice porridge.

September 25, 1942

My dear Mr. Hukle & my memorable friend Mr. Walter:

You languish for the moon in your native land
of Chicago, and I remind you of the blue sky in
my home Dairen.

I'll expect a person every moment the time
of return to my birthplace Dairen, after war.

Will you see in a dream the blue hills and
your sweet home to light of cheerful lamp at
Peria street in Chicago?

"Will be beyond one's power that utter the
everythink toward the mountain of one's native
country.
It's tank loth similar to religion ecstasy."

This poetry is a lyric poet Takuboku's an ode
in New Japan.

I'll be much fond of this, and sometime sing
my faint voice.

For permanently friendship
Your intimately friend,

TADAO IWAMOTO

A letter from Hinkle's friend, Tadao Iwamoto. *Hinkle Archive*

Friday, Oct. 16 to Oct. 24, 1942

Notes of events as they progressed.

1. Suddenly left hospital (all Americans) and went to Malaybalay.
2. Malaybalay to Cagayan by truck — dirty, painful trip.
3. All Americans from Malaybay board dirty ships for Davao.
4. About 900 aboard — all in holds except patients (allowed to say on deck instead of the hold).
5. Went aboard via crane — almost missed!
6. Good chow on ships — rice and soup was ample. Considerate of patients.
7. All filthy dirty — latrines terrible.
8. Colonel Deter and Iloilo and Cebu gang aboard — tales of jail, cracked corn, rice, lopping off of four knobs!
9. On board ships for five days. Off at some lumber yard in Davao Bay. Patients on trucks — rest hiked about thirty kilometers to Davao Penal Colony.
10. Inspection — shake down. Relieved of Perfex,[53] bible, mosquito net, clean shirt, soap box and soap, matches, paper punch, three cans sardines one-and-one-half loaf bread.
11. Sleeping on wood. Chow good.
12. Number of men from up north here. Benson here.

Davao Penal Colony
Tuesday, Nov. 3, 1942

Traded off my watch for twenty packs of cigarettes today. It's a dirty shame to let a Japanese get it that way, but it's better than having it roughly taken away from me, as many have had done to them, with no return. I don't need to know the time, and cigarettes are a boon. Also traded off my pen for eight packs and that about winds up my trading, unless I part with my Rolls and sunglasses. What degradement we're going thru — to hold onto ones self-respect is, I believe, going to be the greatest job of all.

Wednesday, Nov. 4, 1942

About 1,000 Americans from Luzon arrived today, most in very bad shape. Terrible cases of malnutrition, beriberi (swollen, aching feet, swollen testicles), scurvy, dysentery, trachoma. Brought tales of terrible misery from Cabanatuan. Food there was pretty bad — very little salt, few vegetables, little fruit, no meat. Americans treated *each other* like dogs — "Hell with you, buddy, *I've got mine*!!" Men with money able to buy good food, but would not share it. Hospital conditions reported as terrible. MC[54] men were *selling* medicines to our men! This included doctors and corpsmen, who always were fat and healthy. Said fifty to sixty Americans died every day in camp from malnutrition. Tommy Bush died this way. Newt Mathews killed in action. Hooker is here — looks like hell, beriberi, lost seventy pounds. Magee and Sneddon here too as are Al Wolfe, Irv Mandelson, Mark Goldstine, Gordy Myers, Art Holmes (full of gangrene). May I never again in my life be a witness to such a horribly

---

53 The Perfex 1938 "Speed Candid" was the first American-made focal plane shutter 35m m camera.

54 Medical Corps.

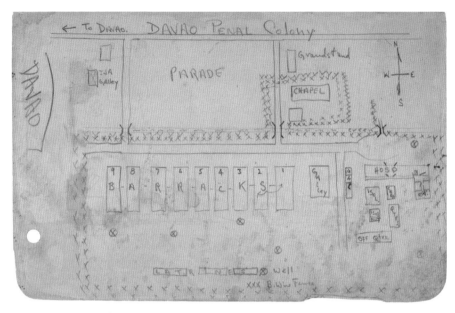

The Davao Penal Colony had a land area of 74,000 acres with a prison reservation of 20,000 acres. The colony prison facility, depicted by Hinkle in this drawing, was laid out in orderly rows with huts lined up much like a military camp. Behind the barracks were three fly-infested latrines, each having thirty holes. Surrounding the compound was a triple fence of barbed wire with a tower at each corner, manned by guards with orders to shoot anyone who approached the fence. Crops grown on colony land included coffee, avocados, coconuts, vegetables, rice, and bananas, most of which was exported to Japan during the Philippine occupation. Little of each harvest was given to the prisoners, who existed on rice, camotes, and whatever snakes, rodents, and insects they could catch and eat. The Japanese worked the prisoners for long hours in the fields, seldom taking into account their diseased and weakened condition, which had reduced many to little more than walking skeletons. *Hinkle Archive*

pitiful sight as is presented by this group of men who actually are skin and bones — who are acidly bitter toward the world, and who just don't give a damn anymore.

Friday, Nov. 6, 1942
With all the bananas, papayas, coconuts, coffee, avocados and sugar around here, the Japanese refuse to put out. We may as well be sentenced to death by starvation. Cassava root and camotes[55] and rice and greens compose our diet. They keep saying the chow will improve, but I can't believe them, and don't.

We've moved to the "hosp." This hospital is a dirty building; hasn't been taken care of at all. Bedbugs and lice abound. Dirt and cobwebs exist in spite of corps men attempt to clean up. Beds are almost all wooden (slats); some are wicker.

[*Continued on page 108.*]

---

55   Sweet potatoes.

The Death March & Camp O'Donnell
by Murray Sneddon

The diary entry for November 4, 1942, marks the arrival of 1,000 prisoners from Cabanatuan. In this autobiographical account, Murray Sneddon describes the horrors he and others from this group experienced leading up to that day.

Sneddon's dramatic story was assembled after his death by his wife, Fiona, using her husband's notes and written recollections. An abridged version of their final manuscript is published here with permission from the Sneddon family.[1]

I remember well my introduction to the Death March. A single Japanese soldier came into my area and pointed toward the road. I understood what he was indicating. I stood up, put my pack over my shoulder, and started walking.

When I arrived at the road I got a terrible shock. There in front of me lay two corpses, both Americans. Their bodies were burned black by the heat from the Philippine sun. The gases generated by decay had blown up both bodies to almost nor-

mal size. The skin had stretched far beyond its capacity, revealing through tears parts of the skeleton within. Maggots in limitless numbers wriggled and crawled over every opening in the skin, making the bodies seem almost alive. Swarms of flies with luminous blue bodies hovered just above the corpses and the angry drone of their flight made the whole scene even more eerie. Then, as my wide circuit around the bodies reached the downwind side, I suddenly caught the horrible stench of death and I quickly clapped my hand over my nose and mouth to keep from vomiting on the spot.

Those who were ill when we started faced a terrible dilemma which we all soon experienced. As we trudged along, each man deep in his own thought, the sharp crack of a rifle suddenly shattered the air. Needless to say, we marchers were really startled. A few men turned and looked back but quickly faced forward again and warned others to keep moving. This was a forced march we were making. Any man who could not keep up the pace, and as a result fell behind the column, was finished. One of the guards who brought up the rear of the column simply placed the muzzle of his rifle against the skull of the

---

1 Murray and Fiona's 168-page manuscript later became the book *Zero Ward: A Survivor's Nightmare* (Lincoln, NE: Writers Club Press, 2000).

faltering POW and pulled the trigger. The prisoner fell immediately into a crumpled heap and the guard stepped over the body and looked for possible new candidates ahead. This was not an isolated incident. Many more of these executions occurred before the day's march was over.

Since the moment one of our members was executed at the rear of the column, a great change had come over our group. The marching pace increased, no man spoke, and every man realized this was no weekend outing. Any one of us could be killed instantly. This was a life and death matter. The guards were capable of annihilating all of us for little or no reason. We had to be as serious in our intent as the Japanese were in theirs. We became wary and watchful.

Later in the afternoon of that first day, our guards led us beyond the side of the road into a dried rice paddy. There they ordered us to stand in rows, to open our packs and arrange every article we possessed in front of us. Pockets had to be emptied with the inside of each left sticking out so they knew we concealed nothing. Those who were slow to respond were slapped around to convince them that speed was essential. Then each guard examined the items displayed by the prisoner in front of him.

At one point I heard a guard reacting strongly to some of the items two of our prisoners displayed. Soon he was joined by other guards, all of whom were voicing loud angry remarks. Then suddenly the two men were abruptly yanked to their feet and the guards began beating them with fists, rifle butts, and hobnailed boots. In only moments they were bleeding profusely and covered with bruises. The guards tied their hands tightly behind their backs and roughly shoved them back to the edge of the road. There they were forced to kneel and remain erect on their knees. Then every Japanese soldier or Filipino coming down the road was required to beat them vigorously on their way by. We learned later that at sundown they were beheaded. They had been carrying some Japanese coins among their effects.

The Japanese brought our first day's march to a close about dusk. No food was offered to us by the Japanese, but to be honest about it, I only wanted to sleep.

The next morning the composition of our group changed some. As soon as the guards started us forming our columns, some of the men who arrived late yesterday hurried into some of the front positions. I guess they knew how important it was to avoid the end of the column.

Just before orders were given to start marching, a young man about two files ahead of me quickly left his position, and ran down the steep bank of the road. As he ran he was trying to drop his pants in preparation for a bowel movement. He quickly squatted and put his head on his knees. Instantly a high powered stream of liquid feces came pouring from his body but quickly stopped. He felt great relief from this initial outpouring and started to pull up his pants, but suddenly he was stricken with violent cramps that held him fast. The column was ordered to move out. He began to expel mucous and blood, a sure sign of amoebic dysentery. One of the guards sighted him and was on his way down the bank. The guard quickly dispatched him with a shot to the back of his head. It sickened me to see it happen, how easily he could have been saved with the proper medicine.

The column continued to move, and the sun bore down on us without mercy. I could tell that despite my week's rest, my body was not used to the demands being made on it during this march.

Fatigue was taking over, and I was bone-tired. I hoped I would catch my second wind and pick up my pace again.

When I started on the first day of the march I was rested, moderately well-fed, and sure that I could make it through anything the Nips required of us. As my body began to tire from the lack of food, and particularly the absence of water, [the march] began to drain my body of energy. At times I began to hallucinate and I could see myself drifting back in the column, then blam, I woke up at the instant the guard emptied his rifle into the back of my head. It took me a moment or two to regain my orientation, to remember where I was at the moment. I knew I had drifted beyond consciousness and I had no way of telling for how long. This really frightened me. I had to be aware of the present or I'd never make it.

The heat was taking a heavy toll on our men. To march all day, from sun up to sun down during a tropical summer, was too demanding for many captives. Many had no head coverings and the Japanese would not allow us to get water. There were free-flowing springs at intervals along the Bataan road. They projected the water two to three feet into the air. Yet the Japanese threatened to bayonet anyone who attempted to collect water at those spots. Water was absolutely essential to soldiers marching under the conditions we were forced to observe. The execution of marchers was increasing drastically.

I lost track of the days and the village names. The only thing I could remember were the various incidents that took place along the route. I could depend on the sun; I knew it would be hot. I knew, also, that if I awakened in the morning I was still alive. If we started to march, I knew there was at least one day left to go; other than that I was in a mental fog. All I wanted to do was lie down beneath one of those springs we'd seen along the road with my mouth wide open and drink until I could hold no more.

Then something seemed wrong; the guards were calling for our evening rest area before dusk. It was a pretty area, by far the nicest we had seen. To the left side of the road, a clump of bamboo was growing much like a giant umbrella and another group of marchers had already occupied some of the space beneath it. When we were dismissed we moved quickly into any vacant space we could find. As I was lying on my stomach arranging my musette bag to serve as a pillow, one of the men next to me spoke.

"Do you see those Jap guards directly across the road from us?"

"Yeah, I see them. Are there about five of them?"

"That's the group. Don't let them think that you're watching them. They've been using us to bury some of those Filipinos over there alive."

"Did you say bury them alive?" I asked with alarm. "That's gotta be the bottom. They can't get any lower than that. I can't think of anything more horrible than burying a man alive."

I figured that must be why they brought us here early: so they could get us to do their dirty work while it was still light. I kept my eye on them while pretending to be busy with something else. At one point they began to stir a bit, so I stood up and stretched and actually tried to be ready to move away from them if they started coming my way. It wasn't long before they began to come across the road. I moved slowly but managed to stay on the opposite side of the bamboo from where they made their selections.

When they had picked four men they moved toward the Filipino area. Several of the guards were carrying shovels. The next thing I knew each American POW had hold of either an arm or a leg of the Filipino the guards had selected and was dragging him across the sand, and out to the drainage ditch at the rear of the area. They placed the Filipino in the ditch, the guards gave the shovels to the American prisoners, then indicated to them by signs that the Filipino should be covered over with dirt.

Well, as soon as the poor Filipino realized what was happening he became terror-stricken and tried to rise up out of the ditch. Instantly the guards motioned to the Americans to hit the Filipino over the head with their shovels, thus rendering him unconscious. While he lay in that state they managed to complete the burial. I returned to my musette bag and tried to sleep, but I kept thinking about that poor native and whether or not he might still be alive and sufficiently conscious to realize what had happened to him.

When we were awakened in the morning I felt tired and sluggish, not a good way to start the day. I tried to keep my mind off the experience I had witnessed last night, but it was impossible.

Once again the heat was really intense, sweat poured from our bodies, and the dust caked over the sweat. It seemed we had barely begun the day and already two of our fellow POWs had been killed by the guards. This was not going to be a good day. This was a day to be alert.

By early afternoon everyone of us was really dragging his feet; this again stirred up a lot of dust. I'm sure this didn't help those who were ill. Even the guards were feeling the heat. They became more irritable and mean. They struck many of the men with sticks intending to spur them forward, but the men, too, had very little energy left so nothing of any consequence occurred.

It was already getting dark, but the guards didn't want to stop until we reached a fair-sized city we could see up ahead. By the time we reached the community ahead it was dark and we were as close to being dead as we had been on the whole march thus far. I saw a sign on one of the buildings in town which read San Fernando.

We heard voices ahead, and the clanking of a metal lock as a creaky gate swung open. We pushed through the gate and found ourselves in a fifteen foot high wire enclosure. The surface of the ground was mud — mud everywhere. Mixed in with the mud was excreta of every type and kind, animal droppings and human feces, both liquid and solid. There were a number of bodies littered around the area, people who had arrived before us. They had fallen to the ground and fallen asleep wherever they could stand the stench. We did the same. I was almost sleeping on my feet as it was. All I had to do was relax my knees, and I sank to the ground and was gone.

The next morning we arose with the sun. The heat helped to intensify the intolerable odor of our sleeping quarters which, in turn, prompted us to stand erect as soon as possible. We were a mess. The foul-smelling mud had thoroughly penetrated our clothing during the night. Some pieces on the outside of our clothing were wet enough and heavy enough to roll off and fall back to the ground. Other pieces on the exterior were already dry and firmly attached as if they belonged there until the end of time. When I attempted to move I felt some of the water ooze slowly flowing down inside my pants on my bare skin. I could feel the mud on my face getting tight as it dried. As I readied myself to leave, I thought of the early lepers who were required to notify all people of their ap-proach by crying "Unclean . . . unclean." I felt so miserable, I wanted to do the same.

The call for our marching formation rang out, and we hap-pily abandoned our pigsty. Sever-al men had died during the night so they remained in their muddy resting place. Thank God their trial was over.

As we began to form our col-umn, many of the villagers stood watching. I had stepped into an outside row, but I felt so ashamed to be seen by the Filipino people in my present condition. Among the people stood a young woman with her shy son who was partly hiding behind her, clinging to her skirt. She leaned over occasion-ally to confer with the youngster. Then he looked up at her ques-tioningly, she nodded yes, and handed him something she had in the pocket of her skirt.

At that moment he left his mother and ran to me. I was ter-rified! If any guard saw him help-ing me, he would beat him for sure. As for me, there was no tell-ing what the guard might do to me to teach the villagers to stay away from prisoners. Fortunately, the guards didn't see him as he slipped a sugar cake in my hand. When he returned to his mother I waited a moment, then when all seemed safe I mouthed the words,

Salamat . . . maraming salamat.[2] Both he and his mother understood and they smiled radiantly and nodded their heads.

We really didn't march very far when they brought us to a halt. Guards then walked along the side of the column counting off 100-man groups. One guard was in charge of one hundred men. When the guard escorted our group to the tracks we couldn't believe our eyes. The train consisted of one small-gauge engine and three or four similar gauge boxcars. The doors on the boxcars were closed tight, and since they sat in the sun all day they were fiery hot inside. The guard opened the door of our boxcar and ordered everyone to get inside. We tried to get him to wait a few minutes until some of the heat dissipated, but he became very angry and started to use his bayonet to force us in.

We could see he meant business, so the majority of our group quickly entered the door and fairly well filled the car. He prodded, and pushed, and shouted angrily at the men nearest the door. As they began to push, the rest of us had to press harder against the men around us. Finally the guard hung to the top

of the door frame, planted his feet on the backs of the last persons in, and pushed with all his strength. When he managed to get all one hundred of us in, he closed and locked the door.

Many men cried out pitifully for air. The heat was so intense we could hardly breathe. The man behind me and the one in front pressed so tightly against me that my feet couldn't touch the floor. I hung in space the whole three hour trip. The boxcar lurched from side to side. One minute I was squashed and gasping for air, the next minute I thought I was going to drop down between the two men who were supporting me and get trampled on the bottom of the boxcar floor.

Men who were sick vomited on the men next to them. Those with dysentery could do nothing to control the frequency of their movements. The foul-smelling gas and liquid excrement they expelled further curtailed the breathing efforts of everyone. I knew even before our trip was over that several men had died. This whole experience was a terrifying one for me.

When the railroad ride from San Fernando to Capas was over, I couldn't remember getting out of the boxcar, or getting in line for the final march to Camp

2 *Thank you . . . thank you very much*, a phrase understood in many Filipino languages, including Tagalog, Cebuano, and Hiligaynon.

O'Donnell. I think I must have been so numb and so close to death that my mind just shut out the memory completely. I felt like a zombie. I was moving, but I was unsure of how I was moving and where. For some reason that didn't become clear to me until later, my thoughts reverted to the poor Filipino who was buried alive. I imagined how he must have felt when he suddenly became aware that he was being buried.

In many ways my experience in the boxcar was a duplicate of his, except that I was being buried in bodies rather than in soil. I remember very clearly the moment the doors of the boxcar were shut and locked. The air was fiery hot and there was little of it. The only way I regained consciousness, now and then, was when the boxcar lurched toward the side which took pressure off my chest and permitted me to draw in a partial breath. So in a real sense I too knew what it was like to be buried alive, but without having to surrender my life.

We arrived at Camp O'Donnell on April 15, 1942, thinking that once inside the camp things would change for the better and that somehow our diet and medical needs would be met. This was not the case; it would never be the case. All of us entered Camp O'Donnell in terrible physical condition. We had been deprived of food, water, and rest, and had been living under conditions no one would subject the lowest form of animal life to. We suffered from diarrhea, dysentery, malaria; our legs were swollen and our bodies covered with tropical sores. We needed medical attention badly, but it was never given by the Japanese.

Of the 7,000 of us who entered O'Donnell, 2,000 Americans died within the first six weeks. Many of those who died could have been saved had a hospital been set up to receive them. Instead, we had a place we called the Zero Ward, where men took themselves, or were taken to die. Zero Ward was a shed in one corner of the compound; it was a place in which no one ever recovered. From the Zero Ward the dead were packed tightly together in common graves in the burial grounds a mile from camp, and they filled those graves at the rate of up to 50 a day.

The huts we lived in were filthy, crawling with lice and other vermin, and acted more as breeding grounds for disease than shelter for us prisoners. The roofs generally leaked, rain blew in through the open sides, and we had no blankets in which to keep warm. Odd as it may sound, pneumonia was a common killer there in the tropics. But then again, in our horribly weakened condition, any disease was a potential killer.

Our diet consisted primarily of a watery rice gruel cooked up in large iron pots. Some days we were existing on 300 calories a day, but in better times we received roughly 600 calories. Basically, we were all starving and anything edible was quickly snatched up and eaten. This included food discarded from the Japs' mess, lizards, the odd snake, some insects, rats and any dogs or cats unfortunate enough to stray into the compound, and sometimes weeds and grass. Anything to keep us going from one day to the next.

We were always hungry and were obsessed with food, so much so that at times it was difficult to think of anything else. We were surrounded by a countryside that produced an abundance of food, but the Japs in their sadistic, mindless cruelty denied us access to that food. And whenever the local Filipinos arrived at the compound gate with gifts of food, they were turned away; some of them beaten in the process.

To make matters worse, there were few water points in the compound and we had to stand in line for hours under the hot sun to get water, which we carried away in coconut shells or the few canteens we were able to get into camp. Water was always a problem; either there was not enough and we suffered from thirst, or it fell from the sky in buckets, turning the compound into a sea of mud, overflowing the already overflowing latrines and stretching their contents and the disease that came with it throughout the camp.

In order to survive, I had to focus my whole being on survival. I tried to conserve as much energy as I could, vowed I would eat whatever came my way that was edible, and worked hard to avoid the wrath of the guards.

There was no reasoning to their grounds for punishing us. One Jap in particular, a sergeant named Hashimoto, was extremely violent and unpredictable. He was also an expert at Judo and would demonstrate his ability in the most cowardly manner. We nicknamed him Little Caesar because he had such illusions of grandeur, picturing himself as a great leader of men and an invaluable asset to the Land of the Rising Sun.

Little Caesar would often punch, throw and kick men in

the groin, head and face just for the sheer pleasure of doing it. One man he beat so brutally that after that the man was never mentally complete and his speech was impaired. The man's crime had been that he was so violently ill with malaria that he could not work and drew Little Caesar's attention. When a man was beaten like that it deeply affected all of us, and we could never understand the cruelty behind it.

So, why didn't we rebel and rise up? By the end of the Death March, all of us were so weak and debilitated that we hadn't the strength to fight our captors; our primary fight was to survive. And shamefully, there were many who would look out for no one but themselves. Fighting often broke out over the scraps thrown to us by the Japs, and there were some who were outright murdered for the food they had, or had it stolen from them and were left to starve. That lawless element in camp only served to compound the horrible plight we were in.

After two months at O'Donnell,[3] many of us were moved to Cabanatuan. We were organized into groups of ten and were responsible for the conduct of each other. At Cabanatuan, I know one man did escape. I assume he got away because we never heard of him again. But the remaining nine members of the group were lined up before a firing squad and shot. Those who were caught trying to escape were tortured for days before being shot or beheaded. So unless a man felt he had a better than average chance of getting away, he didn't take it.

Malaria and dysentery were two major health problems in the camp. Quinine was the only drug available to treat malaria, and it was available from the outside, but the Japs refused to allow us access to it. Those who had been able to smuggle money or a ring or watch into camp were able to bribe the guards into bringing in quinine or extra food, but what they brought was never plentiful and the need was always critical.

Malaria was such a terrible disease that it put some into fevers so high that in effect their brains were fried, and they became babbling, helpless idiots who had to be helped wherever they went and spoon-fed like infants. Cases like these usually died. Those who suffered from malaria never fully recovered from it and regularly went through bouts of high

3 Approximately 60,000 Filipino and 9,000 Americans from Bataan and Corregidor were housed at Camp O'Donnell in 1942. It was here that 20,000 Filipinos and 1,500 Americans died. The Japanese believed the force on Bataan would number 10,000, and were unprepared to care for the 70,000 men who were surrendered.

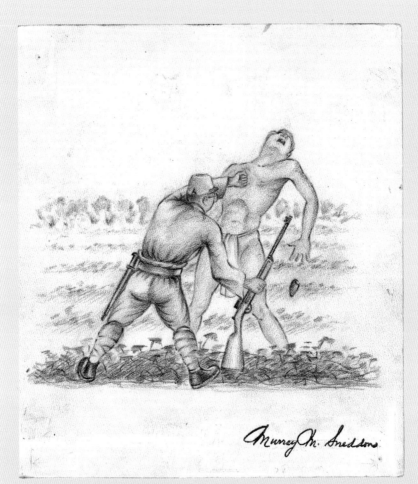

Many times the only clothes that the men wore while working in the fields at the Davao Penal Colony were loincloths, as seen in this sketch by Murray Sneddon. It is titled "Strafed for eating a comote in the field." *Reproduced with permission from Laurie Duffy (Murray Sneddon's daughter)*

fever to bone-chilling cold, shaking uncontrollably until the bout, which might last for days, passed.

Dysentery was a disease many never recovered from. Bowel movements fifty to seventy times a day were not uncommon as liquid excrement streamed uncontrollably from the body. With dysentery, whatever we ate or drank went straight through us, and try as we might to make it to the latrine, we often didn't, and had to squat where we were and relieve ourselves. Those men who were so weakened by dysentery and could not rise to even make it outside their huts, or off the ground on which they lay, were forced to foul themselves over and over, lying in their own filth. Needless to say, the flies surrounded us in clouds, and the stench was beyond belief.

There were only two types of work to be had at both Camp O'Donnell and Cabanatuan: to carry the dead away, and to bury them. In the graveyard, men were packed into holes until they were almost to the surface, and then a covering of dirt was heaped on. In the rainy season, with the ground saturated, blood seeped to the surface and it seemed as if the ground itself was bleeding. Also, wild dogs got at the bodies and it was not uncommon to see them gnawing on human bones.

O'Donnell and Cabanatuan were both the same. It made no difference; each was a dying place. Each was a place to get through one day at a time. We were only existing and days just blended together. At Cabanatuan there were 6,000 of us, and at the rate we were dying, I often felt there wouldn't be any of us left by the time the war ended. Every day long lines of men were taken from the hospital out to the burial sites. All of us were terrified of going to the Zero Ward because we knew we would not come out alive.

We did work hard at trying to keep our spirits up, but we had no access to outside news and didn't know how the war was going. What we got from the Japs was all propaganda designed to lower our morale; the Japs were winning everywhere. But most of us knew what they were trying to do to us, and understood whatever they had to say could not be trusted.

I remained at Cabanatuan for four months. Then I was selected, by what means I know not, to go to Mindanao. There we were to join 1,000 men who had been captured in the southern islands at a penal colony at Davao.

They're moving in cots taken away from the men. The main "ward" can hold about ninety, the "isolation" about thirty (tight squeeze). Operating room is surprisingly good — not germ free of course, but good as compared to the rest of the hospital. We have one "duck" and one bed pan for the whole outfit!!

Saturday, Nov. 7, 1942
O God! I read the lines in my diary from a year ago and I'm ashamed of myself for such words, and would give plenty of money to get food like that again.

Wednesday, Nov. 11, 1942
Removed my cast today — a jack-knife being the instrument used. No more cast to be applied. Foot looks like hell — deformed, and shorter than the left. Hole in right side still quite large and goes into the bone. Doctor says it "looks good and clean," but what the hell?! It's still draining, of course. Jeez, what some butter, eggs, milk, bread and meat would do for me!

Saturday, Nov. 14, 1942
Day dreaming is a great hobby among us, and I'm no different. There is *one* thing that has been on my mind very much; in fact, it is now a fervent desire which I hope to realize after I return. I want an island in the north woods of Minnesota around Jackfish Bay. I want to build a cabin there and stock it well so I can go there any time, or stay year round. At nite, when I can't

sleep, I visualize the cabin, with a big fire place, furnished fairly well; a boat house for my row boat and canoe; the well, cellar, work shop and lumber saw. I can hear the "put-put" of the water pump, the whistle of the wind thru the pine trees; the bark of the cocker spaniel, the smell of bacon and eggs on a wood fire. Away from all the damned conventions of society — dress shirts, dances, so called "parties," and useless hustle and bustle. Just a big radio-Victrola to keep in touch with the crazy world. Flannel shirt and blue denims — cold mornings and cold nites. All of this to me presents heaven on earth. Eileen — you had better like this kind of a life in case you and I meet a priest. Otherwise, we'll never be happy.

Monday, Nov. 16, 1942
I have been doing some very serious thinking lately, working on the assumption that I will get to return to the U.S. I have been pondering the wisdom of having my right leg amputated just above the ankle, and then having an artificial foot. It seems to me that this would be the wisest move — in fact, all seems to be to my advantage to have this done (after I get home, of course). As it is now, my foot is muchly deformed, being smaller than my left foot. In two columns it comes to this.

Advantages

1. With modern artificial foot, can walk normally, with no limp.
2. Without limp will not be object of pity.

3. Will be able to apply for good job, where I can partake of social events if necessary, as with Brown and Bigelow advertising.
4. No trouble in future.
5. Same size shoes and sox.
7. Can dance, golf, ride, drive, etc.

Disadvantages

1. With a stiff ankle I will have noticeable limp.
2. Will be object of pity, and terribly self-conscious — with an inferiority complex.
3. Great hindrance to job and mar on personality, in spite of fact is result of war.
4. Possible pain, like arthritis.
5. May turn fiancee against me.
6. Certain limitations.

Wednesday, Nov. 18, 1942
Major Roper's birthday. Been playing poker — colored chips made from cardboard. Colonel Deter gave Roper a Camel cigarette which was duly passed around. [*In the margin, Hinkle wrote: "Apparently I picked up some vicious germs from it, for that nite I had sore throat, and for two weeks afterward suffered miserably with nasal pharyngitis. Ate hardly nothing for eight days — could hardly swallow water. Broke it finally on Nov. 28 with plugged nose only left over."*]

Monday, Nov. 23, 1942
It's hot as hell here most of the day — sticky. Hospital is the coolest building of all because we have a ceiling to protect us from the heat of the sun. Everything is as usual — "SNAFU."[56]

One day they move the patients around one way, and a few days later they shuffle them around again. Thank God Colonel Deter is in charge of the hospital. Otherwise things would really be in a mess. He is doing a good job under the circumstances, if only the patients could realize it. If they knew him as I do, they'd know that if there's any break to be given the patients, he'll give it to them.

Many of these men who came down from Luzon don't seem like Americans. Their total spirit is "every man for himself." They appreciate nothing. Give them a hand, and they take an arm. They're exceptionally foul in their language, pessimistic as hell, uncooperative and at heart unfriendly, and thinking only of what they might possibly get out of you.

Friday, Nov. 27, 1942
Chow has been terrible — same thing over and over. Breakfast usually stewed purple camotes and rice, no salt. Lunch is rice, stewed camotes and a few greens, "ticki-ticki." Supper is rice, stewed camotes, and maybe dried, foul smelling salted minnows! This, not *one* day, but *every* day. Today was an exception — we got *some* meat and a meat gravy. Sure was good. Colonel Deter has been active in getting us lemons and bananas now and then. With acres and acres

---

56   Situation normal, all fucked up.

of bananas, we are given one or two small bananas apiece, when we get them. [*Written in the margin: "Still true, but getting less. 11/27/43."*]

Sunday, Nov. 28, 1942
Tomorrow we're to have some more meat. We got some ice tonite and we all tasted ice water for the first time in months, and the lads with beriberi and aching feet got the blessing of soaking their feet in some *really* cold water.

Sunday, Nov. 29, 1942
Went to Mass this morning. We have nice set-up for altar here in the open. Talked with Padre Lafleur[57] and he is going to give me instruction in the church, which I much need. Rice and meat for supper! Had seconds! Ate biggest quantity in one sitting than I have for six weeks.

Tuesday, Dec. 1, 1942
Japanese are building machine gun pits, entrenchments, etc., on the corners of the camp where the road is. These fortifications are said to point *away* from camp! *What* is expected? Americans? Guerillas? They wanted a rush job — had a three hundred man detail working on them. They say it's for training their troops. We wonder.

Wednesday, Dec. 2, 1942
Cripes! I'm losing weight hand over fist now — half of the chow they throw together here doesn't agree

with my stomach and so help me God, I just *cannot* eat it. I've tried and tried, but to no avail. It's a helluva thing to go thru too, because my body needs all possible nourishment. My waistline is decreasing rapidly. My shorts and pants, buttoned, can slide down over my hips with just a little encouragement. This has never happened to me before. I'm steadily hungry, craving food that would be at least half way palatable. I lie in bed thinking of good food — of Mom's swell dinners and of raiding the ice box, and when I do this, I get huge tears in my eyes and feel as though my spirit is about to leave me. We pray, and wish, and hope, and swear, and suffer, and again pray that this winter the U.S. will deliver us from our sufferings.

Thursday, Dec. 3, 1942
Traded my Ray-Ban Sunglasses (11 pesos) today for a small size can of Ovaltine, small can sardines and some little hot peppers and bananas. God — the Ovaltine is wonderful; mixed some with some hot water for supper, and had my sardines and rice, and thought I was having a steak dinner. For desert — a spoonful of Ovaltine down the hatch to help satisfy that terrific craving for chocolate. The Glee Club, formed at Malaybalay ("Mindanao Melodians"), came over and sang for the hospital gang. They're very good — excellent harmony, and Major Prichard has directed them well. We were told that the men "over the fence" are and will

---

57   Lieutenant Father Joseph V. Lafleur died September 7, 1944, aboard *Shinyō Maru*. For more information about LaFleur and *Shinyō Maru*, see footnote 111, page 202.

be sending extra food to the hospital as their contribution to help us get well. All in all it was darned nice.

Friday, Dec. 4, 1942
Woke up about 2 a.m. to the tune of a slight earthquake. My bed was being shaken the long way and it seems to me the tremor lasted eight to fifteen seconds.

Well! Today, one of the nicer of the Japanese officers came over to see me about buying my camera, which was taken from me upon arrival here in camp. I had given the ole Perfex up for lost, but it seems to be in the office of the CO here. We talked for awhile and I showed him my pictures and he likes the camera very much. He offered "money," but it is almost worthless here, so I told him I'd like to get bread, fish, sugar, cigarettes and fruit besides money; some of each but most importantly food. He speaks good English and understood my point, and agreed. He is coming again and will bring a "contract," and if I can get the food, believe me I'll sign! My health is paramount in importance, and if I can keep clear of beriberi and scurvy by trading my camera, I'll do it. By the time I get out of here it may not be of much good — and I most likely would not even *get* the camera. J. Honda is his name. He gave me two packs of cigarettes and a box of "vitamin candy" with A,B, and C vitamins.

Saturday, Dec. 5, 1942
Hmm! We had meat gravy and navy beans with rice last nite, and there were actually "chewable" pieces of meat! It was good, liken to steak and potatoes. Tonite is supposed to bring more of the same. Roy Gray and Bill Matson came over and brought me some corn and green bananas. Sure was nice of them! Eight planes in formation were seen flying south this a.m., altitude about 8,000 feet. No doubt Japanese. At about 2 p.m., eight planes seen returning from south — looked like twin-motored dive-bombers, unquestionably on a mission.

Sunday, Dec. 6, 1942
Went to Mass. Have been chiseling milk from Jim Campbell, diluting it heavily and putting some on rice. In this way, I can eat plenty of rice — I can't stomach the banana blossoms, cassava and camotes, etc.! In return I give Jim a cigarette whenever I get any. Got a ripe papaya today and three tangerines. Upon opening the papaya, discovered many "wormy inhabitants!" However, this was a minor detail — merely scraped out the worm and went ahead, and it was a very delicious papaya. A year ago, I would have become sick to my stomach at the sight of the worms — but war, and lack of good things to eat does amazing things to a man.

Monday, Dec. 7, 1942
Mr. Honda brought me six eggs today. Jim will scramble four and we'll split. The other two will be hard boiled for me.

Many prisoners created and exchanged cards at Christmas and New Year. This card was created by Murray Sneddon. *Hinkle Archive*

Sunday, Dec. 13, 1942

On Dec. 10th the mosquitoes caught up with me, and I now have malaria. It's a terrible sickness — diarrhea, vomiting, high fever (105°). Makes you feel like giving up — sever stomach cramps make it miserable. I've never felt as awful in my life, and I hope we get out of here soon so I get no more attacks of it.

Monday, Dec. 17, 1942

Exactly one year ago tonite since I was shot.

Thursday, Dec. 24, 1942

Well, had a very pleasant day; evening. In the afternoon, I went over to Mr. Honda's house. He made up a concoction of boiled water, flour and sugar, and it was surprisingly delicious. While I was there, I showed him how to operate the camera and then we talked about Chicago, and he also told me many interesting things about Japan and some other customs. At 4 p.m. went out to the chapel to practice on the piano. In the evening during lulls, Sanders and I shared "pianofrills." I played my "Night Serenade." Then a Russian song and a melody including the Marine song, and the Marines went wild over it! By 10 p.m. I just had strength to make it to my bunk and slept like I haven't in many months. Kept thinking of Mom and Dad and Eileen, and of how much fun they must be having. God bless you and may God please grant we're together next Xmas!

Friday, Dec. 25, 1942

"Merry" Xmas Lieutenant! Woke up to the tune of the "Winter Song" and it was most certainly beautiful. Major Larry Pritchard did the directing. All morning visitors kept dropping in bringing bananas, oranges and some candy. Roy Gray, Bill Latimer, and Les Moote were all over as well as Al Greathouse and Irv Mandelson. For lunch we really had a feast! I had four pieces of roast beef, mashed camotes, rice and good browned gravy. Coffee milk and *sugar* topped with a deliciously flaky *pumpkin pie with cinnamon*! Oh, and some cold sweet cocoa and a Camel cigarette. What man could ask for any more? Padre Lafleur held high Mass at 10:30 a.m. — I attended and received

Sneddon's 1943 New Year's card — the only known example to have survived the war. *Hinkle Archive*

his blessing. What supper will bring is still a mystery. It can't be better and I suppose it'll be worse. Merry Xmas, Mom, Dad, Eileen — as merry as possible anyway.

Sunday, Dec. 27, 1942

Went over to Honda's today and he set me up with some chow — a couple of packs of Bowlings. Trying to make a deal for a couple of chickens w/the Filipinos so we can have some soup and fried chicken.

Thursday, Dec. 29, 1942

Had hemmoroidectomy (sp?) operation today under spinal. No pain during operation, but about three hours afterwards it started, and boy it is a real pain! I'm on the MSO4[58] every four hours and that helps a lot. I've a sort of G-string on w/"pads" — tsk, tsk, and I'm taking plenty of razzing about it! A box of Kotex is what I need!!! Humph! Tsk! Pfftt!!

Saturday, Jan. 2, 1943

Can't eat for three days, but I'm sneaking some food 'cause our breakfast has been pretty good these last two mornings.

Sunday, Jan. 3, 1943

Two good meals of mung beans today, and I ate quite well. Now getting only one shot of MSO4 at bed time. Wish I could get one after midnite. Boy, never again will anyone carve on the interior of my rectum with a scalpel! My movements are slow-motion, as I roll over, a half inch at a time.

Wednesday, Jan. 6, 1943

Still having a rough time with my rear end. Haven't been able to have a bowel movement yet, and it worries me quite a bit. They keep giving me mineral oil, and today I got castor oil, but no result.

Thursday, Jan. 7, 1943

Today we filled out form post cards that are supposed to be sent home. I sure hope they get them so the folks'll have a little word and renewed hope any way. Wasn't much to say — mostly about your health. I checked off that I'm injured and in the hospital and improving. Did this 'cause maybe the letter I sent out in April got thru and so they'll know about my foot any way.

Sunday, Jan. 10, 1943

Stopped shaving today. Expect to shave again aboard ship bound for home, and not before. [*Note in margin: "Changed my mind 2 weeks later !!"*]

Monday, Jan. 11, 1943

Irv Mandelson and I have been thinking of opening a real nice short order restaurant either in Los Angeles or Chicago. I'm all for it — at least it's this or my delicatessen. Irv would be an ideal partner too. He's a lawyer, older than I, his father is a restaurant man in Chicago and Denver — knows the business pretty well — he's a "white" Jew and can achieve the credit contacts, etc. Besides, I like him quite well and we get along good. We could even live together and make a go of it I think. Wondering if it'll ever pan out. [*Written in the margin: "Forget this, too! Just a wild hair!"*]

---

58   Morphine sulfate.

Tuesday, Jan. 12, 1943

This problem of defecation is finally over! Last nite had a shot of MSO4, then an enema, but couldn't get the H2O in! This a.m., the same thing, and got a little H2O in at a time. Then I sat for 1½ hours and finally gave birth to an elephant and it hurt like hell in spite of the MSO4. Then the castor oil took effect, and kept me busy all day!!

The RC packages are supposed to be in Davao. Only 1,200 for 2,000 men! It's something anyway. Mail is supposed to be there too! Boy, I hope I get some.

Jan. 13, 1943

Issue of one pack of cigs today. Some of the field officers were "paid" last nite — 25 pesos!! Japs. say that 42 pesos deducted for board, fifteen for clothes, and five-hundred in the "bank." I'm in line to receive nothing. Borrowed 40 pesos from Chris Bruun. "Inspected" today by some Jap General and about ten officers. Reason? Outcome?

Jan. 14, 1943

Had a sort of chocolate lugao this morning and I ate a helluva big helping. Traded my Rolls Razor for a "Zippo" cigarette lighter and a pack of cigarettes. Figure the lighter of more use than a razor.

January 18, 1943

All the stuff is unloaded from the RC ships and is in Davao. There is canned

This rare example of a blank POW post card (pictured front and back) is one of the many artifacts that can be found in the *Hinkle Archive*

beef, chocolate, tomatoes, sugar, flour, dried fruit, cocoa, clothes and cigs. Only reason we haven't the packages is that the river is too high and the road and tracks are underwater! Damn! Supposed to be seventeen kinds of chow, toilet articles, soap and cigarettes in the individual packs. May be two men to a pack. Not enuff packs! Colonel Deter and twelve others got letters and sure hope there's more mail and that I'm not disappointed.

January 19, 1943

Bought a can of corned beef for 12 pesos! Can of salmon for 5 pesos! Bananas, eggs and sorghum coming up! The prices are high, but what the hell — if I have to pay for health, I'll buy it as long as I can *borrow money!*

Having a terrible time defecating. The rice makes such terrifically, solid feces, and my rectal muscles are still very tender from malaria. Don't know what I'll do — I "gotta," but the intense pain won't let me. Doctor Davis won't let me have an enema either. Still expecting Red Cross packages.

January 24, 1943
Two-hundred men from permanent details came in yesterday. Doc's going to work on my foot tomorrow — has to go in and scrape dead bone out again. He's going to put me under — sodium pentothal. Still having alot of trouble with my bowel movements. Boy, what a pain that is.

January 25, 1943
Operated on today. Took about forty minutes, and when I woke up in bed, my foot was full of blood and my blanket and sheet were all bloody. Then the pain began and the MS04 shots started.

Thursday, Jan. 28, 1943
Jeez, when those shots wear off, the pain really is strong in my foot. I'm still bleeding. The RC packages and stuff are in camp!

Friday, Jan. 29, 1943
Today, Dr. Davis took off the bloody bandage, and it was partially dried and stiff. It was rather painful. Then he got to feeling around my ankle bone and that was really painful. Later in the day we got our RC packages. Each man got one package apiece and then there

were two more packages, containing different foods, and these were to be divided between two men. A total really of two packages of food per man! Jeez — corned beef, tomatoes, cheese, coffee, cocoa, meat roll, bacon, butter, cigs, tea, sugar, candy, etc. It was a great day, and we were all like a bunch of kids at Xmas. Many will be sick tomorrow *no doubt*! We thank the American RC, the Canadian RC, and the South African RC. The Canadians did the best job of all. Conspicuous by their absence, however, were pork and beans, sauerkraut, peanut butter, and canned wieners. I was sick today too, so I couldn't or didn't feel like opening anything. My stomach felt like hell. I'm bound up — that's the trouble.

Saturday, Jan. 30, 1943
Oh God! Today I had the most painful dressing since hospitalization. Doc began taking the gauze out and it was agony. There was about two-and-one-half yards of it and it stuck to the bone. He finally got it out and then began getting blood clots out with a hemostat and wiping with applicators. He then told me the peroneal nerve was again exposed and he bumped it every now and then and it was just like reliving the days of a year ago. I took my mirror and looked for a split second and the hole is terribly large — about the original size! Then he began packing it — right up against the nerve, and I was shaking so he could hardly do it. At least it was over, and he said I'd taken the dressing better than any other. Then he ordered

the shots. And to think this'll happen every two days! It's knocked my courage down. I had thought the wound had almost healed, and now it's back to where it was a year ago — and no cast material. God give me strength to bear the pain — pain with which I thought I had finished.

A Filipino killed a Jap guard today by hitting him in the back of the neck with an axe. Took rifle, shoes, canteen, and took off.[59] Christian funeral was held, American and Filipinos went. Pino not yet caught.[60]

Thursday, Feb. 4, 1943

Talked very seriously today with Dr. Davis about amputating my foot. He said he's thought of it quite often, too. The hole is so big now and the pain so continuous and strong, that sometimes I feel like screaming. It's obvious as hell that my foot is not turning out as well as was expected, and for me to be able to say, "See, I've still got my *own* foot," seems quite useless. I'd be able to get around, or rather as the

Dr. says, "you could use it." Hell — I'd rather get it off *now* — have a few days or so of pain, and then *know* that operations on my foot would be over with. I'd know that I wouldn't have to own a club foot and a limp, and pain-spells the rest of my life. I'll get the best artificial limb money can buy and be almost "brand new." Dr. Davis is still thinking it over. I think he *will* perform the operation. The only thing I *don't like* is that he said it should be done under *spinal*, not *ether* as I asked.

Sunday, Feb. 7, 1943

I guess Dr. Davis has decided to go ahead and amputate my foot. His big worry, apparently, is infection setting up inside the stump. The situation as to sterility is not too good here. So — I feel that in the near future I'll again be on the "table," but this spinal anaesthesia business has me nervous. I hate to hear the doctor talking and asking for instruments in the operating room, and the noise in my head of metal against bone — God — it drives me wild.

We were each issued two cans of corned beef today, and we're to have raisin pie today too!!

Saturday, Feb. 13, 1943

Damnit! Doc says it doesn't look like he's going to amputate. It's mainly because he doesn't want to take the chance of infection, in which case he explained he'd have to amputate higher and higher. Naturally, I don't

---

59   The Filipino was an Igorot, which in Tagalog means "people of the mountains." The name is collectively used to describe several Austronesian ethnic groups in the Philippines who inhabit the mountains of Luzon. In earlier days the Igorot were known for their wars and practice of headhunting. The prisoner in this diary entry attacked and killed the Japanese guard with an axe, mutilated the body with a bolo by cutting off the lips and arms, and made his escape after taking with him the guard's shoes, rifle, and equipment.

60   This is the first appearance in Hinkle's diary of the informal demonym Pino—his version of the usual spelling, Pinoy. It can be used as a pejorative or as a term of endearment, similar to the way Yankee is used when identifying someone from the United States. Although Pinoy and the feminine Pinay are regarded today as derogatory by some (especially the young), the terms are still in mainstream usage in the Philippines.

want *that*, so I suppose it'll have to be done back home, if I ever *get* back home! I'm determined that the foot will be amputated, and NO ONE will change my mind. Hell, I don't want to appear or act any more crippled than I have to.

Sunday, Feb. 14, 1943

Valentine's Day! — and my love to my three married valentines. We get another issue of two cans of corned beef per man today. Oh Joy!

Damn! Having the nerve exposed again, and my ankle has made life pretty rugged these last two weeks. I can't lie in one position for any great length of time because pressure on any part of the foot highly irritates the nerve. I've been continually on that blasted MSO4 to ease the pain, but I wish there was something else I could get to stop pain.

Some bastard hooked a package of tea out of my box last night. Damn — wish I had been awake and caught him.

Tuesday, Feb. 16, 1943

God! I'm sick and tired and utterly disgusted of being *lousy*! Yes, lousy — damned bed bugs and greybacks, just can't get rid of the bastards. And do those greybacks bite — cripes! At nite is when they raise particular hell, and it's hell trying to get to sleep. Dirty little bastards! When will we get the hell out of here?

Wednesday, Feb. 17, 1943

A Jap plane flew over and around today and dropped pamphlets telling the guerrillas to surrender their arms, but they did not have to surrender themselves because the Philippines would soon have its independence! In short, the Japs seem to be getting ready to pull out of P.I. for fear of Yanks. Give the Philippines "independence," and then they try to raise hell about the U.S. "invading" a neutral country. They keep talking and printing in papers that the independence will come "soon." Hope so.

Thursday, Feb. 18, 1943

Report from Davao — thousands of Japs pouring in there. Supposed to be from Solomons and New Guinea. Hope our troops keep on their tail and spring us out of here! "Then is there good hope that thou mayest see thy friends, and come to thy high roofed home, and their own country." — Odyssey, Book VIII.

Saturday, Feb. 20, 1943

Another idea in my head for what I'd like to do for awhile when I get back. This much I've decided — I'm going to buy myself a good motorcycle, even if I have a car. I've had a taste of driving one while over here, and I'm nuts about it. If I can't fly, I'll have a bike, and take short trips on it on week-ends, or just knock around on it for fun. It'll be my big playtoy — expensive to buy, yes, but I want it, and I'll get it. But what I had in my mind was talking the River-dale Council into letting me paint it up as "Riverside Police," and then after I'd learned the necessary State and Village laws, they'd pass me, give me a star again, and I could do patrol duty for Riverdale, say alternately days and nites, or Wednesday nites and weekends. There's only one car in Riverdale, and I think I could talk them into letting me help out. I'd like that a helluva lot. I'm not planning on settling down for quite awhile after I get back anyhow — I owe myself that much for the hell I've gone thru over here. This idea will probably horrify the folks, and they'll call it crazy. Let them. I'm going to be crazy by the time I get back!

Monday, Feb. 22, 1943

A few things I've learned since arrival here:

1. Cribbage
2. Roll cigarettes
3. Drink scotch and soda
4. Patience.
5. Appreciation of infinite number of things back home.
6. To place little or no faith in rumors.
7. To swallow U.S. propaganda with a barrel of salt.
8. That man is a contemptible fool.
9. That rice and sardines is a foul dish!
10. That the Japanese are human and likeable. [*Hinkle pencils in, "Some revisions on this 2/45."*]
11. That Filipinos are not to be trusted.
12. That pain is pretty much hell.
13. That ankles will not stop .30 cal. bullets!
14. That war is hell on earth.
15. To go without food.
16. That Americans will stab one another in the back for any trivial personal gain.
17. That any canned chow is delicious (except squid!).
18. To eat fried or boiled liver and like it!
19. That life is intolerably short. Make the most of it!

Had another issue of corned beef yesterday. Too bad it'll stop in a few weeks — be better if we could get out of here. They started a PX here and to start with we have tobacco leaves and soda pop. As a result of the following concoction, or combination, I gained a severe belly ache and gas on my stomach: corned beef, rice, mungo beans, onions, chocolate, and milk — and fifteen minutes later, a bottle of pop!! So ate no supper and very little breakfast today, and only tea for lunch. I'm still having a great deal of pain in my foot, especially in the late afternoon and evening. I get so damned mad about it. It hurts so much that I have to get a shot of MSO4 so's I can be still and get to sleep.

Monday, Feb. 23, 1943

Ah, me, if it's not one thing it's another; now I have the runs.

All these rumors that are floating around have the men here in higher spirits. Most of them are now looking for us to be out of here soon. Some "figure" one month; others two. Some say three months, and others "June 1st." Personally, I think six months to a year may see us freed from this.

Saturday, Feb. 27, 1943

The Japanese are having us fill in cards again with all our personal information on it. Wonder what's up now — more specialists to be taken out?

Tuesday, March 2 1943

Alot of men received radio grams yesterday, dated sometime around Xmas. I did not get one and I'm worried for fear Mom and Dad have been notified that I was killed. I sure hope not. It kinda hurts a little not to have been one of the lucky ones, but my day will come. Mine probably got lost somewhere.

Wednesday, March 3, 1943

Have had an idea break forth in my head, and I'd like to fulfill it. After I'm able to get around back home, why not try to get into some Polish relief organization, get sent to Poland and help those people get back on their feet? Dziadzin[61] did it, and I think it would be a fine thing to do. Perhaps I could get Jackie to go along. I've experience of all sorts now, and if my foot isn't, or doesn't turn out too bad, I see no reason why I shouldn't qualify for such a job. I've decided I want to remain a bachelor for quite awhile yet, at least there are too many things I want to do by myself, and if Pete doesn't care to wait for an indefinite result, I won't blame her, and I don't feel she should wait. I've changed — no, I haven't lost my love for you, Pete, not by a bit — but this war has had its effect on me;

my outlook is different. I've been a prisoner of war, and tied to a bed, inactive. I want *liberty* when it's all over. I want to raise hell in my own way for awhile. I want to do what I want to, when I want to, where and if I please. Do you see my point?

Thursday, March 4, 1943

Jeez, my foot certainly has been giving me hell. Especially when the humidity is high is when I have the greater pain. I'm getting MSO4 shots during the nites, otherwise I fear I'd get little or no rest. But soon that's going to have to end and then … ?X?@???!

Friday, March 5, 1943

There are all kinds of rumors running around today. In fact there have been rumors galore the last few days and they are so silly that I have not recorded any except a few. The prize one holds that the guerrillas on this island are in direct talks with General MacArthur and that they are to clean up the Japanese forces here three days prior to the coming of the U.S. troops!!!

Colonel Colvard had a can of M&V[62] stolen from under his bunk. There's been some sonofabitch swiping stuff here. Must be doing it at nite. I'd sure like to catch the bastard and club him with a crutch. Wonder if it was the same guy who hooked my package of tea?

Got a new canteen and mess kit today.

---

61 A friend and physician to the Hinkle family.

62 Meat and vegetables.

Cripes, this afternoon I was suddenly hit with a fever of 101.6° and I felt like hell. Into bed and Doc crammed me full of stuff, including a shot and two nembutals. As a result, by 9 p.m. my fever was down and I felt pretty good again, and slept very well.

Saturday, March 6, 1943
There's been a helluva lot of air activity lately; one plane, three planes, and quite a few planes today. This leads me to believe that there is something going on not very far from here. Perhaps our troops and navy are nearby after all! Anyway, I kind of expect something to happen in April — but only "kind of."

Sunday, March 7, 1943
Damn this climate is hell! You can bet on having rain every day between 4:30 and 9 p.m. You might lose once or twice, but you'd sure win a helluva lot. The water has been turned off all day today. Luckily, I had half a canteen of water for lunch today (corned beef, rice, mungo beans, chocolate-raisin pie). But I and the others are thirsty as hell now (6 p.m.) and there may not be any water till tomorrow!!

Monday, March 8, 1943
I'm selling anything gold to get money with which to buy food and fruit. I can't help feeling that the food is more important to me than the gold. I don't want to get beriberi. I've seen too much of it and know it's very, very painful. So far I've sold

my MPMA[63] ring. Now I've had the stone taken out of my S&B ring,[64] and will sell the gold ring. I hate to do it, dammit, but I can't fill my stomach, or keep up my strength on sentiment. Besides, I can and will replace them when I get home.

Tuesday, March 9, 1943
WELL! I walked a total of about 120 feet with a cane! I used the whole sole of my foot, except under the big toe. I hurt like hell, but I've got to do it sooner or later, so may as well do it now. Doc was pleased and all were surprised (me too!). All ideas of amputation pretty well pushed out of my mind — but, of course, will wait for further developments.

Wednesday, March 10, 1943
Walked twice as far today as I did yesterday. The pain is really something when I put my weight on it. Course, I don't walk anywhere near like a normal person, and I use a crutch (not having my own cane) for support. Doc helps me out at nite though with ¼ gram MSO4 and two nembutals.

Friday, March 12, 1943
Golly, I'll bet prices and wages are very high back home. Sure hope Dad has done some investing, and at the same time I hope he has put some or all of my $ in stocks or bonds. By the

---

63 Hinkle attended the Morgan Park Military Academy, which is located on the south side of Chicago (co-ed grades K–12).
64 While a student at the University of Michigan, Hinkle held the rank of captain in Scabbard and Blade, the honorary military society.

time I get back, inflation will probably be well set in. I just wonder what things are like back home? Wonder if Mom has sold my car? Wonder if the folks have moved? Wonder if the folks are both well and trying to enjoy life as much as they can during these times? Wonder if they know I'm OK? Wonder if Eileen gives me a thought now and then, and whether or not she has completely regained her health? And I go on wondering day and night — how much longer?? Wonder how Eleanor is and if she ever thinks of me? And B.J. and Walt C., and June, and Sally?

Saturday, March 13, 1943
Did my walking today without a crutch or cane! Every time a friend comes to see me, I have to "show off" for him by hobbling a few steps. They're all glad to see me trying to get on my feet again, but so am I! Golly, If ever a goddam ship comes in to take me home, maybe, no, I *will*, walk down that gangplank! Jeez, I fear that will not be for many months though. In fact, I feel that if the U.S. "springs" us from here before the end of '43, we'll be very lucky!

Got a kapok mattress today. Made in camp, using shelter halves to fabricate the outside. Hospital to get forty to fifty of them. Swell haven for lice and bed bugs.

Sunday, March 14, 1943
Another issue of canned beef and M&V. Good chow at noon; rice, mun-

go beans, a little carabao meat and some onions, and chocolate-coconut pie now helps to brighten the week.

Oh hell, there are two old duds that chew the fat loudly nearby, and all their damned chatter is about the '17 War. "Yes, I remember at Bordeaux . . . ." "When I was in France . . . etc. etc." Drives me crazy, and on top of that they also re-hash what should have been done on Bataan, and Christ, both of them got over here in November *before* the war ('41), and neither could tell a Filipino from a Nip by Dec. 8th! There they go again — "All those riot guns and hand grenades I had. Didn't see how the Japs were going to get me . . . ." ALL DAY!!

Signed postcard #2 to send to Mom and Dad. Card all messed up. "Please see that Eileen Clement . . . taken care of." Fault of typist, couldn't change. Supposed to leave Davao on Tuesday. Wonder if they'll go thru?

Monday, March 15, 1943
Golly, I get so lonely every nite when I get to thinking of home, and wondering what Mom and Dad are doing. Whether they're OK — and, on hundreds of little things about home. Oh, what a wonderful day it will be when we're reunited! And Eileen gets her share of thoughts, too. Surely, now Pete must be healthy and enjoying life again; probably peeved because the morning toast is burned!! But, after I get back to eating *real* food again, I'll probably

moan about some of the food preparation. I seriously don't believe I'll *ever* moan about food however. I'll eat any and everything set in front of me! Does she know I'm alive? Do Mom and Dad know? Damn it, Pete I hope you don't hold back in anything because of me — even marriage. I'll try to explain someday just how I mean this.

Tuesday, March 16, 1943
When will we get out of here? That's the biggest question and part of every man's thoughts who is a POW here. All kinds of questions arise on that subject, and the mind is full of them. For example:
1. How will we get out? By trade; by U.S. troops coming; or at the end of the war?
2. If U.S. planes come over here, will they bomb and strafe? Do they (the brass) know we're here?
3. If U.S. troops attack the island, what will be the Japs' attitude towards us?
4. If we get out of here, will we go home, or to Australia?
5. Can we endure this continual nervous feeling of who, where, and WHEN?!!
6. If we're traded, wonder if we'll be sunk enroute.

Everything preceded by IF! Oh, God, bring us peace once again; that we may return to our loved ones; that we may eat again like human beings rather than low-class hogs. Bring us peace and erase this racial hatred that has permeated nations. Bring us peace, for we have learned our lesson

and can return to things which before we never appreciated. Please, O Lord, give us another chance to live in peace.

Friday, March 19, 1943
Damn! Malaria attack again, and it feels like it's going to last for a few days.

Saturday, March 20, 1043
Taking quinine and it's sickening stuff. Have a terrific headache and keep feeling nauseated. Can't sleep nites, in spite of MSO4. Last nite I sweat so much that I soaked the sheet and blankets clean thru!

Sunday, March 21, 1943
Worst day of fever yet. Didn't take my temp, but it was an easy 105° or 106°F. This afternoon was miserable — could have gladly accepted death! God, it was awful.

Monday, March 22, 1943
Doctor Davis birthday. Feel better today, but still don't care about eating. Weight about 129 pounds. At about 5:30 p.m. we experienced a rather severe earthquake, lasting between thirty and forty seconds, I'd guess. The rain is very heavy, the strongest I've seen, tho it comes in "waves."

Tuesday, March 23, 1943
Had the stone and emblem taken out of my S&B ring, as stated earlier. Sold the ring for eight packs of good cigs. Present value of cigs is 2.5 pesos per pack. Am swapping six packs for canned chow. In about two weeks the canned chow will be worth five to 10

pesos, so I'll be able to sell two more cans, have money and eat the rest!

Sunday, March 28, 1943

The Japs held a shakedown on details coming in yesterday, and as a result no "cuan"[65] came in, the bastards. They made a haul of eggs, chicken, radishes, cigs, camotes, etc. !!

Wednesday, March 31, 1943

A Jap guard in a tower shot and killed Sgt. McPhee (MC)[66] today in the other compound. Mac was digging camotes on the outside, had a pass, etc., and someone tossed him a canteen of water. The Jap guard says Mac was trying to get away — in broad daylite under the guard tower!! The dirty bastard shot him three times, twice in the back, once in the chest. They didn't bring him to the hospital, but buried him right away. Mac was from Chicago and I knew him pretty well. Some day we'll even it up for you Mac. It was cold-blooded murder, no getting out of it. Mac was wearing only a pair of shorts and a pair of "clackers," no canteen; and going to *escape*! Nuts!

---

65 This word has several meanings. When used as a shortened form of *cuanto*—"How much"—in the Spanish language, it is something to trade or barter with. Cuan could be food or items from Red Cross packages. Cuan was also used by the Filipinos to fill in when they lacked a word, regardless of the language. In the back of Hinkle's diary is a handwritten dictionary. He defined cuan as a "Visayan word for 'Whatchamacallit.' Used as 'Where's the?' 'Let's cuan it up,' etc. In lieu of any word!" In the following example, a Filipino office worker is overheard using cuan four times in one sentence: "I put the cuan on the cuan, Jose is getting the cuan and Fredrico has the cuan." Translated into standard English: "I put the typewriter on the table, Jose is getting the paper, and Fredrico has the cover."

66 Marine Corps.

Thursday, April 1, 1943

There was quite an explosion last nite about 11:20 p.m. I was still awake — damn bedbugs! It was hard to tell what caused the explosion. To me it sounded rather distant and forceful. Some figure it was a mortar; others, antitank gun.

I should get paid tonite — 40 pesos. They paid the Corps Men, Doctors and 2nd Lieutenants yesterday; 1sts should get paid today.

Friday, April 2, 1943

Dammit! Underlying all our outward expression of optimism, there burns that painful fire of despondency. We all know we were the suckers — the gang the States forgot about and we can't get that fact out of our minds. We long for home, for the ones we love — and what hope do we have? Rumors? They build you up and then drop you flat — best not to listen to them. Almost 1½ years of hostility between U.S. and J and nothing done about getting us "loose." Of course, we're just a handful, less than 10,000 probably, but goddammit we're Americans and we expect America to do something to free us and expect her to take back what was hers. Every day we wonder — "What will today bring? Maybe we'll get some good news." And it usually ends with — "Aw Hell, what's the use?"

Thinking. Thinking of home, of the things we need to have — simple little things; a clean towel, clean sheets, a radio, the ring of a telephone, the noise of a street car, the rumble of traffic. How long can we go on like this, plus the *rice*, before we go crazy? We pray for strength to last it out.

Monday, April 5, 1943
!!! An escape was effected yesterday by ten men, eight officers, two EMs and two Pinos. One of the men was Commander McCoy USN. Another was Dobervich, US Marines. The story isn't complete yet — one time I hear it was mostly Navy men, then mostly Air Corps men. At any rate, 11 of them got away at one wack! What it means is hard to figure out. They may have gotten a contact thru some Pino about a submarine somewhere, or they may have just gone to join the guerrillas. What will the Japs do?? They sent two truckloads of them out searching for the men last nite — no result. The other compound got a "meal" of just salt and rice this morning. There's the thing; we'll doubtless suffer in the chow business. The hospital may escape that part, at least we did this morning — we'll see how the rest of the day and tomorrow go. May hear more about this today. Japs say no one will be shot for this — usual procedure, ten shot for one escape! Jap HQ gave themselves away — said to Col. Nelson, "We see no reason for this escape, the Americans still too far away!!" So, they must be on their way here!

Tuesday, April 6, 1943
No result as yet from the searching party. Lieutenant Uki, the Jap officer who had charge of the Americans and the work details, will probably commit hari-kari to save face for the Jap camp commander. The escape was well planned and all men had their teeth and shoes fixed, had leggings and good clothes, took mosquito nets, and had saved their RC chow. They were all on the coffee picking and plow detail, which had no Jap guard, hence they had an eleven hour start before their absence was noticed. How they managed to get all their stuff out of here is still something to think about. One man was an expert radio man, another an expert all-around mechanic, another a navigator, the others pilots and the Lt. Commander. What their objective was no one can understand. Our chow hasn't been wonderful, true, but we're living on it and that certainly would be no reason for an escape. Then — these were all intelligent men. Surely they must have realized that in some way the whole camp would suffer. The other compound is suffering; rice and salt for breakfast, a few greens for a watery soup, and much less rice than usual. If the men had no other reason for leaving other than getting away from this camp, then I hope they suffer for it and get caught, for this would be criminally selfish and unthinking of them. If however, there's some good reason for it, and there may be because one of the Pinos who went was a doctor here — he left his wife and family here! Why a man just doesn't up and leave his family for no good reason — he can't come back without

a strong force with him. Then I hope they make it safely, which they probably will, or have already. Latest is that if the escaped ones are not found, the Japs will take ten men from Camp and shoot them "one for one."[67]

Wednesday, April 7, 1943

Jeez! They "elected" a "bookkeeper" for the ward, to handle the money for the PX and of all people — W.J.H. got the job!!! Cripes, I've been working at it all afternoon and now I've 244 pesos to take care of! I've got to keep these straight — sure hope I can. The reason for the bookkeeper lies in the fact that we got paid in ten peso notes, and change is the big problem. Now *I'm* the one to worry about it!

Thursday, April 8, 1943

Japs searching party for escaped Americans resulted in three dead, one wounded, and twenty-five missing so far. Guerrillas working! Japs attitude toward this escape is peculiar. They've removed the restrictions on chow, and apparently are treating the men on duty very nicely. Why? Is *fear* behind it all? Could be — perhaps *must* be.

I have fully and firmly decided that the best thing for me to do when I get back to the U.S. is to have my foot amputated. I don't care to go thru a long siege in a hospital with doctors trying different things — things which will never give me a decent foot. I WANT NO LIMP WHEN I GET OUT OF THE HOSPITAL. I do *not* want to endanger what personality and ambition I may have left with an inferiority complex. *And no one is going to change my mind.* I wish to God I had had it done at the outset, or at the latest last year. Now I look forward to it with great anticipation. Why go on with this pain; pain for which Dr. Davis sees no reason?

Saturday, April 10, 1943

Oh no! Everything is getting jazzed up here. I firmly believe we can look for trouble in one form or another very soon. Today they're moving barracks 5, 7, and 8 to the #2 compound, and the "quarters" men are being moved back here to the #1 compound. It was from these barracks that the ten men escaped. Probably this shift is being made so that the men from these barracks can be closely watched and given the more tiring details. Also, other than the hospital, cannot build any

---

67 The escapees included ten Americans: Commander McCoy, Major Mellnik, Captains Dyess and Shofner, First Lieutenants Dobervick and Hawkins, Second Lieutenants Grashio and Boelens, Sergeant Speilman, and Private Marshall. Also included were Filipino convicts Beningo de la Cruz and Victorio Jumarung. They were serving time for murder prior to the war and offered their help as guides through the jungle without any thought of gain for themselves. The escape objective was the mouth of the Agusan River in northeastern Mindanao. There the escapees would contact American/Filipino guerrillas and send a radio message about their escape to South West Pacific Area headquarters in Australia. In July, Mellnik, McCoy, and Dyess were evacuated by submarine to Australia, where they briefed the US military on the Death March and described conditions inside Japanese prison camps. When their story was made public, it infuriated Americans and changed the course of the war, as sales of war bonds soared, service enlistment numbers rose, and absenteeism in the war industry was slashed. Dobervick, Hawkins, and the other escapees joined Wendell Fertig's guerrillas fighting on Mindanao. Bolens was the only US escapee not to return to the United States after the war. He was killed on Mindanao in early 1944.

more fires to warm up peanuts, extra chow, tea, etc.[68]

Good God, the continual pain in my foot is sapping all my courage, optimism, and faith. WHY didn't I have it amputated when I had the chance?

Tuesday, April 13, 1943
Boy, the talk is thick and fast about this prisoner exchange business again! Everyone is speculating.
"Think it's true, Jim?"
"Naw, it's a lotta crap!"
"Hell, it could be possible — chow situation's not so good and the Japs don't want us around anyway."
"Yeah, but forty-five or seventy days — I can't believe it!"
"Where'd it start?"
"The Japs started it."
"Hmmm — maybe it's just to keep us in camp?"
"Who knows??? The undercurrent of excitement is present nevertheless!"

One year ago since landed and got stuck on Mindanao. Jim Campbell and I are going to celebrate with a can of corned beef.

Wednesday, April 14, 1943
Doctor Davis rather blasted our exchange rumors! He said the Jap doctor told Col. Deter that what medical supplies we have on hand will have to last us at least one year!

Sunday, April 18, 1943
Oh damn these bed-bugs! They're in everything: shoes, mosquito net, in between the cracks of these wooden bunks. The latrine is infested with them, and that's one place you can't escape em!! They can't seem to do anything about the situation either. What a *wonderful day* it will be when I can escape all these insects and lice!

Monday, April 19, 1943
SOME RUMORS TO DATE:
Nov. 5, #1: MacArthur's HQ in New Guinea. We have Timor.

Nov. 11, #2: U.S. submarine sank three ships in Davao Gulf.

Nov. (?), #3: Roosevelt makes speech. Says Americans in P.I. will be free by Jan. 18th, '43. [*Note in margin: "BS!"*]

Nov. 25, #4: Americans landed on Pelew[69] Island. #5: Celebs ours. #6: Italy sues for separate peace, refused.

Nov. 27, #7: Americans raiding Pelew. Fighting in Celebes.

Nov. 28, #8: Russians pushed Nazis back 150 miles from Stalingrad, 90,000 Nazis killed. #9: America bombs Jolo, no damage. #10: Forty-three U.S. planes shot down in Celebes.

---

68 Due to the April 5 escape, camp commandant Major Kazuo Maeda (commandant of Davao Penal Colony, November 15, 1942–August 20, 1944) placed the prisoners on a diet of rice and salt. On April 15 he announced that prisoners headed out to the fields would be clad only in G-strings. Maeda believed that future escapes would be discouraged if they were no longer permitted to wear pants, shoes, or other clothing necessary for jungle survival.

69 Hinkle is referring to the 340-island archipelago known officially as Palau, and historically as Beleau, Palos, or Pelew. The rumor was premature. The United States captured Palau from the Japanese in 1944 after the costly Battle of Peleliu.

Nov. 29, #11: Russians pushed Nazis back 200 miles from Stalingrad. #12: Japs had seven ships sunk trying to reinforce New Guinea. #13: Pelew Island story now claimed unfounded. #14: One Jap ship has tried three times to leave Davao, had to turn back. Left once, led by two others — two leaders hit by subs outside Davao Gulf, other turned back. We are apparently cut off here from Luzon by action of our subs.

Nov. 30, #15: Davao has been bombed by our planes! U.S. lost 18,000 men in taking of Pelew Island and forty-one ships. Also have Yap Island.

Dec. 1, #16: The Japanese CO here is supposed to have said that if negotiations for trading us for Japs back home are not completed by Dec. 23, it will be the fault of the U.S. (What crap *this* one is!)

Dec. 7, #17: The "trade" business is picking up in force! There was supposed to have been published in the Davao paper that negotiations for the trade are completed, and that Dec. 23rd is the day. (Excuse me — I'm terribly afflicted with skepticism!)

Dec. 8, #18: Russia declared war on Japan!! #19: Spain declared war on Nazis and is mobilizing.

Dec. 9, #20: This camp is surrounded by about 1,000 Filipino guerrillas under a U.S. Major. They are well armed and are waiting for "the day."

Dec. 10, #21: That permanent details are to be returned to this camp on Dec. 17 in preparation for the trade.

Dec. 24, #22: We sank four ships in Davao Gulf. Americans are flying around the Davao Road bombing trucks and cars.

Dec. 26, #23: Here's a hot one — we're supposed to be on our way to Japan by June 1st!!

Dec. 28, It's really been dead as hell — not a rumor of a rumor.

Dec. 29, #24: The Americans will be here in two months. #25: Guerrillas swarmed down on Malaybalay and killed all the Japs, liberated the Filipinos and took over the camp.

Jan. 2, 1943, #26: Six allied planes over Davao were fired on by Japanese AA yesterday. Naval battle going between here and Celebes. #27: We took Borneo in thirty days! #28: A Canadian Red Cross ship is coming here this month with a package for every man and mail! #29: Sick and wounded here to go out on said RC ships! (Ah me — they come in bunches like grapes, these rumors. What do we believe?)

Jan. 4, #30: Two Jap ships sunk in Davao Gulf.

Jan. 5, #31: One-hundred-and-ten Nazi ship convoy on way to Rommel sunk by Allies in Mediterranean Sea! Italy asks for peace.

Jan. 6, #32: Wake bombed by U.S., thirty-seven tanks landed and island recaptured.

Jan. 10, #33: MacArthur returned to Australia to organize the convoy of American and Filipino and Chinese troops for offensive. #34: MacA. supposed to have authority to make armistice with Japan: conditions — Japs to remove all troops from occupied islands. U.S. to move in army of occupation! (BS!) #35: Jimmy Roosevelt killed. #36: RC packages to start arriving the 12th or 13th.

Jan. 11th, #37: Dutch, English and U.S. navy supposed to have Jap navy bottled up, but don't know where. #38: We have Java blockaded so no oil gets out. #39: Roosevelt makes speech that we will soon strike at Japan and Pelew. #40: U.S. and Japan having peace conference in Peru.

Jan. 14, #41: MacArthur left Australia for an unknown destination. (Hope it's U.S. and we get a real general now!) #42: U.S. appropriated $110,000,000,000 for 1943. #43: F.D.R. says war will be over in 1943. #44: Hong Kong in U.S. hands.

Jan. 19, #45: U.S. bombed Tokyo twice — once on Xmas. We bombed in the Celebes. #46: Roosevelt said that in six months we would have retaken all losses.

Jan. 20, #47: Jap planes supposed to be in Davao. We have bombed the Celebes. #48: MacArthur supposed to have started push in south. (Again?!)

Jan. 22, #49: Berlin bombed with six-ton bombs and one-ton incendiaries. Burning for four days. #50: Russia traps 40,000 Nazis — demands surrender — refused — Russia kills 17,000 — rest captured or wounded. #51: Fall of Tripoli expected any time.

Jan. 24, #52: Japanese civilians are being evacuated from Davao via boat and plane. If true, it sounds good.

Jan. 28, #53: Italy surrendered. #54: We have planes operating out of Celebes bombing Pelew. #55: Chinese coming down Malay Peninsula.

Jan. 29, #56: Turkey, Iraq declare war on Axis. #57: General dissension in Germany. #58: Spain to allow Allies to pass thru her land. #59: Tokyo bombed — in flames. #60: Rommel escapes to Germany. His troops surrendered or trapped. (BS!) #61: Sir Arch. Wavell as Field Marshall in China of Allies.

Feb. 2, #62: Two Jap ships sunk between Celebes and Davao and survivors brought to Davao.

Feb.4, #63: Guerrillas have taken over Cebu, Iloilo and one other! #64: Great naval battle in Solomons or Makassar Straits. Large concentration of planes (U.S.) in this battle. We got fifty-four Jap planes on the ground, sunk one battleship and one cruiser. #65: Roosevelt, Churchill in conference at Casa Blanca, Africa (French Morocco). #66: Ships with food on way here sunk by mistake by Jap bombers. #67: Tojo tells people it'll be a "long war" and everyone must expect all hardships of war.

Feb. 5, #68: 330,000 Nazis surrounded by Russians in Caucauses — twenty-four Generals, one Field Marshall. #69: Naval battle supposed to be over. We sank twelve Jap transport ships and seven warships. Lost one or two. Japs admit that they had to withdraw, because U.S. had surprised them.

Feb. 7, #70: Nazis sue for peace with Russia — Russia refuses.

Feb. 9, #71: Mussolini fires Count Ciano.

Feb. 10, #72: Japs have evacuated Solomons and losses there have been heavy. Since August: 800 planes, 166 ships, 60,000 men, lots of equipment.

Feb. 12, #73: Another Red Cross ship on its way. AGAIN — sick and wounded to be taken out on it! #74: Heavy fighting in New Guinea — Japs supposed to have landed at Port Morseby. #75: Germany had capitulated!!! (This we'd like to believe, but can't — not yet.) #76: We have bases in Turkey. #77: Japan has "warned" Turkey about getting mixed up in the war. #78: U.S. and England bombing Germany in steady waves 1,000

planes. As to Italy — not bombing cities, just roads and railroads.

Feb. 13, #79: All able-bodied Americans from here to go to Japan. #80: Officers with three years service to go to Japan. Majors and Colonels to go to Japan!! (BS!)

Feb. 14, #81: Russians have pushed Germans back to Belgrade. #82: Roosevelt declared that no more aid can be sent to England. Henceforth, the U.S. will concentrate and give more attention to the Pacific situation. China to get more help. #83: Germany reported as getting very weak and ready for surrender. #84: Sick and wounded from here to be sent to Sternberg.[70]

Feb. 15, #85: Mussolini arrested by the Gestapo!

Feb. 16, #86: Russians retake Rostov. #87: Rabaul bombed by U.S. — laid flat. #88: We have heavily bombed New Britain.

Feb. 17, #89: People of Davao ordered to evacuate because room is needed for about 35,000 Jap troops. #90: Russians retake Kharkov sector. #91: Japs evacuated Solomon Islands.

Feb. 18, #94: There is a RC ship in Davao to take our wounded home! (Could I believe it?? — Hah!) #95: About 3,000 Jap wounded in Davao. #96: Several Jap

---

70 Sternberg General Hospital in Manila.

warships off Zambo., apparently wait-ing for trouble.

Feb. 21, #97: Rommel made attack — pushed our troops back sixty miles. #98: Italy sent emissary to ask for peace terms — he was sent back — no talk of peace till Hitler agrees to unconditional surrender.

Feb. 22, #99: We have the Celebes under control. #100: U.S. or allied planes have been flying very high over Davao. Planes have been seen for five successive days. #101: Japanese troops supposed to be coming to Davao are to be for the Celebes. Again, "suppos-edly" six days late. #102: A Jap ship was seen to be torpedoed and set afire just off Davao. The Filipina who saw this said that the Japanese soon expect to lose Davao. Manila and other island ports supposedly cut off from marine traffic because of U.S. subs!

Feb. 23, #103: U.S. counter-attacked Rommel. Pushed him back and cap-tured quite some equipment.

Feb. 28, #104: Madame Chiang Kai Shek in Washington D.C. urging quick action in Pacific. Former ambassador to Japan urges same.

March 1, #105: Japanese are reinforc-ing Jolo, possibly scene of next battle.

March 3, #106: Filipinos expect some-thing to happen in next two or three weeks. Pinos and Moros are ready to take over Davao and Del Monte

airports when U.S. moves in. (BS!!) #107: U.S. grants P.I. independence and declares Quezon sovereign ruler of Commonwealth of P.I., thereby beating Japs to this diplomatic move. #108: U.S. only sixty miles from this island now. #109: There is more food for us down in Davao.

March 4, #110: Sea battle going on between Jolo and Celebes. #111: Rus-sia retakes Kiev.

March 5, #112: Quite a number of Jap soldiers turned up in Davao yes-terday; dirty and poorly clothed and many wounded. Supposed to have come from down South.

March 6, #113: Madame Chiang Kai Shek reported killed in air crash in Lisbon. #114: Ole Capt. (Maj.) Mc-Clish supposed to be out here some-where w/10 enlisted men.

March 10, #115: Rommel has finally surrendered in Africa (again!). #116: Japan asked for peace terms — was refused. (BS!) Jap envoy going to Geneva to "talk things over" with U.S. representative.

March 13, #117: Rommel (again!) has pushed the American and English back and regained some ground.

March 22, #118: At long last, A Jap interpreter told McCartney that these will probably be U.S. planes overhead in the "near future," and that the Americans here in camp should not "become excited!" (Try and hold us down if such should happen!)

March 23, #119: U.S. sub sunk a Jap sub in Solomons — Japs have taken Ceylon.

March 24, #120: U.S. sunk Jap convoy headed South, was continuously bombed by U.S. for two days, one nite, and all ships were sunk or damaged. U.S. claims 90,000 Japs. lost. Japanese claim 25,000. #121: Russia has three spearheads into Poland. Germany advanced in Kharkov area. Russia and Nazis both in Kharkov City. #122: Rommel tried to get away but was chased into the hills. Battle in N. Africa virtually over. #123: One million Americans in Spain, heading for France!!! #124: Another Red Cross ship is in Manila transferring part of its food to another ship, which will be here in about two weeks! (BS???)

March 28, #125: U.S. planes bombed Kobe, Japan. #126: Russia closed the spearheads in Poland and captured a large Nazi force. A few more such actions will end Nazis. #127: If U.S. bombs Tokyo, all American prisoners will be killed! (Happy thought, but *go on* U.S.!!) #128: Americans going thru Italy w/o opposition. #129: Nazi officers conditional surrender — refused, then unconditional surrender! War to be over by June or July! (BS!) #130: We destroyed 240 Jap planes and landed on Rabaul.

March 30, #131: Empress of Japan broadcasts statement that it will no longer be disgrace for Jap troops to surrender.

April 1-3, #132: Red Cross ship now in Davao. (BS!) #133: A huge U.S. air force bombed Pelew Island. Virtually wiped if off the map. All four-motor bombers, also landing. #134: We have taken Amboina; bombed Timor and New Brit. #135: Davao under three-hour air raid alarm. #136: 500 Americans coming to Davao Penal Colony from Cabanatuan. #137: Rommel now in States as POW (America got their supplies via tunnel in desert — fans blowing over opening so couldn't be seen.) #138: Sea battle in N. Pacific near Aleutians.

April 3, #139: Russia doing well in North. Germany heavily bombed. #140: Formosa heavily bombed from base in China. #141: Japan heavily bombed twice during March.

April 7, #142: Japanese will bomb all barrios in mountains around here if Pinos don't surrender the escaped Americans.

April 9, #143: Last week, American planes flew over Davao, and Jap anti-aircraft fired at them. #144: Davao was shelled yesterday by a U.S. sub. #145: Many Jap soldiers, marines and sailors pouring into Davao.

April 14, #146: Manila paper carries Tokyo dispatch to effect that the U.S. is now consuming *horse meat*! (Sounds like a lot of horse-shit!)

April 17, #147: The Japanese have given "the U.S. till May 9, 1943, to decide about the exchange of prisoners, or else!!" #148: Here we go again!!! We are to be exchanged within the next ninety days, according to some Jap interpreter!! (BS!)

April 18, #149: Japanese civilians and Pino constabulary coming to take over part of guarding duties here. (Rumors almost unavailable since escape.)

April 19, #150: Fifteen U.S. planes bombed Manila and Corregidor last week. #151: All nations at war have ceased hostilities for a period while they hold a conference. (BS.) #152: Filipinos to get their independence very soon. #153: Italy having internal revolt. #154: North Africa now completely controlled by Allies.

April 22, #155: In sixty days, the able and well go to Japan — the sick and wounded go to Bilibid. #156: The Japs have given the island their "independence," #157: A Pino told a guard here that "very soon, the storm will break here."

Thursday, April 22, 1943

Wrote another card to send home today. Hard to get any information on the card. Would like to ask Mom to send me a package with food and cigs, but don't dare mention food on the cards. Besides, if I know that swell Mom and peach of a Dad of mine, they've tried to send a package and write to me — but I've never received anything. Hoping you get this card and get some encouragement from it. Card #3.

Saturday, May 1, 1943

Damn! Rice, salt, and so-called tea for breakfast this morning!! Chow is becoming pretty bad. Jungle stew and jungle stew! Where the hell is the RC? Because we received *one* shipment certainly doesn't mean that's all we're to get, does it? And *that* shipment was labeled "package No. 8." *What* happened to the others?? Aw, HELL! I don't much give a damn anymore. Besides, those packages were not meant for us — the Japs apparently hi-jacked the shipment.

Sunday, May 2, 1943

Now I have scurvy! The gums around my teeth get very loose after brushing my teeth, and are quite tender. My body itches for no apparent reason. All I have to get now is dysentery and beriberi!

Monday, May 3, 1943

Something going on. Japanese collected all garden tools last nite at 9:00 p.m., and at 12 p.m. (midnite) they made an inspection. Why, suddenly, and at nite did they collect the tools??

The rumor is quite persistent that we're going to move. Various destinations — Japan, Mozambique? Let's go ANYWHERE the food might be edible!! Rice and salt again for breakfast. Answer to above. Last nite a Japanese major caught some Americans digging out of the new compound.

Among other changes going on within me, as a result of this war and concentration camp and having been wounded, is the increasing desire to be *alone*. I've learned a VERY great deal about human nature, and so far the bad points outnumber the good. I'm probably the same as the rest — I don't know. I've found that "friendship" is too much fair-weather. I've been let down too many times by my "friends." There's so much greed, selfishness, dogmatism, pettiness, and underhandedness among men.

Tuesday, May 4, 1943
Trying to stand the pain w/o MSO4, and the nights are pretty rugged. Can get only one or two hours of lite sleep. Maybe I'll get a shot tonite — at least I hope so. The pain knocks the hell out of me.

Distributed per man: one small towel, one pack tooth powder, and 100 sheets toilet paper!!

Wednesday, May 5, 1943
Went to Mass today — St. Joseph. Thought of home and especially of years gone by when Dziadzin used to take me all over Warsaw.

All these rumors of us going to move are, in my opinion, a lot of "cuan." I fear we're going to stay here for quite some time; longer than we care. I pray I'm wrong. I understand they're putting up a large fence around the whole camp. Why, if we are to move??! Some times I feel we won't be out of here

until June of 1945!!! Cripes — *that's* a *long* ways off!

Saturday, May 8, 1943
Two years in P.I.

Sunday, May 16, 1943
The Japanese have "caused" to be erected around the camp a large barbed-wire fence, about 8' high. It has been constructed very near to all buildings, making our enclosure much smaller. The wire is spread at between 6 and 8 feet. Looks to me as though it may be for purposes of better control over us in case the Yanks start activity around here — I may be wrong tho!

The chow has been pretty miserable the last several weeks. Had rice and salt for breakfast three times last week. Salted fish three times, and it was really salty! Damned near like taking medicine. Had pork and beans, mungo beans and rice for lunch. Have been getting that once a week for the last three or four weeks. In betweentimes the food is *rotten*. The Japanese just won't give it to us. There's coffee, bananas and other things galore, but we can't get it. Damn!

MORE RUMORS:
April 24, #158: A captain here in camp got a note smuggled in from the guerrillas, stating that the Americans will be here in 30 days. (They *must be* in touch with the U.S. in Australia or somewhere.) #159: Nichols Field, Clark Field, and Corregidor bombed

again. #160: Major Maeda (IJA)[71] told someone at the rice fields, "This is last planting America will do. Japanese farmers coming soon for harvest and Americans will go home." (BS.) #161: Russians fighting Nazis on Polish border.

April 25, #162: Commander McCoy is G-2 for guerrillas.[72] Gist is, guerrillas in contact with our forces. Guards told to stand-by and at command to take over Jap stronghold here. Only about 100+ Japs on island. With our forces "coming" and guerrillas we'll have 100,000 men. This to be "very soon." #163: Twenty-five ship convoy (U.S.) effected landing in Celebes and we now have several bases there. #164: Rumor from Japanese kitchen here: there are "*takusan*"[73] Americans and U.S. planes in Celebes.

April 26, #165: One-hundred-and-fifty new U.S. prisoners of war in Davao, from south somewhere.

April 28, #166: Americans in Jolo. 125,000 Americans on Pelew! #167: Again, we are to be exchanged very soon, and are going back on one of the big "Marus"![74] (BS.)

May 1, #168: U.S. lose 25,000 men taking the Celebes.

May 3, #169: Japan has put up another plan for our exchange to the U.S. If it is not accepted, we're going to Japan. #170: We're to move by May 30th, 43!?

May 4, #171: All of us are going to be interned in Mozambique for the duration. (BS!!!) #172: The Japanese have uncovered "much" canned beef in one or two tunnels at Mariveles,[75] and we're to get it. (Yeah??) Rice and salt more likely! #173: In ten days we're to move. Now it's to Macao, port off of Hong Kong! (We'll go around the world, too!) This is a Portuguese port. #174: Americans have definitely landed in the Celebes and Jolo! (Muchly doubt the Jolo business!)

May 5, #175: We're to go to Manila for a layover of a week, then to Formosa! They're to move Pino prisoners here. (BS.)

May 6, #176: Americans have bombed Singapore, and are bombing Jolo.

May 7, #177: There has been a five day armistice declared between the Anti-Axis and the Axis. #178: Officers from here to be moved to Malaybalay. #179: Three barges of corned beef hash and sour-pickles coming up the river for us. ("Sour pickles," right!) #180: Mess officer was told that he would draw his last rations on May 10th. (Not confirmed yet.)

---

71 Imperial Japanese Army.
72 G-2 refers to the military intelligence staff of a unit in the United States Army.
73 "Very many" in the Japanese language.
74 *Maru* is a common suffix to Japanese ship names. It comes from Hakudo Maru, a spirit in Japanese mythology who taught humans how to make ships.

---

75 A municipality located in southern Bataan.

May 10, #181: Navy battle going on between Jolo and Celebes.

May 11, #182: "KGEI," San Fran. has warned Pinos to evacuate to the larger cities, and that since they want a new P.I., U.S. will give it to them.

May 12, #183: A Jap officer in Davao told the mechanics (U.S.) there that the "Americans are very close."

May 15, #184: Jap navy ships in Davao Bay on "maneuvers." They're using the available meat supply, hence we get no meat till they leave. #185: The U.S. "fleet" was seen off of Mindanao! (One carrier!) #186: Three Jap warships in Davao Harbor — all pretty badly shot up. Seen by truck driver.

May 16, #187: "*Takusan* boom-boom" in Davao yesterday. #188: Seven-hundred men from here going to Zamboanga.[76] #189: The men who escaped from here were picked up by a U.S. sub, taken out and have made broadcasts about DPC! (BS!!)

Tuesday, May 18, 1943
At least nineteen Jap planes flew over at different times yesterday, going South. It may be a good sign — who knows?

Wednesday, May 19, 1943
Met Phil Brain, ΦΔΧ '39 today. He was two beds away from me for two days, and we hadn't become acquainted. Today, someone asked me about some Michigan songs. The fellow two beds away asked,
"Are you from Michigan?"
I said, "Yes, where are you from?"
"Minnesota."
With some hope I asked the question I had asked so many times of other men — "Fraternity man?" Then waited for the usual ΣN, or ΦΔΘ.
"Yes," he said. "Theta Delta Chi!" Amazed at having at last found a Theta Delta Chi, I could only exclaim, "Well — bless bless, at long last — a *brother*!"
"Are you a Theta Delta Chi??" he came back at me, in an incredulous tone. And when I replied in affirmative, we exchanged the grip and proceeded into a mess of memories and rapidly became good friends. He too has asked and asked other men, hunting for a Theta Delta Chi man, so we were both happily surprised to finally find each other. I brought out my Shield, and after he had read it thru he said, "Boy, I'm sure glad to see that." He has scabies. 194th Tank Co. Arrived September '41.

Thursday, May 20, 1943
Tenko[77] was at 8 a.m. instead of 6 a.m. today, and all Filipinos around were taken away, to where, we don't know. All Japs had fixed bayonets and there were guards along the road at 50 yard

---

76 Shortly after the end of the Spanish-American War, the United States Army enlarged Fort Pilar and changed its name to Pettit Barracks. It was located adjacent to the business district of Zamboanga City, from which it extended 1,500 yards east along a sea wall on the Basilan Strait. The rumor suggests that the prisoners would be moved to these barracks.

77 Roll call.

intervals for awhile. There may be something brewing.

Last nite, somewhere around midnite, there were some planes that flew over. Came from south, flew over, circled and went back. Japanese or U.S.?

The rumor from several weeks ago has come again — the guerrillas are to strike here May 21st — *tomorrow*!

We'll see. Phil and I getting along fine. He lives in Minneapolis and has cabin on Gunflint Lake. We've spent lots of time talking about the North Woods — fishing, fried fish and other cooking, building cabins, etc. Made both of us pretty homesick I'm afraid! His dad is the tennis coach at the University of Minnesota. Phil is in the sociological line too, but more in social welfare work. Just another little coincidence that binds a friendship closer.

Friday, May 21, 1943
Spent almost all day shelling peanuts in the kitchen. We're to have peanut soup, with onions and mungo beans in it. Should be good. (It was!)

Emperor Tojo visited Manila for three days. More activity in the air the last few days. Earthquake for about ten seconds this a.m. (10 a.m.) Father Lafleur and Chaplain Dawson started a "Fun Hour" for the hospital and henceforth every Friday nite. It's a quiz business, singing, etc. I missed my question

on popular music — the rice brain![78]

Wednesday, May 26, 1943
We had a very severe earthquake at about 8:30 a.m. today. Lasted a minute or more!

There's a list now for officers to sign; those who volunteer to work. They want better chow. The Japs say if they don't work, they'll get less food. It's still unsettled and not clear. Officers voted — all but three or four voted not to work.

Sunday, May 30, 1943
I've been out of soap for six days now, and no hope of getting any. I'm certainly dirty and filthy too! They moved Phil to another bed. A fellow named Lt. Mike Daman is next to me now — had a mid-line hernia operation, post operative.

Monday, May 31, 1943
Daman is driving me crazy. He's quite sick; wants this and that, and he keeps me going day and nite. At meal time, or just when I'm in the middle of something, he wants me to do something. My sleep has been cut down quite some. He belly-aches quite a bit, and gets me very irritated, but I know how he feels. He's getting cans of milk and I make sure I get my cut out of that! Open a can, then he want water — give him water, then he wants milk, etc.!

---

78 Hinkle's handwritten dictionary in the back of volume #2 defines rice brain as "Slow-thinker or forgetful. Fact usually attributed to excessive rice diet."

Tuesday, June 1, 1943

Damn! Now my left ear is giving me hell. There's fungus growth in the canal and on the drum. Doctor D'Amore is treating it. Says it'll take some time. Noticed last nite — seemed to be a little deaf, and continued till today. Doctor Davis is pretty sick. He's passing kidney stones. Been out since Sunday.

Saturday, June 5, 1943

It can't be a happy birthday, Mom, but I pray you're in good health and not worrying too much. I hope you're as happy as you can possibly be. My heart and thoughts are ever with you, Mom, and maybe, MAYBE next year will reunite us. Mom, when I get back, you're going to be No.1 on my "happiness" list. Anything and everything I can do to make you happier will be done, if I can possibly do it. Padre LaFleur said Mass for you this morning and I went to church and prayed that Our Lord watch over you, and keep you well.

Our fun hour program consisted mainly of a spelling bee last nite; there were twenty of us; five doctors, five Corps Men, and ten patients. I wound up as runner-up! The word that bounced me was "innuendo." I left out one "n." Lieutenant Faulkner beat me, after the two of us fought it out for about four or five words apiece after everyone else was out. It was fun, and I was surprised that I did as well as I did. Some of mine were: accelerate, illegitimate, can-tankerous, hieroglyphics, advertise, innuendo, legendarian.

The men from the "new compound" are to be moved over to the new compound here, tomorrow. Will make about two-hundred men to a building.

Japanese are to make some important announcement in the next few days. "Good news," supposedly! And I'm still "nursing" Daman! He's better now. Wish he'd start trying to feed himself!

Monday, June 7, 1943

There's much cogitation and rumors manufacturing about the fact that they're moving the other compound over here. They're moving in double deck bunks, converting the main chapel into a barracks for 250 or 300 men, and the other barracks are to hold each about 190. The move has not yet taken place. One rumor is that the American civilians who were at Impalutao and now in Davao are to be moved up. Another is that the Japanese are going to use the other compound as a rest camp for Japanese Navy. Major Maeda, the Japanese Camp Commander, had a meeting with the barracks and camp leaders (US) and told them that the prisoners of war would really have to "produce," for we cannot expect supplies from Manila or Davao, because transportation is very difficult, since there is a new war front." What conclusions can we draw? Where is the new front? If it's so hard to get stuff in here, why can't we get at the abundance of fruit here???

Quite an uproar in the hospital. One of the Corpsmen was caught selling MSO4 shots! Major W. turned him in because he had *raised the price*!!!! As a result, a vicious circle developed — more Corpsmen were involved, another patient, Capt. Field got in on it. This of course is serious business, and when they get back, charges will, or should, be pressed against both buyers and sellers. Happily, I'm not involved in any way. Didn't even know the racket was going on till yesterday. I've never had to worry about getting a shot when needed 'cause Dr. Davis has been allowing me the amounts I've needed when I needed them. And even if the pain was exceedingly strong and Dr. Davis didn't order a shot for me, I'd never buy MSO4 — I'd rather sweat it out. Once you start buying the stuff, then you've a habit, definitely. I can do without it from now on if necessary, but some relief from pain is needed too. I'll take relief if Doc OKs it.

Tuesday, June 8, 1943
I cannot help but believe that we are destined to remain prisoners of war for at least six months or one year more. The Allies may be pressing or planning to press an attack in the South West Pacific, but I don't believe they'll try to come here till late November or December ('43); that will be the beginning of the dry season if the P.I. are in the attack plans. I think that's when it'll come. Course they could surprise attack between now and then — I wish they would, but sincerely doubt it. God, can't it be as soon as possible tho, for the food situation terrible — no food coming in to the hospital. Men *out working* get some while on detail. Supplies are at a definite minimum. Malnutrition in evidence.

Wednesday, June 9, 1943
Great Caesar, they're putting up a 3rd barbed wire fence around the camp! This one is as high as the last one, and is only about two feet distant from it. The other compound is to come over today or tomorrow. Signed the "payroll" again today, but got no pay. "It" has been "deposited" in my "to my credit." (where?) Cigarettes issued: new kind, the rising sun enclosing areas Japan controls. Pretty fair tobacco. Supposed to be 4,000 Japanese navy and marines in Davao. Lieutenant Uki and a group of his soldiers have been going on what appears to be patrol duty. Maybe we're wrong, but there's no other answer for their "maneuvers." The Japs held a "war dance" the other nite. Perhaps that has some significance.

Thursday, June 10, 1943
Other compound moved over today. 286 men in chapel, all double-deck cages — 3 feet between. Cages doubled. Roy Gray, Irv Mandelson, "Max," Bragdon over to see me.

Saturday, June 12, 1943

We feel something *may* be in these rumors that are rampant. The Japanese seem anxious to listen to the radio Nazi broadcasts — nite and day! They're even running the generator during the day at times! The second fence has been completed. The Japs ordered 900 men out to the rice detail — talking about sending out the Doctors and Medical Corps! Rations have been cut, including rice.

Sunday, June 13, 1943

The fly condition is getting pretty bad here. Seems to be no system of fly control. The increase in their numbers is very notable.

Monday, June 14, 1943

Nasal pharyngitis is setting in on me again. Am gargling with Dormel solution and getting Argyrol in my nose. One of the Japanese officers is supposed to have asked one of our U.S. officers how Americans treated prisoners of war. In the course of the talk the Japanese officer said, "Well, we will soon see how they are treated!" (BS!?)

Rumor that there's to be an inspection of our camp by an IRC[79] representative this Saturday. *If* true, we'll eat good on Saturday at least!!! Probably be a Jap rep. tho!

Sunday, June 20, 1943

The ward men *actually mopped* the floor of the hospital yesterday, and

what a to-do about it! All for this inspection I guess. It's about the 5th time the floor's been mopped this year! Should have heard them, "Don't spill anything on the floor" and "Don't track," etc. Throughout the process they used practically the same water from end to end. As result, floor got mud bath! And, according to my memory of the ways of the outside world, this is Father's Day, so again Dad, greetings to you while you worry and keep Acme going. All I can give you today is a prayer, and I trust you'll know my thoughts are with you.

First shot today for me in typhoid series. Shot included "juice" for protection against typhoid, dysentery and cholera. Arm is very sore. Good music program today. Sanders wrote a good number, "The Yanks Are Coming."

Tuesday, June 22, 1943

The latest J paper reads to the effect that Premier Tojo has told the J Diet that the Philippines will get their independence this year! What that means is hard to figure out. Are the Yanks near? Will J keep an army here? What will WE be — internees in a neutral country? Prisoners of the P.I. under "J protection" or what? Anyway, it sounds good. The whole camp is booming with optimism. Some "figure" we'll be free in 1½ months, others 3 months. General opinion seems to center about October. I've picked October 12, but feel that January - April '44 will be the

---

79   International Red Cross.

real date! Too many rumors to be a "good thing."

Friday, June 25, 1943
Another postcard written today to "send" home. Hope they get it. My wound has finally completely closed. Still pain. Ugly foot. 18 cigs per man issued today.

MORE RUMORS:
May 17, #190: U.S. Troops in France; are in Marseilles. #191: Nazis have been pushed out of Russia. (BS!)

May 18, #192: Roosevelt made a "fireside chat" May 6; said U.S. would be in P.I. in sixty days. (BS!) #193: We have a "spear-head" in Borneo, Java and Sumatra. #194: There are 400 Japanese planes and many warships in Davao.

May 19, #195: According to the Jap paper, Rommel has at last surrendered and has escaped to Germany.

May 20, #196: Turkey has declared war on the Axis! (Again!) #197: We're to receive milk every morning for *everyone*; meat three times a week and fish the other two days. Proved false, of course! #198: The Japanese guards have received orders *not* to strafe any more Americans while on detail here.

May 21, #199: Five-hundred sick Yanks coming here from Cabanatuan. #200: Sick to be traded off!! (False rumor.)

May 22, #201: Jolo bombed by 75 planes last week.

May 23, #202: We had 50,000 Yank engineers and ordinance men in Turkey in previously prepared positions.

May 25, #203: Allies bombed dam in Germany — flooded three cities.

May 26, #204: We have taken back the Aleutians. #205: We have eight-motor cargo planes flying to and from India carrying supplies.

May 29, #206: Germany has capitulated! (Again!)

June 1, #207: Russia has put in 200 new divisions against the Nazis in Poland. #208: U.S. has two fronts in France and are coming thru Spain. #209: There are RC ships in Manila and Cebu, but we will not receive anything because there are some ships in Davao to take us home!! (Here's *that* rumor again! More BS) #210: We are supposed to have gotten in truckload of milk, pork and beans, and mail. Fear this too is BS. #211: U.S. and England to start offensive against Japan this month, this a result of Churchill visit to Washington.

June 7, #212: U.S. troops have landed on Formosa.

June 9, #213: Roosevelt makes speech, said "Americans in P.I. will be home for Xmas." (WHICH XMAS?!?!) #214: Big sea battle somewhere around Celebes, north of New Guinea.

June 10, #215: U.S. and England bombing Italy steadily — people near revolt; Nazis sending troops there to help keep "order." #216: Hitler appeals to troops to hold all fronts, not retreat; Goebbels appeals to people for more sacrifices. #217: U.S. captured Jap air-base within bombing range of Japan. #218: Three places in P.I. supposed to have been bombed recently. #219: Goebbels says outcome of war to be decided in '43 — had not expected to "feel" U.S. till '44, but no such luck. #220: Opinion of Japanese guard here who speaks excellent English is that Japan cannot last after Dec. '43. (hope so!) #221: U.S. troops in Italy. Japanese guard here says, "Italy is no good."

June 11, #222: Roosevelt in speech says Yanks be here in July or August.

June 12, #223: Revolt in Nazi occupied territory.

June 15, #224: Japanese are making "strategic withdrawal" from Celebes — Yanks in thirteen places at once there. #225: Twenty-four U.S. planes have been shot down over Celebes.

June 16, #226: 2,000,000 Yanks on foreign soils. #227: Yanks have two islands in northern Mediterranean. #228: Yanks have a force in Norway #229: Yanks have retaken Guam and Wake. #230: Russian troops massed on Manchukuo border.

June 19, #231: Russia declares war on Japan. #232: U.S.-Alaska road completed. Now has heavy traffic.

June 20, #233: Third attempt for exchange of prisoners of war now going on between U.S. and J. (About time this rumor started again!)

June 21, #234: Japanese losses heavy in sea battle in South West Pacific on June 7.

June 22, #235: A Japanese guard told someone we would leave here in two months. #236: Vichy gov't. has recognized the new Argentine gov't!?! (Nazi??) #237: U.S. sank over 1,000,000 tons of shipping in one month in Pacific.

June 23, #238: Here's a beaut!! Negotiations have been concluded concerning the exchange of prisoners between Japan and U.S., and the Japanese gov't has asked that ten U.S. ships be sent out here to take us home. If true, Japan apparently has no ships to spare and hence, no chance for us to get back since U.S. cannot trust Japan NOT to seize the ships once out here. So?!?! #239: Henry Ford is dead — undulant fever.

June 24, #240: We are to be exchanged in August ('43), and in 90 days the P.I.s to get independence. #241: German troops suffering defeats in Poland, from Russia. #242: The interpreter told four officers that Davao is definitely in the war zone, and Yanks landed on an island south.

June 25, #243: Japanese say we have retaken an island within bombing range of Mindanao. #244: Yanks and British amassing large force down south. #245: Great naval battle in Indian Ocean — J'se lose heavily — not U.S. or English navy — convoys. #246: Japanese have asked several Yanks, "have you heard the good news? Major Anaida will announce in a few days that the negotiations for exchange are completed. Yanks go home next month." (!! BS)

Saturday, June 26, 1943

Optimism is booming forth more and more! Greater credence seems to be placed in the present "exchange rumor" than in previous rumors on the same subject. Maybe there is something in it, but I'll still remain a firm disbeliever, until something happens!

The exchange rumor has (as expected) been thoroughly blasted by one of the interpreters. Now we can sit back and relax and wait for "the rumor about a RC ship with food for us"!!!!!

Thursday, July 1, 1943

Witnessed circumcision and operation on cyst on back. First most interesting. Glad Dziadzin took care of me on that long score ago!!!

Lieutenant Uki sent over a piece of J music, looking for a pianist. It's written for *koto*[80] and violin — no bass clef! Can't hardly read the notes. Said

I'd try, but would need practice to try and work it out.

Yesterday two J's and two A's got sick on some kind of fruit. The detail came, half carrying the guards, and the Yanks carrying the rifles! Rather humorous situation.

Total of 16 J planes flew by today.

Saturday, July 3, 1943

Jeez — I've been trying this walking business again. It's been extremely painful. The last three days and nites have been hell. Doc gave me an ⅛ gram for two nites, but no relief and last nite I got a ¼ gram and finally got some relief. If I'm to walk on it, I know it'll be hell for awhile — but I'd like some relief at nite. There's no incentive to go thru that added hell here — no good food, no good bed to rest in, etc. Hell with it.

Talked my way into a HB egg today!

Sunday, July 4, 1943

Colonel Deter makes speech commemorating 4th to remind us of those who died for liberty, etc.

Monday, July 5, 1943

This rice detail has been taking a great toll on our men. They get a rash on their legs and arms, and it seems to resemble poison ivy. It's vicious stuff and takes a while to cure up. Use hot compresses mostly. Out of almost 3,000 Americans here in camp, only 690 were able to do duty

---

80 A traditional Japanese instrument with thirteen strings, played by plucking them using three finger picks.

of any kind last week, and only 337 were available for the rice detail. The quarters cases have greatly increased in number. Malaria is rampant, and quinine is extremely low. The J Doctor has made several "surveys" of the quarters cases, and if a malaria case had not had a chill for two days, he was sent to duty!

I've quite a beard — haven't shaved since May 18th and am not going to till we get out of here! Note: There is a "work detail" of three officers and two enlisted men assigned to the J kitchen to *swat flies*! Must stand during period of three or four hours.

Tuesday, July 6, 1943
If I had no other reason for being glad and satisfied about having been able to join the Brotherhood of ΦΔΧ, I have that reason in Brother Phil Brain. Our friendship has grown very close, and it's so *very* sincere. Phil comes over to see me every afternoon, and though he's still in rough shape, he wants to know if he can do anything for me. When he and I are together, we never have to make conversation — we can sit and be quiet, or be talking — the company of one another is enuff. So, again — ΦΔΧ has proven her worth to me; and has proven to both Phil and myself that ΦΔΧ means more to her members than other fraternities seem to mean to their members. I know, that when we return, we'll keep in touch with one another, and that one will always be welcome to

the company of the other. I sure wish Walt Clement could meet him, and if Walt pulls thru this fracas, I'll see that they meet. Phil and Walt are pretty much alike; guess that's why we get along so extra well.

Wednesday, July 7, 1943
Have not been doing much walking lately — its very painful. However, I am doing a little every day. Doc has me somewhat worried. I'm still of the opinion that I'll be better off with an amputation. He said he wasn't sure the Army would amputate for me if the x-ray doesn't show enuff destruction, tho' I could have it done privately, on my own. No use worrying, I guess — just have to wait and see.

Quinine situation is extremely acute. Malarial patients suffer thru attacks without. Got 8,000 three gram tablets in today. About three weeks supply. And then?

Twenty Yanks were thoroughly strafed[81] today on bodega detail, for trying to bring in fruits. Tomorrow as usual on the 8th of the month, the J have to celebrate the declaration of war on U.S., so from 10 a.m. on, it's to be a holiday for the Yanks. Chow is still abominable. Kangkong[82] and rice is our main diet. Imagine living on this swamp grass!

Japanese are having a celebration

---

81 Hinkle's handwritten dictionary defines strafed as "to be badly punished, as by slapping."
82 Ipomoea aquatica; a semiaquatic plant grown as a vegetable (water spinach).

party tonite of some kind. Brought in a number of Filipina and Japanese girls, so there'll be fun for them!

Friday, July 9, 1943
Remember these:
1. Doctors dressing wound with used bandages — saving on sponges.
2. Great use of hot water soaks, for rash, ulcers, boils, etc. after long years of med. studying. Fact is ironical.
3. Shea's argument with Dr. Whiteley about MSO4, and latter saying, "See Major Ruth," and Shea left in rush. Suffers pain rather than see Ruth.
4. Daman always arguing about *anything* in hospital.

Sunday, July 11, 1943
Had a busy day today beginning with Mass at 8 a.m. At 9:30 a.m. went over to see eight boxing matches! It's the end of the rice harvest that's been going on, and the Japanese gave a set of 12 oz. boxing gloves to the camp and a holiday today. So, Col. Olson had the matches put on. Damned good show, but I sure felt sorry for the lads doing the boxing — what with this chow, having gone thru malaria, and the living conditions, etc. One did get a bloody nose, however. Another quite dazed by a blow to the head. Baker and Brewton, cousins and members of the Med. C. were matched — all they needed was music! Then, the ten boxers were rewarded for their efforts (thru the Maj. Gen. of the IJA) with one coconut, eight bananas and one orange apiece.

At 1:15 p.m., here at the hospital, another music program. Swell. Saunders and his singing trio — Biggs the emcee, a quartet of accordion, clarinet, trumpet, and guitar. Young Craig singing good, Yaeger whistling, and Hinkle envious and wishing for a piano!!

Jungle stew today.

Tuesday, July 13, 1943
Remembered some of the wisecracks at the boxing bouts on Sunday.
1. "Cigars, cigs, peanuts, popcorn!"
2. "Remember when he short changed ya on the rice that morning, Steve!"
3. "Those guys must be gettin different chow'n me — look at them bodies!"
4. "Got Mother Knowles (Maj.) in the ring."
5. "Don't throw peanut shells in the ring!"
6. H. Rowley announces saying, "This broadcast coming to you courtesy Adams Hats!"
7. "I can see where our ration will be cut, when the J's see em working this hard and looking so good!"
8. "Look at the G-string Kid!"
9. "You guys wanna orchestra?" This while combatants "waltzing."
10. Just before the bell, "Hey, Steve — ya still got time to have a chill!" (Malaria.)
11. "Yaahh, Chief! You're on your way to #7" (Quarters blocks.)
12. "Look at them rice muscles!"

Phil and I keep talking about trying to do some recuperating together when we get back, depending of course on how long I'm in the hospital and how long Phil has to stay in the Army. It'd be swell if we could work it out, but Lord only knows.

Began series of vitamin B shots today. Japanese state that if there is more than five gallons of rice wasted per meal, the rice ration will be cut. They are measuring today!

Japanese have asked for volunteers.

Cerebral malaria case admitted today. Husky lad; been on wood-chopping detail. Delirious, tends to be violent. Took six Corpsmen to hold him down. Definitely objects to being stuck with hypo needles (Baxter). Got another egg!

Wednesday, July 14, 1943
The Japanese now demand that the patients who are able to do so will sit up in bed during *tenko*, a.m. (6:15) and p.m. (7:00) — thusly do we lose those forty-five minutes that seem to give most rest. Takes away doctors right to say who is and who isn't able to sit up.

Friday, July 16, 1943
Quite a bit of air activity last few days. At least twelve yesterday and ten so far today — from north to south, apparently landing at Davao. Lot of speculation as usual. I think it's just patrol activity. Who knows?

Incident of the Corpsmen in the avocado tree last nite, and the guards excitement. The "eating out" of Col. D. that followed.

Saturday, July 17, 1943
Got paid today by the IJA the usual printing press peso. Field Officers 25 pesos, Capts. & 1st Lts. 20 pesos, 2nd Lts. & WO[83] 10 pesos. Had meat at noon and fresh fish at night. Gala day. Dave Montag is a patient — infected foot. Did quite a bit of walking today. Pain not too great. Gave Phil 5 pesos; put 5 pesos in PX. Will give Mickey 2 pesos, and Phil and I'll have to divide the rest.

Sunday, July 18, 1943
Pork and beans at noon! My appetite has left me for some unknown reason. Don't feel at all like eating and this better than usual chow has been "just chow," as far as I'm concerned. Stomach cramps today. Chiseled in on an egg! Three so far in last two weeks! Good program today (music).

Sunday, July 19, 1943
And again — happy birthday, Eleanor Lee, on your 24th year. July 19 is always a strong reminder of pleasant hours and days spent with you and I hope you are having a gay ole time this year. Someone must.

Friday, July 23, 1943
Optimism is going up again because the news in J newspapers from middle

---

83 Warrant officer.

July. United States offensive in SWP[84] seems to be underway. Yanks in Sicily — Germany apparently expected to fall this year. United States six months ahead of schedule. Now, many are talking about us being sprung in Sept. or Oct. '43! I'd like to believe it, but I can't.

Sunday, July 25, 1943

Had a real shakedown inspection today. My diary and films were safely put away, as were many things of other men. They checked mostly on clothes and took books away. Supposed to get them back, stamped. Took my bible, but I got it back, stamped.

Have been having an agonizing time with my scrotum. The skin has become raw, and they're "weepy." Have had calamine, H2S, salicylic acid, glycerine, and sulfanilamide, and some other crap but can't get it under control.

Friday, July 30, 1943

Birthday eventful in several ways — most of them quite trying on the nerves. Padre LaFleur said Mass for me this morning, and later in the morning Dr. Davis came and talked to me about my foot. More was said about amputation, and he knows I want it done, and he's gone over the thing pretty thoroughly. He seems to think my foot can be made fairly usable, but Dr. Colvard (to me) doesn't agree. The factor of the U.S. gov't and "loss of limb" seems

to figure in a lot, though I can't see where he'd be "leaving himself open to the government," as he says. So, next week I'm to have a nerve in my foot injected with alcohol to try to stop the pain. If it doesn't work, the implication is that he will then amputate. God knows I want to get rid of the incessant pain, and stop having to take MSO4 at various intervals for relief. More developments later.

Elocution contest held tonite, for which I've been preparing for ten days. 1st prize is one can of meat and vegetables. 2nd prize is a hand of tobacco. 3rd prize is one peso. There are eleven entries, and I was "on" 5th. Three judges, judging on points system. My "say" was "Gunga Din," given in cockney accent, and damned if Walter J. didn't *win*!! So — having won the can of meat and veg., I'm splitting it three ways. Phil's birthday was June 2 and we had nothing, so he's in on it. Sergeant Shea patiently helped me learn and rehearse, so he's in, and *I* gave the thing, so *I'm* in on it. The feast is tomorrow noon. And again, I deeply appreciate Mom and Dad's looking after me in younger years — those elocution lessons sure came in handy and right on my birthday, when I felt extra blue, and had no way of celebrating. Thanks Mom and Dad, and all day long and far into the nite, my thoughts were with you, and I kept wondering what your thoughts were today. Whether or not you knew I was alive — at

---

84   South West Pacific.

least it would give you some peace of mind to know I'm alive. May God bless you both and keep you well and unworried. Don't change. Don't let the war make you cynical as I have become. Don't change because *if* I get back, I'm going to need you to cling to more than I ever have in my life. People will change — life will be different — my social readjustment will be a very great thing to accomplish, and when I go home, I do very much want it to be the same, or nearly the same home I left in 1941. Again, I say, "maybe next year?"

P.S. — Having won the "M&V," I was suddenly startled, and later seriously afraid at a very apparent change in my personality — *definite cynicism*. I realized it when people began congratulating me on having taken 1st place, and the back of my mind kept drumming — "Yes, go ahead, congratulate me, but when you don't get invited to share the M&V, you won't know me" — or "Huh, another guy trying to work his way into the M&V." So — there's another definite result of this war, and a helluva thing too — distrust of human nature. Nuts!

Sunday, Aug 1, 1943

Injection operation tomorrow. Good entertainment today. Music and then sing God Bless America and they unfolded Old Glory (hidden inside a blanket). Tears and heartbreak — but swell.

Monday, Aug. 2, 1943

Operation today — neuro-section of right ankle. *Very painful* operation because of necessity was not given enuff novocaine since had to tell Dr. when he had the right nerves that led to my toes. He clipped the nerves. Incision about 4¼" long. Took about ninety minutes. Thirteen stitches done on lateral side.

Tuesday, Aug. 3, 1943

Dr. Colvard got five letters from home! Latest was May 18th, '42. A few others got letters — not this chicken tho. God, I hope I'm not reported dead.

Friday, Aug. 6, 1943

Ankle dressing yesterday. Incision area infected — not deeply though and I hope it doesn't spread. The former pain in the toes seems to have stopped except for an occasional twinge.

Saturday, Aug. 7, 1943

Infection under control. Has been very painful, but so far today seems easier. Rubber tissue drains and pressure pads being used to get pus out.

Sunday, Aug. 8, 1943

Doctor took out the stitches today. Infection still present, but seems to be under control. The old pain seems to have quieted down almost all the way. Still some pain from the incision.

Major Maeda had all Americans assembled today and gave speech about lack of food, and that what we eat we must raise; can't get anything from or to Davao. Ration of rice cut.

Monday, Aug. 9, 1943

Doc "spread out" the incision and packed it with gauze. Some of the pressure has thus been relieved. Got *no* sleep last nite, had helluva time. Got ½ lemon zest and today burned my mouth pretty badly — scurvy. Colonel Deter gave me the receipt to RCA Radiogram I sent folks 4/3/42. Says it got thru OK.

Wednesday, Aug. 11, 1943

Malaria hit me again today, at 3 p.m. Terrific chill and fever but no sick stomach. Caused foot to hurt like hell again. On quinine; had MSO4. Left ear has fungus again! Fifty-five men in camp received radio or telegrams from home. Very belated. None for W. J. though. Apparently, however, the folks at home have been notified that we are alive and OK, so I'm put much at ease on this question, which has had me very worried. The report is that there are many letters and telegrams in Manila for those of us down here and that they're to be sent down here soon. Boy — my fingers are crossed and crossed hard.

Three of the telegrams brought bad news for three officers — two wives died, other divorced! Jeez, and things aren't bad enough without that kind of news! Sure sorry for them.

Saturday, Aug. 14, 1943

Cigarette issue yesterday. Supposed to be 1,800 letters in camp for us. If true I sure hope I get at least one. God, it's been a long time. Still on quinine — can only eat a little.

Wednesday, Aug. 18, 1943

Don't forget incident of Japs punishing chickens for not laying expected number of eggs. Chickens given two days w/o food — H2O only! Jap gives tongue lashing to chicken, then says, "*Wakaru*?"[85]

Thursday, Aug. 19, 1943

Inspection by some J general today. Says, "Your diet is very good!" Asked Col. D. if he was satisfied with diet, and he said, "As a doctor, I would be satisfied with more." Japanese general, "But, you must remember, you are prisoner of war, and for prisoner of war, this diet is very good!"

Sunday, Aug. 22, 1943

Doc now injecting me with cobra venom, which is supposed to control pain. Cannot notice much difference good from it.

Thursday, Aug. 26, 1943

Japanese newspapers give the following information — "Rome declared open city. Sicily to U.S. Fighting in Balkans." We are also doing pretty well in Solomons. New Britain and Bougainville apparently ours. "Italy will fight to bitter end." "Evacuating Berlin." "U.S. uses atrocious, inhumane methods." All in all, news is very good — optimism high.

---

85 "Understood?" in Japanese.

Saturday, Aug. 28, 1943

Men coming in at 9:30 p.m. from rice detail: raining, had to push train in! Showed spirit by singing God Bless America and being very loud and in good humor. Awakened Jap Major (one of their intentions). Real Yank spirit. Made all feel good.

Sunday, Aug. 29, 1943

Sanders and gang put on another good show. They work hard and all deeply appreciate efforts. Some good singers. Good arrangements of songs. Last two shows had female impersonators, excellent "Carman Miranda" — (Pvt. Loya) very good.

Sunday, Sept. 4, 1943

Our rice ration has been cut quite a bit. Now we get a *level* scoop full which doesn't fill a mess kit. As a result, a perpetual pang of hunger is present. Today, at noon, we had meat "stew" and *hardly any* rice, and the rice we got was scraped up from the floor of our little storehouse. We had not quite five gallons of dirty rice for eighty-three people!! The men managed to down two carabao this week, hence we had meat twice!

News from papers plays up failure of Quebec Conference, dissatisfaction of Stalin, terrible meat shortage in U.S., Vella LaVella island, China dissatisfied with U.S . . . even disagreement between two U.S. Air Force units in China.

Tuesday, Sept. 7, 1943

On your happy birthday, Pete, I have been informed that on Sept. 9 my foot will be amputated! Doctor Davis finally got some 95% alcohol from Dr. Yashamura, and we're going ahead day after tomorrow. The only thing I'm now nervous and worried about is that he says it's to be done under spinal, and I want *ether*. I'm going to try to win him over to ether before Thursday. Otherwise, I'm very glad that it's to be gone. I'll be rid of pain at last, except of course the postoperative pain.

Wednesday, Sept. 8, 1943

Didn't sleep much last nite — worrying about having to be awake thru it all. Doctor took measurements today, and marked my leg off with silver nitrate. It's about twelve inches below the knee. Operation will give me an "anterior flap" which is supposed to be the best. Know damned well won't sleep much tonite! Sorry, Mom, but I have to lose it. I'll be so much better off without it. Pray for me.

Shaved today after 3½ months. Chow better — more fish and meat!

I *won* — I get *ether*.

MORE RUMORS:

June 28, #247: Rumor is that the exchange rumor has been nullified! #248: Russian troops in Warsaw; now their HQ. #249: Now "they" have us moving to Bilibid (Luzon Prison) in the (near? far?) future. My, my —

how thick is the BS!! #250: Davao is in the war zone, and furthermore, Davao is being used as a base for bombing planes (J).

June 30, #251: The Japanese soldiers here are destroying all U.S. personal property in their possession; watches, blankets, etc. #252: Fighting now on German-Polish border. 253: A number of unidentified planes around Davao yesterday.

July 1, #254: After the present crop of rice is harvested, there will be no more rice planted and only necessary details will be sent to work. About a week more.

July 2, #255: Philippine Islands to get independence on July 9! BS! #256: A naval battle going on down south. Japanese claim victory. We lost two destroyers, one cruiser. #257: Yanks going thru Italy proper. #258: Latest J'se newspaper claims J has bases on New Guinea, and Timor, and planes from these bases are bombing Australia! (Probably true!)

July 4, #259: Gen. Roxas to take over this camp on July 7th–July 9th. Japanese to leave and P.I. independence. (BS!)

July 6, #260: Japan bombing Vladiviostok! Tokyo bombed. #261: Japan bombing U.S. bases in the Caroline Islands.

July 7, #262: U.S. has started offensive in South West Pacific according to Stimson in broadcast, and we took four islands — Solomon group in

one nite's operation, using the "buddy system," said very effective. Landing operations supposed to be very effective. #263: Japan now bombing isles which were hers a few days ago! #264: Davao had blackout Sunday nite — gun emplacements being put in at Davao airport. Bombers in last few days have been leaving Davao loaded — return empty and shot-up. #266: No large ships in Davao for last five weeks. Only few small ones. #267: Greece in revolt. #268: U.S. Navy now 100% stronger and 60% more tonnage than a year ago. #269: We have enuff rice to last till end of Aug. '43. #270: Roosevelt, July 4 speech, "Philippine Islands taken over in 60 days!"

July 8, #271: Four Red Cross ships in Manila. (This and "exchange" come in cycles.)

July 11, #272: 2,500 Yanks died in Cabanatuan of dysentery. Sick moved to Bilibid Prison at Batangas — rest moved to?[86] #273: There are 51 letters in Manila for men in this camp. Doctor Covard told there is one for him — gee, how I'd like to hear from the folks. Please, God, let there be a letter for me.

July 16, #274: The biggest offensive the world has seen being made by U.S. in South West Pacific. #275: The Phil.

---

86 There are two prisons named Bilibid. Old Bilibid, built in 1865 and located in the heart of Manila is where Hinkle was interned for much of the war. New Bilibid was built in 1936 and is located a few miles to the southeast. It is not, as Hinkle claimed, in the Province of Batangas. Both prisons were used by the Japanese as prisoner-of-war camps.

constabulary is moving into our area around here. Some schoolhouse.

July 19, #276: Naples declared open city. #277: United States offensive definitely started on SWP at end of June.

July 20, #278: U.S. has landed in five places on Sicily. #279: United States has taken two more islands in Solomons.

July 22, #280: Three large ships in Davao Gulf torpedoed. #281: Many J troops in Davao apparently waiting for transport, but none available. Been there two and three weeks. #282: United States planes over New Guinea, but no more land battalions firing at them. #283: Japanese planes that leave Davao, comeback w/o belly-tanks.

July 30, #284: Mussolini and cabinet have resigned — King Emmanuel appoints Marshall B. to take over government. Many Yanks in Italy.

Aug. 6, #285: Burma given independence by Japan — declares war on Allies and then surrenders! #286: General Eisenhower in conference w/Italians concerning peace in Italy. #287: United States has Ellice Islands — J sinks five U.S. transports near Sols. We have about 1,000,000 men in South.

Aug. 15, #288: We have Rabaul. U.S. tanks skirting, or in, Hamburg, Germany. #289: Philippine Islands to get independence in 30 days.

Aug. 16, #290: Japanese evacuating, or evacuated Jolo.

Aug. 18, #291: United States gov't to give $1,000 bonus to those in P.I. Also $2.50 a day for all on foreign service during war.

Aug. 21, #292: Now, P.I. independence set for Oct. 1, '43.

Aug. 24, #293: Two carabaos a week to be butchered for us.

Aug. 26, ##294: We bombed Rome w/1500 planes. #295: Russia and J now at war on Manchurian border. #296: U.S. has sub base at Vladiviostok.

Aug. 27, #297: Yanks pouring into France from N. Italy. #298: Allies land on French coast — across English Channel. #299: Russia in Warsaw. (Again!)

Aug. 28, #300: The war in Europe is over ! (BS? or possible?)

Aug. 30, #301: Japanese guard watching ten planes going over asked Yank if they were U.S. planes. "No," so J guard says, "Wait, wait." #302: Some Chinese storekeeper told Yank officer who was in Davao that Yanks will be here soon. "60 days."

Aug. 31, #303: Allies fighting in Belgrade. Nazis now on defense. #304: We have New Guinea. New Britain., Dutch Timor.

Sept. 1, #305: United States on five-pointed offensive to Java, Borneo, Sumatra, and two more places.

Sept. 2, #306: Davao being evacuated and camouflaged and J civilians being sent to some small island. Fox-holes and air-raid shelters being rapidly built. #307: Zamboanga bombed twice recently.

Sept. 7, #308: Churchill killed at sea in plane crash. #309: Japanese supposed to have taken Midway!!!

Sept. 8 to Oct. 21, #310: United States para-troops took main city on East coast of Borneo. #311: Interpreter told wood-cutters to get in all wood possible, because after rice harvest no more outside details. #312: Italy has definitely surrounded our troops on Balkan front. #313: Philippine Islands to get independence.

Oct. 14, 1943. #314: Germany surrenders. #315: Tokyo bombed by 2,000 planes. #316: Nazis not surrendered. Fighting in Warsaw. #317: British navy in SWP.

Thursday, Oct. 21, 1943
This is the first chance I've had to write anything since my right foot was amputated on September 9. It was under ether — a little more than two cans! Second day after, began dressings and Oh God, what pain to these dressings! Stump got infected from the alcohol used in injecting the cut nerves in leg, and

so stitches were taken out and packing put in. Pain terrific. Dressings daily for about four-and-one-half to five weeks; now every other day. MSO4 given. Loss of appetite. "Crud" breaks out on arms, crotch, and left foot and hands. Some pain still present, the "drive you crazy" persistent stuff. And, Oh God, why did I have to undergo this alone, without Mom and Dad near me? It's been hard, discouraging, painful, and I've been so lonely.

Monday, Oct. 25, 1943
Two men escaped today while out on detail. What the outcome will be I don't know yet.

Tuesday, Nov. 2, 1943
Damn! I've left you go Diary 'cause I just haven't felt like writing. I've been unable to concentrate and has been hard to write. So, I'll catch up with notes and hope I can remember details. 1. Oct. 29 — I was *operated on again*! Doc figured I had some infected bone in the stump, so into it he went. He used a *chisel* and *mallet*, and golly, it was the most undesirable experience to hear the chiseling and know it was *my bone* that was being chiseled. He was right — infected! It was extremely painful for a few weeks afterwards, and again I was forced to be under MSO4 influence. To date for the last week, and at present, I still need ¼ gr. MSO4 at nite, so that the pain is erased long enuff for me to get to sleep. Pain is decreasing. Incision healing, slowly 'cause of chow.

2. Hospital kitchen done away with, we get chow from new main kitchen, Better deal; more sugar, salt, "soup" and tea. Chow rotten.

3. New barracks built — compound remodeled to rectangular shape.

4. Once a week we get peanut brittle, each piece = 3" x 1" x ¼ @ 10¢ ea. Get between four and six pieces per man. How we wait for it! And, God how good it tastes! Boot-leg candy sells for .75¢ to one peso *a piece!*

5. Fifty man detail to Davao, in November. Seen hauling coral and sand!??

6. Air corps men now being questioned and surveyed by IJA. Rumor that another detail to go out. *Diary space seems at premium!*

7. *Tenko* now done in Japanese. Commands in Japanese, and we count off in Japanese.

Saturday, Nov. 13, 1943

Thru all this pain am continually thinking of home, of Mom and Dad; and at nite especially, I break down and cry like a baby when I think of them, and long to be near them. Then I visualize Mom in the kitchen, cooking up veal cutlets, or pork roast and mashing potatoes; I hear Dad unlock the front door and call out, "Hello, hello, hello!" Then we sit down and eat — about here I could *scream*!!! Food, *good* food, please God, get us somewhere where we can get good food. Rice and greens, rice and fish, rice and salt . . . oh Christ!

Wednesday, Nov. 17, 1943

Still having quite a bit of pain. Like a tiger cage, no position gives me rest or freedom from pain. Leg healing good, no infection. Now getting only quarter-grain MSO4 at nite. My weight down very much. Doctor talking blood transfusion for me! (Didn't get it!)

Friday, Dec. 3, 1943

Just some thinking: I've often re-read your letter, Eileen, and they always remind me of the struggle you had two years ago — (2 years!!). You mention the monotony; lying in bed; etc. You said I couldn't fail in any battle I faced, because you didn't. This has given me strength. But Pete — and Mom and Dad, *if you only knew* what I've been thru, and am going thru! It's not self pity causing me to write this, merely sheer amazement at what I have faced, and waiting to face more. Think of it: since my amputation Sept. 9, the sheet I'm lying on has not been washed! Eleven weeks!!!! The other sheet, boiled once! A bed of bed-bugs! Ants in everything! Rice and "kangkong" (a wild-growing weed)— practically a steady diet. Monotony? Hah! Try to borrow a book to read! No radio to listen to; no loved ones to come in and keep you happy; no newspapers or magazines; no "smacks" — always that continually gnawing hunger, and, oh hell, why do I go on??

Monday, Dec. 13, 1943

Bought large can of sardines for 25 pesos. Saunders and crew put on good program tonite. And still having pain from last operation, especially at nite. Doc cut me down to ⅛ gr. MS tonite. There are only about forty more capsules of sodium amytal left. I got very little sleep.

Tuesday, Dec. 14, 1943

One hundred man detail to leave today for ___? Colonel Colvard going with them. Japs issued us each: one G-string, one "guest size" toothpaste, some toilet "tissue." The above detail did leave, under supervision of Japanese Navy. Perhaps they'll be treated better and get better chow — the Navy has a better reputation for this, anyway.

Saturday, Dec. 18, 1943

Well, just two years ago tonite I was shot, and when I think of two years, why that's a helluva long time ago! Plenty of water has gone under the bridge since then (my right foot with the water!). A painful two years, both physically and mentally, a hell I never expected to go thru, and I'm not out of the woods yet. My leg still pains me where it is still open, on top of the tibia. It keeps me from sleeping, but it is closing and two weeks should see it healed. Still have to have at least ⅛ gr. MSO4 at nite, and once in a while ¼ gr. I don't think there'll be many more ¼ gr. shots after tonite though. Colonel Thayer, Col. Deter and I hashed over the events of Dec. 18, two years ago, and had a lot of memories to go thru. Rash on face finally cleared up after taking sulfathiazole treatment. Sort of a barbers "itch" affair.

Wednesday, Dec. 22, 1943

Japanese gave us forty cigs per man today. Xmas must be just around the corner! The whole camp is full of Xmas spirit. Saunders and his music gang are to put on a 2½ hour show Xmas day. There's a peculiar type of palm tree in front of the hospital, that's shaped like and looks exactly like a real Xmas tree. It is being decorated with empty toothpaste boxes; tin cans that have been cut into long spirals; strips of cloth for icicles and snow; and from somewhere, some real Xmas trimmings. The effect may be funny to some, but it's *our* Xmas tree. The hospital is decorated in palm wreaths, etc. I've made five cards, with verses for Maj. Davis, Col. Deter, Phil, Joe Garcia, and one card for Stud, Roy and Mac.[87] We're to have good chow on Xmas, but I guess no RC stuff.

Thursday, Dec. 23, 1943

Xmas is shaping up quite well. The J'se brought in more candy and cup cakes to sell to us than usual. Today I traded off fifteen of my snapshots for two packs cigs. The snaps are starting to fade, and besides, I'm counting on my negatives to be in good shape and not stuck together. I think they'll be OK. Many of us are still American enuff to be giving gifts at Xmas. I've a couple of packs of cigs that I'm going to give away, but otherwise I've nothing to give. And thoughts are ever homeward, But what can I say in words? The heart aches terribly at times like this, and I pray for those I

---

87 2nd Lt. Henry Macner.

love and wish I *knew* how they were. Just that *one* little thing I'd like to know, it'd make things easier — how is everyone?!

Sunday, Dec. 26, 1943
Well, Xmas is over, and it was pretty nice. Spirits have been high and morale at the hospital seemed higher than "across the fence." Our chow was not so exceptional — "coffee w/ a little milk and less sugar, rice and sugar for breakfast; kangkong and rice for lunch; some meat, carrots and corn and rice for supper. Alcohol (w/ diesel fuel in it) was going down many throats, including mine! Roy, Mac, Stud and Fred Roth asked me to eat lunch w/them, hence I happily "walked" in on a can of corned beef hash. Gifts were exchanged by many. I received packs of cigs, from Howie Martin, Stud, George, and John Alden. All seemed to like the cards I made for them. In the afternoon, Sanders and his crew put on a swell two hour musical program and that further raised the spirits. Doc gave me a good Xmas nite by killing my pain with ¼ gram instead of the ⅛ gram I've been getting. At nite, when it finally got quiet, I thought of home, but I got so homesick and blue I had to stop. I only hope they were in as good spirits as I was able to be, and I'll try again and say, "Next year, we'll be together." God bless you all.

Had my hair cut real short today. It was quite long, but it began falling out a lot; probably from lack of sun

and lying around. Japanese gave us some U.S. magazines — 1941 issues of Sat. Eve Post, Life, Vogue, Collier's, Pinocchio(!); and there were two bundles of them. Sure good to look thru them, but jeeps!, those pictures of meat loaves, soups, cakes and Whitman Samplers!!!

Tuesday, Dec. 28, 1943
Some of the gang were caught full of "good cheer" by Japs on Xmas nite. They found Mike Milligan's canteen w/alcohol in it. Mike later taken to JHQ and accused of stealing the alcohol, but since he didn't steal it, he denied it and would not give out names of rest of those who were imbibing. Mike now in guardhouse and understand the Japanese told him he may as well tell them how the alcohol got into camp, or they'll torture him till he dies!

Naturally, in my nites and days of thinking, the question that most often pops into my mind is, "What shall I do when I get back and what will I be like?" This much am I sure of — that once my mind is set on doing something, I'm going to do it, or at least try. Some of my desires may (and probably will) seem crazy, or childish or foolish to Mom and Dad, but they'll be things I want to do after having gone thru this hell. I cannot help but feel that *no one* will have the right to tell me what I should or should not do. If I should decide to get a motorcycle, e.g., and then want to do highway patrol duty for awhile at $15 or so a week, *I want to do it*! If I should decide I want to just loaf for a year — I want to do it, etc. In other words, my philosophy on life has changed (or finally taken shape), I don't know which. This much of my philosophy I am sure of — great material gain in the form of money is going to mean *little* to me. I've done without so much for over two years now, that I believe I'll be able to get along somewhat differently than I did before, If I have to. Another thing — I'm not going to worry one damn about what other people think of my activities, or of me. I'm going to be me as I want to be. I'm going to try to enjoy life after I get out of this mess, and how better than by doing things I want to do. Money, I'll have to get, yes, but I'll not be out to make a million! So, perhaps people will get a new Walter in their midst. Perhaps they won't understand him, but I expect that. They'll never really realize what this war and prison camp and pain can do to a man toward changing his ways.

Wednesday, Dec. 29, 1943
Quarantine! The hospital and barracks #8 is quarantined, beginning today! Reason? Infantile paralysis case showed up yesterday, and all possible precautions are trying to be taken. We patients have made masks for ourselves to use when in close contact with someone (Col. Deter's suggestion). No giving away of chow, no visitors from another compound. It's to last three weeks.

I think It'll be an extra monotonous three weeks. Imprisoned within a prison in a prison!!

Thursday, Dec. 30, 1943
Today, my thoughts have been especially with you, Dink — and again I pray that you're safe and sound and not off the continent of our U.S. Needless to say, my memories of all the good times we had seem endless; but what warms me the most is the knowledge that our friendship and brotherhood in ΘΔΧ is closer than any blood relationships could ever be. Walt — I treasure you, as a friend never treasured another. God guide you thru this mess, wherever you are, so that someday you and I and June can again unite for happy days. Don't go off to be a hero as I did — mistake #1!! Remember ole Hackly Butler's single with the verse, "As a rule a man's a fool; when it's hot, he wants it cool; when its cool he wants it hot; always wanting what is not!" I remember you and I both liked that verse especially. I hope this next year may end the war, but I somewhat doubt it.

Friday, Dec. 31, 1943
Well, New Year's Eve and, though it isn't a happy one, we have some alcohol (with diesel fuel in it!) and tho' it wasn't much, it was enough to make us all (six) feel like maybe '44 would bring us some better luck. All I could do was to keep thinking of the happy New Year's Eves I spent with Mom and Dad in the past at the Evergreen, at Woodman, at Jud's and the others.

God, I hope we don't have to spend another year here, but it wouldn't surprise me at all!

Must start a new diary — it will have to be of the "brief note" type, probably. This one can hold no more.

This quarantine is monotonous already, and we're just starting. So long, '43 — and *please* be good, '44.

MORE RUMORS:
NOV. 1–20, #318: Davao bombed. #319: Borneo ours — U.S. troops in Zambo. (BS!)

Dec. 5, #320: Red Cross packages will be here for Xmas or next month (?). Please God, grant *this*.

Dec. 7, #321: War in Europe over.

Dec. 8, #322: Japan surrendered this morning at 3:30!(BS). #323: Nagasaki bombed heavily. Fire seen 200 miles off. #324: Japanese evacuating Manchukuo border.

Dec. 15, #325: Heavy fighting in Gilbert Islands. We lose heavily in naval battle. #326: Japanese have frozen German assets in Far East.

Dec. 17, #327: Interpreter said, "Maybe war will be over before Red Cross stuff gets here." (Yeah??)

Dec. 24, #328: Nichols Field bombed by us. Thirty Yanks killed there. #328: We have Shanghai. #329: Peace conference going on; agreements reached between J and U.S. but U.S.S.R. objects. (Think this is BS.)

Dec. 31, #330: Our troops in the Celebes and heavy fighting going on down there. #331: The peace conference wound up with the Japanese refusing the terms. #332: Senator Knox makes speech. Says war will be over in 90 days, and that P.I. will be in U.S. hands in 30 days. (We've heard this before!)

Saturday, Jan. 1, 1944
Our chow today was supposed to be better than usual because of 2 carabao. However the kitchen didn't do so well and the "meat" (just strings to pieces) was cooked with kangkong and cassava. Incidentally, the J's have stopped the issues of dried fish, so we now face rice and salt for breakfast, every other morning. Darned leg is still open on the tibia, and it still hurts. Dr. Davis did another successful operation on a man's insides and found a tumor the size of baseball behind the stomach. Padre Lafleur managed to scrape up a group for show — wasn't good, we at least had one!

Wednesday, Jan. 5, 1944
Had a good nite's rest last nite. Doc gave me ¼ MSO4. Should be off the stuff in a week or so. The pain is getting a little less, and when I heal up, I believe it will all go away. Am using McNair's pen,[88] and it sure feels funny to write w/a pen. Kind of hard to control, too!

---

88   First Lieutenant Joseph E. McNair.

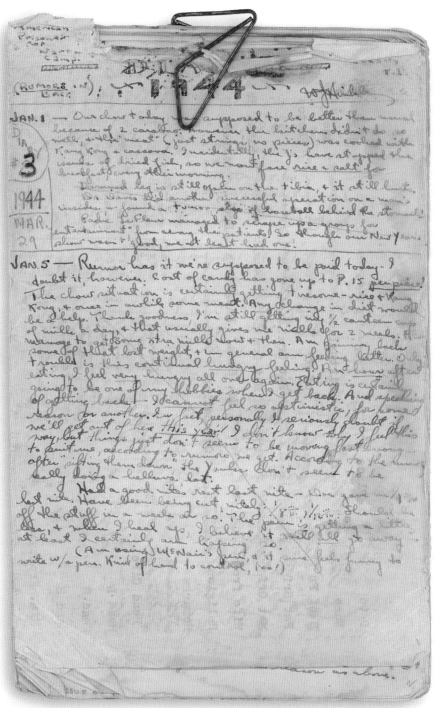

Volume No. 3. *Hinkle Archive*

Rumor has it we're supposed to be paid today. I doubt it, however. Cost of candy has gone up to 15 pesos *per piece*. The chow situation is certainly getting tiresome — rice and kang-kong, and once in a while some meat. Any change in diet would be a help. Thank goodness, I'm still getting my half-canteen cup of milk a day. Also managed to get some extra milk now and then. Am gaining back some of that lost weight, and in general am feeling better. Only trouble is this continual *hungry* feeling. An *hour* after eating I feel *very* hungry all over again. Eating is certainly going to be one of my hobbies when I get back. And speaking of getting back — I *cannot* feel so optimistic, for some reason or another. In fact, personally I seriously doubt if we'll get out of here *this year*! I don't know why I feel this way, but things just don't seem to be moving fast enough to suit me, according to rumors we get. According to the rumors, after "sifting them down," the Yanks don't seem to be doing a helluva lot.

Jan. 9, 1944

For the past 7 days we have had quite a bit of rain. On the nite of the sixth it began raining and did not let up till about 7 o'clock this morning. The rice-fields are flooded. No work for our gang for a change. Everything is mud around camp. Have been playing lots of bridge the last four days. Mac and I decided to learn something about the game, so we got the rules and have been doing pretty well.

Jan. 10, 1944

Quarantine lifted today and seeing the "visitors from the other side of the fence" has been like old home-week! Of course there has been no change in life "over there," but it's been good to see some friends again after ten days of seclusion. Rumor has it that the J's have informed the U.S. HQ of the number of men they'll need to unload the RC ship (when it comes again). The J's have collected — or ordered turned in, I should say, all books — including Bibles and medical books. Excuse is, "Library to be started." We've heard this before and never saw the books again.

Little things to recall from this hospital.
1. Colonel Powell continually tapping away, busily carving out knife scabbards, etc. (his white flowing beard).
2. Colonel Perry playing away on his "coconut uke," which he made from a coconut shell, wood and some metal for frets, and telephone wire for strings.
3. Leo Pentecost[89] and his "dad-gum," "Dang" and "Doggone's."
4. Colonel Powell and his flowers and his garden produce.
5. The "salads" that are concocted.

Jan. 12, 1944

Damn! My leg has been hurting like the devil today, and it's just on that one spot on top of my tibia. Decided to ask Doc if he couldn't operate and see what's wrong. He said if he operated and scraped the

---

89 Died aboard hell ship *Arisan Maru*, October 24, 1944.

bone, the stump would be useless and I'd have to have an amputation above the knee. Said if he operated it would be better, therefore, to go ahead and operate above the knee (amputate). *This* does not appeal to me! He left it at "We'll see." So, now I don't know "what's gonna be!" I sure hope he can do something, and not another amputation!

The library is actually ready to function! Has about 1,000 books, many of them '44 editions and new books. Japanese gave us about 300–400 books. Three of the J'se have formed the "executive committee," "vice-president," and "treasurer." Major Knowles, the American who is to actually handle the library, is a "member of the executive committee, but cannot make any suggestions!" We get a book for 14 days and must return it in as good condition as received, or the J guardhouse will be our home for awhile!!

The rains have flooded out the road to Davao, and the rice-fields, too, except the rice that is ready for harvest.

Jan. 13, 1944

Doc dressed the stump today and took a close look at the area that I've been complaining about, and decision is — to operate day after tomorrow and chisel a piece of bone which apparently has excessive growth. Not a difficult job and it won't ruin my stump, so I'm feeling kind of happy this morning 'cause *THIS* might be the operation that will stop the pain. Sure hope so. I'm *TIRED* of this hell.

Jan. 15, 1944

Operation put off till tomorrow or Monday because of an admission calling for immediate operation, and surgery *does not have enuff gloves for two operations in one day*!! So, I lie and wait, and am anxious to get it over with. Don't know what I'd do w/o Jose.[90]

Issue of ten cigs per man and one banana.

Jan. 17, 1944

Operated on again today, and piece of tibia chipped off. Done under spinal, and worked well. Took about 45 minutes. This operation should be the last one, and it should stop the pain. I sure hope so.

We got candy and tobacco in the PX today. Officers now pay .15¢ per piece of candy, making it possible to give all the EMS their candy free. Tobacco of good grade was 2 and 3 pesos per hand. Got paid today, 30 pesos.

Jan. 21, 1944

Have been having bad luck with the hypo syringe and this has been no boon to my post-operative pain. The syringe leaks if not used carefully, and most of the time it's not used carefully. And there are none to replace it.

---

90 Private First Class Jose Garcia, 515th Medical Detachment.

Another post card given to us to fill out "to send home." New type, with space for fifty word message, and I don't know what to say in fifty words that won't be censored! Post card: "Living under conditions as satisfactory as may be expected. One fraternity bro. here. Most important is that you not worry but try patience and keep your health. Heard from Mich. Ave. group once. (RC) Greetings + Marilyn's birthday. Anxious to return. Keep faith. Love to you, Eileen and all. Wally." Oh — International RC sends "New Years Greetings" but where's the food??? That damned message hurt, but did *no good*. Canadian and Australian RC sent same message to their P of W.

Jan. 22, 1944

Japanese apparently need propaganda badly. All here "asked" to fill in form of "worst part of war seen," "action seen," etc. Also, ten enlisted men and five officers and chaplain allowed to write 200 word letter home. Supposed to go air-mail. Told to stress Xmas treatment. Down to ¼ MSO4 at nite, which is damned good for so soon after last operation. I think this one will knock out the pain, at least it seems to be heading that way for a change. 50% cut in rice ration to go into effect Monday: to be made up with camotes and cassava. This is liable to hurt quite some. Reason for cut is unknown. Many are conjecturing.

Jan. 24, 1944

Rice cut apparently dropped. Instead, we seem to be getting more meat! (Carabao and Brahma.) Today is the first time since we've been P of W that we have had meat in all three meals! Sure raises the morale, even though the quantity of meat, and the way it has to be fixed still leaves a lot to be desired.

In our "letters" for the Japanese, apparently none of us saw any action or "horrible sights," or had any "most horrible experiences," or saw any of our "comrades die," or "saw such suffering." So — we had to rewrite the letters, and the advice was given that we shouldn't "be so cheeky." Still, I put some "cheek" in mine, as e.g., "Japan may make a brave stand, but she will fall in the near future, I am sure." To smooth it, I wrote, "And if she does, it cannot be a disgrace for to lose in fair battle is no disgrace." And — "Inasmuch as the diet is so vastly different from that which those of us here are experiencing, it is not hard to understand the run-down condition of the men here, and their susceptibility to disease."

Hah! The new fence posts that were put up some time ago are sprouting!! They are trunks of kapock trees and have the facility to begin growing again, though branches are cut off and the trunk severed from the roots. Japanese having an inventory of the library Monday! They sure attach import to their library duties. And since we "have the books, no music programs!" Invoice for RC stuff at HQ. Supposed to be 2,080 cases of stuff; 67 shoe repairing outfits; clothes, shoes, *SHOE POLISH*!! (what a bedlam of comment *that* caused!), musical instruments, athletic equipment. (I still *doubt*!)

Feb. 1, 1944

Got candy in today, twenty pieces per man. Smaller pieces, but still .15¢ per piece. Issue of twenty cigs today, too.

Feb. 2, 1944

"Ground Hog Day," but wouldn't have seen shadow here. Has been cool and rainy for two days. We called it "MacArthur Day," — Mac to come out of his tunnel, sees shadow of Jap plane and goes back!

Oh, yes, *the library*!! I knew it was too good to last, but it *was* the Americans cutting our throat again! Order went, "Quarters, barracks and hospital *cannot* draw any more books." Why? Because some dope of an "American" of ours "bellyached to a Japanese that they had all the books and the workers didn't get a chance to read!" (This was wrong, 'cause we got an equal share of the books.) This same thing happened in regard to our getting any more corn meal, except that the whole camp suffers this time. So — close the barn door after Bessy escapes! Our headquarters puts out orders *not* to discuss food situation with any J's. Nuts! We're always just a little late, it seems!

Padre Kennedy had a can of bacon and divided it between three of us tonite. Man!! It sure was good!

Feb. 3, 1944

Have felt very blue and lonely today; leg still paining and fair hunger. Conversations continually turning to food, recipes, etc. Boy, a plate stacked with crisp bacon and about six eggs, sunny-side up!! Jeez! Mc-Nair's birthday (34).

Feb. 4, 1944

Damn! Rice had strong taste of kerosene this morning. Most everyone ate it but I took one spoonful and felt my stomach do a loop, so I quit!

Some more things to remember.
1. The wood-carving craze, using the hard woods nara, camagan to make butt-shooters, knife handles, pipes, knife scabbards. Colonel Powell especially.
2. Familiar sight of Colonel Tom Powell with white beard, and his son, young Tom, with beard at meal time here at hospital.[91]
3. Cutting tobacco.
4. Rolling cigars.
5. Making vinegar out of banana peels.
6. Incident of man smuggling in palay[92] in skivvies, but skivvies come off, and palay spills in front of Japanese headquarters!! Gets 15 days with skivvies tied to beard!

---

91 Thomas Nimmons Powell Sr., lieutenant colonel, Infantry, 61st Division Headquarters (PA). Thomas Nimmons Powell Jr., major, VM Force USAFFE Engineers. In December 1944, father and son boarded the *Oryoku Maru* and were interned together in Japan.
92 Rice prior to husking.

7. Colonel McKeever and Major Miller drinking tea, and eating chow on porch of hospital, laughing gayly and loudly over something suddenly find J guard mad and demanding to know if they are drinking WHISKY!! Shows how the J'se cannot understand our high morale and attitude as P of W.

Feb. 5, 1944

Roy Gray in hospital and pretty sick. Doctors not sure just what it is. He can't keep *any* food down, milk included. Looks like pneumonia in a way. Fifteen more pieces of candy today (2.25 pesos). Hah! The J's classed the "letters we wrote for them into three classes; "A" (satisfactory), "B" (mediocre), and "C" (no good — possibly punishable!). Well, since I was rather uncomplimentary in my letter, I got classed "C"!! Understand about 72 of us are in the "C" club. Some 360 "A's" and the rest "B's." The "A's" were given prizes of *a lemon per man!* Jeez! The nerve of the J's. When the line-up came to get the fruit, the Yanks, as usual started (and succeeded), in putting one over on the J's, and J's kept putting out fruit, ran out and still about 150 men were in line!! The interpreter meanwhile crying, "I'm embezzled!!" Red Cross stuff supposed to have left Manila for here January 30. Padre Lafleur bops Stewart on the nose for calling the Padre "pro-Nip" because of latter's "A" letter.

Sunday, Feb. 6, 1944

McNair gave Roy Gray blood transfusion today. Funny how this gang keeps doing things for one another, even to blood. I haven't shaved since January 16th. Don't know when I will!

R-U-M-O-R-S:

Jan. 5, #333: Yanks in southern Germany, heavy fighting in N. Germany. #334: Japanese bombers w/full load plus pursuit escort leave Davao every day. Many times all do not return.

Jan. 8, #335: Tojo makes speech to House of Peers. Says Jap facing crucial situation, that the Allies are attacking on all points. #336: Japanese still have outpost on Bougainville. #337: Yanks on N. Britain — fierce fighting. #338: Nazis shelling Dover, England from France w/ "rocket" shells. #339: Japanese troops in Manchuria suffering from lack of supplies.

Jan. 10, #340: Germany has surrendered but some of her armies still fighting.

Jan. 13, #341: Bismarck Archipelago ours. Truck Island ours, too. #342: RC stuff to be here in ten days. #343: Rabaul has fallen — now ours.

Jan. 17, #344: Gilbert and Marshall Islands ours.

Jan. 20, #345: Roosevelt at conference in Cairo, says war will be over in 80 days. #346: "Brigadier Gen" Lindberg flying on tour of European countries.

Jan. 28, #347: RC stuff *not* coming in 'cause Yanks too close! (BS!)

Jan. 29, #348: RC stuff to be here next week! #349: Gen Eisenhower in China. #350: Battle in Banda Sea. We lose 2 cruisers, one transport.

Jan. 31, #351: Philippine Islands declares war on U.S. (Hope so — maybe it won't be long now?!)

Feb. 4, #352: RC stuff to be here by Feb. 15. #353: Roosevelt speech — be in P.I. in 50 or 60 days. (BS!) #354: Naval battle off Caroline Islands. U.S. on top. #355: Japan proper being heavily bombed. #356: Russia lost 1,000,000 men in month of January. #357: U.S. troops lose 150,000 men in Sumatra (?!?).

Feb. 7, #359: RC ship in Davao. Stuff to be here soon (15th). #360: Large detail from here to go to Davao to help build barracks for 65,000 J'se coming from south. #361: Work at Mactan rice fields to stop in seven days (Feb. 15). #362: Star men say they will be gone from here between 15th and 30th. #363: United States sinking hospital ships and strafing J fishing boats in J waters.

Monday, Feb. 7, 1944

Roy's a little better tonite, gave him another transfusion, too. Hope he can start eating by tomorrow. Signed pay-roll today — this is, "Deposit in Davao Bank Month!" No cash!

Wednesday, Feb. 9, 1944

Hurray! Roy[93] started eating today and he's holding it down, so we're hoping and praying that the scare is over.

My leg is not paining so much anymore but it is very uncomfortable. Continually feels like boiling water *looks*! Also, the nerves keep giving me the sensation of pain in my absent *foot*! To boot there are the miserable reflexes, which cause the leg to involuntarily jump without my control. Asked Doc today if it'd be OK for Cmdr. Lehman to make me a "platform leg," and he said "OK," as long as I exercise my knee, and don't use the "leg" too much so that my knee will not get stiff. So, we'll see what the future brings. The stump is not yet healed, but it won't be long now. Doc burned it out yesterday with silver nitrate. Also told Doc to stop ordering the MSO4. The last five days he's ordered only $1/12$ gram at nite for me, but it's useless. Don't know what I'd have done or would do w/o Jose Garcia.

Thursday, Feb. 10, 1944

Roy's coming along a lot better today. He's keeping his food down good and has an appetite. Between Mac, Stud, Knowles, Orson and myself, we've been able to get extra things for him to eat. My part has unfortunately had to be small.

Gee, Pete, it's been raining and raining for the last two to three weeks,

---

93   Capt. R. Gray died aboard Hell Ship *Arisan Maru*.

and today I've felt extra blue, downcast, and lonely. So, I got out your letters again and read them thru. But hell — each letter I read just puts me down deeper in the cellar because I sorely felt the distance between us, and loneliness crept over me like a thick fog. Realizing *fully* how much you suffered, kitten, helps me some to keep taking this hell. But good God — this can't go on and see us all live thru this! This futile, uncertainty of waiting, waiting for — WHAT? Yanks? Death? This slow starvation on rice and greens is telling on everyone. If only the Red Cross chow *will get here*, and get here *soon*. It'd raise morale — It'd help strengthen us, and it'd give us new hope and renewed faith.

Friday, Feb. 11, 1944

Woompf!! I'm quite groggy today — feeling just like I've a hangover from too much beer!! Reason? Just some phenobarbital powder last nite and it's the first nite in 26 months that I've slept all nite without waking!

Holiday today — Japanese gov't. 2,000 years old, or something. They issued 40 cigs. per man, some shoe grease per two men (to those with shoes — I got in on this with my one shoe). Also gave the mess a little pork, so we had some pork broth at noon. First pork I've had in over two years! Signed the post cards today, so presumably the cards will leave the island, at least. God, I hope the folks have gotten at least one card.

Feb. 14, 1944

"Will you be my Valentine, Mom?" You'd better 'cause you're the only woman who has command of my heart! My thoughtlessness during past years has shamed me, and from now on, though I guess it's a late start for me, I'll do everything I can to see that you're happy, Mom, 'cause you mean the most to me.

Commander Lehman finished my "peg leg" today, and I got myself strapped into it and surprised myself by walking up and down the ward! Felt odd not to have crutches under my armpits, and I was scared to death of taking that first step or two. But I caught on to it in a hurry and shouldn't have much trouble using it from now on. Doc was quite pleased at the way I was able to handle the leg, and was just as excited as I was, I believe. It does however hurt my leg, since it hasn't yet healed. Also, a number of muscles were brought into play that I have not used in over two years. I can *feel them,* especially in the small of my back.

Feb. 16, 1944

Today at 4:00 a.m. occurred the first death since January 19, 1943. Private Evers died of hemiplegia.[94] Nothing was able to save him. He had many transfusions, and was given plasma a number of times.

---

94 Hemiplegia is paralysis that affects one side of the body, caused by injury to parts of the brain.

Apparently the work in the rice fields is going to stop as far as the Americans are concerned. They've brought the plows in and are now bringing in the carabao. Brought in thirty yesterday.

Well, a thirty man detail went to Davao today to unload the RC stuff, so I guess it's *really true*!! Man, I hope so. I and the rest of us could sure go for some good canned chow. And gee — wouldn't it be swell to get some mail from the folks and Pete! But I suppose that's asking too much of our captors. Bastards!

Feb. 17, 1944

Got candy today; ten pieces for 1.50 pesos. The sun has finally come out some in the last three days. Till then, we'd had rainy days or nites, or both, since the first week in January.

Feb. 18, 1944

Again we come to your birthday, Toots, and I can hardly picture you as the young lady you must now be instead of the young squirt you were when I left. Damn — I'd like to be taking you out for a real birthday party tonite, but I guess I'll have to leave that to the "boy-friend," and *he'd better be* a good Joe, too! So, tho' you can't hear me, honey, I'll still wish you a happy birthday and I sure hope you have one.

The detail came back from Davao last nite, and brought some cigs., tobacco and mail back! The ship is unloaded and the supplies will be here in about a week or ten days. There's many a rumor of what we're to get and it all sounds good. All I'll say here is that apparently each man will get four packages. I'll quote the contents when we get them! But I *am* praying and sweating, 'cause I SO MUCH WANT A LETTER!!

The hospital got three cases of RC supplies today. Supposed to be 252 in all! I looked at the steel-strapping on the first two cases and snorted, "Fooey, Signode!"[95] Then the third case came up, and looking at *that* steel-strapping I could almost *hear* the words, "Hello, Son!" 'Cause it was ACME, and that spelled "DAD," and Dad spelled "MOM," and then I got homesick!! I got one of the ACME fasteners and I'll take it home with me. I'm proud of it.

Feb. 19, 1944

We're waiting for the mail, estimate anywhere from 5,000 to 20,000 letters. It's in Camp but we fear it must be "censored" here and that can take an *awful long time* with the interpreters they have here!! I know the folks and Pete and maybe others have written. We haven't gotten the cigs. yet, but there are Lucky Strikes. Wonder how my old brand'll taste.

The camp propaganda sheet from the IJA states among other things

---

95 Signode Steel Strapping Co., Chicago, Illinois. It was a competitor to Acme Steel, where Hinkle's father was employed.

that "English girls are not wearing underwear!!" (tish!) Also, the U.S. is mistreating the Japanese in the camps in the Tule Lake region.[96] Again, tsh, tsh, *we're* being so *well* treated!! HAH!!

Feb. 21, 1944

A thirty man detail went to Davao yesterday to put up a fence around an airport. I think it is to be gone ten days. The good news today is that a detail is going to Davao to load the RC stuff on barges and bring it up the river, and in about three days it should be in camp! Boy, oh boy — good food in the offing. The packages of food are of two kinds, one of them being marked "Invalid." From the dope so far on hand, here is what each contains. Each man to get four packages.

Regular

2 cans soluble coffee —@ 4 oz.
1 can Klim (or milk) — 16 oz.
1 can salmon — 7¾ oz.
3 cans corned beef — @ 12 oz.
1 package cheese — 8 oz.
1 can jam — 6 oz.
1 can butter — @ 3¾ oz.
7 packs cigs (Chesterfield).
1 package Domino sugar — 8 oz.
1 can luncheon meat — 12 oz.
2 chocolate bars — @ 4oz.
1 can meat paté — 6 oz.
1 package prunes — 16 oz.
2 bars soap (Swan).
1 can opener.

Invalid

2 cans soluble coffee — @ 4 oz.
1 can Klim (or milk) — 16 oz.
1 can salmon — 3¾ oz.
1 can corned beef —12 oz.
1 cheese — 8 oz.
1 can jam — 6 oz.
3 cans butter — @ 3¾ oz.
10 packages cigarettes (Camel).
1 package sugar — 4 oz.
1 can "prem" meat — 12 oz.
2 chocolate bars — @ 4 oz.
3 cans corned pork loaf — @ 3¾ oz.
1 package prunes —16 oz.
8 bullion powder — 10 grams.
2 soap (Swan).
12 vitamin "C" pills.
2 cans ham and eggs — 2½ oz.
1 can meat paté — 6 oz.

That's the forecast. I'll leave this page open for any corrections, which I'll put in *upon receipt of goods*!

February 22

Weighed 122 pounds. Stump still not healed; some pain yet. The detail to get the RC stuff left today.

February 24

Well, all the RC stuff is in camp, and some J'se from Davao came up to inspect it! He opened one of the packages; opened all of the cases; ripped the cigarette packs apart; held the paper over a flame and looked for *secret writing*!! We're supposed to get it when he gets thru "inspecting." It's all inventoried, and out of 2,080 cases of chow (four packages each) only one disappeared. Damned

---

96 The Tule Lake Segregation Center, where Japanese Americans were incarcerated during the war.

good. Of course we haven't received any of the mail yet, and God knows when we'll get it. We threw up our hands at the last rumor — "Letters will have to be copied into Japanese before released!!!!"

Sunday, Feb. 27, 1944
Smallpox vaccine today. We all got bottle of 100 vitamin tablets yesterday (A&D) and began taking them last nite: two a day. The medical supplies are in and the doctors are pretty well pleased. However, more adhesive could have been included. Vast quantities of folded gauze from RC chapters in Tiptonville, Tenn, Meridian, Miss, St. Louis, New York, Crown Pt. Indiana, and a few others. They're starting to put the letters out. So far, some men got eleven, fourteen, twenty letters; so I'm just biting my nails nervously and waiting! Many of the men who received letters were made happier by the fact that the letters were addressed to "Major" instead of "Captain." In other words, they have been promoted by the War Department. Hence, I have another reason for "sweating out" some letters — wonder if it'll be to "Captain WJH??"

NO — we haven't got the RC chow and clothes, etc. *yet*. We're supposed to get it today, but then, who knows?

There's been talk about letters of protest (to the Japanese) about sending this large detail out to work for the Japanese. Major Maeda told Colonel Olson that the Japanese were *not* signers of the Geneva Conference.

Monday, Feb. 28, 1944
Well, the forecast was quite accurate. We got two packages today, one regular and one invalid. The J'se are holding the other packages of chow and "*the Luckies*" for our own welfare, 'cause we have no place to store so much! Well, maybe so, but I'd just as soon have it around me; though I *am* satisfied at present with what we have. And damn it, in *both* my packages I got *Chesterfields*! The lucky ones got Pall Malls or Camels, or Old Golds, or Raleighs. Everybody happy; everybody *swapping* stuff…two packages cigs for can corned beef, etc. I swapped one can of Klim for four butter. First thing I got into was the chocolate, then the cheese and the butter — that's all so far. Everything is top quality, and the boxes are a helluva lot better than last year's. Ham & eggs are Army Ration "K," jam is Crosse and Blackwell & Welches, Spam and cheese is Borden and Kraft, Chocolate is Bakers and Kohlers, Sugar is Domino, Prunes is Calif. Packing Co., butter is Kraft and Company (better than cheese!). Also got the following:
1 comb.
1 Mennen shave cream.
1 Dr. West tooth brush.
1 pencil.
1 safety razor.
10 blades.
1 sewing kit.
1 laundry soap.
½ bar P&G.
1 can shoe polish.

J'se allowed Sanders and gang to put on a musical program today. It was good and also a surprise. Doc started me on various vitamin pills today. Get seven a day plus my regular two "A" and "D" tabs at nite. Camp is very vitamin conscious and badly in need of same.

Tuesday, Feb. 29, 1944
I guess I'll put in writing something that has been in my head for many months and it keeps getting stronger and appeals to me more and more. Yes, I've written other ideas down in my diary, but *this* one is more than just a passing thought. In short, I've been seriously considering going to medical school when I return! It'll take four years of hard study, and two years intern, sure — but so what? Over here I've lost or will have lost two or three years of life *doing nothing*. Why medicine? Well, maybe it's because I've suffered so much. I want to help others from suffering — maybe it's 'cause I feel I'll really like the work. If I do go into it, I guarantee I'll be at school to study. If I do manage to get thru and show aptitude for it, surgery is what I want. At least here's how I figure it. I can try for a year or two, and see how I go, and if I feel I won't make a good Doctor, I'll quit, but I certainly will not count the years as wasted. And besides, It'll be my money and my time and my life. I don't know how well I'll hop this hurdle, Pete, if I choose this path, and *if* you're waiting, and if we click.

Took my "peg leg" for its first walk out doors today, and got along OK. Got pretty tired, too! It doesn't hurt too much except after I take the leg off. I'll soon be healed and I really believe the pain is going to stop!!

March 1
The various and sundry extra and odd items of the RC supplies are being issued by lottery system since there's not enuff for one of everything per man. So far, today, I drew #30 and chose a whole roll of toilet tissue, from a selection of tissue, P&G soaps, GI soap and shaving cream. More coming today. The RC food boxes are absolutely *excellent* and they were well planned and excellently packaged. A 100% improvement after last year. Everyone is well pleased and after all these months of griping, we all express our deepest thanks to the RC. The more I think about it, the more certain I am that the reason we've had to wait *so long* for our RC is — J, not RC.

March 2nd
Today the 650 man detail is leaving for Davao or parts near there. The work is apparently going to be the construction of an airport. Naturally quite a bit of discussion about such a detail, but it's all under duress and the Japanese hold the aces! It may be for a month, or maybe we won't see them again! George Weiland's going. Howie Martin, luckily is sick, so he doesn't have to go. Phil stays, too! Padre La Fleur's going. Patients and corpsmen

gave him box of food in appreciation of his fine help to us here at the hospital. Hate to see him go.

Had ham and eggs for breakfast! Got issued two packages of Half + Half tobacco today. Yesterday in the lottery I drew a little cheap pipe with a curved stem. It says "Briar" on it — maybe so! Looks like "Woolworth stuff," but it's a pipe and I've wanted one for a long time. The Half + Half smells so good that my mouth is really watering now for a pipe full of #79. Cripes — won't that be swell?!

March 3
Got a new shoe today, a little big 8½-D (should be "B"). Damned good GI shoes. Also drew a pair of shoes (my lottery # was #9!) and drew size 11½, 'cause I wanted them for Col. Deter, who has had no shoes and who did not draw a # that would give him a chance to get a pair of shoes. He was quite tickled, so we're all happy

Ed Girzi big-dealed for one towel, one can of corned beef, half-pound of sugar, one pack of cigs. SUCKER! (Example of some of the trades that take place).

March 5
Everyone sure having lots of fun brewing up different mixtures of food. Stuffed egg plant, "salad dressings," etc. I did a little myself, today: made some prune whip, with prunes, Klim, sugar, peanuts and a pinch of salt. Rich?! Boy!!

Looks like another detail for 160 may leave soon. We fear the camp is to be broken up and that we'll go to Luzon. All of which makes us unhappy (don't want to ride on a ship at this time)! Guerrillas around Davao supposed to have been supplied by three large U.S. cargo subs. United States also has G-2 at certain places where they "*fruwaja*."[97]

March 8, 1944
Been playing "knock poker" for cigs. Luck down for first few days. Finally won back 6½ packs today. Since I've last written about RC stuff, there have been various lotteries for different items. Lotteries necessary because only a few items and odds and ends. I got 1 pencil, 1 bar soap, roll toilet paper, and a can of meat pâté. Other items include, 12 sheets (hospital), 1 blanket, 1 mosquito net, plus some *long underwear*(!), a few winter woolen service caps with ear and chin flaps!, wool button sweaters, shirts, sox, hankies, and extra razor (VERY CHEAP) blades, tooth brushes, etc.

March 11, 1944
Supposed to get the other packages soon. Hope so. According to reports, we've heard from the 600-man detail. Things are not going so well for them. Our men are setting up "passive resistance" on their work on the airfield and the J'se don't like it! So far, one of our Lieutenants had the hell beaten out of him, and when it happened the

---

97   Polish for "fly."

rest just stopped work. The J'se were mad and called a meeting with the Americans, and were quite surprised when one of our men stood up and told 'em off!

No letters yet, but I still have my fingers crossed.

Thursday, March 16

Doc has been allowing me to watch him operate, and I have spent several mornings in the operating room. It doesn't bother me at all and I watch every move with a great interest. The med. school idea is still with me, but what will happen when I get home — that's hard to tell!

The J'se are digging L-shaped fox holes around the perimeter of the fence; all the same and in a straight-line.

We're supposed to get our other 2 RC boxes on April 1st. I have enough canned chow left to last till about March 23 (and that's stretching it!).

George Roper back in hospital. A laced barracks bag dropped on his head whilst playing cribbage, and gave him a severe scalp cut!

March 19

Captain McMasters has been raising quite a bit of hell lately. He's in the "booby hatch," with some form of de-mentia. Poor fella, I feel sorry for him but there's not much that can be done to help him. He's not exactly violent, but jeez! He sure raises a racket!!

March 22

Today — Doc Davis's birthday. We fixed up a good party for him. I wrote and fixed up the card. Roy and I set the table with a clean sheet, water glass, flowers and candles, and a side-dish of stuffed egg plant on pechay leaves, surrounded by pork and beans (stuffing included bullion powder, corned beef, cheese, butter). A stew was fixed for him, of corned beef, spam, camotes, okra, egg-plant, onions, bullion and salt and green peppers. Desert was slices of baked squash with brown sugar melted thru it and cheese melted on top. McNair did the cooking. This was served by Remy to Col. Deter, Maj. Davis, Capt. Osborne, and Capt. Rader. It was swell. Ten of us were in on it and we chipped in a pack of cigs. each = carton, and Macner rolled a swell big cigar, and Major Frandsen sent over another pack of cigs. Doc was very pleased and happy, especially as it came as a complete surprise to him. THEN, at 1:30 I developed a fever, and had a temp of 100.6° F. My joints ached and my stump hurt like hell. Smear taken. Didn't get supper.

Mystery — Out at Mactau today, were found numerous bamboo tubes filled with medicines. And there was a letter in one of the tubes! *Where* did they come from? The bottles in which the medicine were packed were unlike any that we have received, and according to invoice, all of our supplies are here. The guards thought they were bombs and tossed them around before opening. Hence, various conjectures are in the making; subs? guerrillas? Stealing? We'll see!

March 23, 1944
Malaria smear = NEG. Another one taken today and also a count of white blood cells. Have quite a headache today, just as yesterday. Stump and whole leg still hurts. Doc put me on sulfanalamide. Right inguinal swelled, but water bottle applied and hot water soak to stump. Second smear negative!!!?!

Friday, March 24, 1944
Feel much better today. No fever. Still soaking stump and have hot water bottle on groin. Guess Doc still isn't sure just what *is* or was wrong with me.

Have not mentioned the various uses to which the used cans and some steel straps are being used for. The strapping is used as handles and the cans as cups and "cuan buckets."

March 26, 1944
Had my right rear upper tooth temporarily filled. Filling OK again. Mac "grounded" today!

March 27, 1944
Seven men escaped today after "bopping" a guard. The men are: Capt. Mark Wohlfeld, Capt. Mickey Ashby [*A line is drawn through Ashby's name*

and in the margin wrote, "came in"],[98] 2nd Lt. A. T. Bukovinsky, Lt. Watson, Lt. Boone, Lt. McLure, Campbell, and Hayburne.[99] They were on a detail, and apparently suddenly decided to take off. Why take off *before* we have received our other two Red Cross packages??? Will regret the RC stuff on April 1st. Much woe about this escape being expressed by rest of camp! They were on the fence detail too. They "got" three J'se guards — at least wounded them in one way or another. It is quite definite that this escape was brought on without previous planning. The J'se guard had severely outraged Watson early, and by 9:15 a.m. he couldn't hold back his anger, when WHAMMO! Most of the seven men were sick in some way. Some had malaria, bad feet, some no canteens, no shoes, no mess gear, and no chow to take with them. Some say there were two Pinos seen in their vicinity. If this is so, they'll undoubtedly make it safely, or if the guerrilla bands are not too far off. Four men from the detail, who did not "take off" are in the "*Chusai*" (guard-house). Among these is Glen Wohler, and if there should be any torturing done to them of any severe nature, Glen may cash in his chips 'cause he has a bad heart.

March 29, 1944
Today, Owata announced that one of the escapees had been shot and killed

---

98   Died on the *Arisan Maru*, October 24, 1944.
99   The Davao camp roster from April 15, 1944, has the spelling "Haburne," while other sources use "Hayburn."

in an abaca[100] field. And they'd have the others in two or three days. The description fits Boone. When US HQ asked to send representative for positive identity and return of body here for burial, there were many tantrums. "It is no concern of yours!" Yesterday, Owata made the classic one when an American asked him a question about firewood. "We are not on speaking terms with the Americans!!" Damn! They've not brought in any vegetables and zest. No work details went out. Later a few did go out, but J'se wouldn't let the kitchen detail have axes with which to chop the wood! We don't know yet just what the J'se are going to do about this escape. Drastic action seems in the offing. Incidentally, a bottle of quinine was found among the clothes of those in the guardhouse. *Salt and rice* promised for supper, but McNair's squash crop has been good and one is being cooked up tonite.

March 30, 1944
Operations that I have watched since March 1.
7 Hemorrhoidectomies.
1 Hernia.
2 Pilonidal Cysts.
1 Removal of left breast (cyst).
1 Appendectomy.
7 Circumcisions.
3 Removal ingrown toenails (hallux).
Amputations; 2nd toe, left, one joint (hammer toe).

---

100   A species of banana native to the Philippines that yields Manila hemp.

The J'se brought in the clothes and glasses of Lt. Boone for identity purposes.

Only absolutely necessary details to work in last three days; Bodega Machine Shop and Japanese Kitchen. No detail has gone out for wood and no operations can be performed because wood is needed for operating the sterilizer. Dr. Yashamura and Mr. Owata made a complete survey of the camp "sorting out" healthy ones from the crippled, etc. At the hospital they were in two classes, A and B; A for those who will be out of hospital in thirty days or less; B for those thirty days or more. Were careful to ask "officer or enlisted man." The entire camp seems to sense that a move is in the offing — a separation of officers and enlisted men, but there has been no info on this yet.

Patients no longer have to count off in *tenko* but those of us who are at all able to, have to sit up as J'se come thru.

For the last few days my thoughts have been with Eleanor. I guess it was brought on by someone whistling, "It's been so long," and that just whisked me back thru the years and my memory became an unruly horse that I couldn't hold back. So, Lady Eleanor, you and I again went to beach parties, MPMA dance, out to O'Henry downtown to see "Snow White," to Harvey Keller's Rathskeller, to Lincolnshire, to Starved Rock, to the J-Hospital, etc. It's been extremely pleasant to recollect these events while lying awake at night as the moon glows thru my mosquito net, my heart repeating, "It's been so long." Oh God, it *has* been *so long* from everyone and thing.

April 1st
Late bulletin by Chaplain Dawson ("The Bull!"). Mr. Owata says: "Americans must not escape because he is responsible for them and cannot protect them when they are far from here!!!" As we expected, part of our punishment is to be "delayed action" as far as delivery of the rest of the RC chow is concerned. We did not get it today as promised by the J'se *before* the escape. WHEN?? Our rations have been cut too. We get rice once a day, and squash and carrots the other meals. Thank God for Mac's garden!!

As I mentioned yesterday, my memories seem to be tugging at my heart more and more. Not just Eleanor, but Mom and Dad, Pete, Walt, Toots and Jackie and all the rest! What is it *but memories* that is sustaining me thru all this, with the fervent hope and prayer that in the future I may experience again pleasantries similar to those of the past? I hunger for memories now. Every nite, when it gets quiet in the ward, I close my eyes and drift off into the colorful sea of memories — and Oh God!, *the memories are so real*! It almost frightens me because I can hear Mom's happy voice, and Dad, whistling. Even in the corners of my memory, Tiny's bark comes to my ears as though she were under my bunk. What shall I call this struggle with my memories? Torture? Yes, torture would apply, because as I live thru my past I fail to see myself returning — returning to go to medical school — for a MA in sociology. But to put in many years of study? No, I guess I want more fun out of life, instead of devoting myself and life to medicine and drudgery. I want to live a carefree life. Life is too short for anything else, I've decided. The pain and hell I have suffered, mentally and physically, has changed my personality I *know*. In short words I presume my philosophy on life from now on can be bluntly stated as, "I just don't give a good damn!" What people think or expect from me will not phase me. It's my life, and these last years have been messed up without my having any control over the situation. The future? IF I EVER GET BACK, I'm going to have something to do and say about my future. Rich, poor, beggar or student, "I don't give a damn, as long *as I feel I'm getting all I want out of life*." People back home better be prepared for a bunch of strange men then — I am not alone in my thinking!

[*Continued on page 188.*]

Escape from Davao
by Mark Wohlfeld

"Seven men escaped today after "'bopping'" a guard." These are the first words written by Hinkle on March 27, 1944. When he named the men involved, Captain Mark Wohlfeld was first on the list.

In this unpublished interview with former POW Manny Lawton, Wohlfeld gives an animated account of the escape. Reproduced verbatim, their conversation changes direction midway through the interview, and the finale to Wohlfeld's escape story is lost to historians forever.[1]

It must have been about midnight, March 26th or 27th, 1944. I had visited the latrine during the night and was the only one in the latrine. I was surprised to find another man coming to the latrine — in what was a 12 cylinder latrine — and sitting next to me instead of up at the other end, depriving me of my privacy. It was Lt. Watson. He was there with his red beard and rags, and thin, and a bandage on his right leg, and a bandage over his left eye. He used a cane when he walked and he looked as though he were ready to pass out.

We sat there, and he says, "Hello." I greeted him. He says, "You're in an escape party for tomorrow." I said, "No I'm not." He said, "Well, I know about you and Booth and Sollenberger, but you're not with them, you're going to be with our escape party." I said, "What makes you think that?" He said, "Well, you just wait and see. Be sure that when you're alerted before the roll call in the morning that you get the stuff you want to take with you, and get ready to move out." So I thought Watson was off his rocker.

I went back to my plank that I slept on in the barracks. During the night somebody pushed me in the side, and then took off down the hallway in the barracks. I didn't know who it was, but it alerted me, and I remembered what Watson told me a few hours before in the latrine, so I did that.

I had my dummy equipment set aside. We all had two sets of equipment in case we escaped. In other words, they would look at our plank where we slept and they would see our mess kit, our little odds and ends, our little trinkets, and figure well, he'll be back to get them. But you also had another set of trinkets, and odds and ends that you kept on your person in the event you did escape. I took what I would need in case of an escape, and at roll call — they called *tenko*. *Tenko* is roll call.

1 Lawton's papers, Clemson University Library, Special Collections and Archives, Mss/Series identifier: Mss 260, box 1, folder 6. The interview took place in 1977. Printed with permission of the Wohlfeld family.

"*Tenko, tenko, tenko*," the Japanese guards out front would call out, with others guarding the back exits. Everybody had to roll out quick and the last man out of the barracks was kicked. Anyone who couldn't get out of his bed was kicked, and if you were too sick to get out, why you just stayed there until you were called off to the hospital — what we called our hospital shack.

WELL, they called, "Fall in," and we moved out to the front of the barracks. There were nine barracks and everyone had to line up in groups of thirty in the front of their own barracks (there were about 100 men in a barrack). The Japanese interpreter, Mr. Tjusekeiwata [*sic*], spoke, "We'll have roll call and then go to the mess hall and promptly return back to your formation." Then the Japanese sergeant (we had a Japanese sergeant who called the roll), he says "*Bango*," (count off), and we'd count off. There's thirty men to an attachment, or unit, and in those days they didn't take our names. We just had numbers, and they didn't care if you were an officer or an enlisted man, but the officers automatically assembled themselves together, and the enlisted men assembled themselves together as we tried to bring some order to ourselves. But it wasn't with Japanese encouragement. They did recognize officers

after a time, though they did not address them as officers.

Then, we went back into the barracks, got our mess kits, and went to the mess hall and got our soupy rice. The rice was watery rice. It was called lugao, like rice soup, and we received a mess kit full of that and a canteen cup full of tea, and sometimes a tablespoon of sugar. We had our breakfast, washed our mess kits, and fell out in the thirty man formation.

The Japanese interpreter then called out, "We'll now have work assignments. Details read off." An American clerk read off work detail assignment #1, and those men fell out. The Japanese interpreter then called out, "Work detail assignment #2," and so the American clerk read off, "Work detail assignment #2 will be under direct charge of 2nd Lt. Mickey Wright. It will be reinforcing a barbed wire fence by digging post holes, putting posts in between the posts presently there." The clerk then called out, "The following men fall out and form in a column of 4s and march to the front gate: Watson, Wohlfeld, Bukovinsky McClure, Haburne, Carmichael, Boone, Buckovinsky."

We formed up in a column of fours, two men trailing, and the work detail marched to the front gate. We halted at the guard shack, and were each issued a shovel from the nearby tool shed. We put our shovels at right shoulder arms, and were assigned four rifleman guards, and one non-commissioned guard with a revolver. Flanked by the riflemen with the non-commissioned officer trailing, we marched off northward toward the railroad tracks.

Watson and Campbell did not tell me how they were going to escape. I knew nothing about it. Just that we were going to escape. I wasn't nervous. It was a game to me — another game coming up. There was nothing to be nervous about. I was trying to figure out what the score was, how I was going to do it. But as far as putting it into effect, I wasn't worried. I relied upon my own reflexes. My theory was that these planned escapes — how many paces a man walks this way or that way — often go astray. The best way to affect [sic] an issue of this sort is to have quick, proper reflexes, and use surprise. A loud shout, like they practice in karate, sets the mental reflexes of your opponent at edge and you have a split second advantage.

So we're walking down the railroad and Watson was marching next to me and I said, "Have you talked to these men here?" He says, "These men are all on the hot list." The hot list was potential escapees. The senior officers kept a list of people who should

be watched so they wouldn't escape because of the reprisals to those left behind. So everyone is on the hot list but they don't know about the escape this morning. So, I said, "We better tell them about it." I asked the Japanese guard if we could sing a song [with the intention of working in conversation between the lines, and to be sure that everyone was in agreement on the plan]. Permission was granted. I started singing;

Mademoiselle from Armentieres, parlez-vous.
This is a day we'll never forget, parlez-vous.

[*As a chorus, the men sang back*]

What are you talking about? Hinky-dinky parlez-vous.[2]

I sang another round, this time inserting . . . *are you ready to go. If you don't do it now, you'll never do it, parlez vous.*

See, this was one month after we received our Red Cross packages in February, and we who had been intending to escape had eaten it as quickly as we could to put strength on us. Usually, you nursed it along a little bit every day, and saved some for tomorrow because of the short rations.

---

2 "Mademoiselle from Armentieres" was an English song popular during World War I. It is famously known by its hook line, *Hinky Dinky Parlez-vous.*

We had eaten the whole Red Cross package within the month, and we knew that if we didn't do something now, we never might do it.

Now one man we banked on was a man who had for months been telling everyone how he planned to escape, and he had all sorts of bizarre plans and methods of affecting [sic] escape, so we sort of assumed him to be the leader, a man who would think things out for us. His name was Carmichael, a naval warrant officer — a big wig. When we saw Carmichael, we felt a surge of strength because he was the man who was always telling us how to escape, how to affect [sic] it, how to serve Uncle Sam.

Now when an officer makes a commitment or an agreement, it's a bond. You don't have to sign a document, that's the theory. So, Watson and I assumed everybody would be in on it. But I'd been in several patrol fights on Bataan where I would lead a patrol, and I would open fire and then I would hear only my own rifle firing. The rest of them had taken off, or taken cover. So I knew that I wasn't going to volunteer to be hero in this escape attempt.

So we marched down the tracks, and after two miles of back and forth, communicating through the song we finally felt that we had the verbal agreement of everyone:

Mademoiselle from Armentieres, Parlez-vous.
Now at the first yasama[3] we're all going to sit down in a circle, Parlez-vous. And you just watch what I do, Parlez-vous.
Remember to stay in a compact circle, Parlez-vous.

[*The Chrous sang back*]

I get 'ya, I get 'ya. Hinky-dinky parlez-vous.

So we halted at the edge of a cultivated area where the jungle began and there was a single strand of barbed wire fence, but the posts were too far apart so there was that much play in the wire that animals could crawl underneath it. So the Japanese sergeant gestured that now the job is to dig out the holes in between the posts.

This was a Monday, so we only worked a half day. And on a Monday, you could wear your good clothes, which in our case were long trousers — we had blue denims, jackets, and of course, caps. We had been issued some American Army caps from the Red Cross that were used in northern Minnesota during the winter. They were wool lined, but we tore the lining out. They looked similar to the fatigue caps of today. We had shirts — not shirts, but the denim blue blouse that the American

---

3 Japanese for "wait here."

Army used at one time. The Japanese issued them to us.

At the first *yasama*, we were assigned off on which posts we were to dig holes in between. We were digging for about an hour and then it was about 8 o'clock. Suddenly, instead of watching our presumed leader, the escape artist Carmichael, they were watching me; perhaps because I was a senior captain. I looked at the Japanese sergeant, sort of waved at him and said, "*Yasunde kudasai*," which means, please give us a rest. "Oh," he says, "Okay, okay." So we stopped working. I says, "Always keep your shovels with you and let's form into a compact circle." So we formed into a compact circle and began singing *Mademoiselle from Armentieres*; some of us singing, while the rest talking. I said, "The idea is that when we're in a compact circle, the four riflemen and the sergeant are going to have to watch us, and they will be rather close because they have a very poor regard for our combat effectiveness. We were debilitated anyway, and no one has struck a Japanese in the last two years. So, at my command I'll say, 'Let's go!' real loud, while some of us are still singing *Mademoiselle from Armentieres*. We'll rush the guards, and take their rifles and ammunition belts, but don't harm them unless you have to. And then we'll head off into the jungle northward, across the tracks, toward the high ground where, with luck, we'll run into Filipinos." We presumed that we would run into Filipinos, but we didn't know for sure. We kept singing *Mademoiselle from Armentieres* for five more minutes and then went back to work. And I said, "The next *yasama* we do this."

It was now close to about 9 a.m., so we worked for another hour and then I asked for a rest. "Okay, okay," said the sergeant.

Now, Carmichael, this great leader of ours, he had gotten the word around to seven of his buddies to move twenty-five yards away instead of forming a compact circle. That left Campbell, Watson and myself. So I'm thinking, Holy Christ! What have I gotten myself into here? And Watson's jacket is full of medicine and he's got it hanging on the barbed wire. All they had to do was hit the thing and find it full of medicine — illegal medicine that friends of his stole from the medical store. See, Watson had been an enlisted man from the 31st Infantry. He was also a gambler of great renown and knew all the enlisted men because he'd been made an officer from the ranks. He had contacts — he knew everything. At that time he had an exceptionally high IQ and was real sharp. Doesn't impress you that way today, but at that time he was very sharp. He knew all the correspondence that went through our higher headquarters and he knew just what was transpiring. He's got everything, and it's hanging on the barbed wire.

Now we have to think of something else. We have to break out and escape now because we couldn't go back into the prison camp. Watson's medicine would be found. I would be found with this knife made out of corrugated iron and sharpened up. You couldn't do any stabbing with it, but it was good for slashing. So there are two riflemen watching the group twenty-five yards away, and the other two riflemen are watching us, with the Japanese sergeant in between. That meant that if we jumped the two guards near us, the two guards near the other group would have a field of fire at us, and we had to engage them in fire, and we didn't know the condition of the rifles if we did disarm our two guards. It would be quite a gun fight.

So we called to the other men, singing *Mademoiselle from Armentieres, parlez-vous,* and Carmichael says, "Fuck you, you go on yourself. The hell with you, we've changed our minds." I replied, (singing) *"You can't change your mind, parlez-vous."*

The Japanese guard then says, "Time up." So I said to Watson, "Now look, we're going to have to do this ourselves. The three of us, we're going to have to do it during the next break, because it's mid-morning now, and if we don't do it now we never will." So Watson, Campbell, and myself, we all agreed. Campbell was also a former enlisted man and was now a 2nd Lieutenant. In fact, this was an officer's detail — we were all officers.

We went back to work for an hour and I saw that there was some fruit growing on a tree near the edge of the jungle. Now, there's a barbed wire fence and then a 2x2 foot wide drainage ditch just the other side of the barbed wire fence, and twenty paces beyond that the jungle started. At the edge of the jungle was this fruit tree. It had star apples on it. So I said to Watson, "The best thing to do is you go in there with one guard and clobber him, and Campbell and I will engage the other guards here." So Watson says, "No, I want you to go." I said, "Watson, I been on plenty of patrols where I fired first and had nobody to support me. You're going to go, and besides, you're the one who has the medicine in his jacket."

Next, I ask for a *yasama* and the guard said, "OK." So everybody stops working, and the other eight men got as far away from us as they could without making the guards feel that something was cooking. Now you'd think that a fellow American officer would co-ordinate and assist each other. But they're scared shitless at this point. They are in over their head. They were paralyzed. But they were talking about this for months and months! All of them! All except Wohlers. And so I said to the Sergeant, "Let one man go up and get fruit off the tree." So the sergeant says, "No." I said, "Look, we're working hard," and I had to pan-tomime what I was saying 'cause he understood very few words of English, and me very few Japanese. So, he said, "Okay, okay." So I said, "All right Watson, grab your shov-el." Watson said, "Aren't you going to go," I said, "No, Watson, you're going." He said, "All right." So he took his shovel and the sergeant says, "Sukoppu[4] down." I said, "No, he needs the sukoppu. He has to reach for the star fruit with the sukoppu." He said, "All right, all right, okay."

Now, Watson went between the barbed wire strings and he went west of the barbed wire across the little ditch there. One rifleman followed Watson through the barbed wire. Another rifleman went through the barbed wire and posted himself between it and the jungle, twenty paces away. Wat-son and the guard made their way through the palm fronds, toward the fruit tree, and then disap-peared. Suddenly, there was what sounded like the cracking of twigs, a loud snap, and the hollering for help: "Tasukete! Tasukete!"[5]

The sergeant gave the other guards the order to open fire. All three riflemen and the sergeant were firing at the exact point where Watson went into the jungle with the guard. So that meant they were firing at their own man as well as Watson. But it was inaccu-rate fire. One of the riflemen was right beside myself and he was fir-ing. Campbell, who was near the sergeant, was depending on me to do something and he says, "Christ sakes, Wohlfeld, you yellow son of a bitch! Do something to help Watson! Watson's in trouble!" But I couldn't move. I mean even with all the mental preparation, I was frozen. This Japanese rifleman was only about a yard away from me and I couldn't bring myself to do anything. So Campbell hit the Japanese sergeant in the mouth with the edge of his shovel, and the blood and teeth sprayed over on to my bare skin (I had my shirt off).

That woke me up! I took my shovel and aimed at the Japa-nese rifleman, who was fumbling around, trying to put another clip into his rifle. I took my shovel, aimed at his head, swung as I would a baseball bat, missed, and landed

---

4 Shovel.

5 "Help! Help!"

on my hands and knees. I stayed there with my eyes closed, waiting for him to put the muzzle of his rifle in my ear and blow my head off, but he couldn't get the bolt closed on his rifle! In fact he dropped the clip of ammunition that he was trying to put in, and started to beat me across the back with the barrel of his rifle. Well, he did this three or four times and I thought, well, enough of this! I turned around, tripped him, and knocked him down. Then I grabbed my shovel and again, swung and missed his head, but gouged him deeply in his left bicept.

We were both covered with blood now, and covered with flies because as soon as there was any blood, feces, or urine about, clouds of bull flies jumped about. As I rolled around with him he slipped away by rolling underneath the bottom strand of barbed wire. Still bleeding, he then got stuck in the drainage ditch because his ammunition belt got stuck in the mud. I rolled underneath the wire and I got stuck in the mud right near him. We were facing each other, only an arm's distance away, and I couldn't tell whether he had closed the bolt or not, but the rifle was in his right hand and he was moving it around, pointing it toward me.

Five-hundred yards away the other American prisoner-of-war gangs were working. One was a sugar cane gang, and the other a railroad section crew, and both were guarded by Japanese military personnel who immediately opened fire. The bullets began bouncing all round, and beyond, into the trees, knocking off bark and leaves and twigs. Birds flew up in clouds and monkeys were jumping about with great confusion. Although this lasted a little more than sixty seconds, it was a life-time in a minute! That's just what it was! The fire was intense and I was hit through my left bicept, but it was numb and didn't hurt at the time.

Bukovinsky was lying on the east side of the barbed wire fence and he was taking cover, lying as flat to the ground as he could, as were the other eight men. Campbell had, although I didn't see it, taken his shovel and struck the Japanese sergeant, and then disarmed and taken the rifle away from the other Japanese guard. The last I *do* remember seeing was Campbell beating the guard with his rifle. The rifle butt had broken off at the small of the stock, but it was still attached to the sling. Every time he swung the barrel, the broken butt followed, attached by the sling. He beat the guard several times. It was in a quick flash that I saw this, and then he must have gotten through the barbed wire, but I didn't see him get away.

Meanwhile, I'm still in the ditch with the Japanese soldier. He's pointing his rifle at me and his left arm is pulsating blood. His cap was off, revealing a crew cut, and with a pained expression on his face he's trying to bear his rifle on me. I could see the bolt was closed, but I didn't know if there was a clip in or not. I said, "Bukovinsky, get up and get this rifle away from him." He says, "I can't. They're shooting at me." I says, "Everybody's being shot at! Get up, you god-damned Polack son-of-a-bitch!" He says, "Don't call me anything like that." I said, "Get up you dirty coward." So he says, "All right, all right, I'll get up." I said, "Now take his rifle out of his hand." He says, "All right." So he got up, and was so confused that instead of crawling under the barbed wire, he goes to the post, climbs over the top strand and gets his pants caught on it. As he untangles his pants he tears them. Once free, he runs over to where I am and grabs the Japanese rifle and says, "Oh, my God, my God," and starts running for the jungle. He took the rifle, but he didn't do anything to the Japanese! He just took the rifle out of his hands! Then Bukovinsky gets hit in the side and I says, "Good for you, you Polack son-of-a-bitch!" He went down, but then got up again and ran into the jungle.

Now I'm all alone and the bullets are flying all around, and I'm bleeding and I had blood and pieces of teeth all over me and the flies were everywhere. I jumped up, grabbed this Jap, and got out of the ditch first, while he was stuck with his ammunition pouch. I took a handful of mud, put it in his face and kicked his head down into the mud. I then got more mud and piled it on his head. As I took one last look before going into the jungle, I saw everyone down on the ground, flat, with their hands over their heads — nobody was moving. But what did happen was that after I went in the jungle, still being fired at — bullets flying everywhere, knocking pieces of bark off the trees, Haburne and McClure got up, crossed the barbed wire fence, and ran into the jungle in the confusion.

So there's Bukovinsky in the jungle, Haburne in the jungle, McClure in the jungle, myself, Watson, and Campbell. But we were all separated.

I ran into the jungle, breaking my way through the underbrush. I was so exhausted and my left arm was pulsating when suddenly I came to a clearing. There before me was a big bog. I didn't know how far it went; it might have gone for a hundred yards or a hundred miles, but I had to get across. I couldn't skirt the edge of the bog because that would be too

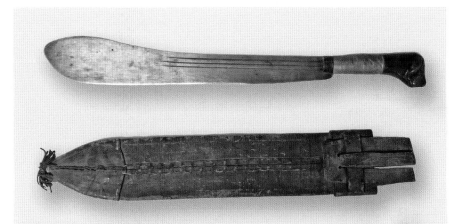

This machete is believed to have been carried by Wohlfeld during his time as a guerrilla fighter on Mindanao. Upon returning from the war, Wohlfeld donated the blade to the New York City Fire Museum. He had been a member of the department before the war and returned to his prewar company, Engine 34, later serving with Ladders 7 and 129. He was detailed to headquarters in 1949 when skin lesions from his service in the Philippines reemerged. Fireman Wohlfeld retired on August 16, 1953. He remained in the US Army Reserves and retired at the rank of full colonel. Colonel Wohlfeld passed away in 1978 and is interned at Arlington National Cemetery. In 1979 the Mark M. Wohlfeld Memorial Medal was endowed by American Legion Post 930 of the FDNY. *New York City Fire Museum collection*

close to the clearing. The bog was still covered with fog as I walked down a ways. The fog was about six feet off the ground, and under it I saw one of these long hardwood trees that the natives had knocked down to span the bog. It was a huge thing, and they had cut off all the branches. So I went to the base of the tree which was about three feet in diameter.

I was so exhausted at this point, and wished it would rain because in that season, the rainy season, it rains for one hour and then doesn't rain for three hours. Then it will rain again for an hour and won't for another three. If it rains, it comes in furious gusts through the jungle and makes so much noise pelting through the leaves that you could move a tractor in there and you'd never hear it.

I make about twelve foot steps on down the top of the trunk, shovel in hand, and then slowly lowered myself into the water, which was only six inches deep, but the silt was at least six feet deep and I sank right into the mud. There was a small branch stub near me and I held that with my wounded left hand as I gathered water lilies around my head, putting my face as close to the tree trunk as I could. The water was clouded from my having stirred up the silt, but fortunately it started to rain and the firing stopped.

As the birds started to come

back I felt I would just hang on here and rest for a while 'cause I knew a patrol would be out after me. But how long would it take the patrol? It would probably take about an hour for them to get organized, and then they would have to go two miles by railroad car that was pulled by a diesel engine on the narrow gauge tracks.

I must have fallen asleep as it started to rain, which washed the muddy tracks off the top of the tree trunk. Suddenly I was startled out of my sleep. I still held the shovel in my right hand and my wounded hand was frozen, clamped around that little stubby piece of branch sticking out of the trunk of the tree. Insects were around my head, but I still had my cloth cap on to protect myself. Suddenly I heard Japanese chatter. "*Koko des*! *Koko des*!"[6]

They had found where I had snapped palm fronds going into the jungle. They located that and then they went into the jungle and found my tracks. "America, comebacku. America, combacku," they cried out. I thought to myself, geez, I don't know what's in the jungle, and they have this code of bushido.[7] Maybe because I fought my way out they'll forgive me, and let me go back to work.

Now, as I was just thinking to myself, maybe I'd better give myself up, I hear, "America combacku," followed by an automatic rifle; rat tat tat tat tat. All the birds rose in clouds and he hollered again, "America, comebacku." And then there was the sound of a couple of automatic weapons; pat, pa pa, pa, pa. "America, combacku." Fuck you! I thought, and then in full packs[8] and wearing split-toed *tabi*,[9] they bounded across the log at about five pace intervals before disappearing into the fog at the far end of the tree trunk — they were very athletic. When they stopped at the far shore of the bog, they again called out, "America, comebacku," and then pat, pa, pa, pa, and I wonder, what the hell? They're trying to lure us back and here they fire a weapon. It didn't make sense.

I then figured, well, if I follow them, I'll be much safer than if I go the other way because I may go around the bog and meet them coming around. But first I better wait because I remembered from the Battle of Bataan that when the Japanese small units move, they had an advance guard of the main body, and then about five minutes later, two or three more Japanese follow along. They use them as

---

6   "Here it is!" Koko = here. Des= is.
7   The code of honor developed by Japanese samurai.

8   A full pack carries 7 kilos of rice, fourteen dried fish, a box of red salt plumbs, crackers, and some sugar and salt, and will sustain a Japanese soldier for about fourteen days.
9   Split-toed outdoor footware.

their getaway messengers and rear guard. So, I waited about five or ten minutes and, sure enough, two more Japanese came along. They jumped up on the tree trunk and followed on across it, disappearing into the fog at the far side.

After they passed, I waited, and a big rain came; one of these warm water rains. So, I took the shovel, pressed it down into the mud (I had an awful job getting out of it because it was like going into a vacuum cleaner) and tried to get back up on the tree trunk. I was really worried because my left arm was so stiff, but at least the bleeding had subsided. Earlier I had tried to put a tourniquet on it by holding some leaves over it and taking some vines and tying them around, but it made it bleed worse. So then I applied some mud and placed a leaf over it, but it came off when I went into the water.

I got up onto the tree trunk, went down to the far end across the bog, took off my trousers (I didn't have a shirt you know. My shirt was left hanging on the barbed wire) and washed the mud off. I had shoes on and socks and I washed them too.

I put my trousers, socks and shoes on wet, and then looked for a trail to follow. First, I saw the wide trail that the Japanese patrol had taken, a man-made trail. I went along it for a ways and then looked

for another. I came across a diagonal trail. This was an animal trail, narrow and wasn't as beaten down as the trail the men had made, the patrol had made. So I followed the animal trail figuring that it would take me somewhere near, deep into the jungle away from where the search party was operating.

At this point in the interview the conversation abruptly switched to the Battle of Bataan. Talk of the escape did not resume.

Traveling along jungle trails, Wohlfeld, Watson, Haburne, and McClure eventually made contact with General Wendell Fertig's guerrillas and joined their forces. As for the other men mentioned in Wohlfeld's story, Lt. Boone was cornered and killed by the Japanese on the second day; Bukovinsky and Campbell joined guerrilla forces in Zamboanga; Captain Wohlers, Lieutenant Wright, and Warrant Officer Carmichael, for reasons known only to them, did not get away.

April 2nd

Finally took the roller bandage off the stump, and now have just a "4x 4" gauze taped on. Practically all healed — still open on the ventral side, distal, but not much. This week should see it healed. PAIN, however, still present and therefore I have suspicion that Doc may operate again, and this somewhat frightens me.

Our chow is vicious. The squash of course is a large percentage water, and besides the individual ration is small. Result — continual, gnawing hunger. God, why don't the Yanks get here?

New J'se camp commander arrived late this afternoon and inspected camp. He is a *Chosa* (Major!) named Takasaki. Tomorrow may bring more news of him. He is short, pudgy, a "humane-looking" face with treacherous eyes, and a chest full of ribbons. He seems, and probably is, severe, and an old soldier. We shall see!

Had long talk with Phil last nite about philosophy of life as mentioned April 1st and we pretty much agree. It's sure swell to have him to talk to because there's a wealth of understanding between us.

April 3rd

De-bugging for bed bugs in hospital today and tomorrow. We wind up in discussion of what would we prefer to have — bed bugs or lice!!! Bed bugs win!

April 4

New J'se commander "invited" or requested Col. Deter, Col. Olson and barracks leaders over to his house for dinner last nite, and all went well. They had beer, egg foo yung, chicken patties, cigs. My! Takasaki said he was sent down here with specific orders for violators of discipline, and that he hoped relations between us would be better. Said that for those who followed the orders of the J'se, he would try to do all he could to help them. Said he's probably here for duration. Said he's open to constructive suggestions, etc. Nothing said about RC chow?

Big load of firewood came in.

April 6

The one thing on everyone's mind is the fact that we again will *eat good* for awhile, beginning Saturday! Major Takasaki yesterday stopped a truck loaded with supplies for our boys at Lasang. He made them unload and he checked the weight and found it to be about ⅓ light!!! Thereupon he strafed hell out of the J'se in charge (Tagamini) to the extent that Dr. Yashamura was called to render first aid!! Apparently our new boss will be *severe* but *just*. We hope.

About three hundred letters were put out yesterday, but still none for me. I'm beginning to feel desolate. Still have hope tho.

April 7

Well, since tomorrow is the "big day," (RC), everyone is madly trading off items of chow and cigarettes for their preferred foods. Yours truly is no exception, and after I make all my deals, I'll record them in my diary. The medium and basis of exchange is cigarettes, and prices are quoted according to cigs value. Klim, of course, is highest at twelve packs. The rest is graduated down. I'll record them tomorrow.

April 8th

Received only one box of RC chow today. Reg box had:

3 cans corned beef.
2 cans Spam.
1 can Klim.
2 cans coffee.
1 can fish.
1 box prunes.
½ lb. cheese.
2 bars chocolate.
7 pks cigs.
4 cans butter.

Made several swaps and wound up with no butter, 3 jams, 2 cheese, 1 coffee. We were also issued 1½ packages of Lucky Strikes per man. First Luckies I've had in two years, and they sure taste different and good! People trading their chow as if hell wouldn't have it! At 8 p.m., Mac, Mc[101] and I each opened a can of corned beef and waded in! Jeez, it was good!! Incidentally, Lucky Strikes can be swapped off at the rate of one pack of Luckies for

two of any other! So even in prison camp, "it's Luckies, two to one."[102]

April 12th

For the last few days we've had a poker game going for cigs., and brother, either someone really loves me or I'm a rotten player!! So far, it's cost me one can of Spam, one jam, and one chocolate bar!! Guess I shouldn't gamble, but I enjoy playing and as a gambler I'll take the losses and the winnings, if any. The poker is an outlet for nervous energy and I've lots of that!! But luck is certainly against me — I've never seen such a run of cards. Can't draw a thing and my hole card in stud is usually a 2 or a 3.

No mail for me yet.

There's something in the air!
1. They check on the bunks in the hospital to see which ones will fold up.
2. Doctor Yashamura makes *thorough* check on patients in hospital, and has "First List." On which list is written the name of Walter J. Hinkle?
3. A clothing exchange was recently made.
4. When Lt. Ulri was asked about replanting the camote field, he said, "There will be no need." So off-hand, we suspect a *move*, with sick staying here. Also, the four men who were in

---

101   First Lieutenant Joseph E. McNair.

102   This is a reference to advertising genius George Washington Hill's advertising campaigns for Lucky Strike. It captured 38% of the US market between 1925 and 1935, using catch phrases that included "LSMFT, Lucky Strike Means Fine Tobacco . . . so round . . . so firm . . . so fully packed . . . so free and easy on the draw. . . . With men who know tobacco best, it's Luckies — two to one."

the guard house (from the detail the escape was made), were released "on probation" yesterday.

The Major also made the following remarks.
1. "Only I know what their sentence is."
2. "If no more escapes are made, I guarantee with my neck to protect the lives of the American prisoners of war."
3. "As to the ditches and fox holes which face south, think what you please."
4. "Any more escapes and I have my orders."
So, that's that. However the ole boy is a soldier and I think relations will be much better here.

Filled out post card #7 to send home. I sent this one to Dad, at Acme; said I haven't heard from home. Maybe my address is new and maybe my cards have been lost, so this way, if it gets there, I know Dad will get it! Message, as close as I recall was.

Well and waiting. Invest all my money in stocks Dad's judgement. You write War Dept. request raise alot. Maximum, my authority, possible retroactive. Don't worry. Greetings your birthdays. Love you, Pete, family, Harriet, Gus, Acme, Cecilia, Wally.

The request to the War Department probably won't work but it's a try. The "greetings" to give the folks approx. date of writing. Hope they get it!

April 13th
Two years ago today I left Iloilo on that B-25 and landed in Mindanao.
Joe Garcia and I had lunch together. Baked a can of salmon, rice, hot peppers, salt and cheese together, and had prune-raisin whip and coffee for desert, and Luckies to smoke. It was a delicious lunch — one I would go for at home. Winning back some of my cigarettes. Was able to buy back my Spam, and that was the only can I really hated to part with. I'll swap it with Phil for corned beef, because I prefer corned beef.

Phil and I figure that there is definitely a move coming our way in the near future. Phil thinks it may be the sick and wounded going out on exchange, whereas I feel that the well men will leave here possibly for Japan, and that the rest of us war "derelicts" will remain here. We're afraid, almost for certain, that we will be separated — in which case one of us may reach the States before the other, and if that happens, he who does get home will get in touch with the other's family.

April 14th
Two years today under Dr. Davis' care. No news. Visiting officer to inspect this afternoon.

April 15th
Issued one bar soap, one pack tooth powder, paper and one "towel."

April 16th
Three years today since I left home and that nite at the airport is as vivid in my

mind as if it was last nite. How long? Doctor Yashamura came thru again checking on who would be in the hospital as a patient and how long. Mine was "permanent." What's up??

April 17th

Three years today since I first saw Pete after such a long span of years, and here we are again — with years between our meetings. Various men have come over to see me and give me their addresses, "in case I should be going home soon."

Hinkle's musette bag, referred to in his entry for April 18, 1944. *Kurt Stauffer collection*

April 18th

The feeling is very strong that the sick and wounded are to leave here soon — destination unknown, but exchange seems to be the theme. People are checking their belts, and musette bags. Double checking their equipment. Several packs of sterile surgical instruments and thirty days supply of pharmacy goods are packed (???). Rumor had it that we were to get our RC stuff today, but so far — no.

April 19th

Well, here's the dope as we have it, and from these items we are doing all our speculating, and most of us are of the opinion that *we are in for an exchange*!!!

1. Doctor Yashamura has been dashing in and out of the hospital during the last week, and it always has to do with a "list." Plus his close check-up on the patients.
2. The hospital underwent a change of patients the other day, and most of those in here now are in some way *disabled*.
3. The pharmacy had to pack up 40 days supply of medicines.
4. Surgery packs three bundles of sterile instruments.
5. Five typewriters are packed.
6. Doctors checking on their bags, belts, etc.
7. Orders to hospital, "No operations, except absolute emergencies, no admissions, no discharges."
8. Rumors have sprung up that 120 patients, 30 MCs, and 6 Doctors to leave here soon.
9. We are to get our RC today.
10. I talked to Colonel Deter and he says he believes I am to leave here soon.
11. Everyone is victim to this undercurrent of excitement and each is trying to figure things out. And out of all of this, the one thing we are becoming more and more certain of is *the patients are going to move*. But *where*? Is it really that lost dream of prisoner exchange coming true? God

grant this — I want it to be this so much that I can't find the words to write it. I am getting things ready though, because there may just be something to this, and if there is, maybe I'll be singing "California Here We Come," by the time my birthday comes.

April 20th
We didn't get the RC today, but we expect it tomorrow. A large supply of medical supplies were sent somewhere today. I won 19 packs of cigs today, and inasmuch as cigs are scarce, I get paid in chow which = 2 packs Luckies, 3 packages Half & Half, and 3 cans of corned beef. So, I'm finally ahead of the poker game, *and eating good.* Still sweating out the move. Rumor has it now that we are to be moved to some small island. Some believe it to be the small isle next to Samal in Davao Gulf — but I do not believe in this rumor at all — it just doesn't make sense. If that's as far as we are to go, why not just leave us here?? If it is to be small isle, more likely it would be Portuguese Goa in the Indian Ocean, or King's Island off Japan.

Won 21 packs of cigs. in poker today, which, plus the can Blackie paid back, equalled 6 cans of corned beef!! So I'm doing OK. The game has temporarily ended since I seem to have placed everyone in bankruptcy!!!

The J'se are packing and loading everything!! Blankets, clothing, scrap iron,

bottles, shovels, etc. We can't figure the thing out at all.

Three years ago today was the last time we were together Lady Eileen, and a beautiful day and evening we had — both ignorant of the hell that lay ahead for you, first, and then for me. Will they *ever* give us a chance to find our hearts? Will they let us live? And who is the "they?" God bless you kitten — I hope you're well and happy as you can possibly be. I had a wonderful dream about you last nite — it was so real that I was heartsick when I awakened and didn't find you near me. You and I were together, and your Mom and Dad were with us. Where? I don't know, but it was the closest to Heaven I've been. And it's dreams like the one last nite that keep the hearts of those of us here in the camp alive — keep us in hope that some day we will return.

April 21st
Colonel Deter read off the list of those going today, and we each have numbers. Mine is #4 as it appears on the list. Roy is #30, Mc is #40. I don't think Dr. Davis is going, and I'll certainly miss him if he doesn't go with us, wherever we're going. I sure hope he will go, however, 'cause Doc has absolutely been more than a doctor and surgeon to me. He's been father, advisor, encourager, and hope itself. Colonel Deter read all 99 names off. Said he believes we will be given only a [*entry ends abruptly*].

April 22nd

Shaved my goatee off today, after not shaving it for three months. The doctors were to get the information as to which ones of them were going — but this has been put off for "3 or 4 days."

They shipped the rest of the RC boxes of chow out today, so now everyone is rumoring that the whole camp is going to move. This I believe is true, but it won't happen at the same time is my guess, and I don't think the rest of the gang will leave this island. Naturally, I may be all wet. April is my month — hope I get the long awaited break *this* April!! No mail for me as yet, nor for Howie or Phil. Guess we're *dead*!!

April 23rd

The extra boxes of RC chow were put out today, and the items were raffled off. For a change, my "raffle luck" was *good*, and I wound up with one corned beef, one salmon, and a half-pound of cheese! Outside of this there is no other news.

April 24th

The J'se asked Major Rotherham for two cooks and four KPs[103] to go with us on the trip. Rumor has it that we're to leave today. And there are all kinds of conjectures about *where*!! Yesterday — we received a communication of the War Department concerning P of Ws and pay, promotions, etc. In short, I guess

I'm still a 1st. Lieutenant — at least my pay is still going on.

Colonel Deter makes announcement, "Some of the J'se officers are very angry because the men on the other side of the fence are packing. So remove all evidence of packing around your bunks. Get the trunks out of the aisle, etc." His surgery was busy all day today packing up their gauze, instruments, etc. So we're still going tomorrow — I'm sure. Received no mail as yet. Some of the fellows tonite received 5, 7, 9 letters apiece, and *all* I ask for is just *one*!

April 25th

Well, this nervous tension for waiting for the word to move is getting to be quite trying. Wish it'd come off. The news is quite persistent about our having taken Pelew Island. If this is true, then we have a chance of getting out of here soon, and I think we won't need J'se assistance.

April 26

Things seem at a standstill as far as an immediate move is concerned. The move is coming — no doubt in my mind. The J'se are all packed and surgery is finally packed. What's the delay??

Gee, I wish I'd get a letter. I hunger terribly for news of Mom and Dad and Pete. Lost 2.40 pesos at Bridge.

Friday, April 28

Still no action on the move. Doctor Yash. is to look us over again today.

---

103 "Kitchen Police" or "Kitchen Patrol" work. Men detailed to KP would work under the kitchen staff by washing dishes, peeling vegetables, and performing other kitchen duties.

Tomorrow is the Emperor's birthday, so I don't look for a move till about Monday. No news. Mail keeps coming in but still none for W.J.H.!!

April 29
The Nipponese Emperor's Birthday!! And thru their magnanimity we were given six green bananas per man, one (or two) lemons per man, one coconut between two men. Wish him many unhappy returns!

May 2
No startling news. Packing up of various and all things *still* going on. Don't know when we'll move. Chow is no good. The "list" has been altered and those "who can't walk" any distance have been put on. Officers allowed one foot locker and one bag. Enlisted men allowed one barracks bag. No bed rolls. So, excitement is the order of the day. We're packing what junk we have and hoping for the best. I'm beginning to feel that we're going to wind up in Manila, or at least on Luzon and no further. Others are convinced it's an exchange. All of us have our fingers crossed. Sold one can corned beef for 20 pesos. Irving Mandelson gave me 5 pesos, and Thane Hooker gave me a pack of Philip Morris! Figure still be a good idea to have some cash on hand, for wherever we go. And I think we're really going to Bilibid, in Manila. Gave Phil a case of corned beef as a birthday present (June 24) for we may not be together then. Howie Martin gave a long line of stuff to tell his folks in case I should be exchanged.

May 3
Today was a holiday, since it was the Japs "Feast for Boys" or some such title — when all the little boys fly kites and banners with a picture of the carp on them as symbol of strength, etc. So — not being able to get any carp to feed us, the *?! Japanese bring us twelve sharks, each between four and six feet long! Cripes — it was necessarily boiled and it was really bad!! Damn — what a taste! Mc and I split a can of corned beef, and that was *much, much* more edible!!

No news on move. Japanese announced that the two men who escaped from Mactau some time ago were killed by natives. (Why tell us *how*?) Japanese RC relays message from U.S. War Department about insurance. According to it my application for the extra $5,000 (to make a total of $10,000) is ineffective because it was put in *before* April 19, 1942. I don't understand this! At any rate, I'm filling in a card here and will send it to Wash. DC.

Losing my "cuan" at bridge!

May 7
The move is coming tomorrow or next day is my guess. Everything out of surgery has been packed; the big light, sterilizers, supplies, tables, chairs (metal). The pipe lines are all being picked up. In short, the J'se are stripping this place of EVERY DAMNED thing that can be of any possible use anywhere! It

seems the move has been delayed, and all I can make out of it is that the Yanks caused some trouble for them between April 10–15, and that it occurred not too far from here. We still don't get any reason for this move nor any hint of where we'll go. 9,000 letters distributed so far, 1,000 left. AND NONE FOR ME! Makes me damned blue. Must be jammed up in Tolay or in Manila.

RUMORS:

March 23, #364: Pelew being bombed by our planes. #365: Pelew is ours. #366: Argentina declares war on U.S. #367: Italian fleet divided three ways to Allies.

April 1, #368: United States has Shanghai, Canton and Hong Kong. #369: United States attacks in South Pacific going good.

April 18, #370: 180 invalided and some medical staff to leave here.

May 6, #371: RUMORS HAVE BEEN CRAZILY RAMPANT LAST 2–3 DAYS. We're going to be moved to GOA. #372: We're going to be moved to Bilibid. #373: We're going to be exchanged. #374: The Yanks have taken Truk and Pelew. #375: The war is over!! #376: The Nazis out of Russia.

May 8, #377: We are to go to Spain, then U.S. #378: Captured Yanks from Wake & Guam have been exchanged. We're next. BS!

May 8

Three years in P.I. today!! Jeez, that's a HELLUVA long time to be away from home!! I miss everyone and everything back there. Nothing today on the move. Won back 4.20 pesos in bridge. Still out about ten!! We've been playing bridge from A.M. to P.M. I'm getting better. Now use Vanderbilt 1 Club system. Stump still not quite healed and the nerves give me a great deal of trouble at nite.

May 9

Eight months today since my foot was amputated. Amazing thing happened last nite — J'se issued us three packs of twenty cigarettes *each* plus one cigarette!! Either they cleaned out the bodega or a ship came into Davao. Chow has been *very* slim and *bad*. Rice — small portion — ounce, sometimes twice a day. Other meals are cassava "glue." Salt rations VERY small. No meat.

May 10

Another "anniversary" today — two years as P of W.

May 12

Wrote post card to Vet. Adm. today for increase in insurance to $10,000. Dad "beneficiary" because first $5,000 was that way. Had first real blow-up with Mc over a bridge hand. I had 5½ and he had 1, and lets it die at "two hearts" when we had three or even six NT[104] *cold*! Jeez, I was mad! I quit!!!

---

104 No trump. Hinkle suggests that they had a very strong hand and should have bid but did not.

Weather has been very hot. Quite a bit of air activity lately. Bombers from Davao daily head north, apparently loaded and on mission. Perhaps the J'se waited too long to move us. Who knows? Rice we're getting *per man per day* equals 300 grams.[105] Bet with Murray Day. He says, "We will be free from the J'se on or before August 24, 1944." I say, "No." Day's 10 gallons pure maple syrup against my $30.

May 13

Today, my stump began to give me some trouble, and a fever started. Had three "knots" in my right inguinal region. Doc put me on sulfadiazine and gave me MS ⅛ gr. The "diozene" really hit me and gave me the damndest headache I have ever had! I got no sleep at all.

Read over Pete's letters again today and got very homesick and lonely. How extremely well do I now understand her hospital trials and pains. But how will she ever be able to understand mine? These conditions will never sound possible to people in the States.

Tomorrow is Mother's Day and it means that I'll be thinking of you just that much more. Lord knows you're ever foremost in my thoughts, and I'm ever worrying for fear that you don't know I'm alive and well. I know you're probably nervous as all get out, but

please don't get too many strands of silver in your lovely head over me. But what else? You are my Mom — nothing will stop you.

May 14

Mother's Day. Had to miss Mass today, Mom, but received communion. This headache is a killer. Doctor has me soaking my stump again! Ate no breakfast or lunch and little supper.

Maybe we won't move! A detail unsacked 90 sacks of camotes two days ago. These had been sacked two weeks ago "for our trip." We're getting more to eat. The air activity has increased even to *nite flying*, and all planes go north. We can't figure things out. The general opinion is that the Yanks have thwarted the J'se somehow.

May 17th

The last of the mail was put out today. So — thru 10,000 letters and none for me. I've felt very sad and disconsolate over the fact, but it won't do much good to grieve over it — should just undermine what strength of will I have left, and the good Lord knows I need everything I have left to see me thru this damned ordeal. It's becoming more and more of an ordeal too, as time goes on the food situation is abominable — no variety and so tasteless.

May 18th

Our "nut-house" has been busy the last few months. First was Captain McMasters, but he is OK now after

---

105   There are 390 calories in 300 grams of cooked white rice. The average adult male needs approximately 2,500 calories per day to keep his weight constant.

he got some letters. Then Baxter, Hall, and last is Colonel Carpenter, who is continually raising hell — howling like a dog — screaming, yelling, hysterically laughing, and most of it at nite. It's hell to listen to, and tears at your heart too.

May 19th

Good Lord — now there's word running around that we're to have a chow cut! We get lugao in the morning now, and every other day is to bring three "Purple Death" (camotes) meals. Our salt ration is very meager. Oh — we did get a little meat today, but only because two carabao got into a fight and one of them broke a couple of legs.

Air activity has slowed down a bit, which may mean something or not — who knows? I know all of us are becoming desperately sick of being POWs under these people! I know we're anxious to live again — as human beings — to laugh, and mean it — to escape our cynicism.

May 20th

Breakfast = Lugao, salt, + "B."

Have I ever described our hospital? It's about 110' by 22', is about four feet off the ground, built of wood, and has a galvanized iron roof. There is a planked lumber ceiling between the floor and the roof, which helps a great deal in cutting out the intense heat of the roof. The building is full of cracks and is dirty. Ants, bedbugs, cockroaches, lizards, and rats overrun the

place. At one time the building was apparently white-washed — perhaps when it was first built. At intervals of about ten feet there are large windows with beat-up screens (of no use!). The beds are made up of army cots, wooden "slab" beds, wooden "slat" beds, and three or four beds with a rattan woven surface. Most of us have mattresses of capok, which are really as hard as wood itself. The main ward has an average of 70 to 80 patients. With isolation and "annex" wards it runs about 98 to 102 patients. The surgery is the most respectable part of the hospital, or was until the J'se moved everything out! And have I ever mentioned that the IJA considers sick and wounded soldiers as a handicap? — men who need only half as much chow, etc.? True!

May 21

Excitement and trouble this morning. Major Charlie Harrison was on rope detail[106] and got into an argument and fight with J guard. Guard probably slapped him. Harrison grabbed the rifle from him and laid the barrel firmly on the J's neck! This caused a swell-wound and had the Nip screaming and yelling and other J's took it up. Harrison took off into the compound with rifle. Nips after him with bayonet. Harrison dropped to knee and leveled rifle at Nips, but gun not loaded and

---

106   When planting rice, a prisoner would stand at either end of the earthen dike with a rope stretched across the paddy between them. From the rope hung strings at 6- or 8-inch intervals, and spaced across the paddy were prisoners pushing a rice seedling into the mud at each string.

only a "click" resulted when trigger pulled. Nips finally overpowered Harrison and took him away. The guard around the fence was immediately increased to one guard every fifty feet. So — we don't know what to expect now. Harrison will probably have the hell beat out of him and camp in general will probably be punished. But it sure showed how the Nips are, and how easy a task it would be for us to take the camp. And I think the Nips are continuously worried about that.

May 22
Roy's Birthday. Straight stuff on Harrison: On rope detail, everything calm, guard bothering no one. Harrison suddenly grabs iron bar and beans Nip, grabs rifle, and runs out. Nip at main gate levels rifle at H who does same to J's. Latter jumps behind a board. Harrison pulls trigger but not loaded. After socking Nip, Major Croger and others kept him from further assault. Nips finally overpowered Harrison and took him away. Camp Commander (IJA) questions whole detail. Detail made to sit cross-legged all day. Harrison reported in Ward.

Today shot was fired at Blackie Grossman and guards immediately surround compound. Blackie was in prohibited area, behind latrines near fence searching for edible greens. Shot missed.

May 23rd
Today the J'se made rectal exams on all the enlisted men except those on hospital list — check for dysentery, typhoid, etc.. This means only one thing — a trip to Japan or Formosa, and men are getting jittery. Patients and Medical Corps not examined. The doctors on the list to go with the hospital are Davis, Osborne, Jackson, Ruth, Barty, Hawk, Col. Deter, and Capt. Rader with main group.

Hungry, hungry all the time!!

Thursday, May 24th
Colonel Olson, Major Schaffer, and Major Traeger in guardhouse to "mediate" over Harrison incident. Col Stubbs (a no-good) is Camp CO. The J'se took Major Harrison to Davao for Court Martial, which undoubtedly means curtains for him. Too bad.

Doctor Yashamura to check over patients today. Had about two spoonsful of rice and fish per man at noon, plus dipper of "squash-camote crap." Never, so help me dear Jesus — never will I again be hungry after we get out of this.

Doctor Yashamura made his check just now and brother it was a long check! Stopped at my bunk and instead of going on as he usually does, he began asking questions and I began to sweat. He was going to send me to permanent quarters, and about then I really did sweat. But Dr. Deter, Davis, came to bat for me in a grand way, and stressed the difficulties of getting around on crutches to get my chow, go to the "Chic Sale Salon," etc. The result was, "Mark him permanent quarters but he can stay in Hospital." Naturally then did I sigh with relief!!!! Ten out of the hospital, seven in. I stay. Played "bingo" all day.

May 26th
Chow is quite poor. White rice and salt mostly. Last nite and tonite we had a *little* bit of tuna. Rice ration very small. All guards on duty now with fixed bayonets. IJA medics who take roll-call at hospital wear pistols, and two guards with FB[107] are with them. Suspicion is that Major Harrison has already been killed. Arises from remarks made by guard during ration issue. When questioned as to why one ration less he said, "One American *inai*[108]. . . no, no, not eat."

May 27
Damn this life! More and more I feel it getting the best of me. Sometimes I feel so desperate and nervous that I fear I shall go mad, as several have already. My nerves are continuously high strung, and my temper breaks loose at the slightest thing. I'm so tired of everything here, and especially the food and boredom. Then, too, the vulgarity of so many of these men gets me down. I've been unable to keep from it, hence I fear I have absorbed some of it. I know my vocabulary has increased in cuss words and phrases and they have become a part of my speech. You just can't keep

from it. Lord help me if I ever get back to decent society!!!

Damn it — I sure miss my piano and music in general. In evenings, after chow, I lay back and spend at least an hour every nite just whistling and humming the tunes I know and knew. It's amazing how much I have forgotten. Can't for the life of me remember the introduction and middle of "Tales of Vienna Woods"! And that's just one. Besides this point, everything I think of brings memories of one kind of another, and invariably I wind up with a greater heartache than when I began. "I'm Sorry for Myself!" Maybe that's it — I dunno!

May 29th
Colonel Olson and crew released from guardhouse on 27th. IJA announced that "Major Harrison died from his wounds." So much baloney.

May 30th
Tobacco situation now like that of chow: ACUTE — none in "PX." Am continually reading anything I can get my hands on, and since January have kept a list of books I read.
Zorro, by Johnston McCulley.
Consultation Room, by Fred Loomis.
Dodsworth, by Sinclair Lewis.
Born in Paradise, by A. Von Tempski.
The Man from Glengarry, Connor.
Rebecca, by D. du Maurier.
Murder on Thursdays, by ?
Ann Vickers, by Sinclair Lewis. (No end in book!)
It's amazing to hear all of us men con-

---

107   Fixed bayonets.
108   People around the world employ euphemisms for "dying." One that is equivalent in Japanese and English is *inai*, which means "to be gone" or "he is no longer with us."

tinually talking about food! No matter what the conversation, it ALWAYS ends in a discussion of food. Someone will sigh longingly and say, "Gee — I wish to hell I could have a big plate of fried chicken." Or — "Man, wouldn't about ten hamburgers and five bottles of beer go good!! NUTS! (They'd be good too!!!) Colonel Gregory just said, "I could eat a boiled owl."

June 1

For some reason or another the J'se allowed us to have two carabao today, so eating was a bit more of a pleasure today! IJA had U.S. detail leaders and camp administrators over to lunch today. "Thanks for helping us with the camp."

Doctor Yashamura again inspected the 200 some enlisted men who previously had the stool exam. They are apparently going to leave here as a work detail. Phil was dropped from their list, since he is not very fit for work. They're sacking vegetables again, and a lot is leaving the camp for Davao.

I lost 25 pesos at poker and .95 at bridge today.

June 2nd

Filled out postcard and sending it to Pete. Message reads;

> Words limited. Future so indefinite. Hope you are waiting but feel it not fair to you. You must judge course for your happiness. Have no right to you except love. Pray you now well, happy. Send nothing, don't worry. Love to

your folks. Send love, notify mine. Ever loving you. — Wally.

June 3rd

The IJA seem to be rushing the post cards! They came this morning and had us sign blank cards! Why? Apparently the move must be very near.

June 4th

The move seems to be more and more imminent — at least so we feel. They're putting up floodlights around the "parade ground." Only thing I figure is a move at nite. Must be an inspection party coming — we have *meat* for tomorrow! Lost at poker game again!! Damn — in debt. What the hell!

June 5th

We got the word tonite — we leave tomorrow morning at 4 for . . . ? Hustle, bustle, packing. No sleep. Kitchen put out all the chow on hand. Dogs and cats are cooked up. Gardens stripped.

June 6th

Our shoes were removed, and we were *packed* into trucks; made to stand, blindfolded and roped to each other about the wrist and waists. The journey was about 25 kilometers in the hot sun. Anyone who was suspected of peeking or talking to his neighbor was promptly beat over the head with rifle butt, bayonet or club. Hospital patients received no different treatment, and I was forced to stand during the journey. At the end of the journey we were forced to march about half a mile. Two of us, who were on crutches were at the head of the column. There were about 1,200 to 1,400 of us — loaded on to a small stinking ship which had been used to transport coal. It was *filthy* — about size of a Great Lakes Steamer. Aboard ship, greeted with a long wooden ladder that had been lowered into the hold. Each man stepped up to the ladder, turned 180° around, and then cautiously descended down the ladder to the floor of the hold below. In our particular hold, we had over 600 men. Patients received no special considerations. Litter cases shoved into the hold also. Their method of packing us in was this: First, all available space from bulkheads to hatch was jammed with men — elbow to elbow, and breast-to-back! The Nips then ordered, "Sit down." All passageways were filled with our men. Appallingly hot. After ten seconds in the midst of the stink and heat of the hold, my face was as wet as if I had just dipped it in water. A number of the men sick, adding to the already foul atmosphere caused by the excessive crowding of sweat-bathed humans. The noise, too, was as complex as the air. Souls in hell could not be expected to undergo much worse an environment, or suffering.[109]

June 7th

Ship still anchored. No smoking below decks. A Red Cross Package per man was issued. Twenty men at a time allowed on deck. Rats running over us at nite!

June 10th

Upped anchor at 11:30 a.m., underway, go to Davao Bay, anchor! Take on ice, vegetables, IJA troops and equipment.

June 11

Still anchor. IJN collects all life-preservers, *they're* wearing them topside. Won 22 pkgs. cigs (or equiv) at poker yest. & today.

June 12

Four a.m. up anchor, underway, but not before Japs change number on the smoke stack. Ship unmarked.[110] Two 37mm guns set up: one fore and one aft. Apparently in convoy. Some say 33 ships. Looks like we're going Zambo way. Convoy actually about five ships. Two or three sweepers. Have slight diarrhea. Won 20 pks. today. Hugging shore very closely all the time — shore on starboard — J'se apparently feared our subs in these waters. Guards on top deck with rifles pointing into the hold. Anchor at 7 p.m. in cove. I would guess we're near Cotabato. Wrote note — put in bottle. Will drop overboard first chance.

---

109 Portions of the hell ship entries are from three pages that Hinkle later wrote describing the journey.

110 Beginning in the early 1940s, the International Committee of the Red Cross recommended that belligerent countries transport cargos of POWs separately from cargos of war materiel. The IRC also recommended that ships carrying POWs be marked with the owner's national flag, painted prominently on the port and starboard, and illuminated when traveling at night. None of the belligerents in World War II agreed to the IRC's recommendations. Their reluctance was based on the assumption that their enemies could not be trusted and would use prisoners as human shields to cover contraband goods.

June 13th

4 a.m. — underway. Good weather. Anchor 7 a.m. Parang. Dropped message. We were permitted to swim in the sea, over the side of the ship; three minutes per man. Anchor 7 a.m., Parang.

June 14th

2 a.m. underway. Rain, some sea. Apparently cutting across bay. Order out to throw nothing out ports. Makes it hard on washing mess kits. Streams of perspiration poured from our bodies at all times. The depth of our position [in the hold] meant that no moving air would pass across our bodies. Yesterday poker; won six packs, one fish, one can pork, half can coffee and two bars soap. Anchor 7 a.m. Zamboanga. Yesterday poker won 6 pks, 1 fish, one can pork, ½ can coffee, 2 bars soap.

June 15

At about midnite Col. McGee escaped over side of ship. Guard fired from BAR, but guess McGee made it OK.[111] All topside ordered below.

Daybreak — all still below. Looks like we're to lay here today and nite.

10:45 a.m. underway.

June 16th

No anchor last nite, kept running. Lt. Wills went over port side last nite about 10 p.m. (while ship moving) and there was some shooting! I heard him hit the water, and heard two

---

111 POWs were permitted to come out of the hold and use toilet facilities built over the edge of the ship's deck. At midnight, while the ship was anchored 400 yards off the Zamboanga City docks, Colonel McGee went on deck, approached one of the toilets, dived over the ship's side, and plunged into the ocean. After swimming underwater straight away from the ship, he surfaced and saw the water was glowing as though lit by a searchlight on the moonless night. When bullets from an automatic weapon struck the water just beyond him, he swam underwater again. When McGee surfaced all was quiet, and while looking around realized that it was phosphorescent particles that lit up when disturbed — marking his every movement. McGee stopped moving and floated with the current toward Zamboanga City, located at the tip of the Zamboanga Peninsula in southwestern Mind-

anao. Zamboanga means "mooring post" in the language of the Sama-Bajau people. They inhabit the Sulu Archipelago, which includes Mindanao as the northernmost island. Their name for the peninsula refers to tidal action that twice daily causes the current to reverse direction. This allows a boat visiting the tip from "up" peninsula to come in on the current of an outgoing tide, moor at the tip, and return on the current of an incoming tide. With previous knowledge of these tidal effects, McGee timed his escape to coincide with the returning current. After drifting for quite a while, he began to swim across the current to reach shore. When McGee turned his head to check his direction, his face nearly struck the outrigger of a Moro fisherman's vinta. McGee grabbed the outrigger, looked up at the startled paddler, and called out, "Americano, Pettit Barracks." McGee had served in Zamboanga City at Pettit Barracks as a Moro Company Commander before the war and knew the city and its neighborhoods well. While still on the outrigger, McGee offered the boatman a reward if he would take him to a place that was familiar. The boatman agreed and helped McGee up over the side, cramming him down in the boat's bottom with the evening's catch. On shore, McGee made his way along the edge of the city and to the mountains beyond, where, with the help of friendly Filipinos, he was put in contact with American-led guerrillas fighting on the peninsula. McGee lived among the guerrillas until September 1944, when he embarked on a mission to aid POW survivors of the torpedoed *Shinyō Maru*. The survivors were forced laborers from the Davao Penal Colony (see Hinkle's entry for March 2, 1944) and were constructing an airfield near the village of Lasang when the Davao Penal Colony was suddenly evacuated in June. Of the 750 POWs who were aboard *Shinyō Maru* when it departed the Davao Gulf in August, only eighty-two survived the torpedo attack. McGee arranged for the submarine USS *Narwhal* to pick up the survivors and take them to Australia. One of the survivors was Hinkle's friend Murray Sneddon. Friends who died in the attack included Lt. George Weiland and Father LaFleur. Much of this information was provided by Brigadier General John H. McGee in his book, *Rice and Salt: A History of the Defense and Occupation of Mindanao during World War II* (San Antonio, TX: Naylor, 1962).

Volume No. 5 is filled with entries from Hinkle's June 6–26 hell ship journey to Manila. The entries were written on the unprinted inside surface of cigarette package wrappers. *Hinkle Archive*

screams. Ship did not stop. Went over port side and they kept firing till he was apparently out of sight. We don't know if he was hit or not. Helluva thing laying there and hearing those shots hit the water just outside the port. Roll call this a.m. So far no punishments. Making good time. Now only 20 men at time allowed topside for smoke. One allowed in each latrine. 2 on deck waiting. 4 or 5 men take all canteens of their companies topside for filling. Chow has been cut. Guards are strafing and bayonet jabbing the men topside. We're jammed to beat hell here in the hold. The odors are vile, morale high, Should hit Cebu tonite. Can't smoke down here, so I've taken to chewing cigs!! Anchor Cebu 6:30 p.m.

June 17th

Disembark. Marched to old Fort San Pedro. Jam about 575 men in building 90' x 40'. Rest of 1,200 outside, exposed to sun and rain during the day. Chow late. Bodega floor dirty w/grease. Many men forced to leave baggage w/clothes and chow behind. I have all my chow, one change of clothes. Am filthy. All ships suddenly pulled out of Cebu about 20 minutes after we disembarked. Rumor of air raid warning.

Sunday, June 18th

Suddenly realized this is Dad's birthday. Maybe we'll be together next year. Hope you're well and have a happy day. Keep taking good care of that swell Mom of mine too. Dagos-

tino and Morelli caught with stolen goods (RC chow). To be punished later. So far I have lost no chow. Have given some away today to celebrate Dad's birthday. I gave a can of fish to Roy and Mc, Veatch; Doc Davis and I split can meat pate. By golly — it's Dad's Day too! Have another drink Pop! Water problem. No washing. Have not washed since June 5. IJA asked Colonel Deter if any men were too ill or weak to travel. If so, they to be left behind. Answer = "No." We can't figure out next move. I fear more walking. If so, and too much of it, also fear I'll never again see Chicago. We're worse than cattle in a dirty pen. Two small rations rice daily. Rice scorched. Morale still good. Medicine low, almost all of it had to be left on ship. Lot of sore eyes, prickly heat, diarrhea. Must be careful of all personal belongings; stealing rampant. Water carriers allowed semblance of "nurse bath" when getting water (no chance for me!!). This place certainly is picture of fictional prison camp. Small old Spanish fort, formerly USAFFE HQ. It's stone wall around, one gate, one bodega in the small court. Many IJA troops. Saw motorized units and cavalry with damned nice looking horses. Air activity slight.

June 19th

God! What a hell-hole! It rained last nite and our bodega was jammed — no sleep. MS ¼ gr. Work detail of 400 men out today to load and unload ships. Seem to think we leave here tomorrow. Still ahead in poker. Flies here are *terrible*. Jumpin Jiminy I've *never* seen or felt so many flies. Our filthy, smelly, sweaty bodies — the portable latrines — the piles of empty cans. All these draw flies. Prickly heat has taken a firm hold on me and Jeez how it itches. My eyes are giving me hell from lack of sleep, sun and dirt. Great life.

June 21st
Major Jackson and I took bath out of 5 gallon bucket, also shaved and Sure felt lots better. Fifteen days w/o washing. Have not changed clothes since June 6, except that today I put on clean G-string after bath. We move to ships after chow today. Wither away??

To ships — underway 3:00 a.m.

June 22nd
600 — small hold. No ports. Two shelves [levels] and no one let on deck. "P" line, crap line, chow line, etc. Air bad. All beginning to physically weaken. Fever and malnutrition. Cases of dysentery spread, since we had no facilities (other than our precious canteen of water) for washing mess kits. Some pork was fed to us, and this caused an exceeding amount of diarrhea. Physically filthy and desperate. Rats of all sizes darted over our bodies at night, and bit a number of men. Bed patients suffering miserably. The number of those unable to find strength to stand or walk increased rapidly and startlingly. Nerves shattered; fist-fights over a

mere spoonful of rice. Sleep with great difficulty. Men unable to control their bowels. The stench in the hold abominable. Skin diseases flaring up. Still, the Nips will not relent. Rice was again cut in ration.

June 23
Anchor Manila Bay before midnite. Hot. Incident of watches and lighters. Shakedown for same. Cut out one meal, one issue of water for some.

June 24th
Still anchor here. None let on deck. Lieutenant Willard Weden and Private George Kohanski deathly sick. Nips would not allow our doctors to take these two men on deck, where fresh air would have been so extremely beneficial. Our group in a deplorable state of weakness, and extremely unruly. Nerves frayed. Phil's birthday (in another hold).

June 25
Still anchor. We're irked. Sleep great problem. Everyone uncomfortable. No wash. Little fresh air.

June 26th
Manila Bay, still at anchor. 6 a.m. Lt. Willard Weden died; fever, cause undetermined. Kohansky now in very bad shape. Am now worried about Phil. Why *do* they keep us below here in the bay? At about 8:00 a.m., our doctors violently raged at the Nips, and warned them that if we weren't removed immediately from the stinking, burning-hot,

disease-ridden hold, deaths would rapidly take place of many men. Guess Weden did not die in vain: we disembark at 11:00 a.m. at the old Pier #7. Here patients loaded on trucks (Weden on my truck) and the others marched to Bilibid Prison. Manila like a ghost city; few cars or horses, mostly bicycles. Much IJA equipment was visible, along with fox holes and old damage unrepaired. Arrived at Bilibid and assigned to SOQ (sick officers quarters). It was like heaven!! I had a shower, a shave, and a clean dressing. All friendly, and the hospital was run entirely by U.S. Navy personnel. It was clean, efficient, with high ceilings, a concrete floor, barred windows, flush toilets, showers, running water, and 5 hot plates in the ward — and still plenty of room. Drs. Langdon and Barret on ward. Tom Bell here. About 70 officers in ward — still plenty of room. The rest of the able-bodied DPC[112] going to another camp. Probably won't see Dr. Davis or Deter again. Chow here is light, but three times a day. We were up at 6:15, and lites out at 10 p.m. They have mail and some personal pkgs ready for us. Nice and quiet, with a good library — books were always invaluable. That was the day we heard the news; U.S. in France and Marianas.

Bilibid Prison — Manila
June 30, 1944
Have not had time to write in diary — when not too busy, too lazy!

Getting pretty well met here, and like it fine. Doctor Davis, Capt. Osborne, Dr. Deter, etc. went to Cabanatuan on the 28th. Keeley (Major) and Belinky (Capt.) going with group of about 1,500 to Japan, expected to leave tomorrow. Everything is run quite efficiently here. The discipline is fairly well maintained, and sanitation is fine. The hot plates in the ward are quite the thing. My coffee and ham and eggs have tasted much better hot. There is mail, and there are personal packages waiting to be distributed to us!! I have mail!! Thank God, in a few days, *I* will hear from home! Lieutenant McCown worked on the mail and told me I had alot of it. He didn't know about the packages, but now I know there is mail. Expect a package and hope there's chow in it. Oh boy, Mail! Hope they put it out soon. It's fine here, 'course I can get out and get some exercise. Not muddy, no slippery boards. It's quite a large place. We now have about 75 officers in the yard. I pay a stipend of 1 peso/week for laundry. Here we'll get paid every month and allowed to spend so much in a commissary. Chow well seasoned, well cooked, but small rations. Had shakedown of baggage yesterday and they were very thorough. I lost a few letters from Mom and Dad, and some papers and notes. Luckily, I hid my diary, address book and map, or I would have lost them. Many did. I had to talk fast to save the rest of my papers, letter from Pete and telegrams. Got 'em through! And so ends the busy, dirty, trying and tragic month of June.

---

112   Davao Penal Colony.

Doctor says I'll probably be operated on (nerves in stump) in a while; after stump area gets a bit stronger. No more drainage. Have stopped taking any dope at nite.

July 1

Ah, me — this has been a gala day!! I'll change my birthday from July 30 to July 1!! Yes — I got my personal package from Mom and Dad!! It was still in excellent condition, except for two things; the tooth powder broken and all over; the candy had melted to some extent and leaked out a bit. Everything else OK. The malted milk tabs are melted together, otherwise fine. You did fine, folks, and sure do thank you and appreciate everything. I've been wondering why you didn't put in cigs or tobacco or pipe, or canned chow, but I figure the RC must have put out certain restrictions. However several men got boxes of chow only, so we can't figure it out. Getting my old harmonica tickled the hell out of me. Glad you thought of it. The cards are a boon too. All in all, I'm satisfied with everything. The only thing I can't figure out are the two pillow cases!! The candy, though sticky as hell, is delicious — I sure hankered for it. The other things are certainly needed. I'm chewing gum right now and getting a big kick out of it. The pencils and clippers from Dad are swell. Thanks for managing the personal touch via "Pitts, Rolls and Lewis." It was just like hearing you say, "Hello, Son!" And Mom, thanks so much for St. Anthony — it means so much to me. You've made "the kid" as happy as can be — the happiest he's been in over three years. Words can't express the joy and thanks I feel. I thank the good Lord for my two swell parents, and this is not the first time I've given Him such thanks. Xmas in July! Hmmm — I can just see the two of you talking over the contents of this box, but I'd best stop here — I'm getting too homesick now!

July 2

Japan detail of 1,000 plus men left today at noon. Many of my friends left — hated to say g'bye!

Am sharing what little chow I have with Lt. Miller, since he did not get a box. Wish the folks had sent some cheese, chocolate, cocoa, or Nescafe and pepper, but then how could they know how little of those things we get from the RC. Gee, some kielbasa would have been swell! Met an old Pole, name of Wolf last nite — a 69 year-old. Born Warsaw — served in Russian army. In Philippines was 15 years a chemical engineer. Speaks *czysta*[113] Polish, and says same of me. Whole conversation in Polish. Surprised myself!

July 4

Inspection by two-star general.

Results of X-ray shows some infection still present in spicula and tibia, right to end, which is needle sharp.

---

113 Clear, or pure.

I definitely need a clean-up job and so I suppose it'll be coming up soon. Mail not out yet. May begin tomorrow. Candy all gone — swell while it lasted. My "melted malted milk" just started to ferment immediately! But good! Chow in this camp sure is tasty, even tho ration is small. Since we've been here, eight days, among the meals have been: carabao and green beans; beef bones and mango beans; two fried fish days; two issues of papaya, avocado, peanuts, coconuts. Lots of grease used here during week's meals (good). Quite evident that the Doctors here feel they're from Jesus, but they're doing a good job, so let'em strut. Hayes, the camp CO seems to me to be tops. Swell man.

Well, diary, here's an entry I never expected to make till I was no longer a POW — I went to a movie tonite!! Yes, Judy Canova in "Puddin Head." True, the movie itself was corn slapstick — it stunk! But it was good to see America again: clothes, cars, men and girls. Quite an experience after 2½ years.

July 5
Doctor Smith, Chief of Surgery, visited me. Looked over stump and said in week or ten days, they'd probably operate. Waiting to give scar tissue chance to strengthen.

July 6
Red letter day! Today, I finally received my mail. 20 letters from old U.S.A. 17 from Mom and Dad,

2 from Uncle Jack, one from Shirley Marvin. It was sure swell. Excited? Cripes, I wanted to read fast, then slowly, make 'em last longer. Eleanor's marriage to Frank came as a sort of a shock — still can't get over it. And a kid! Jeez! Sure glad Dink and June are married, that's aces. Elated about Pete's recovery, but have feeling of foreboding about no letters from her, and just a few lines about her from the folks. I have strong feeling that she's married or engaged. Even if so, good luck gal — don't blame you for not waiting. Best news of all is that Mom and Dad and Grandma and all are in good health. And I'm proud of my new superintendent — "That's my pop!" Thanks for the swell photos. I'm very, very happy at having gotten word at last, and now I hope you'll pay no attention to my last post card! But then maybe you'll never get it! Well, guess I'll let the mail rest for now — I could write pages about my feelings.

July 8
After having fixed up enough paper for this diary (#5), I can carry on with my writing for a while longer. Yesterday, besides mail day, was commissary day and I got some onions, garlic, pepper, and salt. It totaled 5 pesos. Beans and coconuts didn't come in. Yesterday, I also got a chance to play a piano, and from now on I shall have every Friday evening to play. Piano's rather rugged, but I can get some practice and enjoyment out of it.

Back to the mail. Spent half the nite just lying awake thinking over all the news, and the more I thought of Mom and Dad the happier and lonelier I became. Keep saying over to myself, "Gee, Pop's the Boss!" Proud? I hope to die I'm proud. Kept thinking of the change in lines I'll find when and if I get back. Cripes, Eleanor married and a mother of a three year old kid! Kinda staggers me — makes me acutely aware of my age! And Basler a Captain! Jesus — he passed me by in rank, of *all* people. This matter of making time over here and losing out on promotions is aggravating to all of us.

Doctor Waterous has ordered me pair of sun glasses; lenses to be ground to my prescription. He has quite a set up here. Formerly civilian eye doctor in Manila. Now POW here in SOQ.[114] Old office girl allowed in here once a week — takes and fills his orders. Don't have to pay him. He figures after war most of us who get glasses from him will remember the debt. He pays for all of them.[115]

More mail was put out today, but I received no more. I believe there's

still more to come, and I'm hoping against hope that I may get some more. Now I'd like to hear from Pete — get the troubled mind settled one way or another.

Boy — garlic and camotes tomorrow! They sure go good and we use plenty of both. Breath smells like that of a well-seasoned WOP!! But good!

I suspect my operation may be scheduled for July 17, that's a Monday. Just my idea. Incidentally, the convoy of eight ships, including the one with our "boys for Japan" steamed out the other night, and then turned about and came back! We strongly suspect that the action around Saipan — Bonin was responsible for this. The news is so much better this year than it was last year at this time that I'm now looking forward to being home for Mom's birthday in '45, and class reunion at University of Michigan. Boy, that would be swell. Hell, that's only eleven months!

Hmmm — I readily see where I've lost weight. The shorts and undershirt Mom sent me reveal the truth. The undershirt, size 36 that I use to fit into snugly, now hangs loose! Howard, by the way, went to Cabanatuan, as did Phil Brain, whom I miss a great deal. Sure miss Doc Davis too.

July 10

I've something new to think about now — the good possibility of a Captaincy for me. You see, I have in

---

114   Senior Officer Quarters.

115   Major Willard H. Waterous was a US Army reservist and prosperous Manila eye doctor who was allowed to continue his specialized practice during his incarceration at Bilibid. The Japanese and their prisoners had a need for new glasses or repairs, and Filipino technicians brought in the necessary supplies to Waterous from outside the camp. One of his associates, Maxima Villanueva, secured her own pass that granted routine access to the prison. Over the next eighteen months, under the guise of performing optometry work, she smuggled in nearly 180,000 pesos for the prisoners.

my possession an order from General Chynoweth, dated 6 January '42 appointing me to rank of acting captain. Prior to this I had performed duties equal to that rank, and that of Major. Colonel Cain opines that this order is good as gold and that when I return I send a photostatic copy of it to AGO,[116] and that I'll get my two bars retroactive to date of order — pay and all. Gee, that'd be swell. Suggests I also send photostat of report of shooting for Purple Heart under "Meritorious Service" clause. Should get AG at IMA to push this.

Turned in draft for 25-word card — sending to folks. Reads, "Health — Excellent. Message, Mail, package received; thanks. No mail Eileen. Thanks Shirley, Zaleskis. Disregard last message; can use your sendings. Regards N. Jedgine; Mr. Sutliff. Congratulations boss. Love." Hope they catch the plea for chow and smokes.

July 11
News last nite that US has 100 warplanes in Central Pacific, and that we bombed and shelled Bonin group. Hitler speaks about still being victorious. Filipinos advised to be prepared to "fight for their independence." This one I can't figure out . . . i.e. as far as the word "fight" goes.

Gee, I'm sure glad Mom is keeping a scrap book for me. It's very thoughtful and I'd been hoping she did just that.

Tickled to death too, that Dad is taking care of investments for me. Golly, with Dad's new job, and with my $ coming to me, we should be able to make Mom's life somewhat easier and more joyful. Housemaid and travel — if she'll leave it. I know Mom!

8,000 letters in.

July 12
Got myself on the mail detail and have been sorting mail, alphabetically for our hospital, and then do the censor. Naturally saw to it that the "H's" would come to me, and I found four letters from the folks. During the afternoon I managed to sneak the four letters and got them safely to my bunk. The news was swell, but gee, what a let down feeling when I realized that you too, are now allowed only 25 words! Who did it? U.S. or J? More mail coming in too. We're praying now for RC and personal packages.

July 13
Got two more letters today, and best of all Mom's picture. I practically have Mom and Dad with me.

July 14
The post cards have been cancelled. Got coffee and coconuts from commissary today. Five pesos for about 6½ oz. of coffee! Coconuts .80¢ ea.!! The ships with our men on it still in bay. News that we bombed Truck Island, bombed and shelled Guam, and fighting on Saipan. Dewey running against FDR.

116 The Adjutant General's Office maintained personnel records.

RUMORS:

May 26, #379: Pelew definitely ours. #380: We have to leave June 1st.

May 30, #382: Russians on Vistula. #383: The Lasang detail has already left for parts unknown.

June 1st, we get our other RC box here. (I HOPE!)

June 12, #384: We have 200 miles of China coast.

June 29, #385: Germany has asked for separate peace, but J says J will fight on. #386: Japanese ambassador leaves Italy. #387: Japanese admiral says things in SWP "grave."

July 15

News that 2,500 to 3,000 more men to go to Japan on marked ships. Port area detail in, and 800 or so coming from Cabanatuan.

Hear Yanks 50 miles from Paris.

Can't seem to get a date for my operation. I'm getting anxious and kind of nervous. Want to get it over with. I don't seem to click with Dr. Langdon either. Too impersonal, too young. Only about thirty or so I guess. Not like Doc Davis — can't beat *him*.

A gang from here going to Cabanatuan. About 15 from SOQ. Specks, and Bill Prickett going. Mc and Ray stay. Wrote note to Doc Davis.

This photograph of Hinkle's mother, described in his July 13 entry, was found inside the billfold that he carried as a prisoner of war. *Hinkle Archive*

Monday, July 17

About 1,100 men, "Japan draft," left here early this a.m. This is a busy place at the moment — like Grand Central Station. Men coming in, going out; for Cabanatuan or Japan. Men going to Japan will buy any chow you have for all the pesos they have. I sold a coconut last nite for 22 pesos! And this was cheap! All the men going to Japan issued a set of J'se clothes; shirt, long-short (or short-long) pants. Come just below knee with drawstring around calf; fit any and everyone! I have a hunch they're going to send everyone (Yanks) to Japan, except the "PDs" (that's me — Permanently Disabled).

Our gang from Davao now at Cabanatuan is branded as "bad." Result, a 30 day period of "meditation," separation from rest of camp; must turn their backs when "non-Davao" Yank passes them; cannot speak to any other than DPC men.

July 18
Well, Dr. Nelson looked the stump over today and said that the operation will be in two weeks!! DAMN! Reason — he must make sure the scar will not break loose and do any draining. Safeguard against infection. So, I *wait*, I'm *always waiting* it seems. Caught cold yesterday, too.

July 20
Well, got my 28th letter today and it's late news! From Dad dated Jan. 23, '44. Hell, that's only six months old! Glad everyone's well. So, no more 8201 So. Peoria Street! Gee, I'm going to miss that. It won't be exactly like going home now. Golly, I wonder where they've moved to? I hope it's to Beverly Hills, or over East. Guess they wouldn't buy a house out Flossmor way, but that'd be swell too. Well, good pickin' folks and we'll really warm the place up when I return. No mail from Eileen — and that's the goddamnest thing for me to figure out. Her getting married is the only solution to the problem that I can see and she doesn't want to let me know for fear I've enuff worry on my mind now. That's O.K., but I'd like to know. Kinda hope she is married.

Gee, if we should all pull out for Japan, I don't know what in the hell will do with my various "pieces" of DIARY. I've sneaked them thru thus far, but I'm scared to try Japan, and I do hate to think of losing three years of memories and thoughts and facts. It's a problem.

Latest news (rumor) is that our men on the Japanese draft left in a 33 ship convoy. Attacked by USN — 5 ships sunk, one ship with our boys.

July 21
Just another idea for something to do when I get back — a riding stable. Quite an investment but worth thinking about.

July 22
Boy, the news last nite sure pepped us all up and made us feel that the near future may yet be bright. I refer to Tojo and cabinet resigning and some generals taking over. To me, this says that the J'se have suffered too many successive set-backs. I'll be home for Xmas yet!! France is also good news, as is Saipan.

The rainy season is setting in more and more here in Manila, and it's pretty cool.

HAH! We understand that POW in P.I. are to be given the following:
From Ford — one V8 car.
      "   GE — $300 credit.
      "   Budweiser — $100.
      "   Philco — $100.
      "   Greyound Bus — one cross-country trip.

" Standard Oil — 500 gals. gas,
" 50 quarts oil.
" Parker Pen — Pen, pencil sets
" Remington — one typewriter.
" Iver Johnson — one bicycle.
" Hart Schaffner Marx — one men's suit.
" National Hotel Chain — 24 hrs. free service.
" US Govt. — 3 mos. leave/w pay.
    6   "   w/½ pay.
    12 "   w/o pay.

Base pay doubled since June '42. Bonus under consideration. These items are supposed to have been in a letter a Yank PW received at Cabanatuan. Sounds too good to be true and if true must be catch somewhere! But, supposing it's true, the ones that interest me most are doubling base pay (that'd be something!); and the gas and oil, the Ford, GE, Bud, and Philco.

Further dope on Tojo's resigning is quite heartening, and between the lines we read "peace negotiation." Understand that the Generals and Admirals now heading the J gov't are former members of the Konoye cabinet, and this fact should be a considerable driving force toward ending the war. I believe Japan has already realized that she has gained everything she possibly could out of her belligerent actions already, and now wants to end it. Certainly she has bled the P.I. of everything she could, money, foods, iron and steel scrap, vehicles, arms, ships, and many other materials. Doubtless she has likewise enriched herself in like manner from Japan Sumatra, New Guinea, and elsewhere. Now she's being hemmed in and the party is over. All she's lost is some men and ships, but gained greater world recognition as a world power (though belligerent, ruthless, and brutal), tin, rubber, quinine, gold and other such important minerals. Yes, I believe the sun is about to set. Amen.

Gee, the chow situation is what I'd call acute! Yes, tasty and well prepared, and we can buy garlic and onions and pepper to flavor the chow. But the three meals we get per day, night, just about be satisfying as one meal, if all three were put together. The rice ration (under any other condition of ours of starvation) would be funny. Doesn't even make half a mess kit. Besides, our spending power is finite as far as the commissary goes. They take the total amount paid per month to the officers in camp, divide that by the number of men in camp, then pro rate that — so much for field officers, Co. officers. Last month allowed 14 Pesos.

Sunday, July 23
The item of importance today is that I received eleven letters from Mom and Dad. That makes a total of thirty-nine letters from the U.S. NONE FROM EILEEN.

July 26
Had a surprise yesterday. Vernon Booth, from Iloilo is here in camp —

on the work detail. Booth married Millie Heise (Pop Heise's daughter) and he and Millie are the parents of little David. He looks well, and 'cause I knew him well in Iloilo, hence he'll probably do all he can for me. Millie is in Santo Tomas. Jackie and Max Klinger are free, on the "outside."[117]

Wah! — Coconuts have gone to 1 peso each! Prices are going way up! Blackout last nite. Wish it had been a real air-raid.

God! The chow ration we get isn't enough to keep a bird alive. I've had a headache for the last five days, steadily, and it's nothing more than a "banger headache." Jeez! What I'd give to get my belly full just *once*!!

RUMORS:
News today — 600 planes at Clark Field. Naval battle in N. China Sea near Japan. If we win that one, we'll be out of here shortly.

Shirley Main, you little devil, you've got me thinking about you more and more. I've re-read your letter over and over, and wish to hell you'd write more. Maybe we missed somethin', who knows for sure? I know I always enjoyed being with you and we did have lots of fun at 3 Rivers and in Chicago. Maybe we passed

something up because we practically grew up together. Anyway, what I'm trying to say is that I hope you don't get married while I'm away. I'd like to see more of you and see if we couldn't make a go at things. You see, I figure I probably made quite a mistake on Eileen. There's really nothing on except my wild stubbornness and romantic ideas. Then again I might be right. Christ! I wish I could hurry up and get back and straighten out this problem.

Always, always I get into the goddamnest situations with females!! Must have a gift for it!! But by George, there's none to call me "Daddy," that I know of !! (I hope!)

Lunch is light ration of *plain rice*!

July 27
Paid by IJA 30 pesos. Cabantuan gang got their back pay — 90 pesos!! Not us though. Draft 400 to go to Cabanatuan Aug. 2. Not "PD's" though — I hope. News that we have Guam. Good. No confirmation on China Sea battle, or France. About 200 J ships in bay, including two carriers. Quite a bit of air activity. God! I've never yet gone thru the hunger pangs that we're going thru here! There have been times when I thought chow was bad and meager and we called them "starvation diets." But sweet Suzy! Those were banquet days, and days of plenty compared to the present chow situation. I live from meal to meal. My energy is

---

117 The former campus of the University of Santo Tomas housed a diverse group of internees that included business executives, bankers, plantation owners, writers, beachcombers, prostitutes, and mothers with their children. German nationals, however, were allowed to live freely in the Philippines. These included Hinkle's friends Jackie and Max Klinger.

very low. I've experienced stomach cramps from HUNGER. Get up suddenly and you get dizzy, and sometimes black-out for a second or two. Continuously I hear these remarks abound me,

"God, I'm hungry!"

"Well, only 5½ hours to supper!"

"If I ever get a chance to feed those sons of bitches, they'll find out what starvation can be! Christ, if they don't put out more chow than this, none of us will be here to see the Yanks come in!"

"I'm so goddamned hungry I'm shakin like a leaf in October wind!"(This from Colonel Cain, and he was and does shake from it.) So you see, our rations are extremely short. There's no exaggeration. It's *just barely* enuff to keep us alive. Well, maybe it won't be long now. Here comes chow, and Maj. Ruth just said "Boy — it's small rations again tonite!" So, there you are.

July 28

News today that attempt made on July 20 to assassinate Hitler, general killed, but Hitler just injured. Damn! Why the miss?

July 29

One of the USN corpsmen here on duty is Harry Payne. Was on duty at Great Lakes and knew and dated Beverly Hills girl — Dot McDougal. Lives around 111th! Also, knew Virginia Belser, a 111th gal that Snelly used to date quite often. Payne's quite a nice young lad, too. I like him.

Aye laddie, it looks like a rotten bleak birthday coming up for you tomorrow. Chow'll be short.[118]

July 30

Hi ho! 27 years old today and feel 37! Fourth birthday in P.I., sincerely believe it will be my last here, if the news I've been hearing is correct. Went to Mass, blessing of Padre, prayed for Mom and Dad, the best in the world.

Fifteen British POWs arrived in the hospital today. They are part of the 45,000 who were captured in Singapore. Three ships of them on way from Singapore to Manila, took six weeks! Have been in Bay six days, during which time the J'se tried twice to leave the bay. Had to turn back both times. Bay has 1,000 of ships, some damaged. The Limeys were working on railroad in China; cholera epidemic — between 20 and 30,000 out of 45,000 died. Have suffered about same as us; beriberi, malnutrition, etc. 2,000 on one ship, 750 in another, other?? Much of time spent topside in rain. One died before getting here to hospital.

Entire American fleet and parts of French and Italian in Pacific. Hitler severely wounded in 3 places.

July 31

Rumor — Just came in that the IJA gave orders to the Filipinos that 80% of Manila must be evacuated in next 48 hours. (True?) It is true that they

---

118   Walter J. Hinkle was born July 30, 1917.

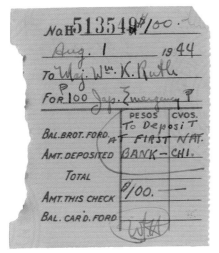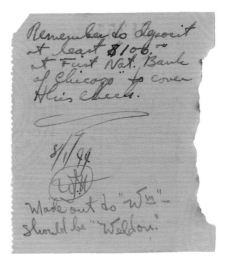

This check stub—pictured front and back—was Hinkle's reminder to fund the check to Major Ruth after liberation (mentioned in his August 1, 1944, entry). It was found in Hinkle's billfold. *Hinkle Archive*

(IJA) are painting big red crosses on the buildings here at Bilibid. I was *watching* them do *that*. This to me is extremely significant, and I'm willing now to bet that I'll be home for Easter.

August 1

Draft leaving for Cabanatuan tomorrow morning. Twenty out 500. Mc among those going, dammit. Will give us more room here, tho.

News — The men on the work details here no longer allowed to work around docks, speak or sign to Filipinos. IJA guards have fixed bayonets and are elevated while guarding so can't be rushed. Americans told that in case of air-raid siren, they are to lie flat. If run they will be shot.

Gave Maj. Ruth check for $100 in exchange for 100 pesos Japanese. I need the money desperately so I can get something extra to eat. It was robbery, I know, but what can I do? Made the check out to "First National Bank of Chicago." Must remember to deposit some $ there. Couldn't remember the full name of Riverside Bank or Mutual. Major Ruth, incidentally (Dr.) is quite a hop-head, being addicted to liquid codeine. He has been "drunk" for two days now, and a disgrace to us. Report turned in on him. Means he'll be cashiered.

August 2

Draft left at 4:00 a.m. for Cabanatuan today — 300. More mail in. Some few personal packages come in (about six). Johnny Winterholler (my messmate) got one, and we're hoping for chow!! IJA claims 16,000 packages were lost in sea. They probably looted them and threw'em overboard!! Damn! Boy, I could sure use one now.

Slight drainage on part of stump scar — result raw spot infected some. This may delay operation. Again, Damn!! Johnny's box in good shape except for damned tooth powder all over. He got two packages Chestertons, one pound cheese, six packages noodle soup, malted milk tabs, two packages prunes (I washed tooth powder off each one with tooth brush!), gum, pack orange life-savers, vitamins, sox, etc. And boy, the chow is good, and I am lucky to be in on it!!

August 3

Have been working on mail today. Oh boy, I got sixteen more letters from the States! This afternoon I sneaked out six more letters from U.S. to me. Most of these Feb '44 (only 5 months!). They were from Mom and Dad, Aunt Bess, none from Eileen, and again I say __." Might as well figure you're a free man Walt, in more than one way once you get back! And how my Toots doesn't write? Or Jackie?

Oh, on Aug. 2nd the IJA announced that our water here was contaminated and we've been ordered to drink boiled water. Sometimes, however, I've found myself too thirsty to drink the damned boiled stuff, so I've gone ahead and used regular tap water. Still alive too! Besides, I've had my CTD[119] shot series this year.

August 4

Bought four pesos of peanuts today = about ⅕ canteen cup. Paid 20 pesos

---

119   Clostridium perfringens type C&D, and tetanus.

for coffee can full of Batangas coffee (black market). Have dressing on the little spot that's started to drain on my stump. This will delay things for another week or so. GODDAMNIT!!!! Weather has been very hot last three days. No rain. Nice bombing weather.

Oh yes, the letter that *really* threw me for a loop was from Agnes Griffin, 8201 S. Peoria Street!! I couldn't for the life of me figure that out. *Who* was Agnes Griffin, and what was she doing at our place, and how come she was writing to me?? The *upstairs part* never occurred to me. My suspicions, however, lead me to believe she is a young item — between 15 and 18. We'll see. At any rate I did appreciate the letter, even though it did frighten me when I saw it signed "Lovingly!!"

August 5

Golly. If I eat garlic back home the way I do here, I'll have no friends at all! I use three to five cloves each meal. I use it on everything and love it. Use garlic salt — damned good. Also seems I'm always busy around the hot plates — putting on coffee, toasting coconut, drying salt or cooking up soup. John still has a little Klim left, and it goes good with prunes in coffee. Heard the news Turkey now on our side. That Poland has established democrat gov't. That Goering new Reich-Chancellor. Goebbels = Reich Minister.

August 9

It seems I may have that great disease at long last — beriberi!! Noticed last nite that my left foot was quite swelled up to about the ankle. The indentations made with my finger by pressing into the skin would stay and slowly fill back in. Symptoms of wet beriberi. Some little pains in my toes. Urine and other lab tests today. Doctor starting me today on thiamin, and nicotinic acid. I hope it's not beriberi.

August 10
Himmler now in charge of Nazi army. Number of Nazi officers executed for revolt on Russian front. U.S. had bombed Pelew steadily for last two weeks. U.S. commentators say P.I. to be next for attack; also give Nazis sixty days more live. Our planes sank two J convoys off Saipan. Davao was recently bombed.

August 12
Well Mom and Dad, it happened 28 years ago today, didn't it? Wish I was home to celebrate your anniversary with you. My wishes for you are many. Next year I know we'll be together — I feel it in my bones.

News — Roosevelt says "No more RC chow to Far East. Nips looting it." God damn! General Eisenhower and staff HQ in occupied France. Fighting in E. Prussia. We just bombed three J'se cities. Conference in Washington on Aug. 21 with FDR, Churchill, Chiang Kai-Shek, Stalin.

Payne gave me about 5 oz. cooking oil last nite. Now trying to get rice and will make flour. Then will make hot-cakes, using flour, salt, rice-yeast, and soda-bicarb — it works!

Finally got tinted glasses today with prescription from Dr. Waterous. They're pretty nice and I like 'em fine. Perhaps my headaches will cease if I use them continually and cut down the glare from the windows and white washed walls. At least I plan to wear them all the time. Have to pay Doc 30 pesos IJA, if I can, but must pay up in $ after war.

Ten sacks of mail in today. So far I know of three letters for me. Swell.

Sunday, August 13, 1944
Missed Mass because of heavy rains and wind in early morning. Worked on mail rest of day. Found three letters from Mom and Dad; those were December '43 and two of March 12, '44. There are more for me, but they've gone to the censor so I'll have to wait. It sure was swell to get the letters — makes life so much more valuable and worthwhile. Guess by now my folks are pretty well established on Green Street. Gee! It'll be swell to get back! This hellish waiting will someday be rewarded and home is certainly going to be heaven, and Mom — just wait till you see me eat!!

August 14
Had eye exam today. Dental appointment for Wednesday, 8:00 a.m. Got five more letters yesterday making a total of eight out of the batch, and I think that's all I have coming.

August 15

News — J'se withdrawing from Borneo. Stump quite painful today.

August 16

Slept good last nite. Had temporary filling replaced with silver by Dr. White, the dentist here. Tomorrow I start on vitamins and shots to help out eyes.

August 17

Began vitamin therapy: 2 shots a day and 5 vitamin tablets — 4 capsules, 1 pill. Also am being treated by skin specialist for a fungal growth on face — sort of a barber's itch. Draft coming in for Japan. 150 men from Clark Field arrived today. 500 expected from Cabanatuan.

What a cook I am — John and I managed to get some rice smuggled in; course we paid for it. So, I dried it and made it ground into flour. I put the coffee on, then made "hot-cakes" out of rice-flour, rice-yeast, salt, soda bicarb. and salt. The mistake came in the form of soda bicarb. Boy! I sure loaded the batter with it and didn't realize it! They weren't too bad, however in spite of the fact that I've been burping ever since!! Going to make some flour gravy tonite (mess has some meat in it). Chow ration has been damnably small last three days. Weather has been pretty fair lately — not too much rain.

Pupils of eyes still quite large from dilation, but can read. Expect to give $200 check on First Nat. of Chic. for 200 pesos tonite. John and I need the pesos. We've turned into great coffee drinkers, and I love the stuff more. We have four or five times a day. You know the mess cup holds one pint, and my cup is almost full each time. So I figure I drink at least 4 to 4½ pints of coffee a day. At breakfast especially I have to have one pint, so Mom — take heed!!

$200 check transaction accomplished. Hope I don't wind up in a prison for bounced checks!!!

515 in from Cabanatuan. Well, Phil Brain is on this draft going to Japan. It sure was good to see him again, but I certainly hate to see him go to that place. Hate to see any of our boys go. Major Jackson in charge of detail and he says he'll fix me up on the "cuan." (Thank God!).

Had another temporary filling replaced with silver.

Doc. Jackson really is fixing us up and boy it'll come in handy. Hope I don't get caught, 'cause sure as hell will be hung by the neck if I'm ever nailed. But to get any extra or tasty food, I'll take any damned chance. The result is good already. John and I have had three batches of hotcakes (4 apiece), we have all the *good* coffee we want, we've had some peanuts, sugar and mungo beans and tobacco. Without the "cuan," we'd have NONE of these. With this stuff we can get some protein foods of which none are for the owning from the kitchen. I should be able to maintain weight and possibly *gain* some. Gee — the hot-cakes, coffee, sugar, and some of John's milk sure tasted good this morning. Best breakfast I've had in 2½ years!

Gave Phil a pair of shorts and bottle of vitamin capsules. I sure hope he pulls thru the trip OK, and for recovering our health together in Minnesota still holds if we both get back — I don't see why we shouldn't.

August 22
Have been busy as hell on the mail. I got 14 more letters including a card from Boots and Lyman, which made me very, very happy. Sure glad they gave me a thought. I do wish Dad would send pictures — all the photos around the house and none forthcoming. They'd really help. Anyway, I am glad to get the news that all is well.

The men in the draft were given their packages. Phil unhappily did not get a package. I did manage to swipe three of his letters for him. It's the only mail he's had so far. He looks quite dressed up in his new Jap clothes. He gave me some socks, tooth powder, shave soap and coconut, all of which will be quite handy. They may leave today — we're not sure. There are about 1,200 extra men in camp now. Chow has been very slim. Practiced piano last nite and get to practice today at 12:30. Face is all cleared up.

August 24
Well, Phil and Doc Jackson and the J draft are to leave today at 11:00 a.m. Doc sure turned into a much faster friend than I had hoped for. Certainly hope their trip will be better than ours was. They're destined for a camp near Yokohama, I hear. They've been outfitted in J uniforms, been given blankets, canteens, etc. if they had none. Good med. supplies for 25 days. Doc brought over some more cuan last nite, too. We've been having coffee every nite for our visitors. Now we may be able to make our coffee last longer.

Boy, the trading that's been going on! Tobacco, shirts, pants, soap, etc. for *coconuts*. Coconuts 20 pesos, peanuts 50, coffee 20, etc., while draft is here. Tobacco in the PX yesterday for first time since we've been here; ½ sack per man at 2 pesos per ½ sack. So John and I now have one sack. Five more big, full sacks of mail await sorting beginning today! New and better time for working on it has been put into effect — we'll work ½ day. I work afternoons. Got haircut.

Draft marched out at 3:30 p.m., and then at 5 p.m. here they come marching back *in* again! Some reason or other for delay and they had to lay over here at camp, get up at 3:00 a.m. and finally at 5:30 a.m.

August 25
They marched back out, this time for good. Their spirits were high and they all carried their luggage cheerfully on

their shoulders and backs. So the last cup of coffee Phil and I had together was at 8 p.m. August 24, in Bilibid Prison, 1944. Where will our next get-together be?

Mail turned out to be 2 sacks for us and 3 for IJA, so we'll be thru today. Fact I shouldn't have to work. Hope not, 'cause I have some beans to cook. Weather has been very nice lately. Warm and sunshine, with cottony clouds. Lots of air activity. At nite, the searchlight batteries are busy practicing. For the last three days, anti-aircraft batteries here in Manila have been practicing all day.

A memorandum put out by HQ concerning behavior of POWs, in regard to escape, punishing POWs, insulting superior officers, conspiracies, violating oaths of parole, etc. I feel this has something to do with the nearness of our forces. Why else would the Nips suddenly put such a memo out?

Just three years ago I was busier than hell getting ready to leave Manila for Iloilo.

August 26
Something comes to bother me all the time it seems. Now I have a little conjunctivitis in my right cye, right in the proximal corner. My stump is just about healed. Another three days to a week, I'd guess.

News — Paris and Marseilles ours. Romania has fallen. Japan bombed again. Davao being bombed every day — Del Monte field bombed.

August 27
Mass this a.m. John and I ate pretty well today. I cooked up a mess of mungo beans in the a.m., into which I had put salt, a little soda, garlic, three chicken bullion cubes, and a spoon of oil. They were excellent. We had them at noon and also enuff for supper. At supper, Doc Waterous made three big hot-cakes apiece for the two of us, and they were damned good. Had cornstarch, bean and rice flour and some oat meal in them. But good! John and I also made seconds on rice, and what with a couple of cups of coffee apiece, we were for once, *full*!!

August 28
Had black-out last nite and the Nips were very serious about it. No one allowed out of buildings after dark. Our chow servers were stuck in our building till 11:30 p.m., when they finally managed to talk a guard into taking them to their quarters.

Rained all last nite. Chow late this a.m. because of no fires last nite. Lugao was just like soup!! Blackouts to be every nite from now on. To me, this sounds like damned good news, for I feel that it means the Yanks are seriously threatening Manila, and I hope soon.

August 29
Blackout again last nite, and searchlight batteries were busily practicing.

[*Continued on page 236*]

Reflections of a Survivor
by Phil Brain

Phil Brain first appeared in Hinkle's diary on May 19, 1943. His last appearance was on December 12, 1945, when Hinkle wrote, "I often think of Phil Brain and pray he is safe and in good health in Japan or wherever he is."

After the war, Phil Brain wrote about his memories of captivity—an emotional ordeal that began in 1965.

Subsequent attempts to lay down thoughts that he was unable to express earlier were made in 1983 and 1986. Even then, Phil was unable to put into words feelings he most wanted to convey: "This is a reality I have come to accept without fully understanding why, and must beg forbearance by those who may read my words."[1]

The following story is from these postwar recollections.[2]

The line between life and death is very narrow. At times it disappears. I believe that many of the prisoners of war living today stepped more than once across that line with at least one foot and were brought back by a voice, a touch of another man's hand, a

memory or some other incident.

In the collection of these thoughts, a well of memories was opened. It has also brought to the surface some emotions I didn't realize were there. I believe that as one goes through an experience like this, he builds a shell around himself, and emotions are suppressed. The shell must be hard, and it must be tough, because once it is pierced — once a crack has been made — a man does not usually live much longer.

It isn't easy to take three and a half years and wrap them up in a little ball and say here it is. Indeed, there are some high points and low points and a lot of things that just can't be included in a summary of this kind.

Our problems in the Philippines began prior to the time of surrender on April 9, 1942. We had been in Bataan since January 1st. When we moved in, we immediately went to two meals of rice a day. By the end of January we were down to one meal a day. We supplemented this by foraging. At the time of surrender, it's safe to say that there wasn't one living thing other than man in Bataan. The cavalry no longer had any mules or horses. There were no dogs. There were no lizards. No living creatures that were edible remained at the time of surrender. The men who surrendered were

---

1   Philip S. Brain Jr., *Soldier of Bataan* (Minneapolis: Rotary Club of Minneapolis, 1990), 7.
2   Phil Brain's postwar recollections. Printed with the permission of his daughter Beth Moorhead. *Phil Brain Family Archive*

weak and sick. They had had little sleep. If they stood up suddenly, they often blacked out. These were the men who were trying to hold the lines when fresh Japanese forces were brought up from Singapore to finish the job.

On the night of April the 8th, the order was given to destroy all weapons and move back further into Bataan. We destroyed our weapons and started back. I remember a group of us discussing what the future held and wondering what would happen next. It was almost as bright as day. We could have read a newspaper if we had one because all the ammunition dumps were being blown up. That night I had the best night's sleep in many a month because there was no worry about Japanese infiltration. The shelling we had been under day and night for weeks had stopped, and the planes that had been bombing and strafing us continually were no longer there. I slept like a baby.

On the morning of April 9th, I was awakened by a jab of a rifle butt. I looked into the eyes of a Japanese soldier, and I knew he wasn't saying, "Get up son." I got up, put on my shoes and glasses, snapped on my canteen belt, and fell in line. The Japanese started walking up and down the line searching us. One took my duffle bag, one took my glasses, another took the ring my dad had given me. All that I had left were a pair of fatigues, shoes, and canteen belt. In the bushes I spotted the lid of a mess kit; I tucked that in my hind pocket in hope that there would be food. Then they lined us up for chow, and issued each of us a tablespoon of raw rice. We gathered in small groups, found tin cans and cooked the rice, every man taking his share.

About 11 o'clock we lined up to move out. I'll never forget the sensation as we stood on the road, in a kind of gully, with hills on both sides. On those hills were Japanese soldiers with machine guns. One couldn't help but wonder, "Is this it? Is this to be a massacre, or do we still have a chance?" We had a chance, and we began what came to be known as the Death March.

Men who were too sick or too lame to keep up were eliminated with a rifle shot or a bayonet. We quickly realized that one kept going or else. Water became our toughest problem. In the Philippines there are many artesian wells alongside the road — wells with beautiful, cool water. As we came to the first one of these and tried to break rank and get water for our canteens, rifles were fired and bayonets were used. Many men were left dead at the first artesian well. We realized, as we came to a second one, that the thing to do was to take the canteen cup by the handle and, as we passed the well, make a dash, try to scoop up some water and get back into line. We did this. Again the rifle shot, the bayonets, and some men remained behind forever.

The march continued, and the Japanese soldiers changed their tactics. They stopped us in the middle of the road at a resting point for a half hour break under the midday sun, alongside an artesian well — well protected with rifles and bayonets. Farther along, as we came to stagnant pools in which lay the bloated bodies of soldiers and of animals, they allowed us to fill our canteens and to take a drink.

That night we were marched into a Philippine estate that was enclosed with stone walls. We marched in columns of four. We were marched to the back wall and were told to turn around, sit down and stay there for the night. As the men kept coming in, it got more and more crowded. With no latrine facilities, the area began to get pretty filthy. Then, in the blackness of the night, a soldier cracked, and a shriek rang out. Rifles were fired in the direction of the shriek by guards walking on the wall, and then there was silence. One begins to realize that he is living only minute by minute

and that he does not have any control over the situation.

As the days went by and the march continued, the Japanese again changed their tactics. Trucks came along and picked up the men who appeared to be too sick and too weak to keep going. The men who were taken onto the trucks were never seen again.

Our part of the Death March lasted five days. We ended up at the railhead town of San Fernando. We went into a sugar warehouse where we stayed the night. Again, no latrines. There was a lot of dysentery and sickness among the men by this time.

In the morning we were loaded into railway cars. These were small steel box cars. The Japanese used bayonets to make sure each car was loaded with as many men as possible. We were crowded so close together that it was almost impossible to move our arms. The doors were slammed shut and bolted. The air vents were closed, and we started on what became an eight-hour trip. As the sun began to beat down on the freight cars, it became almost unbearable. When a man died, and some did, it was impossible to lay him down on the floor. After eight hours we reached our destination, the train stopped, the doors were opened, and those men still living climbed out. Some Filipinos were there,

The San Fernando railway station in Pampanga served as the ending point for the 63-mile march from Bataan. It was here that Phil Brain and other American and Filipino prisoners were packed into boxcars and carted to Capas in Tarlac, en route to their final destination, Camp O'Donnell. *Photograph by John Roux, ca. 2010*

and they said, "If you have any Japanese money throw it away." We marched about six kilometers into Camp O'Donnell.

O'Donnell was a Philippine army camp that had been under construction before the war but never finished. It had few buildings and no latrines. There was one water line with one faucet, and the Japanese were moving all of the Bataan prisoners into this camp. We established a hospital in one of the few buildings that were there. The rest of the men lived out of doors.

Some men were well enough to work. There were just two work details: bury the dead and dig la-

trines, and neither could be done fast enough. More than 1,600 men died in that camp the first month.

The nights were restful, and for me, very important. One could lie on the ground, put a canteen under his head for a pillow, look to the stars and be in a different world. Then one began to realize the relationship he must have with his God and the need of God to find His way with men. I imagine this is one of the reasons that nights mean so much to me now. Nights provide the chance to be alone, or as I suppose my wife would say, to be a wanderer. She says that she never knows whether I'm in bed to stay, or whether I'm

Death March boxcar, Capas National Shrine, Capas, Tarlac. *Photograph by Estan Cabigas, ca. 2017*

going to be up reading or looking out the window. Nights still mean a lot to me.

On some nights at the camp, the tropical rains would strike. The first thing we would do would be to fill a canteen, then we could face one of those cold tropical rains. As one lay on the ground and tried to roll up like a ball to keep warm, he couldn't help but think about the number of men who would die that night, men whose strength was almost gone. For the weakest, the cold rain would bring an end to life.

We received word that Corregidor surrendered about May 6th. The Japanese then began to send work details out of the camp. A few days after Corregidor surrendered, I left Camp O'Donnell. I was glad to get away from it and went with 400 men assigned to various work details. We were divided into groups of 50, and my detail ended up in the town of Calauan, south of Manila. Our job was rebuilding bridges that had been destroyed as we withdrew into Bataan. We were housed in the village hall which was a building about 30 feet square with a concrete floor. Fifty of us stayed there. They say that home is where your hat is. Well, for three and a half years, home was wherever you could put your body. There were no blankets, no cots, no pieces of furniture of any kind. Home was a spot on the concrete floor.

After arriving at Calauan, I contracted dysentery and at this point weighed about 95 pounds. My job was carrying sacks of cement, mixing concrete on a steel plate with a shovel and loading gravel trucks. I don't think any of these things are prescribed for the treatment of dysentery. You see, we learned a couple of things. One is that if you're too sick to work, you're too sick to eat, and your rations are immediately cut. Second, if you don't keep moving and thinking, you go downhill fast.

We learned that one of the other details that had started out with us — the one stationed next to us — had been attacked by a guerrilla band a couple of nights before. One of the American prisoners of war had escaped when the guerrillas left. The Japanese commander ordered all the men remaining in that group of fifty to be executed. The Americans protested, and the commander reduced the number to ten men. If any of you who were officers in World War II were to receive an order to select ten men to face the firing squad, try to imagine what your reaction would be. The alternative: have the entire group face the firing squad. This happened again about a week later to another of the work details.

The Americans then organized all prisoners into what were known as "blood groups." Ten men to each group. Interior guards were established to prevent escape. If one man escaped from any "blood group," there would be no need for selection. The remainder of the group would be designated for execution. Some months later, Japan agreed to follow the Geneva Prisoner of War Convention, and the order to shoot ten for one was lifted.

After about three months, we returned to the main camp. Camp O'Donnell had been closed because of its unlivable conditions, and a new camp, Camp Cabanatuan, had been opened.

When we went to Cabanatuan, I took a bag of Philippine pipe tobacco, found my commanding officer, Colonel Ernie Miller, and gave it to him. There were tears in his eyes as he accepted it. Colonel Miller was a great soldier and a great man. Unfortunately, after a serious bout with dysentery and after at least two severe beatings by the Japanese, the Colonel's health was never the same.

At Cabanatuan we slept in double-deck screened bunks with sliding screen doors. We just slid the screen door open and crawled in and joined the bedbugs for the night. Separated from others, we had some time to ourselves. I was assigned a bunk that was located near the spot where a Regular Army Sergeant got up on his soapbox almost every night. As a young punk fresh out of the University of Minnesota, I had my opinion of regular Army Sergeants, and this man didn't do anything to change that opinion. He maintained that American GIs kept away from women for over three months would go stark raving mad and that there was absolutely nothing wrong with us except "lack of malnutrition." As I said, he did nothing to change my opinion of Regular Army Sergeants.

I worked at Camp Cabanatuan for a month and then was among 500 prisoners sent on a prison ship to the island of Mindanao to work the rice fields at Davao Penal Colony. That trip lasted 12 days, after which we had a 26 kilometer march from the dock to the penal colony.

It was there that I began to have trouble with malaria — and dysentery. We never seemed to have one illness or one problem at a time. We always had them all together. We worked in the rice fields on the farm details as long as we could stand upright, because if we did not work, our rations were reduced by one half. We needed the food so we kept working.[3]

At this point, with malaria and dysentery I was put in the hospital area. One day as I lay on a cot with my eyes closed, thinking of nothing, I heard two men speaking. One of them said, "This man will die next." And the other said, "Ah so?" I opened my eyes to see who they were talking about. Looking down at me were an American doctor and the Japanese camp commander.

After they left, I got up and went to the American officer in charge of the hospital and said, "I want to go back to work." He said, "Are your sure?" And I said, "Yes." The line between life and death is very thin. Often only the will to live keeps one alive, and that will to live can easily disappear without one even being aware of it. The comments by the doctor and the Japanese Camp Commander

---

3 A typical rice-planting detail had thirty prisoners, two rope men, and two seedling carriers. Seedlings for the day's planting were gathered as they floated down water canals from where the seedlings were grown, and then tied into bunches. When planting, a prisoner would stand at either end of the earthen dike with a rope stretched across the paddy between them. From the rope hung strings at 6- or 8-inch intervals, and spaced across the paddy were prisoners in calf-deep water, pushing a rice seedling into the mud at each string. The prisoners in the paddy (who were not allowed to wear shirts) were spaced apart so that each was responsible for planting twelve seedlings. When a row was filled, someone hollered, "Ho!," the planters backed up, the rope was moved, and the prisoners started planting the next row. This rice-planting description comes from Hinkle's friend and fellow prisoner Calvin Jackson, in his book titled *Diary of Col. Calvin G. Jackson, M.D.* (Ada: Ohio Northern University, 1992), 111.

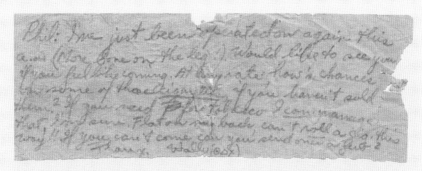

"Phil: I've just been operated on again this a.m. (more bone on the leg!). Would like to see you if you feel like coming. At any rate, how's chances on some of those cigarettes, if you haven't sold them? If you need pesos for tobacco I *can* manage that, I'm sure. Flat on my back, can't roll a cig this way!! If you can't come can you send over a foot? Thanks, Wally (ΘΔΧ)." *Phil Brain Family Archive*

made me realize what was happening to me.

Later, while lying in bed, I heard the man on the cot next to me singing a song that was familiar. He was singing one of the songs of the Theta Delta Chi fraternity. His name was Walt Hinkle.

We became acquainted, and two days later I went back to the main compound. Later, as I was returning from the farm detail on a very rainy day, someone handed me a note from Walt, and I still have it. It says, "Phil, I have just been operated on again this a.m. More bone off the leg. Would like to see you if you feel like coming." So I went to see him. He had had a foot amputated and, because of the conditions, the doctors were having trouble with infection. That day they had to take a little more bone off the leg. No anesthetic. Walt exemplified the kind

of people the POWs were. He had undergone a very painful operation and just a few hours later in the day could send a note to me.

I went over that evening to see him. It was raining, and the roar of the rain on the tin roofs of the barracks was so deafening that one could hardly hear anything else. The mud was ankle deep. I waited till dark so it was easier to slip past the Japanese guard who stood between the camp and the hospital area. As I neared the mess shack, I noticed that the light was still on over the rice kettles. Then I remembered that the men were not back from the rice fields. This was nine o'clock at night. They had been out in the rice fields since six o'clock in the morning. The only clothes each man wore was a loin cloth. After working in the cold rain all day, their lips would be purple, and their fingers would be shriveled up like dried peas.

For several weeks there had been contact between the guerrilla forces and the men working in the rice fields. There was a good chance that the POWs, with the help of the guerrillas, could subdue the guards, take over the camp and then head for the jungle. But we knew that meant sure death for every man like Walt who was lying in the hospital and could not be taken into the jungle.

I visited Walt. As I returned about ten o'clock, I was thinking about the chances of the guerrillas and the Americans taking over the guards in the rice fields, and wondering when this would happen. Everything was certainly right for it. The men had been out in the mud and cold all day long. Something had to give. As I stood in front of the mess shack, I heard a noise above the roar of the rain on the roof. Then I saw the light of the diesel locomotive. The rice fields were a few kilometers away, and we were always taken to them on flat cars drawn by a small locomotive. I thought the POWs had taken over and wondered what would happen to Walt and the others.

Then as the train pulled to a stop, I began to make sense out of that noise. I realized that the men were singing. They were singing as loud as they could. They were sing-

ing "God Bless America." I felt very proud to be among men like that.[4]

The next morning the Japanese commanding officer came toward the gates of the camp, and with him were some of his men with wheelbarrows. In the wheelbarrows were bananas, avocados and some of the other foods we craved. The officer went up to the POW headquarters and asked for the American commanding officer. He saluted him, and said, "I salute the soldiers of Bataan." He pointed to the wheelbarrows and turned and walked away. It is impossible for me, to this day, to hear . . . the singing of "God Bless America" without seeing again in my mind those men coming back on that train from the rice fields.

There were some light moments on occasion. I remember an instance of a work detail consisting of two Japanese guards and eight Americans. The detail found berries. The Japanese asked if the berries were good to eat, and the Americans said they were, especially if roasted. The prisoners recommended roasting, because it would take time and offer some respite from hard labor. In any event, the Japanese ordered the berries be picked and roasted. When all of the berries had been picked and roasted, there was a good sized pile. Then the Japanese

---

4   See Hinkle's August 28, 1943, diary entry.

divided them: one-fourth for eight Americans and three-fourths for the two Japanese. When the work detail returned to camp that evening, the Americans were carrying both the rifles and the Japanese soldiers. The berries that the Japanese had eaten so heartily were actually castor beans. The Americans had simply followed the oft repeated military directive, "Clean out the enemy."[5]

The Japanese seldom allowed the Americans to gather in mass meetings, but on one occasion they let us have a talent show. There seems to be a lot of talent among American soldiers, no matter what the circumstances. So, we had a rendering of *Dugout Doug*, a well-known poem by an unnamed poet that referred, of course, to General Douglas MacArthur. There were songs and skits, often directed at certain of the Japanese guards. At the end, two men, facing away from the audience, turned around and unfurled an American flag. Where they had kept it hidden for two years I never learned. That day the men spontaneously broke out in song and sang "Oh, say can you see . . ." in a way I shall never forget.[6]

Ten months later the American Forces coming up from the South were getting very close. The guerrillas were active in the jungle around the rice fields, and the Japanese decided that they had to move us back to the main camp on Luzon [Bilibid]. We were loaded onto flatbed trucks, three men across, 12 men deep.[7] We stood with our hands on the shoulder of the man in front, tied together with ropes at the waist to the man in front and the man in back. Before we were blindfolded we saw the Japanese soldier sitting on the truck cab roof with a rifle. We had a 26 kilometer ride to the port of Davao, standing up all the way under the blistering sun.

At the dock, we got off the trucks, and as we were being herded into the hold of the prison ship, I became very weak and began to faint. A captain from California named Kaiser, who had been a member of one of the units which surrendered on the southern islands and with whom I had become acquainted, grabbed me in his arms, pushed past the surprised guards and carried me down into the hold.

Fourteen days later we arrived at Manila. We were taken off the ship and to Bilibid Prison. There was a Japanese doctor standing at the entry door to the prison. He selected several men in front of

---

5   See Hinkle's entry for July 1, 1943.
6   Mentioned in Hinkle's entry for August 1, 1943.

7   Hinkle and Phil departed on June 6, 1944. See diary entries for June 5–30, 1944.

me and pulled them aside. When I came to him, he took a look at me, started to laugh, and motioned me into Bilibid Prison. I later found out that the men picked in front of me were being selected to go to Japan. They were put on board a ship that remained in Manila Bay for one month. Every morning the bodies of the men who died during the night were dumped overboard into Manila Bay. That ship, by the way, never reached Japan.

We went from Bilibid Prison to Camp Cabanatuan to work the rice fields. One morning when I awakened, I had a very high temperature and was disoriented. When I tried to talk I could not put my thoughts into words. It must have been something similar to a stroke. I went on the rice detail and while walking on the dike between the rice paddies, I heard somebody behind me whistling *Intermezzo*. I couldn't believe it. It was absolutely beautiful. As I turned my head to see who was whistling, I stumbled and slipped off the dike into the mud of the rice paddies. It was cool and comforting. I really didn't care at that point what happened to me. Then I heard a voice, "Come on, Buddy, you can make it." I looked up and there was an outstretched arm. My eyes followed up that arm, and there was the Sergeant [the same

Regular Army Sergeant who got up on his soapbox almost every night]. I took his hand, he pulled me up on the bank, and I made it.

In August of 1944, as American forces were getting close to the Philippines, the Japanese were moving things out as fast as they could. We were among the last to be shipped out from Japan.[8] This was to be my third prison ship trip. If I had any choice, I would take three death marches to one prison ship trip. During the course of three-and-a-half years as a prisoner of war, I spent 36 days aboard prison ships. It seems that very little has been said about them, and I will just try to give some idea of what prison ship conditions were like.

We were loaded aboard small freighters in much the same fashion as we were loaded into the railway freight cars earlier. The Japanese stood on girders above and, with bayonets and poles, pushed men back into the corners of the cargo holds as far as they could get them so they could keep loading more and more men. It was so crowded and hot that one did not believe he could continue to breathe or live.

We picked up room during the course of these voyages. Men shake down much as sugar would in a bag, and we began to find

8   August 24, 1944.

an extra inch here and there. As men died, and their bodies were passed over the gangway and up on deck to be dropped overboard, one gained a little more space. Near the gangway they placed big wooden buckets. These were the latrines for those men close enough to reach them.

Once again there was a saving factor, at least for me. On some nights the Japanese would remove the hatch covers, and one could look out and up at the beautiful stars and the deep blue sky. As I looked up into that sky, I wondered whether or not there was any place on the face of the earth that was still clean — whether there was any place where there was still laughter, where there was still love.

And as you look out and up, and begin to communicate with a force greater than yourself, you begin to realize what is important in life. It isn't a matter of man trying to make a deal with God, saying, "If I get out, I'll do this or I'll do that." Instead, one's sense of commitment becomes a sense of something new beginning to develop within one's self. And as dawn breaks, you feel a new strength in order to face the day a little bit differently.

And then came a night when there was the sound of scurrying up above. The hatch covers were slammed back on, and there was the sound of depth bombs. Then the POWs became a yelling, shrieking, and praying mob. All of them wanted the same thing — a direct hit from an American torpedo. They were willing to take their chances on sudden death, or in the open water — anything to be released from the situation they were in. But then there was silence, and nothing happened. Another dawn broke, and probably a deeper despair set in. These men had steeled themselves not to think of freedom, but for just a moment Lady Freedom had looked at them.

We reached Japan in September of 1944 and were sent to the copper mines of the northern end of Honshu. How many steps do you climb in a day? Ten, fifteen, twenty? We went down 478 steps into the mine each morning and back up 478 steps each night. There were elevators, but they were used only by the Japanese. When a prisoner was caught between two ore cars, or otherwise injured, it wasn't a matter of putting him on an elevator and taking him up; it was a matter of getting him up those 478 steps with the help of the men around him.

How do you climb 478 steps when you're weak and sick and have spent the day working with a pick and shovel in the copper

The Hanawa Prisoner-of-War Camp #6, Honshu, Japan, September 14, 1945. *National Archives photograph #71875ACA3315*

mine? Well you do like you do on many other occasions. Whether you're in prison or not, you lock in your mind on something. You recall a poem, or the sonnet, "How do I love thee, let me count the ways." Or a speech you learned as a boy beginning with, "Four score and seven years ago . . ." Or you plan a meal, a Thanksgiving dinner. This was a favorite. You planned, prepared and cooked a Thanksgiving dinner, being very careful to select the vegetables, the kind of potatoes and the dressing — sage, chestnut or whatever kind that appealed to you. By the time you worked at this until you could almost smell the food, you were at the mouth of the mine. The cold winter wind and snow blew through your clothes and you knew that you were at the surface again. And then, as you faced the mile walk down the mountain side to the camp, you set your mind back or picked up a new subject; and many were the times a man would go from the bottom of the mine to the top and never remember taking one step in the course of the whole trip.

On August 15, 1945, we were awakened at 4:00 a.m. and had breakfast as usual. Then they passed around the second meal, always millet, a good chicken food. This meal we would put in our mess kits until noon to eat down in the mine.

As usual, we went out to line up and start the march up the mountain. Gone were the regular guards — "Pick Handle Pete," "Popeye," "the Owl," the men who had made life miserable for us. They were all gone, and in their places they were just kids without any weapons. They said, "No mine today." We went back into the barracks.

Later in the day they lined us up again, and the Japanese commanding officer announced that the war was over — that "America had surrendered." We knew this was not true, but we didn't know what the truth was. We didn't go to the mine the next day, or the next.

After three days, they again lined us up, and the Japanese commanding officer said, "The war is over. America has won. You are going home." We put "POW" on the roof of the barracks. A short while later an American Navy plane buzzed the camp, and the next day B-29s came over and parachuted food and medicine. By the way, we had not previously seen any planes larger than B-17s, and those were lined up at Clark Field on December 8, 1941, for the Japanese to destroy.

On September 12, 1945, the Japanese told us that we would leave camp the next day and return to American control. In preparation for lunch, I went to the latrine and washed my hands. I went back to the barracks, climbed up the ladder to the second bay and was sitting with some of the men, talking and eating. Suddenly I had the sensation of having left my ring someplace. I climbed down the ladder, went halfway back to the latrine to get it, and then I remembered a Japanese soldier had taken that ring three and a half years before. Then the realization hit me for the first time. The Death March was over, and I was going home.

Made lucky contact with IJA guard, Hirata, formerly with us at Davao. At 10 a.m. I asked him if he could bring in some coffee (1 kilo) for some "*kusuri*."[120] He said, "Yes," and we agreed on three per. Asked if I had 100 pesos. Said, "Yes," and forgot about it. At 11 a.m. he comes to window and says, "Sugar 25, coffee 3 — OK?" I answer. He points to wall, says "You buy now," and pantomimes pulling up rope!! At noon I went out and he brought the goods! Cripes, there was a load! He kept whispering, quite raspingly, "Hurry, inside, INSIDE!!" An enlisted man happened to be there and he carried it to the end of the building and I told him to duck it in the bushes till I got help. The rope was still tied to it and I was in a helluva sweat lest we get caught. Got Roy Gray to bring it in. Checking over it we have about 25 or 28 lbs. of sugar, and about 2–3 lbs. coffee. This for 118 pesos. A good deal, and sets us up pretty well. Now I'm worrying about someone (or ones) in the ward causing me trouble, that *would* be fatal. However, will now try to get some other things in. Best of all — NO MIDDLE MAN! Weighed 135 lbs. (7 lbs. gain). Gave cup and ½ to Roy and Doc Waterous. The Doc is making some more hot-cakes for us tonite. Wonderful!!

August 30
Paper states we will have blackouts every nite till further notice. DeGaul goes to church service at Notre Dame.

Russians passed Krakow. Davao, Del Monte, Celebes bombed heavily. Deal for more sugar, maybe beans.

August 31
Received one more letter from folks. Guess that closes the mail deal. Started giving Dr. White (DDS-USN) piano lessons! I'll never be a teacher!! I could hear Gus giving me hell and putting her point across, but I just couldn't. Oh well.

Trying deal for more sugar. Our contact not working out! John and I are eating better now. Sugar in our lugao and coffee, and plenty of all. Coffee's getting low and harder to get. The rations from the IJA are certainly small.

Been practicing piano about twice a week now for ¾ hour at time. Can't get any more, damnit. Got hold of Manila paper (today's) and on the front page, nearly 5 lines — "Anti-Axis Foes Take Paris." Have been taking sun-baths every day for last week and am now getting a little color back. I look quite well especially after adding seven pounds last month. Now proud of my 135 lbs.! Will be well built-up for my operation — if they ever get around to it!

September 3
Yesterday afternoon I broke out with 101° fever. Felt like dengue. Today, however, I feel pretty well. May have been a passing "cuan" — I hope. Payne gave me a helping hand last nite and what a time I had! Didn't sleep but

---

120   The Japanese word for medicine. Used by Hinkle as a euphemism for "money."

one hour, and this after I corked off at about 1:30, and startlingly awakened at 3:45. Sleepy as hell now. Fever now = 100°, aches returning. Draft of 400 plus in from Cabanatuan last nite. More coming from there, and Los Baños and Pasay. Working party here to go out on draft — no more working party. Expect some familiar faces in today or tomorrow. Made hot-cakes today, came out pretty good, though "weighty." Recipe: 1 cup rice flour, 1 cup bean flour, 1 cup toasted shredded coconut, guess at salt 2–3 tbsp., sugar — 3 tbsp., rice yeast, water or milk. (Anything else you have to throw in.)

September 4

Hi-ho Another gang in from Cab'tn. last nite, heading for Japan. Included are Doc Davis, Deter, Osbourne, and Raider!! Sure good to see Russ again. He looks fair, but kind of tired. Has beriberi. Brought some sugar for me, well, and for John too. Lucky he had his foot locker with him, 'cause that carried the ten kilos of sugar down to me. Boy it'll come in handy. Don't know how we'll ever repay that. Glad he had received my note to him. Still running a fever — not feeling good. Hot plates busy as hell.

September 5

Strong rumor tonite that Third Reich has fallen. We sure hope so! Got two kilos coffee in today. Made some damned good hot-cakes. Also, Fast[121] made us some coconut fudge!! Fudge

in prison camp!! Jeeps!!! Good?? Man, it was exquisite!! Our "chips in" was two canteen cups sugar. Got 34 one inch square, ¼ inch thick pieces.

September 6

Books Read (with star review)
1. *Captain Caution* — Roberts.*
2. *Stories Behind the World's Great Music* — Spaeth.
3. *Captain Horatio Hornblower* — Forester.**
4. *Drums Along the Mohawk* — Edmonds.
5. *Kings Row* — M. Bellamann.*
6. *Rubber Band* — Rex Stout.
7. *The Robe* — L. C. Douglas.**
8. *Case of Velvet Claws* — Gardiner.
9. *Punch and Judy Murders* — Carter Dickson.
10. *Peacock Feather Murders* — Carter Dickson.
11. *Chinese Orange Mystery* — Queen.*
12. *Young Renny* — De La Roche.*
13. *Fort Terror Murders* — Van Wyck Mason.
14. *Drivin' Woman* — Chevalier.*
15. *The General* — Forester.
16. *Sad Cypress* — Agatha Christie.*
17. *Arrowsmith* — S. Lewis.
18. *Whiteoaks of Jalna* — De La Roche.*
19. *Finch's Fortune* — De La Roche.*
20. *Master of Jalna* — De La Roche.*
21. *Sodom By The Sea* — Pilat & Ranson.
22. *Buried Alive* — Arnold Bennet.
23. *Song of Bernadette* - - Frans Werfel.*
24. *Three Harbours* — Van Wyck Mason.*
25. *Wild Geese Calling* — White.

---

121   Chester Fast, pharmacist's mate second class, USN.

Expect draft of 800 or 900 officers in from Cabanatuan today sometime. Original draft seems to be delayed for infinite period. Everyone optimistic as the devil, because of Germany rumor. We expect to see (or hear) the war in Europe end in 30 days, here by January. I expect to get some sugar in tonite. Hirota said he'd bring it in. Don't know where I'll stow it, but we'll *have* it! 30 kilos!! I've been taking cure — baths everyday, and am getting browned up a bit. Look 1,000% better. Feel better and at last, eating a little better. Cooked up some beans today with ginger root in them. Pretty good. Guess whose birthday it is tomorrow?!

September 7
Happy Birthday again Eileen darling. 27 years old, or rather young today, and by Jupiter, if we're not together for next year's celebration, I fear we'd best give up!! I pray you're in the very best of health. Pete, my prayers for your well-being and happiness surely won't go unanswered. And, kitten, if you are waiting, I hope you're not sacrificing any possible good times for my sake. I'd like to know that you're having dates, lots of fun, enjoying life, and at the same time working hard as you're able, and somewhere along the line giving Uncle Sam a hand. But, if you should be married to someone else (here I go again on this) I want you to know that ever in my heart will be a pilot light, burning for my kitten, and ready to burst in to a roaring flame. Anything for you Pete,

just so you're happy. Incidentally, it's John's girl's birthday, too; and she's 27. So, we're celebrating in our own little way. Upon waking this morning, we congratulated each other and drank our toasts to you with coffee. We don't forget.

Last nite saw the accomplishment of what was one of the hall-marks of Bilibid deals! Hirota came stomping into the ward at 10:20 P.M. (lites out at 10 P.M.), and awakened me. "Hinkoo, Hinkoo — I bring thees gate, OK?" "OK, Hirota, you give this man, I meet you." So Matheson and I waited at the door. The ward was dead quiet, and dark except for the black-out lite at the desk. Soon we heard the sound of hob-nailed shoes, moving toward us with heavy staccato steps, crunching gravel and stones with a ferocity that could only mean that heavy weight was bearing down on the shoes. As Hirata came up he was carrying the two sacks, about 25–30 kilos each. Matheson took 'em on in and I paid Hirata, and he said, "OK — very good — you good, sank you. I breeng calindy soon." And thus ended the tale of the nocturnal adventure.

September 9
Oh boy! Got a swell surprise today — received a radiogram (the second since surrender) from Mom and Dad! Sure made me happy, because I realize it was sent as late as July, and being only two months old makes it seem like a telephone call! And knowing that "everybody is well" as of July

```
TO:   FIRST LT. WALTER J. HINKLE
      Rec'd Bilibid Prison 9/9/44

MSG:  "BIRTHDAY GREETINGS EVERYBODY WELL AWAITING YOUR RETURN PRAYING LOVE
      KISSES DAD MOTHER SOPHIA HINKLE."
```

Radiogram. *Hinkle Archive*

'44 makes my time easier to serve. God bless you both. Message was, "Birthday Greetings Everybody Well Awaiting Your Return Praying Love Kisses Dad Mother Sophie, Hinkle." Incidentally, today marks the one year anniversary of my amputation! Golly — in many ways it doesn't seem possible that 365 days have gone by since that long morning on the operating table. On the other hand, it seems just like last week. Vivid in my mind are the memories of those painful dressings, and those hours, days and weeks of excruciating pain. God, what a nightmare! But it *is* over! Today, I feel fine. I'm healthy enuff, tanned, and mentally adjusted to this life of hope and waiting. Eating pretty well — thru no fault of the kitchens!!

Draft still here. Expect they'll leave tomorrow or day after. No news lately. Sources limited since working party done away with. Still having black-outs, but don't understand IJA's practice of nightly searchlight drill, too! Last we heard was the U.S. troops fighting in Germany; this knocking out the "surrender" hope. Fast (Pharmacist Mate) made some damned good peanut, sugar and banana flavoring fudge today! Don't forget: Hirota sending note last nite about beans and sugar; "8:20 p.m.,"

"18 House enter"; "after put to the fire sir," etc. Right ear now infected from previous session of swabbing out wax. Damn!

September 12
This, unless my memory fails me, is Grandma's birthday, and I certainly wish you many happy returns of the day, Grandma. I hope and pray that your health has improved some. At least, God grant you some relief from the pain; I now know how terrible it is to suffer, and only now do I realize how brave a woman you have been. Think of me today Grandma — "Junior" is with you in thought anyway, and next year I'll be right at your side.

In the last few days we've had two air raid "alerts." The sirens blew this morning at about 10:30. Thru a reliable source, we hear that the alert of two days ago was the "real McCoy" and that the Americans were close. We hope they get closer and closer. Whereas we once dreaded and feared the sound of and destructive power of bombs, we are now all anxiously awaiting the advent of a bombing raid!!

You know — I'm just busier than a cat covering up his doings on a tin roof!! Here's an example, or shall I call it — "My Day."

6:15 a.m. — Get up, roll up net, put coffee, wash up, fill sugar jars, smoke.
7:30 — Breakfast.
7:45 — Go get vitamins.
8:00 — Put beans on.
8:15 — Grind or shred coconut, or mix hotcake batter.
9:30 — Put coffee on.
10:00 — Beans and coffee off.
11:00 — Coffee on. (If "Hot-cake Day," start frying!)
12:00 Noon — Chow.
1:00 p.m. — Sun bath.
1:45 — Toast coconuts.
3:00 — Shower, Shave.
4:00 — Coffee on, cut garlic.
5:15 — Chow.
6:00 — Coffee on, *Bango*.
6:15 — Wash beans for tomorrow.
6:30 — Coffee off.
6:30 to 9:30 — Bull sessions.
9:15 — Shower.
9:20 to 10:00 — Hit the hay.
In between times, I try to read, sew, write, or rest!

September 13
Stump raised merry hell last nite. Trying to speed up the date of operation, but can't seem to make headway. Doc Davis said he'll throw in a word and see what he can do. He's the only one here who really gives a damn as to whether or not I do have pain. So we'll see.

Nipponese furiously digging foxholes in front and around their guard house in our compound. Worked on into nite. Must be expecting something mighty soon!

September 14
Today has brought us our first *real* air-raid alarm! Since 7:45 a.m. the sirens have been furiously sending forth their curdling wails. To our ears, the siren's scream has been a beautiful symphony. We started with the siren sounding six times (real McCoy); everybody has to stay in the buildings at such times, and doors to buildings closed. Guards wearing steel helmets. Sirens blew "Beat to Quarters" twice, and "Secure" three times. At present moment (11:30 a.m.) we are alerted but "secure" from immediate attacks. Of course all of us are optimistic as all get out, tho at the same time we are definitely querulous! However, U.S. planes most definitely cannot be far off. This is not practice, and it's easy to see the Nips are jittery. Bless Bless! *Wouldn't* it be something to be out of this by Xmas?! Wheee!

We got some "bread," peanut brittle and cigs last nite (John and I). Good.

September 16
Don't forget 11:30 last nite and the oleo margarine. "I speak weeth heem. Start at 60, end up 17 and undershirt. Got in, cannot take back. Sergeant not sleep!"

NEWS — So far only rumor: U.S. landed at twelve places and took over Mindanao. Four U.S. planes over Manila September 14 (air-raid alarm). Germany surrendered September 7th and 9th. Draft still here. Expect they'll stay. Can't tell, however. Doctor Langdon says I may expect to be out in ten days. Sure hope so.

LATER NEWS — Supposed to be in paper as follows: Iliolo, Cebu, Negros, several places on Mindanao all bombed by U.S. Also, we are fighting in Germany and have met the German "Home Guards."

Had carabao today. One for the camp.

Monday, September 18
People expect that the Japan draft is to leave Wednesday of this week. A second draft is supposedly to go too, but it is to be formed right at the ships, and will meet "our" draft on ship-board. This, we gather, will bring a total of about 2,500 men heading for Japan. Uncle Sam's gang better get moving this way.

Got a good pair of Lts. bars from Charlie Osborne. (Cost me a bit of coffee.) Woke up this morning to sound of anti-aircraft fire. Practice of course, but it sure sounds good. A 26-fighter-formation flew south this morning.

September 19
Last nite seventy more men came in from Cabanatuan. Eighteen Doctors and some medics included. Beattie with them, as well as Major Ruth! "Our" draft got issued clothes yesterday: flannel shirts, woolen (heavy) pants and coats (IJA issue). Dope above about "two groups" apparently correct. They expect to leave tomorrow or Thursday.

NEWS — Admiral Halsey's force attacking from south. Nimitz from East. Nimitz takes two of Pelew groups, bombs and shells Iloilo and Samar and Leyte and Negros. Halsey bombs and shells Mindanao. Heavy fighting in East Prussia. Blugaria folds. Half Czechoslovakia ours. Cologne under siege. Halsey and Nimitz forces in efforts down South got 500 IJA planes on ground, sank 120 ships. Roosevelt, Churchill conference in Quebec. Both to meet Stalin in Paris soon.

September 20
The draft was supposed to leave this morning, but was postponed indefinitely. About 2,300 men in this camp now. FAR too many! Men from Palawan came in yesterday.[122]

---

122   On August 12, 1942, 300 American survivors from Bataan and Corregidor arrived on the island of Palawan. They were interned there by the Japanese in the old Filipino Constabulary barracks, known as Palawan's Prison Camp 10A, or Palawan Barracks, near the city of Puerto Princessa. The POWs spent the next two years building a nearby runway, using hand tools, wheelbarrows, and two small cement mixers. In September 1944, half the prisoners were sent to Manila, and their arrival at Old Bilibid was noted by Hinkle in his diary. In October 1944, the Palawan airstrip was attacked by American aircraft. As a result, the remaining 150 prisoners were put to work digging three air raid shelters—slit trenches 5 feet deep, 4 feet wide, and 100 feet long, and roofed with logs and covered with dirt. A tiny crawl space entry at either end of each trench admitted one man at a time. When the trench was filled, each man was tightly packed inside with his knees tucked under his chin. On December 14, 1944, the Japanese on Palawan came up with a plan to prevent the rescue of prisoners from the advancing Allies. During the midday meal the alarm sounded, but when the prisoners looked to the sky, they saw only two P38s flying high and away from the island. The prisoners, who by this time had become adept at judging the risk from an aerial attack, ignored the signal and resumed their meal. A few minutes later the alarm sounded again, and when the prisoners consulted the sky, they saw an American bomber flying far off into the distance. Again they ignored the siren and resumed their meal. The alarm rang out a third time, but this time a Japanese lieutenant and his men marched in with swords drawn and

Chow is going down. Wish the Yanks would come in or a Red Cross Ship would arrive, or something!

September 21st, 9:45 A.M.
This is the day! We are, at the moment, undergoing our first air attack, perpetrated by U.S. planes! It began with a few anti-aircraft explosions.

---

rifles bayonetted, insisting that everyone obey the signal. The lieutenant screamed, "They're coming! Planes—hundreds of planes!" The prisoners were puzzled and became suspicious. In the past when American planes attacked, the Japanese dropped what they were doing and lept into their slit trenches, often making the prisoners continue their work until the last moment. The lieutenant continued shrieking, "Hundreds of planes! Hurry," and so the prisoners went to their three trenches and crawled inside single file. One POW refused to go in and was set upon by the lieutenant, who cleaved the prisoner's head in two with a blow from his sword, stopping midway down his neck. Those seated at end of the trenches then saw several Japanese soldiers approach with buckets, flinging the contents onto the trenches. Before the prisoners could react to the smell of aviation fuel, other Japanese soldiers tossed lighted bamboo torches to ignite the fuel, and the trenches burst into flames. As the prisoners writhed and burned, the lieutenant scuttled from trench to trench, sword drawn, issuing commands to his men who approached the trenches, throwing grenades into the flaming entrances and showering them with gunfire until they were sure all of the prisoners were dead. Those who managed to escape with their clothes smoldering were bayonetted, clubbed, or gunned down. Weeks earlier while digging the trenches, some of the prisoners tunneled one of the trenches a few extra feet to the edge of the cliff overlooking Puerto Princessa, plugging the opening with sandbags and covering them with dirt to conceal the exit from the Japanese, thinking the secret exit might come in handy one day. As the trench burned, several prisoners broke through the sandbags and escaped, jumping down to the beach and hiding in rock outcroppings. Most were hunted and killed by soldiers, but several managed to elude the Japanese by swimming across the bay, where they were aided by Filipino guerrillas. One prisoner who was shot at in the water and was hit in the armpit and thigh swam for nearly nine hours until reaching the opposite shore. In the Palawan massacre, 139 POWs were killed and eleven escaped. When news of the massacre reached Allied commanders, it sparked fear that prisoners in other camps would suffer the same fate. A series of rescue campaigns were then devised by the United States, including a raid at Cabanatuan on January 30, 1945; a raid at Santo Tomas Internment Camp on February 3; and a raid at Old Bilibid on February 4, which resulted in freedom for Walter Hinkle.

No Sirens. Then we heard some MG fire (in air) and some of us went outside to see what the Nips were doing. I went out, joking about practice air-raids. Then I noticed a flight of planes, counted 52. They went toward port area, and AA let loose right into them. Doctor Waterous saw one go down in flames. I was watching a dogfight, but no damage done. Everyone out of barracks watching, most of them figuring practice. Next saw flight of at least 100 planes in one direction, and over farther a flight of 50 or 60. Looked like Navy. From ground came AA, .30, .50 and 5" fire, sounded like 4th of July. Heard some bombs, but no big ones. Planes most likely Navy dive bombers.

Now 10:45 a.m., and it sounds like another — yes! It's another flight. Man! They're sure shootin' at em! Feel not too scared, just slightly nervous. Reaction hard to explain: happy as the devil about the raid — first step towards our release . . . sort of bubbling with excitement. At same time, when all the gunfire broke loose, I got that "old feeling" in my stomach — frightened cove of quail! IJA sure has some big guns around here. Then I could hear the guards firing their rifles, and also heard some fool fire his pistol. Just as panicky as we were at first. After we witnessed the first wave come over, the prison authorities finally realized they were U.S. planes, and chased us into barracks, locked us in, and closed all windows. However, thru one of the upper windows I watched a flight of dive bombers going thru AA fire, and just as they began to wing over for a dive, saw one of them go down in flames. May God give him a peaceful rest, and I pray his life did not go in vain. Our thanks to that pilot go with our prayers for him. All during this time — 1½ hrs. — I had a pot of beans on, and was nervously tending to them! Too, the reason the sirens didn't blow is attributed to the fact that the electricity was off. Maybe our boys bombed the main line, or it may have been sabotage. During the first wave a stray AA shell lit right outside our building with a WHAM!! Just after it, a bomb lit not far off with a KA-WHOOM!! When these events happened I had my spoon in the beans and did a furious act of agitating said beans!! Jesus — I did jump! It wasn't till then that my pulse rate really began a climb. I put on my wrist dog-tag and medal Mom sent me. Hope it doesn't have to be used. Gee — those U.S. Navy planes sure looked good in formation, and when they'd wing over it gave me a real thrill. Please God, don't have them bomb our camp. We've come too far thru this to be killed by our own planes and bombs.

It's all quiet now (11:30). Raid lasted 1½ hours, and brother that is a L-O-N-G time to sweat! I expect that this 'ill keep up every day or every few days now, and by Harry — we *might* be free by Xmas!!

When first we sighted the planes, it seemed we saw flights in all directions.

Some of the chatter that went on:

"Boy, quite a practice the Nips are puttin' on."

"Practice? Hell, I think it's *real*!"

"Hey, look over there. *Christ*! Fifty-two of the bastards!"

"Jeez — goodamn Nips firin' right into their own planes. Must be usin' blanks. Boys are really usin' alot of ammo for just practice. Maybe its real."

"Wonder why the sirens didn't blow if its real? Probably forgot to press the button!"

"Jeezus! Look at that flight! Must be about one-hundred! Nips planes hell! Those are OURS! Look, LOOK — There's three of 'em wingin' over, and one other goin' down in flames! Jesus! This is it, boys! Don't let anyone bull you! Xmas turkey in Albuquerque!!"

"Yessir this is just the start! Now they know where their AAs are, their guns, ships, etc, and from now on they are going to really work 'em over!"

"God, it's really happening! I'm speechless!"

"Well Andy, what do you think? Real cuan!"

"Golly, Lt. — I don't know what to think. Seems like it's pretty real for practice, and if it *is* practice the IJA are damned good showmen!"

"Golly, look at that dude wing-over! That's the Navy, awright!"

"Well, I hope they take time out so's we can get our chow anyway!"

"What's chow — steamed corn? Hah! I'm sittin' on em!!" (Bucket of boiled mungo beans await him on table!)

"D'ja see the lil' Nip guard squattin' under the tree? Had his rifle pointed straight up, and peeking at the lanes from behind the trunk of the tree, scared silly."

All during the raid, the inside of the ward was a bee-hive of talk. Conjecture, prophecies, hopes, fears and jokes filled the air. Those who had pots on the hot plates were apparently tending them without being too much perturbed. Others hit the deck at the sound of the two shells previously mentioned which hit nearby. As a whole, though, no one was actually fearful of *our* being bombed. Fears were expressed, however, about stray shots, or ricochets coming at us from the AAs and from the panicky rifle fire of the camp guards. For the most part though, activity in the ward went on as usual, except for the excited chatter, the great orations brimming with optimism, and the futile efforts of some to watch the planes thru narrow slits in the shutters. All in all, a damned good raid. We expect the Big Boys next time. Then we *will* hear a racket! How will we be affected by all this? Will our treatment be different? Will our chow suffer? Will the drafts leave? (No!) Thus we wait: anxiously, hopefully, and slightly fearfully.

Two casualties among our men: one man badly injured in jaw by piece of shell that dropped thru roof of barracks #3. Piece of shell in leg of another. 1:00 p.m. Water turned off. Probably need H2O for fire-fighting. Reports: smoke billowing from Camp Murphy and Nichols. Port

area worked over well. Andy says, "Just think, just several thousand feet above our heads this morning were men from *our* country!"

Air Raid #2: 2:55 p.m. Three waves came over this time (it's now 5:00 p.m.) and really gave someplace a working over! Some damned big ones dropped and the air certainly did reverberate. We saw the smoke out Paudacau way — oil dump. What's funny about these raids, is the fact that our boys are receiving no opposition from the "Wild Eagles"! All their trouble seems to come from ground fire. Further, our planes are flying comparatively low, maybe 15,000 feet.

Our boys have sure done a good job today, and we'll expect to see them bright and early tomorrow. But golly, I can't get over my nervous feeling. I feel sure that they won't bomb us, but there's always the chance of a slipup. And God, I don't want another injury. Please dear God, if something is to come my way again, make it a clean trip out of this world. I believe that fear of being injured again is the cause of my nervous tension. It's not fear in the normal sense of the word. It's an excited feeling like you get riding a roller coaster. Hell, I've gone right on with my chores of cooking, while the MGs and pom-poms were blasting away at a diver. Jeez, the activity sounds so damned close by! Course some of it is, but still, not too close. Exceptions are some AA guns nearby, and the guards outside our windows firing at diving planes. These guards are what actually worry me, as I said before. Never know *where their* fire is going!! John's going thru it swell. Been reading except when the wave would come over and hell would break loose. Sleeping rest of time! I've been unable to read — can't concentrate.

So far, now for today: Morning three different waves. Afternoon three waves. Total for day would probably come close to 400 planes, I would estimate. At noon the guards escorted the chow servers to and from the chapel so we'd be fed. Galley crew brought it to Chapel. We cannot leave building during raids. Commander Baltzly pulls bed away from wall and he and Spriggs get up against wall during all firing. Big explosion from Port Area at 8:30 p.m.

September 22nd, 7:23 A.M.
Air Raid #3. So far I've heard just the sirens and bell, and a few explosions of some kind.

7:55 a.m. — They're here!! And the boys are really doing some snappy dive bombing. Man! When Hell breaks loose it's really bedlam. One peeled off and dove down near us — apparently at the RR station. His motor sounded like a symphony; so smooth and well-pitched. As he came down, the engine seemed to scream and we thought he'd never make it, then we heard him pull out after which we waited breathlessly. Then came the "ka-woomph!"

Here's another wave and the AA is firing to beat hell! (Note my writing — kind of nervous.) They're pretty low — it's a very overcast day and the ceiling's about 10 or 15,000. Yesterday was overcast too. Jeeze! Sounds like hundreds of planes up there. God, listen to those MGs!! (I'm writing this during the activity, and my pulse is really up there!) The concussions of the bombs are echoing. Andy says, "Boy, all you could see anywhere you looked was planes." We have to look thru cracks in the shutters to see — very unsatisfactory. Told us this morning that upper half of windows could be left open, but when the alarm went, our guard shut 'em all!

Men from Murphy went thru the raid there in trenches. Had about eighteen casualties, all of which were from accidental pieces of frags. Said it was really worked over. Several of our planes were seen to come down near Bilibid and wobble their wings in salute to us! Sure glad to hear — it shows they know we're here. Wouldn't be surprised to hear about the Marines landing on Luzon somewhere, and I fully expect to be under U.S. stars and stripes before Xmas, provided the Nips don't move us out of here before-hand, and I don't see how they can if this activity keeps up. Bless Bless! This is certainly one of the most thrilling and hair-raising events I *ever* expect to experience. Of course I realize that the rescuing of the American POW is not the primary aim of our forces, but it sure is nice to think so! Then every little bit I get to thinking, "Gee — it's really happening! Yank planes, Navy fighters from *carriers*! They can't be far away! These thoughts are all interwoven with thoughts of how soon I'll be HOME, how soon I'll see Mom and Dad. I won't believe I'm *really* back till I hold both of them in my arms again. And Pete — soon I'll be able to find out about her. Is she waiting or has she married?

8:15 a.m. — All quiet.

9:05 a.m. — They're back! Out of a clear sky!

9:20 a.m. — All quiet again. Did a lot of strafing this time, and some good bombing. Helluva big fire out toward port area.

9:40 a.m. — Back again!

10:00 a.m. — All quiet.

10:20 a.m. — Back.

10:50 a.m. — All clear again.

12:50 a.m. — Secure.

Bombs did lots of damage this morning. Fires going strong. One along Pasig River where bodegas are, another out Pandacan Way. Black smoke has been rolling heavily since last raid.

Now 2:00 p.m. and the smoke still thick enuff to block the sun. Doubt they'll be back today. Quite a wind blowing and the weather may stop

the boys. IJA general was here in the morning for inspection. Several heavy explosions have occurred since planes left. Probably oil or gas or ammo.

3:00 p.m. — Sirens sound "all clear."

4:50 p.m.— Air raid alarm again!!

5:50 p.m. — All clear. No activity.

September 23rd
8:25 a.m. — Air raid alarm. No planes over during alarm. Probably over Luzon or elsewhere. Or, perhaps landing being effected?

Now have job of ward librarian for air-raids, and regularly during afternoons, 2–4 p.m.

September 24th
8:27 a.m. — Air raid alarm.

10:15 a.m. — Temporary "all clear."

Last nite 200 British and Dutch POWs were brought in. They are survivors out of about 1,200 POWs who were on Japanese ship heading for Nippon. About 90 miles out of here, hugging shore, with convoy when U.S. dive-bombers came over. Sunk two cruisers and the POW ship (unmarked). About 1,000 POWs lost, rest picked up by J'se fishing boats. Then planes strafed fishing boats the next day, and many of the POWs were wounded. They say that about 500 of the POWs were paralyzed by dysentery anyway. This gang has been lying in the bay since July!![123]

Went to Mass, confession and communion.

Learned that Peralta[124] has been active with 63rd Infantry guerrillas on Panay. Radio contact with Australia too!

September 26th

News — Philippine Islands declare war on U.S.!! President Laurel with OK of cabinet declare war because of bombing Manila, and because Iloilo, Samar, Leyte, and Cebu were *again* worked over, and because Legazpi had been bombed and strafed. Nips paper says U.S. has fifteen carriers "believed" to be operating off of Mindoro! Jeepers, not far!

I was to be operated on tomorrow or Friday but now an order has come out that only absolute emergencies will be done, so's to keep the number of disabled down to a minimum. Doctor Langdon says if things stay quiet for a little while, he may try and have the order modified so I can go in.

September 27th

"Alert" alarm in afternoon — now secure.

123   They were survivors of the *Hofuku Maru,* sunk 80 miles north of Corregidor on September 20, 1944.
124   Macario Peralta Jr. joined the Philippine Commonwealth Army in 1936. In 1940, he attended the Philippine Army Infantry School, finishing at the top of his class. After war broke out with Japan, Peralta was assigned as the commander of the 61st Provisional Regiment of the USAFFE. In July 1942 Peralta (then a colonel) organized and led the Free Panay Guerrilla Forces in Duenas, Iloilo. When the Americans returned to Panay on March 18, 1945, his guerrillas controlled much of the island. For his heroism, Peralta was awarded with a Distinguished Service Cross and the Silver Star.

September 28th

Wrote and signed post cards to folks today, but fully expect to get home before cards do! Message was, "Everything fine. Received radiogram. Chin up, don't worry now. Health = "Excellent." Friends of John Powell. Morale high. Regards all! Love to you and Eileen, from Walter J. Hinkle."

Find myself hoping it stays quiet for awhile, so's I can have operation!

September 30th

It seems they're getting ready to move out the drafts! We'll see. The news of importance is this: we begin, today, having two meals a day! At 8 a.m. and 3 p.m. Reason — shortage of wood for fires in galley. No cut in rations. Paid $35 pesos.

October 1st

One of the drafts pulled out today at 3:00 p.m. About 665 men left to board ship, presumably for Japan. They're to go to Lubang by barge, and then get on ship from there. Gee — it's a funny feeling to say "so long" to your friends and realize that they may not reach their destination, but may be killed by bombs and guns from our planes! We hope and pray they have a safe voyage. At the same time we hope our forces are very near at hand. The feelings associated with this parting have been very complex in this respect. The other draft (Doc Davis's) is rumored to leave day after tomorrow.

Our two-meal-a-day program is NO good. You can't tell me we're getting as much to eat now as we did for three meals. All of us are sure we've had a cut of one third. Firewood shortage surely *can't* be the reason.

October 4th

No news, just very cool weather and almost steady rain. Stump's been giving me lots of trouble and haven't been sleeping well. On the 2nd, a number of officers came in from Las Piñas. Among them is Al Lawhon who came over with me on USAT *W*. We were together in "E" Co., 31st and good friends. He looks good and feels pretty well. Had long chat with him last nite and we had a good time going over our Manila memories. Al received a flesh wound in calf of leg in Bataan, doesn't bother him now tho.

October 7th

Haven't kept up diary last few days. Haven't felt very much like writing. Not getting much sleep nites, and little chance of making it up during day. On Oct. 5th, had inspection by Dr. Nogi.[125] His inspections usually precede a move. What??!! Just received two more letters from Mom and Dad! Both dated January '44. Old mail dug out of dark corner! About ten cases of bacillary dysentery of some sort here. Hope it gets under control.

October 10th

A draft of 150 officers and 50 enlisted men in from Cabanatuan yesterday.

Two-hundred more to come today. All to join present Japan draft and to leave Wednesday or Thursday. Also, eighty-eight Navy corpsmen, three doctors and one Pharm. going. Further, dope has it that Army is to take over Bilibid after draft leaves. If this is true, and I fear it is, this will no longer be a pleasant place, because our Army medics can't hold a candle to the Navy, in attitude, discipline, appearance, and industry. Anyway, I'm not looking forward to the change.

My IJA boy says, "Patients stay here. After fighting, all friends here — patients still alive." Good — hope he's right!

Yes, the eighty-eight Corpsmen from here are going. The three best ones from our ward, except Fast (nite duty) — he stays. The two left are "dupas,"[126] stupid as hell!

Wednesday, October 11, 1944

Well, the draft (1,800 men) left today at 1:00 p.m., Japan bound. I sure got tears in my eyes when I said "good-bye" to Doc Davis. That really hurt. Roy Gray went too (14 out of our ward). Hated to see him go especially. All the "good-byes" went to the core of my heart for I kept thinking, "Will they make it? Will I ever see them alive again?" So many friends on this draft; Colonel Deter, Major Davis, Dr. Osborne, Dr. Rader, Al Lawhon, Russ Patterson, Roy Gray, Dennis Shea, "Andy" Anderson,

---

125 Naraji Nogi (IJA); director of the Hospital for Military Prison Camps of P.I.

126 Ass or arse in Polish.

"Jughead" Byrd, Jim Dobbs,* Jack Jenkins. Good luck, and God guide and bless all of you.[127]

Thursday, October 12, 1944

We've been on "alert" since yesterday afternoon. Much IJA air activity, too. Oh oh — 247 officers came in from Cabanatuan. Another draft in the making. So many friends on this one, and more are coming tomorrow and following days. Major Howard Pahl (Capt. Pahl of "G" company) is here and it was great to see him

again after three years. (3 years!!!) He looks thinner but well. Says "Ev," his wife, has been living in Mexico City and likes it there. Others I have seen of this group today include Cols. Thayer, Greathouse, Majs. Caruthers, Mandelson, Utke, "Pappy" Knowles, Fred Roth, and lots more. Look fairly well, however.

October 14th

At midnite last nite another draft of officers arrived. A lot more friends this time out. McNair, Bill Prickett, Speck, Utke, Thayer, Magee, Burlando. Took some coffee over to Mc and Bill. Mc tells me stories of cliques and graft at Cabanatuan. They're all hoping for another raid to occur, to keep them from going to Japan. Each draft thru here has had this hope and it has been ours too. Golly, we ought to get a raid sometime again. Visitors over *all* day. Same stories over and over, but it's been like old times.

Sunday, October 15

Went to Mass this morning.

AIR RAID #4 — 8:55 a.m. First the sirens sounded "Alert," and we were disappointed. The camp bell, however, suddenly took off with ten rapid "ding-dongs," which signifies "Air Raid," and sirens joined in. I was baking some coconut, kept trying to hurry it up in case our planes should come!

10:20 a.m. — Here they are! Welcome, boys, welcome!!! Couldn't see many of them. Personally saw only about six in

---

127 The prisoners marched to pier 7 in Manila harbor, where they boarded the *Arisan Maru,* descended into its holds, and were packed together tightly, with enough room to sit but not enough to lie down. Food was a teacup full of rice twice daily and a canteen of dirty water. Toilets consisted of four 5-gallon buckets, and many prisoners became afflicted with dysentery in the cramped and unsanitary conditions. After a lengthy delay due to air raids in Manila, the *Arisan Maru* joined a convoy that departed for Formosa on October 21. Three days into the voyage the convoy was attacked by American submarines. When the first torpedo struck, Japanese sailors prepared to abandon the *Arisan Maru* and cut the rope ladders to the no. 1 and no. 2 holds. This angered the prisoners, who shouted at the guards but grew silent when the ship groaned, buckled up in the center, and nearly split in two, with each half tilting away fore and aft. One athletic prisoner shimmied up a stanchion to get out of the hold and was followed by another five or six men. From the deck they saw a Japanese destroyer dropping depth charges, and later, the destroyer taking aboard Japanese sailors who occupied all of the *Arisan Maru's* lifeboats. The prisoners searched the deck for a rope, which they then lowered into the hold, tied to the severed rope ladder, and hauled up—making the ladder fast so others could escape. After climbing out of the holds, the prisoners jumped into the water, grabbed onto floating debris, and paddled toward the Japanese destroyer. But Japanese sailors aboard the destroyer jabbed at them with long poles, keeping the POWs away from the ship. Darkness came fast as a bitter wind blew up, and screams of men calling out to one another could be heard. Donald Meyers, one of the nine survivors, later wrote, "It was a strange bereft feeling with so many of my friends drowned all about me." All of Hinkle's friends who were mentioned in his October 11 entry perished in the largest loss of American life in a single disaster at sea—575 more than from the sinking of the RMS *Lusitania,* and 273 more than the RMS *Titanic.*

their dives, though of course there were many more. Sounded like they worked over Nichols Field, and Cavite. Don't know. All hell broke loose around here again, but I wasn't near as nervous as I was during the other raids.

10:50 a.m. — All quiet again, but not secure! We'll expect you back today, fellows. Wish they had come three days earlier and kept the other draft in.

12:05 p.m. — Temporary "All Clear."

12:15 p.m. — Air raid bell again!!!

October 17
8:10 a.m. — Alert.

8:35 a.m. — Air raid alarm. We wait. No planes.

11:05 a.m. — Temporary "all clear," and finally "All Clear."

Two hundred men from Cabanatuan yesterday and two hundred more today — all officers. Quite clear that Cabanatuan to be broken up and all but "PDs" slated for Japan or somewhere. Today's group saw three flights of U.S. planes over Baler Bay. Heard bombs. Nips claim sinking three American carriers and four other ships east of Formosa. Claim 18 U.S. planes downed over Manila on 15th.

I have a very bad cold today. Feel like hell! Slept soundly from 6:00 p.m. yesterday to 7:30 a.m. today!!! Didn't help. Howie Martin came in today

from Cabanatuan. Looks pretty thin, but well tanned. Only got a few letters.

October 18th
Rumor of U.S. landing at Baler.

8:00 a.m. — Air raid alarm.

10:15 a.m. — Here they are again! (Raid #5). Those Yanks! Sounds like some heavy stuff and most of it around Nichols, Cavite and port area.

10:45 — Fairly quiet again. Very overcast day.

12 noon — Temporary "All Clear" bell in Bilibid.

12:10 p.m. — Yanks back, raising hell!!!

12:25 p.m. — All quiet. (Brought in another group from Cabanatuan.)

1:25 p.m. — Temporary "All Clear" bell in Bilibid.

2:30 p.m. — Air Raid! (No planes yet! 2:45).

4:20 p.m. — Here's a few back, dropped some big ones; a few minutes of AA and MGs, and all over. Short and snappy but effective. (Raining all afternoon.)

5:45 p.m. — Back to "Alert" status.

October 19th
7:50 a.m. — Air Raid #6!!! Our boys took Manila completely by surprise

a little while ago and really gave the city some Yankee Hell! We heard planes overhead just as we began eating breakfast and we assumed that the "Wild Eagles" were up for a little flight. This was immediately disproved by the sudden sound of bombs! It was about 5 minutes before the city's sirens went off. Meantime our planes were all over the place — no opposition. Some heavy stuff was dropped today too, in fact lots of it. Boy, what a racket! Certainly becomes obvious that we're in the middle of a war! I wouldn't venture to guess how many planes were over yesterday — maybe 150. What irritates me is my *eyes*! I can't see the planes way up, like the others can. It's not until I spot some in a dive that I really get my thrill, because there I'm *seeing* the boys. They must be flying higher than they did on the 21st and 22nd of September, because I saw that gang clearly. Nonetheless, it looks as tho they're here to stay and we can soon expect a landing. Already thoughts of home and loved ones now takes the front. I've been thinking how great it will be to see the Golden Gate again, and see who's waiting on the pier. Gee, it *surely* can't be very far off *now*!

8:30 a.m. — Things quiet again.

9:45 a.m. — Temporary "All Clear" Bilibid bell.

10:30 a.m. — Back again! Dropped some big ones and at 10:35 they were gone!!

12:25 p.m. — Air raid bell at Bilibid.

1:40 p.m. — Here they are and boy they really dropped something on the port area. I saw four of 'em go into their dives and the bombs sounded like "block-busters"!

1:50 p.m. — Quiet again.

2:30 p.m. — A gang of about 15 or 20 came back and raised more hell! This seems to be getting the aspect of a nice habit! We like it!!

3:15 p.m. — Dong! Temporary "All Clear."

6:00 p.m. — Back to "Alert" status. About 280 more came in from Cabanatuan today, mostly medics.

6:20 p.m. — "All Clear." Thus ended October 19th.

October 20th.
7:15 a.m. — Well, the gang that came in yesterday brought most of the Corpsmen from Davao. It was good to see all of them again, especially José Garcia. All the men on the draft are terribly anxious for the Yanks to keep coming, so the Japanese won't be able to get them out. This is not at all hard to understand. If they do get out, they figure it may mean another year or 1½ years before they get out

of this. And take McNair's case. Mc's wife is only six kilometers away from here, in Santo Tomas. If he leaves, this one move may separate them for another two years.

Of course all the talk is about the planes bombing Manila, and else-where. Yesterday, over Las Piñas, Yanks dropped some kind of packs of cigs that had American and Philip-pine flags on them, and a note, "I shall return," Douglas MacArthur. We're just on edge, momentarily waiting for the sirens or the planes. No one seems afraid, although hopes are often expressed that bombs don't drop here.

9:30 a.m. — "Secure."

2:00 p.m. — "Alert" again. No planes over as yet but apparently they're working over Luzon somewhere.

October 21st
7:30 a.m. — "Alert."

8:35 a.m. — "Air Raid" alarm. No planes.

9:30 a.m. — Back to "Alert."

3:50 p.m. — "All Clear." Some more men in from Cabanatuan and brought *real good news*! MacArthur with 150,000 U.S. troops landed at Samar and Leyte on October 17th!!! Osmeñas and P.I. cabinet with him. Mac made broadcast three hours after landing! Boy! That's wonderful! It's like living a dream and having

it slowly come true. We've waited and waited, and still we wait. Some have gone to Japan and are waiting there. But those of us who will be here when our boys get here will certainly shed tears of thankfulness and joy. It's not over yet, but God, it can't be more than a *month or two*!! Mom — keep those home fires burn-ing, because your son will damned soon be coming *home*!

Saw the cigarette packages Mac's pilots dropped.

October 22nd
All quiet, not even on "Alert." Got eight letters from Chicago, six from Mom and Dad, two from Eleanor and Frank. NONE FROM EILEEN! DAMN! I can't understand that! Has she written?? Is she married? Why doesn't she write anyway? Mom and Dad's were dated April and glad to hear they're well. Glad Eleanor's well. Lucky Frank. How the hell does he do it? Got a funny feeling in my stomach when I saw "Mr. and Mrs. F. Boslu." Sort of a feeling of resent-ment somehow. No right to, I don't guess; but I did.

October 23rd
Damn it, Eleanor. Those two letters of yours kept me awake till about 4 a.m. last nite. I dug out your '41 letters to me; the one where you "just wanted to talk" to me (full of "remember whens") and the one tell-ing of meeting Frank at the sorority dance. My memory did some fancy

maneuvering inside the last few years, and I lay here in bed feeling lonelier and lonelier — like a lost orphan who has nothing to his name but treasured memories, and now someone has stolen the treasure! Gee, Eleanor, I do hope you are happy. I can't exactly say I'm glad you're married — that wouldn't be true. But I surely am not surprised — I don't know *what* it is — let's call it "bewildered" or "dazed." I keep saying to myself, "Eleanor's married, Eleanor's married! But I can't seem to come down to earth and *realize* it. I know I will when I return, though!! That's liable to be a bit of a jolt.

Got six more letters from Mom and Dad today — March and April '44. Glad you got my 5th card, but apparently you didn't see thru those unusual statements and spot the code, 'cause none of your letters had any bewildering statements in them. However, enuff that you heard from me. Sure glad you like the new place. Mom sounds very well pleased with it. I'm anxious to get back and begin life again. And still no letters from Pete. Enuff said on this, I guess. I just can't figure it out. If she's written *why* haven't I received them? Wrong address? No sabe. I'll have to wait to find out.

October 24th
6:15 a.m. — "Alert."

7:30 a.m. — A few Yanks came over and dropped some busters, and then took off. More activity is expected from now on in however.

9:20 a.m. — Back to "Alert."

10:20 a.m. — "Air Raid" alarm. No planes.

10:55 a.m. — "All Clear."

12:40 p.m. — "Air Raid" alarm. No planes.

1:30 p.m. — "Alert."

4:00 p.m. — "All Clear." I've had a pretty severe case of belly cramps for the last six days. Doctor Langdon started me on sulfathiazole couple days ago. Some relief now, but appetite is gone. Can't figure out what cause them, but great Harry, they are Hell!!

October 25th
7:15 a.m. — "Alert."

11:10 a.m. — "Air Raid" alarm.

12:10 p.m. — "Alert." No planes.

2:40 p.m. — "All Clear."

3:25 p.m. — "Alert."

October 26th
8:00 a.m. — "Alert."

3:30 p.m. — "All Clear." No planes today, but apparently the boys are buzzing around near-by.

John and I really had a treat today. I swapped 1½ cups sugar and 1 cup beans for 12 oz. can of Spam. Fried the Spam with garlic and peppers. Then made some bean flour gravy, and that, with some yeast, rice-corn,[128] soup and coffee really made good eating. Chow has been pretty bad here lately. Lugao at 8:00 a.m. and rice and corn, sort of a mush, at 3:00 p.m. The ration is small and besides it's so damned monotonous and decidedly tasteless. And of late (last 5–6 days) I've had just a terrific taste for canned food and *any* good American food. Most especially have I been thinking of *rye bread, liverwurst, mustard* and *beer*!!!! Amazing how one's thoughts do run sometimes. Last couple days I've been unable to eat much, because of the sulfathiazole. But as soon as I began getting hungry, I began thinking of those things to eat. Boy, I'm really and truly looking forward to having a lot of fun in our kitchen when I get back, Mom!! Just wait'll I start drumming up some of my concoctions.

We've heard rumors that the Yanks have landed at Lucena (Luzon), but discredit this, because it's so close to Manila (3-hour drive) that I'm sure we'd have had lots, lots more air activity around here. I'm looking forward, however, to being under Old Glory by Thanksgiving (Nov. 30, 1944), but I wouldn't be surprised, either, if it wasn't till Xmas. There is one hope, though. I feel that the election may have a lot to do with this West Pacific attack by Nimitz and Halsey and MacArthur. It's possible, of course, that Roosevelt and MacArthur have promised the folks back home that they'd have "the brave boys in the P. I." back home for Xmas, or some such dribble. At any rate we KNOW the Yanks *are* on their way here, and it's very trying on our patience. We want them to HURRY, of course. We've been caged so long. We suffered so many things for over 2½ years: hunger, filth, disease, loneliness and misery in general. We're all pretty well beat up — we may not be the men we were in December '41, but we still have some traces of humanity about us (most of us, that is), and *we want to go home.* We've fought for Old Glory, we've suffered many, many injuries for Her, and for our loved ones. Now we want to go HOME! We want PEACE, QUIET, and SOLITUDE! We don't want to talk about the war in the P. I. We're *not* HEROES, we don't pretend to be, no matter *what* the War Department says!! We know of the blunders, cowardices, and foolish mistakes, as well as the *few* gallant and smart things done over here. These things we'd as soon keep to ourselves. In short, we're just a gang of Americans who have realized what a wonderful land America is, and how much that land meant and means to us, and we want to RETURN, and STAY PUT!!! Thus ended the Hinkle lecture. How I do run on!! They're my feelings, though — "Them's my sentiments!"

---

128   A rough-cracked corn that Filipinos cook like rice.

October 27th

8:10 a.m. — "Alert." This is "Navy Day," and all the Navy personnel here and the camp as a whole in fact, have been looking forward to this day for a big bombing or landing nearby. So far (9:00 a.m.) we've merely been "alerted," but we still have hopes.

5:00 p.m. — "All Clear." No planes, but it's significant that for two days now Manila has been on "Alert" *all* day. Made another swap today; one cup beans and 1 cup sugar for one 12 oz. can of corned beef. Many plans for tomorrow!

October 29th

7:50 a.m. — Surprise Air Raid #8! I was at Mass this morning and waiting to receive Holy Communion, when I heard a lot of airplane engines. Figured it was a group of J'se, till I noticed a number of Americans pointing to the southeast. Then I could hear planes diving and also some bombs and AA fire! About that time I began "excavating" the vicinity of the chapel, (have to be in your own building during raid and I had a good half block to go!!). As I got about half way to SOQ, the sirens sounded as did our bell, but hell, by then the Yanks were all over Manila, and the war was on again. I saw some of the planes, but not all of them. They dropped some heavy stuff, too. May have been some land based planes in the fracas today. The raids don't get me all excited any more — just routine! Keep coming Yanks! Wanna be home by Xmas!!

Hear we have Cebu and that PT boats are operating around Manila Bay.

9:30 a.m. — Pretty quiet again. Some fires started around the port area. Incidentally, did not receive Holy Communion. There are two good sources of news in the camp, and I hesitate to say more here, in case this should fall into the wrong hands. I'll trust my poor memory about Mc and S.

I fried up the bean sprouts and canned beef yesterday, and also put some canned beef into the pot of beans, and John and I really ate! I felt like I was ready to burst. The meat sure makes a difference. Today I shall fry up some Vogts luncheon meat and celebrate the raid!! Yesterday we celebrated the end of my 4th year of duty! Gee, Eileen, I *do* so hope you're waiting. My past notations on my feelings about this have been mostly for "morale building" purposes. Now, with rescue and return in very near sight, I get a terrifically excited feeling inside when I contemplate seeing you again. Kitten, if you are waiting, and I feel you are, we'll make a happy, happy path thru life, come what may. We both deserve a break. And golly — my plans!! I want to take Mom on a real shopping spree! Wherever she wants to go; New York, Hollywood, or elsewhere. I'd like to pay the folks back for my university education, though I know what their answer will be. I'll talk 'em into at least part of it, or buy 'em a new car or *something*! And Pete, if

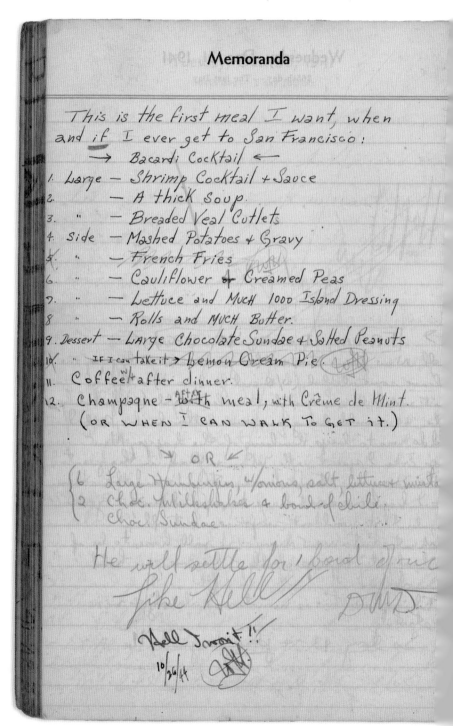

Memoranda

This is the first meal I want, when
and if I ever get to San Francisco:
→ Bacardi Cocktail ←

1. Large — Shrimp Cocktail + Sauce
2. " — A thick Soup.
3. " — Breaded Veal Cutlets
4. Side — Mashed Potatoes + Gravy
5. " — French Fries
6. " — Cauliflower + Creamed Peas
7. " — Lettuce and MUCH 1000 Island Dressing
8. " — Rolls and MUCH Butter.
9. Dessert — LARge Chocolate Sundae + Salted Peanuts
10. " IF I can take it → Lemon Cream Pie.
11. Coffee after dinner.
12. Champagne — with meal, with Crème de Mint.
    (OR WHEN I CAN WALK TO GET it.)

→ OR ←

{ 6 Large Hamburgers, w/onions, salt, lettuce, mustard
{ 2 Choc. Milkshakes + bowl of chili.
    Choc. Sundae

He will settle for 1 bowl of rice
like Hell

Hell Dammit!!
10/26/x

The last eighteen pages of Diary #2 are filled with lists and recipes. *Hinkle Archive*

1ª LUCKIES!   **Memoranda**   Kosher Dill Pickles

ITEMS I MOST DESIRE TO EAT, BACK HOME!

(FRESH)

1. Veal Cutlets (Mom's)
2. T-Bone Steak
3. Filet of Sole
4. Filet Mignon
5. White Castle Hamburgers
6. Country Fried Chicken
7. Roast Pork (Mom's)
8. Baked Beans (Mom's)
9. Pork Chops. Saud
10. Pig Tails & Spare-ribs (Mom's)
11. Italian Spaghetti "
12. Macaroni (")
13. Mashed Potatoes
14. French Fried "
15. Hash Brown "
16. Shoe string "
17. Potatoe Chips
18. Peas
19. Cauliflower
20. Lettuce
21. Brussel Sprouts
22. Sauer Kraut
23. Slaw
24. Lima Beans
25. Carrots
26. Celery
27. Apples ✓
28. Peaches ✓
29. Oranges ✓
30. Tangerines

31. Strawberries
32. Cherries
33. Raspberries
34. Watermelon
35. Cantaloups
36. Shrimp.
37. Grapefruit.

CEREALS
1. Oatmeal
2. Grape Nuts
3. Corn Flakes
4. Bran Flakes.

DAIRY STUFF.
1. MILK
2. CREAM
3. CHEESE (ANY)

OTHER BKFST STUFF.
1. Eggs
2. Bacon
3. Ham
4. Rolls (Sweet)
5. Toast + Butter.
6. Peanut Butter
7. Pancakes Brookfield & Caro
8. Apple Butter
9. Orange Juice
10. Coffee
11. French Toast
12. Strawberry Jam (ANN PAGE)
13. "Cinnamon Toast."

SODA FOUNTAIN
1. Chocolate Sundae w/peanuts
2. " Soda
3. " Shake
4. " Marshmellow Sund.
5. Banana Split
6. Pie à la mode
7. Cake " "
8. Root Beer + Ice cream
9. Choc. Marsh., peanuts + whipped cream Sundae

"Sweets"
1. Whitman Sampler
2. Salted Peanuts
3. Hershey Bars w/almonds
4. Clark Bars
5. Baby Ruth's
6. Camels
7. Plain Milk Chocolate
8. Hard Candies
9. Taffy Apples.
10. Pop Corn
11. Fudge
12. Peanut Brittle

Drinks
1. Black + White
2. Carioca Rum.
3. Coca-Cola
4. Scotch + 7-UP.

you are waiting, and we get married, I'll see that you get a real wardrobe too! God, what fun it's going to be to spend that back pay!

1:00 p.m. — "Air Raid" again, including our planes! Dropped some heavy stuff pretty far off — Nichols Field or Cavite. Maybe they'll land somewhere on Luzon today?

2:10 p.m. — Back to "Alert."

3:40 p.m. — "Air Raid," and our planes working on something in the distance, and dropping some more heavy stuff. They've been quite busy today.

4:50 p.m. — Back to "Alert."

October 30th
Today brought us a shake-up in administration, much to our dismay. The Navy staff, doctors and pharmacist mates have been relieved, and the Army is taking over Bilibid. The Navy have all been put on the drafts. Four doctors and 15 pharmacist mates to go with draft of field officers to Japan in three days or so. The others to go with the rest of the draft to Japan. It certainly has messed things up here, and I hate to see Dr. Langdon leave us. I've gotten so I like him alot. I don't see *how* the Japanese expect to get this gang out! Damned if I do! These Army Corpsmen certainly are a bunch of stooges after experiencing the efficiency of the Navy. Most of the Army men are untrained for hospital ward duty, they're all field men and

poor at *that*. Well, I *can't*, CAN'T last much longer!! I'm still carried as "Unwell Cripple," so I need not worry about moving, and the list of "Well Crips" does not affect officers anyway.

Bet George Roper a 5 lb. box Whitman Sampler we'd be in US hands on or before December 1st, 1944. This is one bet I want to win!

November 1st
More on the Army Corpsmen! They have so little (if any) training that they do not know the meanings of PRN, QUID, TID, Q4h, etc. They don't know "sterile technique," how to use instruments, take temperatures, nor ever heard of catheter, etc.!!! Oh, it's going to be great in here, I'm sure! They're sloppy and dirty — not nice and neat and clean like our Navy men were. One of the doctors has been putting out the medications, because a couple of the Corpsmen never had seen or handled medicines other than aspirin! The new doctor (Bruce) is making an ass of himself with his "Ward, Attention!" (at *tenko*, in pipsqueak voice!) and statements like — "Those were Navy orders. These are our orders." The quality of cooking the chow has already dropped — very watery lugao. So, one can readily understand that we are *very* anxious that the Yanks *hurry* and get here, so we can get to decent living and trained personnel again.

NEWS: We bombed Legazpi with fifty land-based planes. Japanese "attacked" us at Lamon Bay 950 miles east of Manila. We had ten carriers, with retinue. MacArthur says he has 225,000 men in Visayas.

November 2nd
I did the dressings on Johnnie today 'cause the new Corpsman had never dressed a wound in his life!! Great stuff! Men on the draft were issued wool clothes today (old IJA outfits). This is usually preparatory to leaving, but I'm certain in my own mind that this draft will never leave the island of Luzon. I figure these J'se here are merely obeying orders to "have the draft ready at minute's notice." I don't think they can get a ship in or out of the bay.

November 5th
7:30 a.m. — AIR RAID #9 !!! Our planes came over Manila and again dropped some really heavy stuff. Most of it was off in the distance — can't figure out where. We sure needed the sight of those planes — we were getting pretty down in the mouth. The last raid was last Sunday, just a week ago. I know the men on the so-called draft will be happy as hell. And if you think it doesn't make *me* feel good and full of anticipation of home-coming and all, well, you're off the track!!

8:30 — Quiet.

9:30 — BACK! Real heavy stuff dropped.

9:45 — Quiet again.

10:45 — Back to "Alert."

12:50 p.m. — Our planes *again* took Manila by surprise and bombed the hell out of someplace with *land-based bombers*. Boy! What a racket!

1:15 p.m. — Quiet again. All books turned into library, we have to inventory for some reason. Not knowing what will happen, I hooked two books, "Divine Woman" and "Roll River." We're all hoping the Yanks are landing on Luzon today.

2:30 p.m. — Back again! These *must* be land-based bombers. We hear the roar of engines, a string of bombs (heavy), a scattering of AA fire, and then all quiet again. There are a couple of AA guns VERY close by here. Make me jump whenever they go off!

5:15 p.m. — "All Clear." Yes, indeed, we all raise our voices in prayer for our Yanks, and hope that they have landed on Luzon today. The raids today bucked-up everyone's disposition. Our nerves had been getting quite strained. Arguments and friendship-breaks would occur over the smallest things. The strain is somewhat gone now. Again, our thoughts wander into the field of "going home" and "home." As Colonel Edwards said, "All I'm worried about now is what they're gonna feed us on the ships goin' home!!?" Food! Fondest of our hopes, and dearest of our dreams is to be found in the phrase, "Xmas at home!" Wouldn't that be wonderful?? Hell that's only seven weeks, and *lots* can happen in seven weeks. If I knew I'd be in a U.S. hospital seven weeks hence where Mom and Dad and Eileen could visit me, I think I'd say, "Impossible; there is no U.S., no such place!!" These years of hell make those years of peace, happiness and security seem like something I've read in a story book, or a figment of the imagination. I so anxiously want to be a part of that world again — and yet I can't fully picture myself as belonging over there. Hard to explain. Something else I've decided. 'Course I want to have my ole Pontiac for awhile, but my heart's desire is a Pontiac Convertible! I said before that I didn't want another convertible, but I've since changed my mind. I especially want it if I marry and go to school. We'll see.

November 6
4:30 a.m. — AIR RAID ALARM #10.

4:45 a.m. — Several planes over and dropped bombs.

7:30 a.m. — Air raid alarm.

7:45 a.m. — Many planes back this time. Lots of firing going on. At 8:05 a.m. a group of dive bombers came over and did some damned good work. I saw most of them dive, and I'd say it was the hottest contest seen here yet. More AA fire than I've ever seen and others remarked the same. How our boys can dive thru that bombardment and come out unscathed beats me. Certainly this is

a prelude to a Luzon landing. Come on boys — this is good election day stuff, too.

8:30 a.m. — Quiet again.

11:00 a.m. — Back on "Alert."

12:30 p.m. — Our planes back again. All dive bombers, I think, and lots of 'em! Boy, this *is* swell. Mom, I'm on my way home!!

2:15 p.m. — "Temporary All Clear." (No activity).

5:15 p.m. — "All Clear."

November 8
Well, wonder how the election came out? No doubt FDR again, and this time I'm in favor of keeping him in. Tobacco situation very acute. We have no more. Have to bum what smokes we get. Our supply of beans, sugar and coffee (John and I) will run out by next week too. The ration from the guard mess has been cut a couple times and it's really small now! Yanks *better* hurry.

November 9
It began raining during the nite and has kept up all day. The air is chilly and a high wind has been blowing. Quite obvious that a typhoon is in the not-far-off vicinity. It's very unpleasant weather to say the least. Brings out the pessimistic angle to everything. Top of all this, I feel another cold coming on, which will be of no help.

I've given up hope of being free by Thanksgiving; am even quite dubious about Xmas. I fear I was carried away by the wave of optimism that hit us at the sight of our planes! Now I feel that our boys are going to meet up with some fairly stiff (though useless) opposition and that we may expect two or three (possibly even six) more months of this life!! DAMN THIS WEATHER! See what I'm writing? Best I stop before I begin dragging my chin.

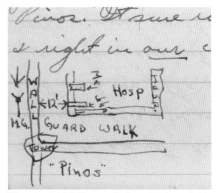

November 9, 1945. "It sure raised a racket tho, and right in *our* corner, over the wall." *Hinkle Archive*

Woof! A few minutes ago (5:35 p.m.) all hell broke loose just outside our wall. It began with a single shot — a pause, then a couple more — and then *I almost* hit the deck 'cause a MG let loose!! Following this was rifle rapid fire, an answering MG, shouting and BAR fire. The "Bilibid bell" chased everyone inside. We don't know what it's all about — probably just a bunch of over-anxious Pinos. It sure raised a racket tho, and right in *our* corner, over the wall.

November 10th

The rain and wind has been incessant, and it's quite cold. It's down to 65° or 70°, and seems like 40° to us!!

12:45 p.m. — Blow me down. ALERT!! Wind and rain, typhoon or no — seems our boys are flying around somewhere nearby, for the sirens just sounded two "shrieks," which is the "Alert" signal for Manila. The rain is slowing up some, and the sky seems a little brighter.

I had a poor nite last nite — didn't get to sleep till about 4:30 or 5:00 a.m. My stump was raising quite a bit of hell. Being unable to sleep, I spent the nite thinking of home, and imagining how it'd feel to be pushing down mashed potatoes, gravy and fried chicken, a la Mom!

November 11

Ironic Armistice Day! We got ⅙ package tobacco per man today, which equals one coffee can full, loosely packed (= .80 pesos). It's damned hard going without smokes AND without much chow. John and I ran out of coffee today. Beans go by Monday and sugar by end of next week. Hunger — our greatest enemy and most persistent.

November 13th

7:45 a.m. — Air raid #11. The boys stuck again! Just a roar of several motors. Someone remarked, "The Nips must be practicin' dive bombing."

There followed a few "ka-whooms" and then a rapid ringing of the bell here at Bilibid (for "Air Raid") and about five minutes later the sirens took off. There were many planes over and I saw quite a few of them diving and coming out of dives — about ten or fifteen. Those I saw were all Navy dive bombers and they went thru the AA without any trouble. The IJA threw up a helluva lot of AA too, and I could see the high explosive AA shells flash as they exploded into white smoke, w-a-y up high. The planes seemed to be working over the bay — maybe got some more ships there, like they did last week. Jeez — I hope they land on Luzon *soon*. I'm *so* damned tired of this life. Had shakedown today, looking for rice. J'se missing one sack from galley!

8:40 a.m. — Quiet again. We had to close our top windows — able to see too much of the slaughter!

9:20 a.m. — Another small wave of planes over.

9:30 a.m. — Quiet again.

10:25 a.m. — Back again! This time they must be heavy land-based bombers from Leyte, because no AA fire is even being sent up. A couple of times we couldn't *hear* the planes, but the bombs were quite evident. This group was working off in the distance — maybe Cavite.

11:00 a.m. — Quiet again.

1:20 p.m. — "Temporary All Clear" Bilibid.

1:28 p.m. — Planes BACK! Big ones, too!

1:38 p.m. — Quite a flight of divers over this time, and I had ring-side seat thru our window. Only got to see ten of our planes, but they just seemed to fly serenely thru the AA fire, and the Nips put up a *very* heavy AA barrage, too. Port area and the bay apparently worked over. Some of this heavy AA fire from nearby still makes me jump! See how shaky my writing is?

3:15 p.m. — Another flight is raising hell someplace on outskirts of Manila right now. We're having a short rain now, and at same time part of the sky is blue and sun shining. Wish they'd let up so's we'd could get our chow, even tho it is poorly. Get damned hungry on two meals a day, and those are sparse and unchanging. Lugao at 7:30 or 8:00 a.m., and corn and rice lugao with fried "stink-fish" or "greens-soup" at 3:00 p.m.

4:10 p.m. — "Temporary All Clear" Bilibid.

4:25 p.m. — Air raid bell Bilibid — heard no planes this time. Can see smoke from two big fires. One out port area way — the other around Nichols Field.

7:00 p.m. — "Alert" (Manila sirens).

November 14th

7:30 a.m. — Air raid #12. Sirens sound off.

8:00 a.m. — Our planes appear. Quite a few dive bombers and again work over port area and bay. Started another big fire in the port area. Smoke billowing forth. Saw AA make a direct hit on one of our planes. Just a flash of flame, and he was gone. They've also been doing a lot of strafing of AA battery positions. Jumpin' Joe — the sound of those .50 cal. MGs sends dreadful shivers up and down my spine! Hope I *never* get in the way of one of them!

8:30 a.m. — Fairly quiet at moment.

8:50 a.m. — Here's another group back, with MGs blazing! My oh my, what a racket!! It's wonderful!

9:10 a.m. — Quiet again.

9:55 a.m. — Our boys are back again! can't see anything right now. Guards made us close our top shutters. (But we *aren't* deaf!!)

10:30 a.m. — Another group of U.S. planes over. "Temporary All Clear" Bilibid at 11:00 a.m. No planes yet.

12:20 p.m. — A few of our planes just flew over, dropped their bombs and shoved off. It's been that way all day. They just pop in an out at their leisure it seems. Sometimes a large group, sometimes just three or four. Or — just a few first and then thirty or fifty planes not far behind. Maybe they really mean business on Luzon at last??

3:20 p.m. — "Temporary All Clear" Bilibid. Our planes have given Manila no rest today — just in and out every little bit. They've been here at times other than those I've recorded in my diary, but they were so numerous I considered them as parts of raids the times of which I have written down. You can feel the wave of optimism that is sweeping the camp! It is not, however, as wild an optimism as in the past. Some figure it may be a month yet before they land on Luzon. Others think the landing has already been effected. Personally, I feel that we may expect to hear of landings in two weeks or so. I figure that if they can send over the great number of planes that they have, to keep Manila under control, they must already have Leyte and Samaras well in hand. It shows both Naval and air superiority, so what's to stop them? Won't be long Mom, and I'll be able to call you up — and I'm going to do just that from the first place I can, if it's permitted by the authorities. I think I'd best call Dad, though — shock might be too much for you Mom! Best thing to do would be time it so you'd both be home. *That's* the answer!

5:00 p.m. — "Air Raid Bell" Bilibid. A dog-fight started way up high. Heard MGs; nothing else yet. Must have been an eagle clearing guns!

5:10 p.m. — Manila siren = "Alert." City hasn't dared go "All Clear" for two days now! Swell!

November 15th
Group of 172 left Bilibid today to go to Fort McKinley. Included "well-cripples" Enlisted men and civilians. Can't figure out why they're separating us this way. It's 9:45 a.m. and no air activity yet.

November 16th
Sent glasses out to get new prescription. At time they went out, got dope that Arch-Bishop's place and Guerria residence completely demolished. This Colonel Art Carlton turns out to be a good friend of Doc and Marty Bona!! Small world! It still doesn't make me like him too much: too big a line of gab and *always* right.

Understand that last nite's raids have netted fourteen ships sunk in bay; destruction of fuel and ammo dumps in and around Manila, 164 planes (in air and on ground) and Krueger said, "The offensive on P.I. is well under way and headed for a swift conclusion."

November 17th
I'm in the doghouse here with my doctor and the administration as a whole, over trying to get Jose Garcia assigned to this ward on night duty. It's a long story — too long to waste paper on, but here's a few parts of it, in brief. Joe assigned to night duty at #3, Dunning [Floyd]. I asked

Edwards, Ch. M/IC about getting him (Jose Garcia) changed to here, so Johnny Winterholler could have some really good care at nite. Present man, Spencer, stupid and slow. Edwards asks Dr. Bruce, latter says, "Can't do it." Hinkle goes to 1st Sgt., who goes to Doc Dallace, and they say, "maybe." Meantime several other requests for JG's service come in, causing irritation, Garcia being on draft and not Bilibid staff. Dunning on nite duty last nite was hopped up — Spencer "nite off." Bruce calls me out and gives me hell for interfering with administration — for "trying to run the boys," "going over my head," "you're just a patient here, etc." Bruce, further, "None of your business," "Sneaking behind my back." Hinkle back with, "Intention only looking out for Johnny Winterholler, and chance to get capable men. Present nite-man ignorant of many things, untrained." "No idea of running boys" (do have some ideas on that thou!). Didn't see why shouldn't go 1st Sgt., time was short. Never thought of "sneaking" or "going over head." In short, I'm in the doghouse, no matter how reconciliatory our words were near end of conversation. All because I try to help Johnny — try to get a good man on the ward. I hope it doesn't cause him to mess up my record in any way that would foul me up later.

November 19th
5:50 a.m. — Air Raid #13.

7:40 a.m. — Temporary "All Clear" (Bilibid).

7:45 a.m. — A few U.S. planes showed up, drew fire and left.

9:30 a.m. — Temporary "All Clear." Planes showed up now and then dropped some heavy stuff. Didn't sound like it was right *in* Manila. Belly cramps started again last nite and still have them. Slept poorly. Stump still hurts.

10:30 a.m. — "Air Raid Bell" and our planes doing some bombing.

11:00 a.m. — Here's our gang! Yippie! What a racket!

12:25 p.m. — Temporary "All Clear" (Bilibid).

1:40 p.m. — Our planes back, doing a little work around the port area. These sporadic raids are becoming tiresome. I feel now that it will be at least three months before we have a chance of being out of here. And probably NO CHANCE of a Red Cross shipment this year, and God, we need it this Xmas as we have never before! Food is so slim. Tobacco is terrifically short. I've had three smokes today — all butts! Saw a man give a damned good watch for fifteen cigarettes! Mungo beans (black market) are $20 U.S. a kilo. Sugar is $5 U.S. a kilo.

4:45 p.m. — Temporary "All Clear."

November 20
"All Clear" Manila sirens, 9:30 a.m. Various rumors out about Red Cross chow. There are 300,000 individual boxes in Japan. Lotta good that'll do us! IJA Quartermaster supposed to have said, "Not to worry if supplies for soups, etc. get short, because there will be RC food issued." Sounds phoney to me! Still having belly cramps, but nothing being done about it. Good ole Army rat-race! Once you get on the wrong side of the clique, you're *screwed*!

November 21st
4:30 a.m. — "Air Raid" Manila sirens.

10:00 a.m. — "Temporary All Clear," Bilibid. No planes. Beginning tomorrow I go on rice and lugao diet for one week; see if it will stop cramps. Could easily be the corn causing them. I'll get the lugao three times a day, smaller quantities at a time. Still get soup and whatever else the mess puts out.

11:40 a.m. — "Air Raid" bell (Bilibid).

12:25 p.m. — "Alert" status (Manila sirens). Here's a little recipe of my own, which I am certainly going to whip up when I get home. Let's call it, "Hinkle's Hashburgers." Two lbs. round steak, 1 lb. ground pork, 4 eggs, some mashed potatoes, breadcrumbs, grated and sliced cheese, onions, hot chili peppers, three tomatoes, salt, pepper, vinegar, butter, and a small can of pork and beans can be used, too! Beat up yolks and two whites, mix with meat, add chopped peppers, onions, chopped tomatoes, grated cheese, salt and pepper, and mix well. Then add spuds, vinegar, butter, and make into patties (burgers). Dip in beat-up egg whites, roll in bread crumbs, fry in deep fat. Just before done, put slice of cheese on each and let melt. A little garlic and paprika's OK, too. Serve with cucumbers (sour creamed), sweet spuds and lettuce and 1,000 island dressing. Howzzat?!

November 22nd
Manila still on "Alert." The Jap HQ from the Far Eastern U have moved to Bilibid, ousting the patients of Building #18. Said to have burned some of their records. Perhaps this is beginning of end? Rations to mess were a little larger last nite.

NEWS — Large U.S. convoy sighted off east Luzon. Nips attack and do some damage. Leyte battle at halt for awhile 'cause of typhoon. Last raid on Manila netted three ships sunk in Manila Bay. U.S. has seven divisions on Leyte (150,000 men); casualties so far = U.S. 5,690; IJA = 45,000. C'mon Yanks! We want a palatable Christmas!

2:35 p.m. — "All Clear," Manila sirens. Damnit!

November 23rd
Nothing doing today as far as air raids are concerned. Sergeant Null, USMC, died today at 12:00 a.m. Had cancer of pancreas. Post mortem showed

pancreas 14 inches long (normal 4½). Had been failing for some time.

Meals yesterday and today fair. A little more in quantity. Had some fried cassava both days. Good and filling. Rumor about getting some meat twice a week from now on, but no one knows source of rumor. Tobacco situation SAD! All kinds of swaps with Nip guards for cigs. New toothbrush = 1 can shoe polish. Other items being swapped include sox, shirts, watches, rings (diamond), pens, glasses, everything!!!!!!!

November 24th
Four letters from Mom and Dad today! Almost a Thanksgiving present. Best of all, they're all June '44 letters, and full of good news. Only five months old — like yesterday. While Mom and Dad were writing the letters, I was going thru hell on that ship-ride from Davao to Manila. Glad to know that everyone is well, especially Grandma. I hope Mom meant one statement the way it's written and punctuated, "Pete writes don't worry," 'cause that definitely shows she's waiting!! And I do believe she is, because *I believe in her* so faithfully. Oh! How wonderful it will be to get home and be with them again — to step into a new life too, a life together at last — Eileen and I. Please Yanks — Let's go!!! Mom also says, "Dad promoted." I wonder if she means *again*? That would be something truly great. Much relieved to know allotment, car and investments are all OK, too. Pete and I will need

these investments, and it's going to be a thrill spending the cash for *us*!

Received the birthday wire Mom mentions. (Really got *that* in a hurry!) It's an exciting thrill, causing a strong pang of loneliness, to see Dad's familiar signature, and Mom's hasty printing of that loved word, "Mother." Happy the new house is so satisfactory. Maybe four of us can soon enjoy it together for awhile. Lately, my thoughts have dwelt on the possibility of a nice, small home of our own for Pete and myself. Gee, that would be grand. 'Course that can't come for a few years yet, till after I either go to school for my MA, or go to work and settle down somewhere. At any rate, I want you to know, my kitten, that you're constantly in my mind and plans. Love is certainly powerful, and I find its tenacity positively amazing!! I hope you do, too.

November 25th

7:45 a.m. — "Air Raid" sirens, Manila.

8:05 a.m. — "Air Raid" #14!! Our planes appeared and began working on Bay, a little on port area, and looks like Nichols, Cavite, Murphy and Pandacan. Sounds like some horizontal bombing and divers. Bombs sound like some new kind. Have a somewhat "hollow" sound when explode.

8:50 a.m. — Quiet again. Fast brought us a can (¼ lb.) of coffee this morning and I brewed some. It sure tasted good after such a long lay-off.

9:15 a.m. — "Temporary All Clear" — Bilibid bell. Planes have been back on and off. At 11:00 a couple came in and dropped a heavy load and took off.

Now 11:20 — my lugao is due at 11:30 and I'm hungry as hell, and it'll probably be late. It's a beautiful, sunshiny day. Just a few cottony clouds up high. I've been unable to see any of the planes, inasmuch as my new glasses have not yet arrived. Doc's girl hasn't been in this week; may come tomorrow if no raid. Should have been writing like this all the time — saves lots of space.

2:05 p.m. — Here's some more of our planes again! Damnit! I still haven't gotten my 11:30 chow, and I'm RAVENOUS! Man! The boys are really dropping some HEAVY ones!! Concussion is terrific! Working over Grace Park — Nips have landing field there, and many planes have been coming in and going out of there at nite.

3:00 p.m. — Quiet again. Fire raging out at Grace Park-way. No chow yet, but when I *do* eat tonite I should have a full mess kit! God! How I wish the Yanks would hurry and land on Luzon and take Manila!! Food!!

5:00 p.m. — "Temporary All Clear," Bilibid bell.

Sunday, November 26

Good ole Fast came thru for us again, bearing gifts! Gave us one cup of mungo beans, which we will cook up for Thanksgiving, and also gave us about twenty-five saccharine tablets. It sure makes a difference! If we only had some smoking!! Supposed to have been paid yesterday. IJA paid off in 100 and 10 peso bills. Whole payroll turned over to senior U.S. officers = 88,000 pesos; to be used to buy us salt, garlic, tobacco and coconuts. "Indigent" fund = 56,000 to be used to buy beans for mess, if possible.

November 28
Eight sacks of beans (@ 100 kilos) and coconuts into the mess yesterday and some rice flour. Garlic and salt also in. Cigarettes are in front office, but not yet put out. This tobacco hunger is almost worse than body hunger. In last two days, counting "drags and butts," I've had a total of about two cigs! Nerves of everyone on edge. Morale picked up some when the beans, salt and garlic and coconuts came in, but in general I should say we're a pretty disappointed gang of Americans. Two months ago we had great hopes, and visions of great deeds by our forces in Southern P.I. But here we sit, on starvation diet, so monotonous you feel like screaming when it sets down in front of you. If it weren't for books, I'm sure I'd already be in the nut-ward! It's absolutely amazing and unbelievable how the lack of food can sap you of your energy, ambition, interest, general vitality and hope! I get tired so easily from the slightest exertions. By 7:30 p.m. I'm ready for bed and usually can't

sleep till long after midnite 'cause my stump raises so much hell. Got about 2½ hours sleep last nite. Oh — it's *Hell*! And I want release! I'm fed up. It's crazy, useless, inhuman and its wrecking my life and the lives of the rest. God — I feel on the verge of tears right now. I'm so incensed!

At last, they're putting out the cigs. One pack of 30 cigs per man. These will be broken up (by most men) and re-rolled into smaller smokes (I'll do likewise!). It's 1:30 p.m., and I'm so hungry I'm sick! Remember, Dad, on Thanksgiving noon, how we'd sniff around the kitchen, and be real hungry (we thought), and you'd probably say, "I'm so hungry, my stomach thinks my throat's cut!" Well, multiply that feeling many, many times and *that's* how I feel right now! Put out the rest of the stuff too. Per man = 5 bulbs garlic (1 large, 4 small), ½ cup salt. Also had our first ration of bean soup flavored with ginger. It was good, but *skoshi*;[129] less than ½ cup per man.

November 30, Thanksgiving
Mass and Holy Communion at 7:00 a.m.

8:15 a.m. — "Alert," (Manila Sirens). Thanksgiving breakfast began (rather was) watery lugao with a few stray bananas in it. Thanks to Fast, however, John and I had coffee, with saccharine, and milk (from diet kitchen). I cooked the pot of beans last nite, and we'll have them this afternoon. Keep thinking of how the table at home would be

---
129   The Japanese word for "little."

set today: roast turkey, mashed spuds, gravy, candied sweets, oyster dressing, creamed peas, mashed beets, and maybe sour-cream cucumbers, lettuce, pumpkin pie, whipped cream and coffee. WOW! Amen. Next year?? Damnned right!

Johnny passed a kidney stone today!! In one way it's lucky he's paralyzed because he never felt any pain at all!! The way our lad Fast takes care of us is heart-warming! He just brought us six pieces of candy he made for Thanksgiving. Damned good, too. It's nice to know someone in this motley crew who thinks of you and is willing to share or *give* part of what he has.

Fast again! Brought us a couple of Luckies for after chow! Kitchen put out rice and corn, thick bean soup with ginger, a camote and other vegetable "pudding" with ginger. I'm FULL for a change. Hell, with our beans and the mess, John and I each had 1½ cups of beans alone!! I couldn't eat the pudding — too much ginger. Here's my real Thanksgiving gift: three letters from Mom!! June 4, 5, and 11th. That made the day perfect. But Mom — WHY mention the strawberry preserves?? Golly Mom, when I think of you making preserves I tingle all over. Just think what I've been missing! Please make lots of them and save some for me. Gee — how good they'll taste on pancakes, French toast, waffles, and in sandwiches. I hope you make some currant, grape, blueberry and

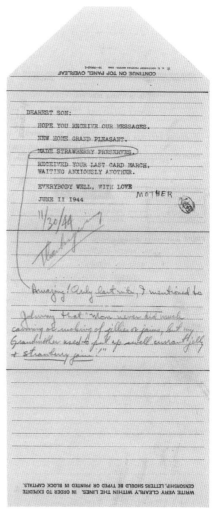

In Hinkle's entry for November 30, he wrote: "Here's my real Thanksgiving gift: three letters from Mom!! June 4, 5, and 11th." Pictured above is his mother's letter from June 11th, 1944; "Dearest Son: Hope you received our messages. New home grand pleasant. Made strawberry preserves. Received your last card March. Waiting anxiously another. Everybody well, with love, Mother." Hinkle would often add a written remark to these letters. On this one he wrote, "Amazing! Only *last nite*, I mentioned to Johnny that 'Mom never did much canning or making of jellies or jams, but my Grandmother used to put up swell currant jelly and *strawberry jam*!'" *Hinkle Archive*

apple jellies, and some rich black-berry Jam. You know, strawberry and blackberry are my favorite jams. What a blessing it will be to be home again, and what fun and an adven-ture in good eating it is going to be! I'm going to drink milk and eat dairy products and eggs till they come out of my ears!!

December 1

Damnit! A spot on the scar tissue of my stump festered up and broke thru today. Looks a bit deep to me. Pains more than usual now, too. Doctor hasn't seen it yet, but when he does tonite, I doubt whether it will "excite" him in any way. It's worrying the hell out of me, though. Incidentally, Dr. White (31st) is my doctor.

Japanese want 25 khaki shirts, pistol belts, and overseas cap. In return we got a short sleeve shirt and some rice. I turned in the tropical shirt Mom sent me and told 'em I wanted RICE. Anything to get something to eat, even if it's just a mess kit full of rice. Can't quite figure what they want these for. My only guess would be they're going to film a propaganda short and need costumes.

Half hour later — Now IJA says they'll give tobacco instead of rice! Well, I need "smokin" just as badly.

December 3rd

"Pay off" by IJA for shirts, belts, and caps = 18 cigs per article!! If *that's* not a laugh!! Rumor about getting some RC

boxes this month, but I can't believe it, however, they'd be more than welcome.

December 5

A wave of chronic constipation has taken over the camp. I'm a member of said wave. Must be the corn and lack of oils in our so-called diet.

December 6

Quite a bit of excitement last nite, and none of us is certain as to what took place. Around 10 p.m. we heard a few planes in the air, (not unusual), and then a number of terrific explo-sions; some of which sounded like bombs. Lites went out and Nips got quite excited. About 2 a.m., more explosions, said to be bombs, but I slept thru this.

This chow situation is certainly abominable! It looks like a very, very poor Xmas all around! DAMN. Colonel Carlton got hold of some beans and sprouted some. Today he brought 'em over and I'll cook them up for him, Johnny, and Jim Daly and myself. Pretty nice of him. I think Jim's making some banana peel coffee for chow, too! Mom, you know I'm going to be a helluva big coffee drinker when I get back, and something's going to have to be done about it. I'll have to hunt up an old fashioned "Dad's Cup," for that's the only size cup of coffee that can possibly satisfy me henceforth, after having used a canteen cup for so long (1 pint). Found a small amount of coconut oil I'd forgotten about, so I fried the bean sprouts, and they were delicious. After we finished eating, Col (Art) Carlton and I began talking about smorgasbord, etc. Talked of Kungsholm's on Rush and Ontario Street, The Golden Ox, and Matt Schulleins. (Man, will I ever forget Uncle Guy and the gold fish?!!!) Sure got homesick and very, very hungry for a delicious smorgasbord. Also talked of Phil Schmits, which I shall frequent when I return. Bit of Sweden, Red Star Inn, and the Chinese restaurants around 22nd Street, which ALSO will know me as a steady customer. Boy oh boy, a plate of egg foo young, and some chicken chow mein! Hunger HUNGER!! A TERRIBLE ENEMY!

December 7

After 11 months of wearing a mustache, I finally got mad this morning and whacked it off! Actually feels and looks funny to be without so I'll probably grow another right off!

December 8, 1944

Three years of war today, and here we sit!! When *will* we get out? News report stated that Red Cross has two-way radio communication ready to operate between released POW on Luzon and their families!! But first, we must be released, and given some good food. God, what hell this starvation is — true realization of starvation. Food and love — that's what I need. Understand that bastard William Winter, radio commentator of KGEI is on Leyte! Someone of our gang is just liable to "cuan" him off!!! Well, I had at least hoped to be on my way home, by the time I reached the end of this notebook, but, woe is me!!

December 9

Because of wood shortage, galley ordered to put out steamed rice instead of lugao. Tasted damned good this morning, but it's still such a pitifully small looking amount in my messkit!! Hunger will really take hold between now and 4 p.m. Guess I'd better switch to my new notebook, since space is getting shot and cramped here. Tallyho!

Books Read (cont.)
26. *A Peculiar Treasure*, by Edna Ferber.*
27. *The Last Man Around The World* by Stephen Longstreet.*
28. *For My Great Folly*, by Thos. Cosbin.**
29. *The Citadel*, by Aid. Cronin.*
30. *Captain Paul*, by Cmdr. Edw. Ellsbery.*
31. *The Bishop's Jaegers*, by Thorne Smith.
32. *The Lively Lady*, by Roberts.*
33. *The Neutral Ground*, by Frank Hough.*
34. *Berlin Diary*, by Shirer.*
35. *Anthony Adverse*, by Herr. Allen.*
36. *Five Tongue*, by Sax Rohmer.
37. *Sound of Revelry*, by Cahen.
38. *Count of Monte Cristo*, Dumas.*

We're supposed to get some tobacco today — 2 packages. Picadura per man; one today and one held for us till Xmas. When I get back, I'm going to fix up some needy family each Thanksgiving and Xmas, if I can. I know now what hunger is, and I can't think of a greater pleasure than allaying the hunger pangs of some family, even though it's only for a day or so. Gee, I'll have fun loading a basket in the A & P !!!

I'm exceptionally homesick and lonely today. These moods of loneliness have been coming to me more and more often during the last few months. During such a mental struggle with loneliness, my heart feels like it were being torn to shreds, piece by piece. Oh — it's been such an eternity of Hell, and many's the time I've wondered at our powers to withstand all our sufferings. Life is so dismally empty for me here. True, I have such a great deal to look forward to, and to hope for, but at the moment those things are not tangible. Besides, I've been in this state of anticipation for nigh onto three years, and after just so long, one tends to definitely lose any sense of reality when it comes to these anticipations. After an interval of time, one begins to wonder if that outside world actually exists, that world of loved ones, new faces, autos, good and plenty of food, newspapers, friends, movies, comfortable homes, radios, etc. This sense of detachment from the world seems to grow stronger as each week passes. We continually converse about it, true, but it (the conversation) has an undertone to it such as

is found in a conversation among a group of eager youngsters, who are planning a vacation trip to a place new to them, and their speculations are tinged with excitement because of reports that they have gained of their vacation spot from reading or pictures or conversation with others. For example, this morning I've conjured up a swell picture of myself at home; and this is how it looks. I'm parked in our new living room, and I hope it has a fireplace with a roaring fire. My parking place is in a big overstuffed chair, and on one side of me is our new radio, safely playing good music, preferably, Strauss waltzes. On the other side of the chair is an end table, peanuts on it. Also on said table, my pipe, some #79,[130] a magazine, and I begin to think it's time for chow! In the kitchen, Mom and Pete have been busy for some time, and soon Pete comes in to me, and after favoring me with a heartwarming kiss, says; "Hungry? Supper's ready; antipasto, spaghetti, meat-balls, peppers, lettuce, bread, butter, cheese, chocolate pudding and devils food cake and coffee. We're just waiting for Dad!!" W-O-W!! To my mind, that's a beautiful picture — seems almost like a fantasy! Can it be at all possible that such a thing may someday happen to me? Within six months or a year?? Cynically, I almost scoff at the idea. I'm a POW, and seems I've ALWAYS been a POW!! There's *really* no Pete, no Mom, no

---

130   Sutliff Tobacco Company—Mixture No. 79.

Dad, none of these things. I'm just a dreamer and nothing will come true. And so I think, and think and think. My thoughts go round and round till finally I come to my senses, and tell myself, "Snap out of it Walt! Of course these things will soon come true. Have faith, and just a little more patience. Don't let the HUNGER get you down. Don't let the *pain* in your stump drive you daffy. Don't let the petty arguments in the ward, the short tempers and the pessimists floor you. You'll soon be out of this, and the sun again will shine brightly. A turn in your luck is coming — all for the good — for you and Pete; you both deserve it." And so, my chin struggles to stay up. I say a short prayer, and sit back again to wait.

Tobacco finally came in today, and as usual, per Nipponese custom, not the amount promised, but 1/6th. thereof!! Instead of two packages per man, they brought in 700 packages for 2,048 men, which = .34 or 1/3rd package per man. When, or if we'll get the rest, we know not.

SUPPOSEDLY RADIO NEWS
1. William Winter says within two weeks he'll be broadcasting from Luzon.
2. Marine Division lands at Ormoc Bay, Leyte, and cuts IJA forces in two.
3. 200 IJA paratroops land and get knocked off at Ormoc.
4. Our torpedo boats raising hell with IJA and IJN around Leyte.
5. IJA tries reinforcing Leyte, lose 4

cruisers, transports with 4,000 men: U.S. Marine pilots did the work, some of whom have 38 planes to their credit.

Sunday, December 10th
Went to early Mass this morning, but before I could receive Holy Communion, we got heavily rained out. Last few days have been very chilly and rainy.

The old Red Cross Box rumor is out again, to the extent that we're to get some tomorrow! I get so fiery mad when I hear this rumor 'cause there's no basis for it, and no one in authority has had any word of it. Sure, it'd be swell to get some, but where will it come from? Damned fools don't think of that: just believe and spread any nonsensical rumors that spring up. Mess got ten bags of salt last nite.

NEWS REPORT — Largest earthquake in history of world hit Japan, around Osaka! Nice work! Should shorten the war some. Hope the bastards all suffer!

POST CARD — Wrote out message to folks to be sent on post card near future. Hard to say anything. Hope they tell Eileen. "1. My health is fair. 2. Xmas greetings. Received June letters, None Eileen. Thanks. Taking care of everything. Am alright. Prepare menu, together soon. Regards all. Love you both, Eileen, Grandma: Wally." [*Note in margin: "Forced to change "Prepare menu" to "Hoping we're."*] Just between me and the graveyard, if I don't beat this card home, I may as well give up all hope of getting back!! Seems it takes these cards about five months to reach their destinations. S-o-o-o?!?

December 11th
Nothing much to report.

NEWS — Goebbel's speech to the German people more or less hints at throwing in the towel. Hope so.

RUMOR — The draft is to leave in three days!! Can't hardly believe this, but anything can happen.

I've been going thru two cook books, and found many things that sound good and look worth trying. Things like baked eggs, apple pudding, Brown Betty, divinity candy, ham, baked in cider, donuts (home-made), etc. Mom, you and I are going to have lots of fun!

There's one thing I want very much to get for the house, and that's a small size, or portable soda fountain. At least a freezer unit that will hold ten gallons of ice cream. I'd like to have it with the water and soda spigot, and at least two syrup spigots for chocolate and another (marshmallow, butterscotch, Coca-Cola). I think this is absolutely practical and handy, especially since I plan to do a lot of fattening up on ice-cream, milk shakes, etc. So, we'll have something new in *our* home.

December 12
The change in steamed rice has been quite welcome, but the amount is so small. I can safely say that I could sit down and eat three, maybe four mess-kits full of just steamed rice and salt. God, I've gotten so I love steamed rice, and I really hope to eat my fill of it when I return. It's so terribly long between 7:30 a.m. and 3:30 or 4:00 p.m.! About 1:00 p.m. I get a helluva headache and belly-cramps — a case of being simply ravenous. But, there's nothing one can do about it but *take it*. But in the back of my mind keeps ringing, "SOMEDAY!"

NEWS — 1. Cruiser (IJN) supposed to have been sunk in Cavite. 2. Ormoc, Leyte supposed to finally be ours. 3. U.S. now has four Field Marshalls: MacArthur, Arnold, Marshall, Eisenhower.

RUMOR — Doctor Nogi (IJA), to inspect those *not* on draft to see *who can travel*. If this is true, I don't like the sound of it! This proposed move of the draft to Japan (again) is no dream! Patients who are already listed on the draft (and always were) were looked over today by Dr. Nogi. Tomorrow all members of the draft will again be subjected to a stool exam (rod test). Only good feature in this that I can see (and this arises from purely selfish motives, but such are the workings of war!) is that *if* a ship does come in, it may bring a cargo of Red Cross food, mail and supplies. I often think of Phil Brain and pray he is safe and in good health in Japan or wherever he is. Often think of "Jughead" Byrd, and "Andy" Anderson, too.

December 13

Well, today has been the unlucky day! About 1,200 men, mostly officers, left Bilibid today and will board a ship for Japan. We never thought this would happen — never believed that our forces in the South would permit such a thing. Yet, there it is. Martin, Mc-Nair, Howard Pahl, Art Carlton — all gone. They left just before noon, and never have I seen such a down-in-the-mouth group, and why shouldn't they be? Almost all of them felt that America had really let them down, and I agree with them. Fast is gone, too, and we'll certainly miss him. His parting shot to us was a gift of about two kilos of beans.[131]

The camp is like a morgue now. Quiet and muchly de-populated. Census now is about 430. Seems as tho they'd be able to feed us better, or at least more. However, I have no hopes to see this come true. I know these devils too well. All we can hope for is some

Red Cross food from the ship. Again, this year, the IRC sends "Season's Greetings." If they only knew how much said "Greetings" go against our grain, they'd cease! We want food! the hell with radiograms.

San Fernando, La Union, transported to a dock, and put aboard *Enoura* and *Brazil Maru*—two ships that had been hauling livestock, with holds still covered in manure. Left behind were fifteen weak or wounded prisoners who were loaded onto a truck and told they would be transported to Bilibid for medical treatment. Instead they were taken to a nearby cemetery and beheaded, and their bodies dumped into a mass grave. During *Enoura Maru* and *Brazil Maru*'s voyage to Takao, Formosa, twenty-one prisoners were buried at sea. On January 9 an air raid siren sounded when the ships were undergoing repairs in Takao, just prior to their departure for Japan. The alarm spread panic among the prisoners. As the men in the hold of *Enoura Maru* struggled to remove the hatch covers and save themselves, there was a sudden flash of bright orange and a deafening explosion caused by the attack. Debris flew through the air and one floor gave way, dropping prisoners 30 or 40 feet below. When it was over, hundreds were dead from the aerial bombardment; bodies were piled three deep and pinned down with large steel girders, hatch covers, and debris. When both ships arrived in Japan on January 29, only 497 of the 1,619 prisoners who had boarded *Oryoku Maru* in December were still alive. Of Hinkle's friends, McNair and Pahl died when *Oryoku Maru* was attacked in December, while Martin and Carlton died in the *Enoura Maru* January attack. Fast survived and was liberated from a POW camp in Japan at the end of the war. *National Archives Photo*

---

131 The POWs were divided into three groups before boarding the *Oryoku Maru* on December 13. Group I (which included Hinkle's friends Martin, McNair, Pahl, Carlton, and Fast) filled the rear hold, while Groups II and III filled holds in the forward and middle. As the unmarked ship left port and neared Olongapo Naval Station in Subic Bay on December 14, it was attacked by US Navy planes from USS *Hornet*. It was attacked again the following day, and survivors could be seen swimming to shore by American pilots in their Hellcat fighters (seen in the photo that accompanies this footnote as white dots between ship and shore). The prisoners were then held for six days at a nearby open tennis court (appearing in the photograph as a white angling rectangle at the lower right-hand corner). The prisoners were then moved to

RUMOR of NEWS (not sure which) — 1. Germany surrendered as of yesterday. 2. Leyte campaign over.

Thursday, December 14th
8:00 a.m. — AIR RAID #15!!! The Manila authorities must have foreseen the raid today, because we had a 6 a.m. roll call instead of 6:30. People said they heard some bombing last nite. I can't say, I slept pretty well. At any rate, our planes are about 20 hours late. It may be that our gang that left here yesterday is still aboard ship in Manila Bay. If so, I pray the ship is well marked and that our planes know Americans are aboard. This is the 2nd time planes have shown up the day after a draft has left Bilibid. Nonetheless, the other draft pushed on to Japan. Wonder what will happen to this crew? It wouldn't surprise me to see them come back to Bilibid.

I sincerely hope that the raid today presages a landing on Luzon, or is coincidental with it. These raids have gotten to mean nothing to me except a deal of mental strain and speculation. The taking of Luzon is our prayer, and please God, hasten the realization of our prayers. Bring an end to our loneliness, our hunger, and innumerable sufferings. Bring to us, thru liberation, a renewal of our faith in America, her power, and her beliefs. Grant us, O Lord, that we may soon be back with those we love, and grant us Peace.

The planes today seem to be high-flyers; very few divers. Hence, I assume that these are land-based bombers. Today, I was to receive my new glasses. Fat chance now. Don't know when I'll get them now, or if I will.

8:45 a.m. — Still a few bombs dropping around, but for most part, it's quiet again. Air Raid or not, my ear eavesdrops on conversation in the ward, and as usual, the predominant topic being discussed is food. "Yes, I've a swell recipe for roast goose, the way the Mexicans cook it. Got another for vegetable-meat-loaf, that sounds pretty good." "Say — any you fellas ever had an 'Alaska Bake'?" Etc. etc.

11:00 a.m. — There have been planes over all morning. At times quite a few; otherwise just a couple or so. There has been no fifteen minute period when there hasn't been some activity. Strafing has been very heavy today, and what bombs we have heard also carried weight. Much AA. Perhaps (again the ever prevailing hope) they've landed?

Yesterday morning and today we've had lugao again. I hope THAT stops pronto! Runs right thru you.

11:15 a.m. — Temporary All Clear, (Bilibid Bell). Bet it doesn't last long!

11:25 a.m. — HAH! "Air Raid" Bell again!! Looks like all day session.

2:30 p.m. — The planes keep coming back, and keeeriste! What a job of strafing they're doing! They must certainly be heavily armed, for when they let loose it sounds like a 4th of July at Riverview![132] I'm sure these are Army or Marine planes; they sound different than the Navy drive bombers — heavier and more business-like. They've been so busy over Manila today that I'm beginning to think that they may have landed!! HO! That's TOO CLOSE!! A fragment or bullet just bounced off our barracks!!!! We're fortunate to be in this type of building — stone of some kind, and plenty thick. I still marvel at the manner in which we in the ward take these raids. We engage in our usual activities: some napping, others playing cribbage, reading, talking of chow, or cooking something. Of course, we know by now that we're in a pretty safe place, and we patiently sit back, relaxed, while the world just beyond our walls is being expertly and ruthlessly shot to hell! It's grand!

4:35 p.m. — "Temporary All Clear" (Bilibid). It has certainly been a hell-raiser of an afternoon! Without a doubt this has been the most vicious working-over Manila has yet seen. The MG fire from the planes has been positively deafening! Must be a lot of casualties today. Heard the fire engines clanging en route to some scene of disaster. Wonder if they're thru.

December 15th
7:45 a.m. — AIR RAID #16 (planes here and bombing). Everything is all screwed up this morning. The prison authorities wouldn't let the kitchen start their fires till dawn, so we have not yet received our chow. Now that some of our planes have come over and done some bombing already. Lord knows when we'll eat. I will say this though — it's easier to go without chow till 10 or 11 a.m. than it is to eat the watery lugao and then wait eight, nine or ten hours. I hope they put out steamed rice today.

What planes that have been over this morning have been bombing port area. Yesterday, from what I can gather, they especially worked over Nichols, Neilson and Grace Park airfields. *At least* 54 planes were over yesterday for sure; Payne counted that many himself.

John and I did a lot of talking about candy and owning your own home last nite, and once again I got the longing to have a home of my own. By that I mean that I wish Mom and Dad would buy or build a house when I return. *Why not* move out to Flossmoor, or Palos Park? Gee, it'd be great, I think. Plan the house and yard, have a little garden, a living room with a real nice fire-place, a library-den, a "sewing room" for Mom that would be well-lighted and a thoroughly modern kitchen for Mom. I'm sure going to talk it up to the folks when I get back. Think how wonderful it would be to be able to say, "This is *our home*!" We shall see.

---

132   An amusement park in Chicago.

8:20 — Fairly quiet. Hah! No sooner wrote "8:20, etc." when some more bombs dropped! If this keeps up steady for a few more days, I'll feel fairly certain that the Yanks have landed on Luzon, in which case 30 days would find us once again free men. Freedom! What a wonderful day that will be.

9:20 — Again, I was about to say, "All quiet," but I just heard a couple more bombs drop! I hear a call outside for chow servers, so maybe we'll soon get fed. (I hope!)

9:45 — Chow finally here — if you can call it something to eat. Goddamned cracked rice lugao — not even a mess-kit full of the stuff. It's exceedingly disheartening to go on waiting for the Yanks to *come in*, while having to starve on the rations we're getting.

3:30 p.m. — The strafing and bombing has continued all day again today. Not quite as much as yesterday, still and all it's been plenty. We meet no air opposition from the Wild Eagles. I stood outside and watched some of our planes work. In groups of 2 or 3 they's come over, seemingly diving and strafing when good and ready — no rush! Actually, the AA bursts I saw fired at two of our planes were from ½ to 1 mile BEHIND them!! The Japs here in the compound are a completely unworried crew. Hell, they're stationed in the safest place in the city. I hear them singing and mimicking MGs during the raids.

Today, they didn't seem to care much whether or not we stood outside and watched our boys work. This is a new attitude!?? Perhaps we *are* getting close to the end of the trail. Just rang the "Temporary All Clear" bell.

I've had the most terrific taste for salt water taffy, fudge, caramels and butterscotch patties of late! I feel that I could eat my weight in any or all of them. Life will certainly hold many, many joys for me, if I ever do get out of here!!

HA! About 10 minutes after the "Temporary All Clear" bell rang from here at Bilibid, some more of our planes showed up and did more strafing and bombing. The amazing part was that the Japs *didn't bother* to ring the bell for "Air Raid" so as to chase everyone inside!! Planes appeared and left, shooting and bombing took place and ceased — all at intervals till about 4:30 p.m. I think that we've had all we'll get today. Never can tell though — a lone wolf may drop in at around 6 or 7 p.m. like one did last nite. I can't stress too much the fact that strafing seems to have been the main mission of our planes, both yesterday and today. My guess is that a landing is being covered, and the mission in Manila is to strafe transportation, airfields, boats and personnel. God, if America only knew how anxiously we await the news that the "Yanks are in Manila!!" What a grand and glorious thrill it will be to see Old Glory waving overhead again and to hear an American bugle call. (Especially Mess Call!)

We've had a little more quantity to our chow during last three days. Not rice, but soup (greens, camotes and soy bean mash. Real hog-feed!!!). Getting some dried, stinky-fish too, which the galley grinds to a powder, making it much more edible. I think they fry it first.

Lots of moving around today. Eight officers from Ward #11 moved in here today. Looks like they're consolidating people, keeping us together.

December 16
7:45 a.m. — AIR RAID #17! Our planes came back over this morning, making it three days in a row of raiding. This has happened only once before; on Oct. 17, 1944. However, all last nite, at intervals, one or two planes would come over and drop and load and a good burst of MG fire and take off again. This nite activity is new, and I like the sound of it! Deep inside me I feel a stir of excitement, which is being kindled by hope and strictly wishful thinking. My mind continually harbors the hope that at long last Luzon is being attacked by a landing force. I want so desperately to have this happen, that these three days of raiding practically have me convinced that it has already taken place. What a truly wonderful Xmas gift it would be for us . . . the taking of Manila, or just landing on Luzon. I'd like to think that within a month I'll

be eating food: corned beef, pork and beans and all the rest. I fear I'm getting to be a mental case about food! I think of good things to eat practically *all* day, and worst of all, I imagine that I can actually taste the chow!!! Well, no use continually writing down how hungry I am, or how much I'd like to have a dozen cinnamon buns and a quart of coffee. I believe I've pretty well covered my hunger problem in previous paragraphs. I just want to make it clear that I'm ready to do some right smart eating from the word "go." I merely, impatiently await the "word," and the word was, "Yanks!"

9:05 a.m. — Our air activity still going on at intervals. We still await breakfast! (Got it at 10:15.)

This tops all! MG fire and bombing and AA going on all around us, so, we got the phonograph out and now it's gayly playing, "I've Got Plenty To Be Thankful For."

4:55 p.m. — "Temporary All Clear" Bilibid Bell; first time all day. Planes have been active all day again, up till about one hour ago. There's been a little more bombing today along with a goodly amount of strafing. More and more I get the feeling that something *big* is happening for our good fortune.

A new order out now. "At sound of one bell only doctors, corpsmen, technicians allowed outside buildings, and only for twenty minutes at time." Us patients have to wait for more bells, which may mean quite a wait since they haven't rung more than one bell during last three days!! If this activity continues tonite and tomorrow and a day or two more, I'm just liable to become infused with a bit of Xmas spirit!

December 17
Well, the air activity ceased today, and there was nothing doing last nite. Result, everyone in camp feels rather let-down. It's not a question of "never being satisfied," it's just that we want so much to see the end of this farce. So, we wait for the next raid. One thing makes us feel better: Manila is still on "air raid" status.

A little nervous excitement and worry today, occasioned by the following Nip activity in camp: loading trucks with uniforms, canteens, mess-gear, barbed wire, and sending out a detachment of Nips with extra ammo. Along with this, a guard pantomimed a ship being sunk by our planes. Opinion, fearful though it may be, is that the ship with our draft on it was sunk and that all the above items are for them, along with guards. From what I gather, this is supposed to have happened off Bataan. We pray this is not so, but it is so damnably in the realm of possibility.

Been working on old mail today, and will be for a few days. Most all of it is for men in Japan, and has to be sorted as to camps. Good chow today: "almost" steamed rice, steamed gabi, powdered fish, and soy bean–in–ash-camote soup.

NEWS — We landed on Mindoro yesterday (I hope). If this news is actually true, then it shouldn't be very long before our dreams come true! We're supposed to have landed at San José, on SW Mindoro: about 150 miles from Manila. If only they keep coming!

December 18
Three years ago tonite since that damned bullet and I were introduced to each other. Three years of hell, for which I'll spend the rest of my life in trying to make up for lost pleasures.

December 19
Nothing new. Manila still on "Air Raid" status: sirens have not sounded once since morning of 14th! That's swell. Xmas comes closer. What will it bring? Extra chow? Red Cross (American or P.I.)? Air raid? Landings? Nothing?? (Most likely).

December 20
I've been looking at a 1941 Thanksgiving issue of "McCalls," and the recipes and pictures of foods in it have been driving me crazy! Here's something I've thought of staging at our house, and having it every week: a "Confection Nite," which would involve fudge making, taffy-pulling, popping-corn, eating pie and ice cream, cookies and cocoa. Sure sounds good to me. I'm going to try making my own fudge and taffy when I return.

Latest "scuttle" on the draft ship is this: it was sunk, and *all* American POWs accounted for except 135. Now at Marivales. Many Nip women and kids aboard. Whether or not this is straight stuff, we don't know.

December 21

Ole tobacco situation is extremely tight again. John and I have been swapping off our powdered fish rations for cigs (5 cigs for heaped tbsp.). 1,093 coconuts came into galley, enuff for about 11 mornings of coconut-lugao. Chow has been a little better if only there were *more*!

Great day in the mornin'! Tobacco came in and we got it tonite! Two whole packages of "Picaduro" per man and one box of matches per man. Don't get me wrong — this is not IJA gift — we paid for it and have long been waiting to receive same. The matches were a nice surprise though! This might last us till Yanks get in. Will be allowed church services Sunday and Xmas. If under either, Padre Thalbot will say Mass in each barracks, beginning here. I don't see how we can have High Mass. Doubt if we will.

December 22

Once again Jackie, I give you my fondest birthday greetings, and wish we were together in this meleé. I'd sure like to see you soon, but maybe that will come truc shortly. At any rate, I pray you're safe and enjoying yourself if possible. God Bless you and look after you.

December 23

10:10 a.m. — As yet cannot call this an "Air Raid," BUT a big flight of U.S. 4-motor planes just flew over accompanied by fighters above them. They look like B-24s, twin-tailed. I was outside when I saw 'em first. All silvery and not too high in beautiful V-formations. Got to count 21, but there's lots more of them. Planes are still apparently going over (10:20). Were coming over from northeast going southwest. Manila obviously not target — not one shot fired or one bomb dropped. Man, what a thrill to see those big boys! U.S. Land based, meaning no opposition!! That's almost as good a Xmas present as we could wish for. Just the sight of them has stepped up the moral around here, and the hubbub of speculations is underway.

10:30 — AIR Raid # 18!!!!! WOW! I was wrong! Manila is starting to catch it now, and bless bless, the stuff sure sounds heavy. It's quite a ways from us, but it's sure good listening!

There are quite a few "personal packages" for men who have died, men on detail in Japan, etc. These packages have been here for almost a year! Now, at Xmas-time, the Nips unlock them for us and we're to get what's in 296 packages. Results = about two bushels of moldy cigarettes; socks, clothes, etc. wormy candy, soups, etc. Also 12 Xmas tree decorations for the ward!!

Hinkle's engraved POW canteen. *Kurt Stauffer collection*

Ole Hirota came thru last nite with a handful of chocolate-peanut candy (God it was good), and five cigarettes. Tomorrow he said he'd bring us half kilo sugar, or candy and beans. Soy, sugar, salt and rice rigidly controlled in Manila.

Results of promise = five bananas and sixty cigarettes.

Made three Xmas cards today: George Roper, H. L. Payne, and John. Hope they like them.

Ho! Bedtime story! Between 9:30 p.m. and 10:15 p.m. we had several big planes come over, sounded like around port area, and drop some juicy loads! This is really the first nite raid of importance. It's the first time the Nips have fired AA at nite. It was slightly cloudy, but a swell bright moon at the time.

December 24
Mass and communion. Altar nicely decorated with Xmas tree doodads and nice little crib. Thoughts of home go rushing thru my mind so fast, it's maddening. Thinking of what a nice weekend Dad will have if he can get off Sat. Sun. and Mon. Picture Mom busy as the dickens with dinner preparations, 'cause probably the Zalekis and Harriet will be over, and then just a chance that Grandma could make it for dinner. Think of Pete going to Midnite Mass tonite (with whom?) and again tomorrow. Wish we were doing it together. Think of it and am thankful for the prayers I know Mom, Dad and Eileen are saying for me. I'm doing same for you and hope my prayers and yours are soon answered. Think lovingly of the beautifully lighted Xmas tree; of the happy exchange of gifts; of the delighted and excited expressions on kids' faces and of that Xmas dinner. I'm gonna stop — I'm crying now; it's too much for me. I've waited so long.

10:15 a.m. — Manila sounds "Air Raid" sirens. Bilibid bell, too.

11:15 a.m. — No sign of any planes yet. None at all today.

Crazy old fossil of a Dr. Bruce! Damned sawed-off runt! About twice a week I've asked for a sedative, to ease off the pains in my leg. Sometimes it's been only once a week. My nites of late have been rather rough. Now he's given orders that I'm to have no more sedatives, that I'm becoming a dope fiend!! Christ, what a lot of sheer nonsense! He says, however, that I can have the operation done if I want. I've known this for about a week, and I have been doggedly thinking it over. Gee, I want the damned operation, but how soon will the Yanks get here? I think Dr. Bertram, the surgeon, is capable enough — at least Payne says he is, and I'll take his word for it since he's working in surgery and has had a chance to observe plenty. Frankly, my mind *is* made up; I *will* let them operate, because otherwise it will be at least three, four, maybe six months before I can get it done in the States, and by that time I'd be a nervous wreck because of lack of rest. Stupid damned Bruce, forcing this decision on me at a time like this — rotten chow, poor Corpsmen, and Yanks due anytime. Aw Hell!! What a Xmas! Jeez! I'd give anything to have Doc Davis here — things'd be different.

About 8:30 p.m. it sounded like some bombing but not sure. "Twas the nite before Xmas, etc."

Monday, December 25th, Xmas
Mass and Communion. Thinking of Mom, Dad, and Eileen, and praying for their good health, happiness, and early reunion. Breakfast quite something; real thick lugao with raisins,

prunes, chocolate, peanuts, and everything else in the boxes, plus a tooth-powder taste! Also, some hot-chocolate. Got a nice card from Payne, and also a can-and-a-half of coffee!! Boy, that was really a golden gift. Our share of the various items from the personal packages was raffled off today, and as a result Xmas turned out much better than anticipated. Most of us were able to get things which we needed and could use. My "take" was: 2 handkerchiefs, 1 towel, 3 packages gum, 8 razor blades, 2 bars Lifeboy, 1 bar Ivory, 1 tooth brush, 1 small Colgate tooth powder, 10 Luckies (good), and 1 pinochle deck. Chow was really something! In the 1st place, I cooked up some beans — cooked 'em way down, hardly any juice. For flavoring we put in green hot peppers and a little black pepper (courtesy Doc Waterous), garlic and salt. Boy, they were good. We asked Jim Daly to Xmas dinner and here's what he had: 1. Almost a double ration of rice, steamed! 2. Steamed camotes (one per man). 3. Soup (bouillons, bean, dehydrated soup, etc.). 4. Sweetened camote "cake" (damned good bake job). 5. Hot chocolate.

Air Raid alarm. Some planes over. No bombing.

Well sir I really got full! In fact couldn't eat all my camote cake (a little of rotten camote spoiled everything), nor all my soup (too much tooth powder taste for me). But I did go thru the beans and rice "firsts." The "seconds" I saved over for morning. Topped the meal off with coffee and a Lucky and was more than satisfied. God, what a nice new feeling to be uncomfortably full! Had a little bottle of flowers on the table and one in front of the picture of Mom and Pete. All-in-all, a good day and we're thankful for being lucky enuff to have received all that we have. Merry Xmas everyone.

December 26th
Had a good filling breakfast, inasmuch as I had a mess-kit of steamed rice from yesterday, plus the lugao and coffee. Colonel Beard had a jar of camote cake stolen from him last nite. A number of thefts have recently taken place during the nite here in the ward, of tobacco, beans, salt and now the camote cake. Suspicion lies heavily on that U.S. "officer and gentleman" Major Primrose, a no good oaf if ever one lived. We can't catch him with the goods though.

Thinking back, visualizing yesterday's raffle, I can't help laughing at the same time feeling sorry for most of these dudes here. They were just like a bunch of old women at a Goldblatts. Basement Fire Sale! Picking over everything, getting the table all disarranged, making caustic comments about the goods, quality, etc. "I'll take this," "Nooo — I think I'll take this other one." "Can I exchange this for the," etc. OLD DUDS!!

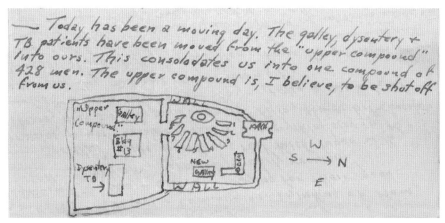

December 26: "Today has been a moving day . . . ." *Hinkle Archive*

10:05 a.m. — Air Raid sirens and bell. No planes. By golly, maybe January will see us out??!

And last nite, after all was quite quiet, I lay back and sadly thought again of home, and grew terribly lonesome. I hope you all had a good Xmas and haven't been worrying too much. I'll be home for Mother's Day, Mom — I'm counting on it!

6:15 p.m. — "Alert" sirens. Today has been a moving day. The galley, dysentery and TB patients have been moved from the "upper compound" into ours. This consolidates us into one compound of 428 men. The upper compound is, I believe, to be shut off from us.

December 27

Rumor has it that the civilian internees from Los Baños or (and) Baguio are to be moved into the upper compound. Don't suppose we'll get to see them if this should be so. Milk supply almost out. John taken off list. This hurts us, since we used it to get down the morning lugao! Incidentally, had this sedative business straightened out, and apparently Dr. Dwyer had misunderstood Dr. Bruce. At any rate, I can still continue to get sodium alurate if I don't need it any oftener than about every three or four days. Since that's settled, I'm not too anxious to have the operation done here. Rather keep hanging on till Yanks get in.

December 28

This morning they called for six man officer detail to work cleaning rice for the Japanese. I immediately "signed up." I knew that such a work detail could be worthwhile, and it is so proving. By a bit of sleight-of-hand I managed to make off with about a cup and a half today, and we consumed the half cup already. Furthermore, this detail looks like it may be for some time, in which case we'll get extra chow — "worker's rations." That consists of a mess-kit of rice at noon, and I hide a quarter of it.

Johnny puzzles me and gets on my nerves a great deal. He's a great one to "receive," but he *does* hate to *give* anything. When the draft was here, someone gave him a practically new Kaywoodie pipe, and since then it's been laying around here in its flannel case. I smoked it a couple of times but he never did. Any number of times I expressed a desire for a good pipe, but he didn't say a word. So, the ass goes and swaps it yesterday for 30 god-damned cigarettes to Commander Bicknell! Rather than make a gift of it to me, hell, as a token of appreciation if you will, he lets it go for 30 measly cigarettes!! 'Course I only managed to keep us in beans, sugar, coffee, oil and tobacco for almost two months. I only do the running around, the cooking, the catering to his little, crazy whims, the cleaning up around his bunk and at times taking care of him when no corpsman was around. In everything I've given him an equal or better share. If I hadn't done this, I'd *still* be eating good myself! Appreciative?? Hell no!! Takes this for granted, damn him. That pipe business hurt. He real-ized I wanted that pipe pretty much, but still he let it go for 30 cigarettes. On the rice deal today, he goes and gets the half cup cooked up without even asking me if I felt like eating it, or what I wanted to do with it. Sono-fabitch — I'll have to soon tell him off if this keeps up and I hope it doesn't come to that. Oh hell!

December 29
At 12:15 a.m. a number of truckloads of civilians from Baguio came in to move into the other compound. Men, women and children were seen.

Got extra ration of rice at noon — "workers' ration," about 500 grams rice.

Three hours work on rice cleaning today. Six U.S. planes flew overhead. "Air Raid" sirens, but no action.

December 30
Another "workers' ration" today. Also cooked up my first pot of steamed rice for John and self. Made it a little too wet, *but good*. Not get-ting any kind of news of late. Don't know what goes on outside the walls. Manila has not yet come off "Air Raid" status sounded yesterday.

!!!Saw a WHITE WOMAN today for first time in over two years!!! At a distance of course and without my new glasses (not in yet). I couldn't recognize her. She waved to me, and I waved back. She was in 2nd floor win-dow of Building #13, which overlooks intervening wall.

Financial statement for November and December of this camp shows that seven sacks of beans cost 7,600 pesos each! Garlic 100 pesos per kilo, salt 150 a sack, and all in all, between November 26 and December 22nd, camp out of 150,244.65 pesos!!!

About thirty kilos of meat into galley today, and coconuts, and pechay. Perhaps this is our New Year's feed, courtesy IJA. As to the New year, we're all looking forward to an early release from our penal servitude. Surely within three months we should be out of this mess and eating regularly. We may not be reunited with those we love in that short a time, and we may not even be on our beloved native soil, but we should be under American control, and *that's* what *counts* at first. I won't dwell on how my thoughts keep winding back over past "Happy New Years," nor how much I'm thinking of everyone back there and of the plans they're probably making. It goes without recording that I'm lonesome and wish I were back with them, and I'll leave it go by saying, "I trust in God that this new year of 1945 may bring us an early reunion, and peace to all."

December 31st

Mass this morning. While at chapel, could hear voices of children in other compound, apparently having a gay old time playing, despite all hardships. But such is the happy irresponsibility and armor against stark cruel reality of children. It was good to hear their shrieks of laughter   but then a morose feeling crept over me when I realized the condition under which all in that compound are living. it must be plenty rough.

After yesterday's "wet steamed rice," a product of my inexperience with rice, I took over two thirds of a Klim can

to Owens (diet kitchen) and asked if he'd steam it up for us. He did, and a beautiful job it is, too! Each grain separate and now we'll have a real feed this afternoon, especially if that 30 kilos of meat makes any kind of a decent taste in the soup. Best surprise was when Owens put four *muffins* in our Klim can for us, and said, "Happy New Year!!!" Will these go GOOD with coffee!! (of which we still have enuff for tomorrow).

News in camp that our "draft ship" was sunk. 270 men lost. Stayed there eleven days and then sailed on in another ship. List of missing or dead in camp being kept "secret" by IJA. So far have heard only that Frank Dixon is O.K.

Meat soup was pretty good. First meat we've had since sometime in early September!! News of draft casualty list no longer "secret." 78 known dead; 300 missing. Among missing so far these I know: Schweich, Bolin, Compton. Dr. Nelson (the orthopedics surgeon, USN) and Major. Goldtrap, USA Inf.

G'BYE '44!! Thank God that's over!!

Monday, January 1, 1945

With the echoes of the phrase, "Happy New Year" ringin' in my ears, I look forward to the happiest year of my life: the year that will bring about the reunion of myself with Mom, Dad and Eileen. How soon will that be? I suppose I should feel satisfied with the almost definite assurance that sometime this year the yoke will be lifted from my shoulders, as well as from those of my comrades-in-hell. Please God, hasten the realization of our hopes and prayers. We know when to say "Uncle," but the opponent doesn't seem to know when to let us up!!! But chin up — see you three damned soon-quick!!!

Mass and Communion this morning, and most fervent prayers for repatriation and peace. Wonder who took Eileen to a gala New Year's Eve dance and whether or not she gave me a thought? Begrudge that customary "midnite kiss," and hope that's *all* there was. I know Mom and Dad were thinking of me, and probably recalling the last New Years Eve we spent together, N-Y-s eve of 1940, at Woodmar, with Ann Hinkle (beautiful almost but dumb) as my partner. A swell dance and feed — the big ice-mold and smorgasbord on the table. We had a pretty damned fine time, as I always had when I went out with the folks. Wait till *this* New Year's Eve! WHEEEE!!!!

Lugao this morning, instead of pancakes and porkies! Lugao had coconut and some dried fruit from packages, but not much. Also served coffee for breakfast. Chow this afternoon to be pretty much like Xmas, plus tea. Knowing this, and hoping it's right, I'm not cuaning anything today. Friend of John's gave him coffee can and half mungo beans yesterday. We'll have those and rest of our rice tomorrow.

10:30 a.m. — "Air Raid" sirens. No planes over Manila yet but several flights of planes were seen coming north, then they swerved and headed east. Total of around 30 planes. "Happy New Year, IJA!!!!" Somehow I feel that our boys won't bother about Manila very much until the "Zero" hour. Bet we don't even get raided today.

10:50 a.m. — "Temporary All Clear" Bilibid Bell. The Bilibid guard is becoming less panicky over air raids, as have stated before. It's easier on us, saves a lot of opening and closing of the wooden shutters. There's a good New Years' spirit among the men in camp. Keep hearing remarks such as, "Well, it's a safe bet: *this is* the year, and within the early part of it, too!" "By golly, we've lived thru almost three years of poor chow, we can go on for a *few more months!*" "Damnit, we *gotta* get out soon, stands to reason, what with our planes only 20 minutes flight away!" And my own hopes — I'd sure like to get back pronto, and out of the hospital by June 1st — grab Pete and make off to Ann Arbor for the first class reunion of the class of '40. Great Caesar! It has been four-and-one-half-years since I graduated! And look what I have to show for it!! Pete, I take back earlier what I said about the New Year's dance. Unless you've changed your ways, and as I recall, you now spend each New Years Eve at home. We may keep that up when I get back, or I may try to change your mind on that. I will guarantee you at least, no wild driving on my part!

1:15 p.m. — Manila sirens put us back on "Alert." No planes overhead. Chow this afternoon was good, though not as much in it as Xmas. Camote pudding was actually excellent.

January 2, 1945

At noon today we saw three flights of B-24s flying very high and seemingly going east. Did not fly over Manila. Bilibid rang the bell, but Manila did not sound sirens. About twenty of our old Japanese guards have been replaced by new ones. I fear Hirota is gone, damnit. He had just promised to bring me candy, or cigs, or anything he could when he came on guard duty around our ward. New camp commander. Don't know his name yet. To make inspection tomorrow morning. Following day, inspection by general.

January 3rd

5:40 p.m. — I guess I can call this an "Air Raid," inasmuch as four dive-bombers just worked over Grace Park Field, with only AA fire as resistance. Manila did not sound sirens. Bilibid rang the bell, but rang the one bell at 5:55 p.m. Inspection never came off. Indefinitely postponed.

January 4th, 1945

At 5:15 p.m. the Bilibid Bell rang rapidly, as it does for an air raid. At this signal all American POW have orders to immediately get inside their own barracks. Tonite, however, the ringing of the bell came just after we heard a couple of trucks pull into the camp, hence it takes no great amount of imagination to realize that these trucks were loaded with Americans and most likely civilians. At 5:25 p.m. the one bell sounded, so they must be all unloaded.

This is the camote season, and though we're getting a goodly number of camotes, about 50% are not edible: wormy and rotten. This food situation is rugged. How I came to gain four pounds in about six weeks is more than I can figure out. During that six weeks I've had less beans and "extras" than even before and no sugar. Perhaps it's due to the periods of tobacco shortage. Usually gain weight when smoking is cut down.

Food, food, food! All conversations either start with, pertain wholly to, or end with, *food*! Officers glibly quoting recipes to others who sit listening with a look of ardent longing. Arguments about sauteing, basting and baking. "What's different about an omelette and a soufflé?" Men sitting down and diligently copying recipes — everything from Japanese suki-yaki and enchiladas to lemon meringue pie and chocolate custards! Plans being expressed that sound like "what I will do in the kitchen when I return." It's funny; its sad; it's laughable and tragic. All of it brought on by starvation.

Doctor Bruce coming around asking about eyes and their condition. Told him mine were getting worse, and that I had been at one time on "massive vitamins eye therapy." What this is for, I don't know.

Friday, January 5th
Swift eye exam this morning. Eyes are both 20-70. Damned poor. The extra personal packages were raffled off today. I drew a tube of toothpaste. John got a razor. Prize of all was a two pound box of chocolate in good shape! 'Course I didn't get it. Each man will get two cigarettes and one stick gum apiece. General to inspect at 3 p.m. 400 patients coming in this afternoon from somewhere. Surmise it's McKinley.

January 6
I just returned from Mass when a few Navy dive bombers came over and did some bombing and strafing. We saw four, but there were more than that. Broke my horn-rimmed glasses this morning. Doc says my new glasses will finally be here next Thursday, if his girl can get here. I sure feel lost without my specks. Guess I'm doomed to wear them the rest of my life.

419 men came in from McKinley last nite. All the men we sent out from here a few months ago and some who were sent there from Cabanatuan. They've had poor chow and no tobacco. Were being worked digging gardens. Gives our camp a total population of 848 men now. Chow will probably drop now to a new low.

Headquarters received orders to crate 70% of the remaining medical supplies and have them ready to go today or tomorrow. Naturally, this is causing us some unrest and nervousness since our first thoughts were that some of us are to be sent to Japan. I can't agree with that opinion, however, since I don't believe the Japs will try to take any more of us out, especially since at least half of us or more are permanently disabled. At any rate, I was glad to see our planes drop around today!

8:05 a.m. — Our planes back with a vengeance this time! Big ones.

9:55 a.m. —Bilibid "Temporary All Clear."

11:00 a.m. — Another large flight of our planes but apparently just passing over. Probably returning from mission.

11:00 a.m. — !!!They're *not* just passing over! Some of them just dropped a load. Quiet, immediately after.

1:30 p.m. — Back again come the Army dive bombers, and really dropped some stuff on Grace Park Airfield. They had one fire there this morning. I'd like to think today's bombing really and truly means a quick change of our luck from bad to good, but I hesitate to so prognosticate. The Japanese interpreter at McKinley told the boys last nite before they left that "The Americans will be here *very, very, very, very* soon!" I hope he knows whereof he speaks!!

1:45 p.m. — Bilibid "Temporary All Clear."

2:50 p.m. — Another large flight of planes over right now and doing some heavy duty!

3:15 p.m. — Bilibid "Temporary All Clear."

3:55 p.m. — Our planes come back with a few more kisses for the "slopes."

5:00 p.m. — Bilibid "Temporary All Clear." Well, it's been quite a day of bombing, what with our planes coming over six times today. The question in everyone's mind is, "Are the planes covering a landing, and is the landing at long last on Luzon?" I realize that thru-out my diary, questions such as the one above, as well as the hopes, fears, dreams and sufferings that we have experienced — such subjects have come into my writings with an unquestionable monotony of repetition. This, however, is justifiable when one realizes how limited is our field of conversation. We're anxious as all hell for the day of our liberation, and hence we talk of it, and food, more than any other things.

For about the last month the mosquitoes have been ferocious! By 7 or 7:30 p.m. I have to get under my net for protection! We've been having pretty nice weather as a whole inasmuch as it's the dry season here, but still the mosquitoes *and flies* have been nerve-wracking.

Steamed rice, and a camote soup with slight meat flavor today. Damned good, but also damned small — about ½ usual rations. Japanese peculiar in this respect. If there's 400 in camp and 400 more come in, they don't increase the ration to take care of the extra men. After a few days, it may be straightened out.

January 7th
7:05 a.m. — "Air Raid" #20! A few of our planes came over and worked over Grace Park Field, bombs and strafing. I just got back from Mass and Communion.

8:15 a.m. — Bilibid "Temporary All Clear."

8:25 a.m. — Another flight of our planes just came over and unloaded. (Breakfast not yet here.)

8:50 a.m. — Here's some more of our planes over to leave some calling cards. A fair amount of AA fire, but also a goodly amount of deadly-sounding MG strafing from our planes. Now I can hear them diving; now the death chatter of the MGs and then — Ka-Woompf!! Woa! *That* bomb sounded somewhat *close*! I'm sure glad we're in a safe place! Am being stirred up by the feeling that this renewal of bombing activities around Manila may mean the real beginning of the end. Many feel the same way, but it is all well counter-balanced by skepticism! Understand that two truckloads of American chow went into civilian camp yesterday. Where do WE come in?

9:05 a.m. — Another group of planes. Action pretty close. Sounds like some Nip planes are in the air at the same time as ours! Probably be some dog-fights if they get close enuff to each other. And me *without my glasses*!! It's a fine day for our planes . . . weather favorable. Fairly cloudy, some sunlite and yet a little haze. All during last nite kept hearing giant explosions. What they could be have no idea. Good news behind this: there were 4–5,000 Jap troops at McKinley. Last week they evacuated.

9:40 a.m. — The big boys (4-motor) just came over and Manila finally found out that there *is* a war going on! That the U.S. is playing for keeps. God, what a terrific bombardment those planes gave to Grace Park Field! The concussions were very strong, and when all those bombs began drop-ping and going off I experienced the well-known sensation of panic & fear for a few seconds. The bombs were evi-dently not of the heavy class, probably 100 lb. bombs. But there were so *many* of them it sounded like the rapid firing of a string of Chinese firecrackers.

9:55 a.m. — Two more flights of B-24s, of 21 and 26 planes came over, and again the horrors of hell broke forth. Now the planes seem to be working over Nichols and Nielsen Fields. Looks pretty systematic.

10:30 a.m. — More planes! Boys are certainly busy this morning and this convinces me that a landing has been made or that this is the softening up process before the landing. If the latter I would say that the landing will take place in a few days. All is in favor of it — dry season; good weather, and no moon. Japanese sergeant told Jim Bray this morning, "Tomorrow you may be free!" He may know what he's talking about, but it won't be tomorrow! Rumor out that the Nip troops (guards) here to shove off tomorrow: Nip civilians to take over?? Last couple of nites we heard them singing their "farewell" song, so, might be.

11:05 a.m. — Hear our planes again. This time working on the western end of Manila. Sure is good to hear.

11:30 a.m. — Yanks back over again, around Grace Park. I'll possibly miss them in the next couple of hours, 'cause I'm getting sleepy.

1:35 p.m. — Bilibid "Temporary All Clear." I went to sleep alright. John says the planes have kept up their activity while I was sleeping.

1:45 p.m. — Planes back! Seems to be true enuff that the Japs are going to leave here very shortly. One of my guard-friends named Āwă is to give me seven kilos of rice. Gave me a pack of cigs and I gave him a cross on a chain I had. He's a Christian, and if he does leave, he'll need it!

I've seen guards throwing things out of their quarters into the rubbish heap. I've seen a couple of them up in their quarters rapidly draining a bottle of "spirits." Others I've seen in new rolled leggings and new shirts, and one of the sergeants carrying a camouflage netting. Guards seem excited and *cheerful*! News or rumor is strong that we've taken Marinduque Island and landed at three places on Luzon.

3:15 p.m. — Here's another large flight of big bombers! Aw Hell! I'm starting to get all excited inside and look for better days right ahead. Latest dope is that the Red Cross is to take over tomorrow. We have rice for two more meals and that's all, and Nips won't give us anymore. Everyone feels the end is near. Talk and hopes are rampant.

5:35 p.m. — Pretty quiet now as far as air activity goes, but the camp is all atwitter. I'm as nervous as a whore in church — anxiously awaiting to see what tomorrow will bring. Will the Nips leave us? Will we be able to go outside the gate? Will we be allowed to see the civilians across the wall? When will we see the Yanks?? And when do we start eating and most important, WHEN DO WE GO HOME?? !!!!*HOME*!!!!

January 8th
9:30 a.m. — Air Raid #21!!!! Had just about given up any hope of an air raid today, but — lo and behold, a flight just flew over and dropped about five or eight bombs on what sounded like the port area. So — *that* keeps up our high spirits. (Just found out it was a flight of twenty four-motor planes *w/o escort*!!) There've been several flights of big ones without escort, and that in itself is not only very unusual and unorthodox, but seemingly shows what little, if any, air resistance the Nips are able or care to put up. Also expresses American contempt for Nip air force.

Got five kilos of rice yesterday, and will pick up another two tonite. Āwă said he has to stay here, and would "sabis" me anything he could. Hope he gets us some sugar! Naturally I took enuff rice over to Owens for a big blowout today, a big pot of steamed rice! Tomorrow I'll take a kilo over to him, and he'll grind it and bake a form of muffins for us . . . no sugar, however. The thing is that we've such a taste for baked things and bread, cakes, anything. Āwă also gave me five more cigs.

I think possibly all of us were fairly well carried away by the wild rumors that were flying around yesterday. Last nite, upon reflecting some, it doesn't sound reasonable that they will pull ALL the guards out of here and leave us on our own. A skeleton guard will probably be left. What the chow situation is to be I don't know.
9:40 — Here's another flight coming over. The AA firing away at them. MAN!! What a load they're drop-

ping!! Jeez — I'm certainly thankful not to be on the receiving end! When that long string of big bombs drop, the atmosphere just seems to be shattered. The explosions are so rapid it's impossible to count the number. Still quite a bit of AA around Manila yet. Major McL. saw one of our planes get hit and come down — wing separated from fuselage. Too bad. In general, however, the AA has been totally ineffective. I suppose our planes will be coming over off and on all day today as they have during last two days. I feel, however, that the landing has already been made.

10:00 a.m. — Bilibid "Temporary All Clear." Manila has sounded no siren since the "Air Raid" on 6 January. A number of the officers saw five parachutes blossom out of the plane that was hit. The other four?? Planes were very low this time, and were apparently bombing Nichols. Five chutes seen, one of which caught fire causing the man to plummet to the ground. The plane exploded upon being hit.

5:30 p.m. — Well, after the short period of activity this morning, nothing further happened during the day. In a way it's somewhat of a disappointment, but no great drop in morale. No question about our boys being busy elsewhere, and that not far off. Brought on USN Chief Radioman in today from University of Phil. He's been here working for the Nips. Says they've been busy burning papers and records and have loaded everything they had on seventy-five trucks and evacuated! Doesn't know to where. His general impression was that the Nips are evacuating Manila. Gun positions still to be seen, but no guns.

January 9

9:45 a.m. — Air Raid #22. Not directly over city, but some planes on outskirts. Have done some bombing. Nothing like two days ago or even yesterday. One lone P38 was seen directly overhead about 9 a.m. — w-a-y up. I didn't see it. From 10:30 to 11:30 several more flights came over. In one of the flights over four B-24s were counted. There was some bombing around, but most of the racket was caused by AA (No escort was seen). Manila apparently not objective, but sure good to see the boys flying over and hear the harmonious symphony of their motors. We know they're around!

5:00 p.m. — No air raid activity since this morning. Rumor has it that we have landed at Tayabas, Lingayen, Appari, Batangas, & Baler. This is supposed to have come from a Nip. We hope it's straight stuff. One Nip told one of the boys (who was trying to make a "deal" with him) that there would be no need for mungo beans in six days. Again — hope this is true! Acted as middle-man in a deal today which netted me one kilo sugar and one cup beans. Naturally, I split with John. Sure has been a busy day for me because of this: been on the go all day! Owens baked us twenty-eight "muf-fins." Boy, they taste just like cake to us, though actually I guess one would call them "unleavened bread." Filling anyway. I steamed off some rice in an aluminum pot today and did a damned good job thereof! Took only a short time, too.

10:15 p.m. — A lone wolf flew over Grace Park and dropped a good load! Thru-out the nite you could hear bombing in the distance.

January 10th
9:45 a.m. — Air Raid #23!! A flight of twenty-five or more came over once and dropped a helluva big load. Shortly afterwards another flight came along the same path and did the same.

10:20 a.m. — I hear another flight coming and sounds like lots of 'em. By Golly, I think we'll be free men by Feb. 1st. Really do!

11:40 a.m. — Two flights of planes have been over here since 10:20 and all big. I counted twenty-two big ones in one flight and they sure looked pretty. Some of their loads have been heavy; some light but plenti-ful. They're flying quite high today. The Bilibid bell has been quite busy! Ringing rapidly when the planes appear and then one bell when all's fairly quiet. Gee, Mom and Dad, I'm so sure we'll be seeing each other soon! God, how wonderful that will be. This month, maybe only a mat-

ter of days, I'd wager that we'll be in U.S. hands. Those not in our position can never, never appreciate fully the feelings that are surging thru us. The anticipation, hope and excitement.

5:00 p.m. — Quiet all afternoon ex-cept for a number of explosions.

5:30 — Newspaper found its way into camp. WE HAVE LANDED AT LINGAYEN, and Task Forces seen off Bataan and Mindoro. YANKS ON LUZON!!!! CALIFORNIA HERE WE COME!!!!! Batangas also facing or already invaded. My oh my!! It's happened! What a morale raiser this news is!! Jiminy! Pete • home • U of M • dates with the folks • ACME • my Pontiac • a piano. KEEERISTE!! I'M HAPPY!!!!!

→ "Voice of Freedom" broadcasts from Luzon!! General Krueger Com-manding large force!! Large Nip force completely surrounded!

Today, while watching some of the big boys we could hear the "howling" noise of the bombs as they were com-ing down. Sent shivers down my back!!

Headlines from Manila paper → I saw the paper!
January 3rd — Started bombing and shelling coast line of Lingayen area.
January 7th — Attempted invasion was repulsed, Batangas, Bataan, and Lingayen.
January 9th — Increased American activity in Lingayen Bay area indicat-

ing invasion as convoy draws close to Lingayen shore. One transport sunk south of Negros . . . many war ships and transports seen ablaze . . . by Nippon air force. Furious attack squadron and Nip air force drove enemy into China Sea. Other details lacking !!!!!!!!

January 10th. "Foe Withdraws West-ward."

Thursday, January 11

AIR RAID #24!!! Have been busy cu-aning rice and beans today and have failed to record times when our planes were over. There was some flying this morning but not much. We could hear more of it in the distance though. At exactly noon, two P47s zoomed right over Bilibid, only a few hundred feet in the air! I missed them, but I heard them coming and was all set to hit the deck!!! At 3:00 p.m., I saw a flight of eighteen dive bombers and they were flying exceptionally low. They did their work without hindrance. Absolutely no AA fire at them today. No Nips planes of course! We seem to completely rule the air, thank God.

3:25 p.m. — Here another flight doing some strafing now, around Grace Park Field. Between the sounds of MG bursts, bombs, and roaring motors, you can hear the horns of autos in Manila. They give me the impression of a driver madly honking his horn, but not knowing which way to go!

Morale is wonderfully high! I'm sure it's only a matter of days now till

the gates of freedom are opened to us. Just sitting on pins and needles. Boy oh boy! I don't seem to be able to find words to express my feelings. As soon as I begin writing I become excited and restless, and words just become forgotten!

Friday, January 12th

9:55 a.m. — AIR RAID #25!!! Sounds like quite a flight of big boys and from the direction of the sound I'd say that Nichols and Nielsen Fields, Camp Murphy and maybe Cavite are being worked over. Forty-two planes counted so far, working west of Ma-nila. 7th day in the row!! We'll soon be in clover!

At 11:00 a.m., just after I finished cooking up some rice for John and self, I got a terrific headache! It was just as though someone had clipped me behind the ear. Spent the rest of day in bed! Took aspirin.

January 13th

9:40 a.m.. — AIR RAID #26!!! A flight of approximately twenty-five big boys came over and dropped part of their load about port area. After they went over we heard the main load drop somewhere off in the distance. *Eighth day in succession*! Everyone getting a restless feeling of impa-tience. We always figured that the last weeks would seem the longest, and it certainly is coming out that way. How many thoughts fly when I think of freedom. Home, of course, is paramount — Mom and Dad and the fire we'll have. Home itself, with big chairs, radios, pictures, magazines and newspapers. Friends calling in the phone, swell odors from the kitchen, a box of candy, our cars — why it almost drives me crazy. And Pete, well, my thoughts don't know which way to turn. I want to be all optimism and happy at the thought of seeing you again — but the lack of any mail from you frightens me into a slight pessimistic mood. But I still believe you're waiting for me. Can't picture throwing me over because of the war and us being separated. Gee — I know I'll have to be in the hospital for awhile when I get back, maybe three or four months, but I hope it won't be longer than that. Pete, what hospital shall I ask for? I'd really like Chicago 'cause Dad and Mom would be ever near by. If I stayed in California Mom would come and stay with me, and you'd be there, too, but what about Dad? Pop means too much to me to leave alone. I want him near me, too, 'cause he's more than just a Dad, he's the best pal I ever had or hope to have, so I believe I'll try to get Chicago. Pete, if you are waiting, there's no reason you can't come to Chicago and stay with the folks. That way, we'll all be together.

Hah! It's about 1:10 p.m. and there's another flight on the outskirts doing some heavy work. You can't realize how much it reassures us every time we hear those bombs. What do I look forward to most on the day the Yanks free us? Well, some American

chow first, of course. I don't think communications to the States will be possible at first, or *that* would be my first choice. After that, other things pop into my mind: to see the Yanks, what they're saying, what the news is from home, what their uniforms are like, see the new weapons, try to get to Santo Tomas to see Mrs. Davis, Mrs. McNair, Miss Earnst, the nurses (U.S.) from Davao and other friends. Try to get word to Alfonso, my old houseboy in Manila. In short, I'll be like a chicken with his head cut off!

DAMN! — For chow this afternoon, all we had was a mess kit of corn, in the form of hominy. I couldn't eat all mine, hungry as I am. Lucky for us we still have some rice — but that damned corn! I hear it's to keep up for a week or so!! C'mon Yanks.

A fairly large flight of planes came over and dropped a "good-nite" load at about 6:30 p.m. Had cholera shot today. Whole camp getting them. Plague?

[*Continued on page 304.*]

My 3 Lonely Years

by José Lanpacu

The subjects of war and memory remain sensitive topics in the Philippines. Controversial issues include collaboration with the Japanese, Japanese war responsibility, and America's failure to defend the islands.

In this illustrated story, three years of Japanese occupation are described by a Filipino named José. He made a copy of his story when the American army landed in his town: "This copy was made especially for my American friends as a souvenir, and to let them know how me and my people had suffered during the Japs occupation in my country."

José's story is presented here with its original phrasing, spelling, and punctuation.

Monday, Dec. 8, 1941, was the day of my greatest excitement in my life when our public radio had broadcasted that our country received bombs from the Japanese planes.

I was that moment in our public market of this town to purchase what I need and that hour the people instantly scattered screaming, crying and most of us were running home.

I too hurriedly went home which was five miles away from the market and that hour I felt flying home of thinking my family left in the hills. My home was situated in the village hills for I was appointed that time as a teacher of adult education for my people who were illiterate.

When I arrived home I didn't know what to do. I felt nervous of the alarm. Days and nights I couldn't sleep of just thinking and what kind of war was coming to us. Japanese airplanes flies freely above our valleys, towns and hills, bombing down the roads, beach, bridges, buildings and especially where our soldiers were. Few of our planes could be seen, we didn't knew what became to others, no news available.

After a week we heard from our soldiers that Japanese army had landed in the northern part of this island and we civilians must hide well. The Japs landed a town there where civilians were brave enough to share the fight with our soldiers against the Japanese invading army.

Dec. 23, 1941, the Japanese advancing had reached a place just five miles away from this town.

We could clearly hear the roaring of big guns and machine guns, like lion and cats that day. At night the dark sky was full of shooting light of fires and smokes so thick. We civilians trembled of the situation in which we thought we would not live any more that day. We made fox holes behind the bushes and in deep creeks in the hills for our families protection. We could see far away the running trucks and tanks and horses, men that looks like a long parade the whole night through.

Some of the Japs passed by our railroad trails, but their trucks were weak enough to roll on the rails. So they destroyed some of our buildings for boards crossing they laid flat on the rails, where their trucks rolls on.

Our armies the Americans and Filipinos fight too bravely against the Japs although they had no more fighting planes to protect them from the air. They killed too thousands of Japs on the roads as they retreated and wait for them in the two towns eastern part which was 30 miles away. Three days and three nights we could hear the exchange of firing there too terrible that we trembled.

After several months had passed these Japs had nearly taken the whole islands except Bataan and Corregidor. Bataan that time was so strong enough to defend itself. All troops of these Japs went there had never returned. Japs officers were worried about Bataan. Some of them were discourage and commits

"Cover and illustration were done by me too." — José. *Hinkle Archive, with help from Rob Morgan*

suicide of themselves by hanging their own necks.

But not long, Bataan had given up because the soldiers there needs their airplanes. But no planes available. No protection from the air and so Bataan was captured. Corregidor too had the same story of it. Most of our soldiers in Bataan had escaped to other villages and disguised themselves as civilians and so these Japs does not know how to pick them up from us.

We civilians had a pity full situation in our hide out. We were afraid to returned to our homes. Some of our women and children got sick of illness due to the unhealthful and crowded place.

Jan. 5, 1942, we heard shots nearby we hid. Five of us went out to see about, but we saw ten Japs soldiers coming to the jungles where hundred of people were hiding there. One of my companion was frightened and ran away but the Japs shot him to death.

We thought these Japs were good people as they were before the outbreak of the war but we had known it that time they were so bad and savagely behaved. They catch and seized anybody they saw. They get our jewels, watches, clothes and money. At our houses they get our pigs chickens and ducks with out any words. They seized too our women and if they could catch one they did what they like to do.

These Japs too wore funny uniforms made of German khaki which was in the same sizes whether a Jap small or tall. They had too long and sharp bayonets and swords. Their eyes were slant in shape so fierce that anybody would be frightened of him. They cut off their hair and their heads were all shinny. They spoke language which could not be understand by us. Few of them could speak English.

We were too surprised of things these Japs did. They burn their own dead instead of burying them. If any Jap soldier happened to lost his one leg or an arm their officers would burn the crippled soldier to death although he can still breath.

During the year 1942 to 43 these Japs issued to us their money (war notes) instead of our Philippine money. We were compelled to use a badge on our clothes where ever we roam. We were ordered to bow low when we met or pass by a Jap and say (*ohio*) means good morning. Nobody could complain the price which the Japs gave to your chicken or anything you sell or if he says (*sabis*) means you could never wait the payment of it. Any one disobey these orders means a severe punishment.

The year 1943 had a bad and good days. Lots of guirellias warfare were in action to all towns which worried the Japs. Weekly lots of wrecked trucks with dead Japs in it could be found by roadside. No body knew who had done it.

Our soldiers especially the Filipinos were fond of guirellia fight because they were accustomed of all places how and where to shoot those passing Japs. But after several months this situation had angered the Japs and so they ordered all civilians not to leave their places. If one Jap been killed, ten civilians shall be executed by them. Wearing khaki suits and holding with firearms

The Japanese officer says, *kuroru sapaho*, which is gibberish. *Kuroru* means crawl in Japanese, but *sapaho* is not a word. José leaves the reader wondering what it was that he intended the officer to be saying. *Hinkle Archive*

by an civilians shall be punish by death. But still our guirellia fighters were not frightened of this law. They continued their duties to revenge what these Japs had done to our people and country. So many of my people too suffered death because of this, but its all right.

December, 1943, one evening two American soldiers with several Filipinos came and hide in my house beyond the hills. They told me that they were engaged in guirellia some place that day. I saw they were so tired and hungry so I gave them food to eat. The next evening before they left I gave my blanket and shirts to the Americans and they thank me for it. They said they will repay me someday for my kindness.

After a week I was reported to the Japs that I am helping some U.S. soldiers by some spies so that time when I learned it I stole away down the city far away with my family to escape the death punishment. But sorry to say when those Japs found me not more at home they burned my house and killed my father.

Those things done by the Japs could be never forgotten in my heart although this war will be over. That's the sense in we Filipinos. We could never and hard to forget the past time especially the wrong done to us.

We were given too an Inde-

pence by the Japs although we were not asking from them. They thought they could fool us. We knew how, where, and when to get our Independence. We want it if we were able to stand with it. And if we all Filipinos have our unity of feelings, opinion and aims.

In the city, all activities and recreations were vanished away. No more music, bars, taxis, hotels, apartments and dances. City roads were dirty. Most of the people were jobless. Stealing, and murdering were going on. Prices on foods were too high. Everybody in the streets were having a sad face except those Nips walking so boastfully along the streets like boss.

My sister's husband who was an American engineer from Los Angeles, Cal. was put imprisoned too in the city. Once when I went there to see him in the camp I pitied him too much that tears dropped from my eyes. He was thin and pale with long beards. He works all day long with meals once a day. Japs didn't treat their prisoners well.

1944, when I returned to the province I found out that thousand and thousands of Japs had moved northward of this island. They scattered themselves among the towns, villages and hills. They drived out the civilians from their home and Japs lived in it. They were all busy all days and nights making fox holes, tunnels, placing of cannons and transferring their ammunitions. Every man were seized along the roads, farms and hills for hard labor. Our native carts, horses and water buffalos were seized too. They collects food from all civilians every day.

One day Dec. 1, 1944, the Japs had placed a big cannon near my house in the hills. I felt nervous of that thing for to be near with the Japs means danger. We didn't believed all the Japs's propagandas. We heard that these Nips were driven out of Leyte by the American Navy and Army. We saw too American fast planes flying over us and shooting the Japs planes. We could see all Japs planes down in flames.

The next day I transferred my family down near the beach where no Japs stayed. But one morning, Dec. 30, 1944 when I happened to climbed a coconut tree, I sighted something which I nearly fall. I sighted a vast American battleships along the gulf of this town. I went down at once and told my friends about it. We at once made large deep holes for our families.

Jan. 6, 1945, the American Navy bombarded our town, beach and farms. American planes sent bombs and bullets down. Japs in this town all fled to the hills. For three days shells and bullets came upon all places like rains. Sharpnels burst everywhere. We thought no one will live among us. Many were hurt and was killed too.

Jan. 9, 1945, American Army had landed in our beach. Filipino men, women and children met the American happily with hot smiles. As for me my tears dropped from my eyes for happiness, not because I was not hurt by sharpnels but I am happy because I could imagined now that my children and my people shall share again the liberty and freedom in which shall be their happiness in their life after.

I thank God for this, next to President F. Roosevelt, to Gen. Doug. MacArthur and to the Admiral who brought the American ships back to our islands. God bless America.

End.

January 14
2:05 p.m. — AIR RAID #27

Not much of a raid, still I'm glad I wasn't on the receiving end! Three planes came over and dropped some stuff around port area, I think. They met no resistance whatsoever. There wasn't even any AA fire. If the boys aren't meeting much resistance here I doubt if the Lingayen theater is giving them much trouble. As soon as the planes disappear nowadays, the Bilibid bell dings once, thereby releasing us from being continually cooped up in the buildings.

Water pressure very low today. Must be using it to supply fire fighters. A big fire was seen last nite about 11 p.m. Lit up the whole sky.

Y'know, I have my radiograms to Mom and Dad and to Pete all composed and ready to go. Just waiting for the chance!

Had some more muffins baked up today. Galley got in sixty kilos meat and bones and fifteen kilos of greens yesterday. We'll have 'em today. Not much for 800+ men. Still I'm thankful we're eating any thing at a time like this.

Nips came in the other nite and took out a sergeant Hansdshew for some reason. Haven't seen him since. Everyone thinks it was because he was contacting Pinos on the outside. Lots of explosions and shooting during the nite tonite. Rumors that we have taken Tarlac.

January 15th
So far can't record an "Air Raid" for today. The Bilibid bell rang the alarm this morning and two P38s flew over Manila. Later a few more planes flew over but no bombs were dropped that I could hear. Sooo — without bombs, I can't say "Air Raid."

January 16
News: We've landed at Bataan; taken Tarlac, and recaptured 500 POWs, which of course would be Cabanatuan. Everyone mad as hell here because Cabanatuan retaking first. Now our hope is that they don't send them home before us! Vanity, glory-seekers? After all this hell, damned right!

5:00 p.m. — Planes been on the outskirts of Manila most of the day, doing some heavy-duty work. Also, from very early this morning we've been hearing distant "booms." Sounds very much like artillery fire. People now making bets that the Yanks will be here Sunday! That's too soon, even for me. I still say February 1st.

Swapped 1½ cups rice for a can salmon today; so John and I finished up the last of our rice in a blaze of glory — rice and salmon! Man, it was *good*!! Seems like the Nips are loosening up with chow. More rice than usual came in, also some say — bean mixture in bags.

January 17

No actual bombing in immediate vicinity of Manila. However, the bell rang the alarm when a flight of our planes went over. Had teeth checked and cleaned. No cavities. Damned good record for my teeth thru out this period of hell. Spent day alphabetizing list of articles lost, for gov't claim. Some more gunfire (small arms) last nite. Tonite, lots of MGs. Japs here raise squawk about our recent lack of "military courtesy" to them (bowing or saluting). This to be corrected.

January 18

May get my glasses today. Been going to Mass and Rosary every day last four days. Having Novena to Holy Mother — prayer of Thanksgiving.

Did not get glasses, damnit!

Friday, January 19

Can't call this an "Air Raid" day as yet but at 9:00 a.m. we began hearing things south east of here, and it kept up for ½ hour. Could hear strafing and bombing. The bombs sounded very heavy — actually, I believe I *felt* these more than I heard. Seemed as though something kept fluttering against my eardrums! We'll probably hear more of it from that direction today. Our gang may be working from that direction, or may be planning a landing down South. Night by night my thoughts and dreams of the U.S. grow warmer. I think of that hospital room, with a radio, box of candy, sandwiches, books, magazines,

newspapers, Mom, Dad and Eileen. To begin with that's as close to heaven as I'll ask for, to begin with.

Mom — I've been trying for three days to think of the name of a favorite cookie of Dad's and mine too — and I used to buy so many of them. Remember these: a vanilla wafer for filling, and coating of chocolate and a walnut on top? WHAT *ARE* THEY CALLED? What I wouldn't give for a dozen of them and a quart of chocolate milk.

A number of planes have flown over today, but no AA fire *at all*. Did some bombing and strafing but far off — possibly the bridges.

Should record this — in last eight days there have been nine deaths here. Just what these causes have been, I don't know. Starvation, however, was a possible prime cause, I'm sure. A number of diarrhea cases have arisen in the ward. About six. Plasma being freely administered. Also, one case of dysentery developed in camp yesterday.

Something up!! Nips asking for lists of "well" patients, "amputation" cases and some list of medical officers. Can they possibly be planning on trying to move some more of us to Japan? God forbid!! If you Yanks *are* on Luzon, for God's sake get a move on and come to Manila!

Another lad died today: total now is ten in nine days. All died from dysentery, and all came in from McKinley.

January 20

For Manila this has been a cold, damp, day. Felt like I was freezing at mass this morning!! Wore a T-shirt and khaki shirt almost all day — very, very, unusual for me. The day has been very quiet, too. Some planes were heard, and about 4:15 p.m. we began hearing some strafing and what sounded like artillery fire, north of here, and south! God, how anxious we are for our troops to come marching in! That first issue of emergency rations and first rolling kitchen are going to be mighty popular events!!!

Announcement out from HQ today — "Mild bacillary dysentery epidemic in camp. Soap mess-gear; wash hands with soap and water before eating; be careful about food." Hope it doesn't strike at John and me.

I *swear* that's artillery fire! It's beginning to sound like a steadier rumble than usual. Hope it's closer by morning.

Why are rumors *always* whispered from one to another? Whispered or not they (the "news") always get spread! Here are some "Authentic"

RUMORS:
1. The U.S. landed a force of 300,000 at Lingayen. One part headed for Cabanatuan, the rest coming toward us.
2. U.S. also landed at Olongapo!!!

Sunday, January 21

Here are some names I am copying from the official of "Dead and Missing" from the sunk draft ships. Who's dead and who's missing, I don't know. These are all men I know! Those with a "✓" are friends, those with "x" are good friends.

Lt. Colonels

Marron
McKeever
Nelson x
Phipps
Powell ✓
Tally

Majors

Bickerton ✓
Carruthers ✓
Filizof
Jones, Sam x
Mandelson x
Moffitt x
Pahl x
Powell
Stensland ✓
Utke x
Weil ✓

Captains

Goldstine ✓
Myers x

C.W.O.

McMillan ✓

W.O.

Mayberry (PhM.) ✓
Dr. Nelson (USN) x
Bruun x

Staff Sgt.

Cohernour x

Cpl.

Biddons

Pvt.

Kuskie

Rumor out now that the second ship was sunk near Formosa and all hands perished! I pray not. All those whom I could call my friends were aboard; McNair, Martin, Thayer, Jordan, Fast, Garcia and others.

"News" — the convoy that landed on Luzon had 3,300 ships, largest in history. Krueger in command of largest motorized force ever. Large flight of B24s over today, more than thirty-six. We could hear their bombs drop in the distance. A number of explosions have been heard this afternoon. Sounded like dynamite. Probably blowing up bridges or supplies.

Wrote out a commendation for Payne.

A number of very loud explosions tonite.

Monday, January 22
Rather a quiet day. Some planes were around in the offing — heard them drop some bombs. Supposedly "reliable" news: force of 75,000 landed on the 17th down south of us, around Mabini. Three Nip guards came in yesterday. Supposedly they are "evacuees" of Cabanatuan, because the Yanks took over and they didn't want to be caught! Chow is a little better. Some onions coming into kitchen, makes the soup palatable. Kitchen does poor job of cleaning rice and greens, however. Chow full of rocks and dirt. Navy did a much better job.

January 23
9:40 a.m. — AIR RAID #28. A flight of planes came over and dropped their load in the near vicinity of Manila, probably air fields. Hence, I call it an "Air Raid" day. Afternoon brought unusual amount of rain. Chow very poor today. Watery corn meal mush for morning and afternoon. Soup was straight camote tops; something I can't stand the taste of. Swapped it all for three cigs. Boy, it'll be great to get back to a hot shower! Do you realize I haven't had a hot shower in over three years??!! And back to bread and butter and milk! It's all like awaiting the realization of a fairy tale — a fairy tale written in blood and hatred. It's rather difficult these days to fully appreciate that freedom and good food are just around the bend in the road. Perhaps fifty miles or less? Life goes on, such as it is in here — the talk is the same as are the hopes, gripes, fears, plans, and poor food. Yet I kneel thankfully before my maker for His goodness. For if I hadn't been shot, I would possibly not be alive today, or I'd have been in Japan or drowned on the way there.

After Rosary, stopped over to see Payne, as I usually do at nite. Had coffee and a general bull session.

January 24
Our planes were around early today, about 8:30 a.m., on the outskirts. Strafing and bombing. Also distinguishing sound of AA.

NEWS — We're eight miles north of Stotsenburg. We shelled Infanta.

Stayed awake half the nite last nite because I just couldn't get my mind off food. Most persistent vision was hot cakes, bacon and syrup!! More than anything, however, my mouth waters for meat, potatoes, bread, coffee, sugar, milk, pie, and cake. It begins to look however that I may have to wait till sometime in February to get any of these things, unless the Yanks really get a move-on. These are torturous days, indeed. So near and yet so far! Never before have I felt the full impact of that saying. We know the Yanks are coming as rapidly as they can, but each day drags slowly by and all we see is our planes! We now take the sight of *our* planes for granted but we the starving, nervously and impatiently await that all important military outfit — the *infantry* and *rolling kitchens*!

12:40 p.m. — AIR RAID #29. Ha! Here's some of the big boys over and giving some part of Manila a bit of a going over. Anti-aircraft guns active today, too. Major Wilson seems to be overstepping his authority. He placed five men on half-rations for three days for eating rice that the Japanese gave out under the heading of "garbage."

He can punish in any way, but I don't believe he has the right to deprive a man of his rations or part of it. Especially here.

Latest report — Quite a tank battle at Calumpit. Our tanks now out and dive bombers take care of rest.

Thursday, January 25
Nothing today except a few planes in outskirts. Novena begins today. Prayers for "immediate liberation."

January 26
Rations supposed to go to 176 grams of grain per day per man. Mostly corn meal coming in now. At same time, a large load of rice, corn and soy beans came in today. Supposedly a 28 day supply. If this is so, we still don't know on what basis it will be put out. Made check out to Payne for $100 dated Dec. 24, 1944. Was to give him this for Xmas but forgot it!! He has done many things to make my life here more comfortable, and I feel that the $100 is well spent. (Must not forget to deposit $300 in checking account at First National Bank of Chicago!!)

January 27
9:00 a.m. AIR RAID #30!! Don't know how many planes were over, but all hell broke loose here for about ten minutes, abruptly followed by quiet. Artillery heard last nite as well as some *big* explosions.

REMEMBER: Last nite — Āwă coming, and I try deal watch off for Harrison (*Dupa!*). Āwǎ takes watch to show friends. Returns at midnite w/ watch, sets down on bunk, gives out cigarettes and asks me to write him "pass." (A letter of recommendation in case he's captured! This I do.) He says he's going to desert — change into Filipino clothes and shove off. He and 8 other Taiwanese. They hate the Japs. Said Japs have badly mistreated Taiwanese in Davao. Said, "Americans come soon. Now they eat many carabao, cassava, camotes, etc. Have chow very swell. If I go mountains — no chow. If I stay here, 'patai' (killed).[133] If I go fight, *patai*! No good! Poom Poom no like! Americans kill, hurt many Japanese. Many, many Americans in Luzon! MacArthur speak on radio (I missed what he was supposed to have said). Manila, chow very high! One camp, Manila, 600 Taiwanese. Many, many Japanese, but go fight. Many *patai*. You writing pass for me, OK?"

Roughly that's part of what he said. Some sense can be gained from it. Most interesting to me is the is the desertion part and the rift between the Ts and Js. I tried to tell him to stay here, that he'd be safe and that I'd put in word for him. He said, "Ah, but you go home, then all same, I *patai*!" So, I wrote a "To whom it may concern," saying he had helped me with food, sugar and tobacco. That he was non-combatant and didn't

want to fight. That I'd never seen him abuse a U.S. POW in any way, that he had kept all promises made, that he might be of value to our forces. This I signed and pray now that I get in no trouble over it. He said the J'se had badly beaten up his two brothers in Davao and his family is suffering a great deal. So you see, each side suffers like things. At 2:00 a.m. he brought me a big plate of rice with pork and egg plant mixed in. John and I split it. Was damned good. Gave me more cigarettes too, and tomorrow he *may* get me some salt and sugar. (If he doesn't shove off!!!). Result — I got no sleep last nite.

Ration cut in effect today. Very noticeable difference. Only 600 grams of cooked, watery corn meal as against previous 800 grams.

9:30 a.m. — I hear another flight of planes. Artillery flacks visible last nite and from reports between flack and explosions, we estimate about 8 to 10 miles. One BIG GUN fires at same intervals around here. After given explosion, takes one minute and forty-five seconds to hear shell. Chow is very small. Lousy greens. Soup.

Sunday, January 28
Oh, this food cut is terrible! The ration of watery cornmeal mush this morning amounted to about three-fourths of a canteen cup! That must carry us till 3:30 p.m.!! If the damned Yanks don't speed things up, we'll be having a number of deaths from starvation

---

133 Hinkle wrote "*patai*," but there is no such word in Japanese. He likely meant *takai*, which in English means "next world" or "other world." "*Ta*" = "other" and "*kai*" = "world."

I'm sure. I'm saving my "breakfast" till later. I can endure the hunger pangs better to about 10 or 11 a.m. than I can endure the period between 8 a.m. and 3:30 p.m. in spite of eating the few spoons of corn meal.

While I was at Rosary last nite, Āwǎ brought over about two kilos of salt for me. That's a help — we're out of salt — but hope he *also* manages to get me some beans or sugar or rice. Anything to eat!

My optimism is now on the skids. Looks like MacArthur is in no great hurry to get to Manila, in spite of his radio speech of "being able to come in at will!" What the hell is he waiting for? "Will" is here so c'mon in! Things are probably all SNAFU. In short, I wouldn't be surprised if it took them another month or two to get here!! Guess I just feel down today, but it's pretty hard to keep dragging the old chin up, in the face of this chow. Suffering and starvation — how well I know now the full meaning of those words!

8:45 a.m. — AIR RAID #31!!! Several short raids all morning. Āwǎ sent for me and said every day now, 3x a day, I should go to building #18 and the Nip cook would give me rice (cooked) and anything else he had. At noon today, I went. Boy! Got a bucket full of rice and burnt rice, and inside was a fried concoction of vegetables and meat and two sort of "pigs-in-blanket" affairs. Pork, and the dough was sweet.

God! It was good! Did we enjoy it!! Going in half-hour to see if I can get more tonite.

Didn't score tonite, damnit! Weighed: 125 pounds. 5.5 pound loss in 25 days.

January 29
I'm having to miss Rosary and Mass because of my seeking food from the J's at just those hours. I pray the good Lord will forgive me — John needs *any* food I can get him, and I can sure use it too. But the Japs didn't bring out any chow for me this morning either. At noon I went back resolved that if nothing came out of it, I'd quit and give up. At 12:15 p.m. out came burnt rice and two *chicken patties*! Chopped chicken, seasoned, rolled in thick batter, fried in deep fat! Boy, it was good. I bet I could have eaten ten of them. John enjoyed his too. Hence I shall try again tonite. At any rate, it looks like he'll show up each noon, *which will help a lot.*

The American guard near the place Nip brings me the chow beat me out of the chow that was dedicated for me. Nip came down purposely to tell him to give me so much out of the bucket. The Nips left just as I got there and this dude said the Nip had merely said to take it to the diet kitchen.

Patient died today.

January 30
Got a full bucket of burnt rice at noon after much arguing with above Ameri-

can guard. Said, "There's lots of fellows hollering about you, an officer, getting this stuff and they're not." "So what?" I replied. etc. etc.!! It is a heluva feeling I get, getting the chow with a score or more of bugging eyes watching me — but there I am getting it not just for *me*, but for *John,* and today I lit on a way to help George Roper who is skin and bones, 92 lbs!!! Doctors not giving him plasma, milk, or special diet. Others better off than George, because George won't holler and moan like the rest of the men. He says, "I'm damned if I'll knuckle down to any of these no good sons-of-bitches!" And he's right — that's just what they are. Anyway, George is slowly starving. He can't eat anything hard 'cause he lost his fake teeth during the POW siege. I gave him my chow tonite (lugao w/ chipped cassava and soy beans) and I ate my fill of burnt rice. If I could do this just a couple of times a week for "Gramps," it may keep him from "going west." But Lord — I sure go thru the miseries of hell when I go out to that gate to get the damned rice!

January 31

Some air activity; bombs in distance, confirmation of explosions.

"Straight Dope" — we're this side of San Fernando (Pampanga), and only 25 air miles away. We landed on Bataan. Heavily bombing Cavite.

Didn't get anything from Nip kitchen today. My man Friday was off duty. Made arrangements to get it at noon only henceforth, because there are fewer men "watching me" at that time.

February 1st

A number of planes around Manila today. Heard bombs in distance and some artillery. Could hear artillery last nite. Big fire northeast of here. Thick, rolling black smoke, like an oil fire. Keep hearing explosions. May be oil drums going off.

Got my bucket full of burnt rice today, OK. Swung a deal for Commander Harrison which gained us a cup of beans. John also got a kilo of beans for 20 pesos, so we eat for a few days.

Each hall now has "mess representative" to be present in kitchen all day and watch preparation and weighing out of chow. Has no authority, however, cannot investigate, but must go to mess officer who of course can "head" him off. Hell, the leak of chow from the kitchen will continue, and nothing can stop it. Ration this morning was very small and watery, and yet we have a good supply of corn, cassava, soy beans, and some rice. True, it's on a ration basis but it surely would be better handled than it's now. *Every* man working in the kitchen is fat and the staff has been gaining.

February 2nd

Many things came my way today (should say our way). My Nip brought out a bucket with burnt rice, and under the pieces of rice was a pillow case with about five to seven kilos of cooked rice!! Man, what a surprise! Had given the pillow case for the burnt rice to be put in, and he misunderstood, I guess, and just put the *rice* in!! OK by me! John'll have a good birthday tomorrow.

More of this later → Cmdr. Harrison is going to cook up a pot of beans and he has a can of Class "C" ration (hash) which will be put in to beans. He also has the coffee. I'll cook the rice and am also going to have Jim Owens bake us some more muffins.

Āwă said tonite, "maybe go soon." He gave me two packs of cigs, some matches, and a flint. I have lighter: now have flint, gotta dig up fluid!!

About 11:15 p.m., it really sounded like a war!! Whether it was artillery, bombs or what, I don't know: but it was *close* and made everyone feel good.

Novena completed. I've done pretty good; missed only two rosaries and one or two masses. These were when I was in quest for food, and Father Talbot has forgiven this.

Saturday, February 3rd
John's Birthday (29). People expecting Yanks any time now! You can get bets on anything from 24 to 96 hours. I took one on ten days (Feb 12), with Lutich for 5 lbs. candy. Hope and pray I *lose*!

Boy! Did we have a good feed at 1:00 p.m. — John's birthday feast. My steamed rice turned out better than ever, in fact perfect; the Commander did an excellent job on the beans with beef and vegetable hash (can of "Class C"), the coffee with milk (John's back on milk!) was excellent, and the muffins were swell! Each of us had a fully-packed mess-kit of rice, and brimming also of beans, three muffins, and two cups of coffee. Full? I hope to whistle! It was delicious to taste and went down the hatch quite easily. Payne brought Johnny a pack of cigarettes. The Cmdr. gave him a chain for his locket. I had nothing to give him except my services and friendship. A group came over to his bunk just as were getting ready to eat, and sang "Happy Birthday," loudly and lustily, causing Johnny to blush a beautiful deep red!! As a result of our excellent meal at 1 o'clock, I gave Roper all my issue soup and half my grain ration.

I haven't downed my grain ration yet (4:30 p.m.), don't know if I'll ever eat it!! If not, it too will go to Roper. Didn't get anything from Nip kitchen today.

Planes have been around all day in small groups. Many explosions coming at irregular intervals. Reports are that the Nips are blowing up public buildings in Manila. Can't hardly credit that.

Lt. Baumgardner supposed to have spoken over radio from Cabanatuan. The landing down South is straight, they say. ANY DAY NOW!

February 3rd: Evening and All Nite!!
Went to Rosary night after 6 p.m.
About twenty minutes after six, I
heard some random MG fire. By 6:30
there were rifle shots, too. At 6:45 I
was over at #6 talking with Payne and
Horn and drinking coffee. A minia-
ture hell broke loose in near vicinity,
all around fire: ricochets could be
heard plainly. I decided to get back
to my ward, and just as I got near, a
bullet whistled over the walk and the
hair on the nape of my neck stood on
end! Everyone was becoming excited,
for the action seemed to be increasing. Commander Harrison, John and
I sat down to coffee and some more
of those muffins, and about that time,
you could hear what I believe were
tanks. MGs were blasting away (.50
ca.) as were .30s, mortars and other
small arms. Some heavy artillery and
explosions added to the terrific fire.
I was getting a slight nervous feeling
and was "gulping" my coffee and muffins! Every now and then, a few rifle
shots sounded like they were being
fired from in the compound, which
worries me more than anything. The
guards made a skirmish line in the
compound, part of it being in front
of our building, rifles pointed to gate.
Dr. Bruce strongly advised, almost
ordered that we place our mattresses
on the floor for our own protection.
They moved Johnny on to the floor,
and I followed! Had a helluva time
rigging up my mosquito net, but
finally got more or less settled. Was
getting more and more jittery, too.
Well — for ten minutes the war

would be in full swing — my God
what a racket!! Then there'd be a
dead silence, and I mean *dead*!! It'd
be so quiet that the silence seemed
to weigh heavily on the shoulders.
About the time I'd heave a sigh and
begin to try to sleep — WHAM,
BAM, BOOM, RAT-TAT-TAT-TAT,
KER-WHOOM!!!! Off we'd go again!
I kept singing "Happy Birthday"
to John! Ricochets kept whistling
madly about and I was keeping up
a pretty constant prayer! The ward
was well under control, and quiet
and the talk ranged from, "Here they
are, boys!" to "What a helluva time
to come in. Why don't they wait till
daylite?!" Electricity went out about
midnite. The nite was hot, but clear.
Fires began in various parts of the
city — lit up the whole sky. Flares
kept going up and providing light. At
first, all the action was right around
the neighborhood of Bilibid. Then,
later in the nite, we could hear it
in other and more distant parts of
Manila. Many places blew up. Thus
passed an unforgettable nite; the beginning of our liberation. If it's going
to be such a noisy affair, our rescue
and liberation may cause us some
unpleasant moments! God grant
none of us be harmed in any way. I
fully expect to see the Yanks in here
by early morning.

Sunday, February 4th
Damn me if we didn't have *tenko*
this morning!! I figured we were
done with that! No Yanks, either.
Hirota on guard duty today. Said that

was guerrilla activity last nite, that the Americans will come in tonite, tomorrow or next day. Japanese from here supposed to leave tonite. Desultory firing this morning. Some bombs, explosions, and MGs. One patrol observation plane came over low (I saw it) and circled Bilibid several times. Kitchen put out big ration of lugao (getting optimistic!). Hirota after civilian clothes. Says he wants to escape. Plans to stay in guardhouse tower tonite when Nips leave.

A FREE MAN!
February 4th, Noon
At last, no longer officially a POW. Below is the official bulletin:

The Bilibid Hospital
Manila, P.I.
February 3, 1945

General Orders No. 1
1. This compound is now under military law, and the undersigned hereby assumes command. No one without exception, will be allowed in or out of this compound, nor will the civilians in the outer compound be permitted in here temporarily. American guards are posted in the compound and at the gates and their orders are to be obeyed.
2. This situation should exist but a few hours when it is anticipated that the American forces will be here, and this hospital will be turned over to the surgeon of the expeditionary force.
3. The following message has been received from the Japanese:
#1. The Japanese Army is now going to release all of the prisoners of war and internees here of its own accord.
#2. We are assigned to another duty and shall be here no more.

#3. You are at liberty to act and live as free persons but you must be aware of probable danger if you go out.
#4. We shall leave here foodstuffs, medicines and other necessities of which you may avail yourselves for the time being.
#5. We have arranged to put up signboard at the front gate, bearing the following contexts "Lawfully released POW and internees are quartered here. Please do not molest them unless they make positive resistance."

Warren A. Wilson
Major Medical Corps, Commanding.

Yes, We are emancipated! But on paper only, so far. Don't feel excited though. Just can't seem to realize the fact that as there are no more Nips here to tell us where, what and how. Can't picture the fact that possibly within the week I'll be able to contact Mom, Dad and Eileen, and the prospect of going home, maybe in a week or two, seems beyond the realm of reason!

First thing that happened today, after the Nips left, was the beginning of three meals! The ration has been huge today, and besides, the Commander, John, and I had an aftermath of yesterday, with more steamed rice and mungo beans!! This afternoon an Army (U.S.) observation plane (same "parasol" plane of a.m.) came over and flew VERY low over Bilibid. We were happily and excitedly waving to him, and he returned the salute. I could see that beautiful white star on the blue background, and as the plane slowly "put-putted" over, I felt chills up and down my spine! Several American flags have shown up in the compound. Good to see.

People, including myself, did some packing up of stuff today, at least straightening up of gear, so can move when ordered. Gee! It's slowly sinking in — I'm practically *on my way home*!! YIPPEEE!!!!!!

Monday, February 5

Firing all nite. MG, rifle and mortars. Mass this morning said by Father Heindel of the "Liberating Forces." All the men look very worn and tired. They've marched on foot all the way from Lingayen, 15–20 miles a day. Bridges all blown out. All are tired, but look good. Very interested in new .30 cal. carbine and new helmets. The boys have been passing out cigarettes all morning. Also got two pieces candy and a bullion packet. Almost all from Ohio 148 Regt., 37th Div. Been fighting for three years, no leave.

At 11:00 a.m. Brig. Gen. Charles Craig came into the ward and said (approx. quote).

> Gentlemen, We're honored to be here with you. Food and medical supplies will be here in two hours. The U.S. Gov't is proud of you, all of you, for the great stand you made here. You have first priority on any and everything! Your families have been taken care of by the gov't. Your back pay will be waiting for you. We evacuated some prisoners of war at some other smaller islands, and they went to Washington. Anything they wanted was theirs; automobiles, free rations, and the gov't paid for transportation of their families to Washington for the reunion of POWs and their families. A complete list of POWs has been sent back to the States during the nite. For the present we are not going to move you. The conditions here are better for you than Lingayen. Be patient for a day or two and we will all be happy to join in reunion with you. General MacArthur will be here in a day or two, maybe this afternoon. His staff is holding him back because of the sniper fire. He wants you to know that your wants are his prime concern. He will wish to speak to you personally and will do so as soon as he comes in. You all look kind of thin — so *don't overeat when the chow gets here*!

BOY, AIN'T THAT SUMPIN'?!!!

Sniper fire all morning. Some Nips up in the buildings. One man got shot in leg here in compound. Bullet whistled right by me while I was outside, and I came inside, pronto. This is not time to cash in my chips!!!

Bless Bless, I think I'll be on my way home in a week or less! And the U.S. at our feet! God! Life is suddenly becoming a ray of beautiful light. My brain keeps singing, "Mom, Dad, Eileen." Hell I'm so excited and impatient I can't write straight! Our luck is at long last changing. God grant we safely pull thru this foray, and get home to enjoy the fruits. There's war still going on outside these walls, and damned close. In fact, too close. Mortar shells and MG raising hell. Damn Nips fight to last man I guess. Well, that last man is not far off, I hope.

Yessir the month of February will be my 2nd Thanksgiving, and it's the month of your birthday, Toots. Don't think I've forgotten it either. JESUS! A mortar shell just exploded outside the wall and *really* exploded! A helluva fire has been started just beyond the walls. Looks pretty close.

6:00 p.m. — Went over for Rosary, but just then all hell broke loose just over the walls; MG fire and carbines. Jim and I headed back for the ward. The fire was gaining in intensity and nearness: just across the street from outer compound. Engineers blasting with dynamite, trying to control it. Plenty difficult to try to fight a war, keep under cover and fight a fire too!

8:00 p.m. — Fire raging madly! Looks like our compound is endangered. Plans to evacuate #18, #1 and #2 are made. I hear #18 will be hit first if wind blows it our way. Wind strong tonite and shifty. Lightning but no rain. Sky lit up a brilliant red like a busy nite at Gary![134] Can feel the heat of the fire inside our place. Am getting a bit worried!

About 9:00 p.m. — Everyone ordered to get ready to evacuate within five minutes; "Litter cases (John) to go to #13, those who can't walk go to side gate (us). Take one handbag; take as little as possible, but hurry up, we're leaving Bilibid!!" I was all stressed

and in bed. I came out of the net like a young cyclone, and began dressing: long pants, long sleeved shirt, peg-leg. Helped get John straightened out. Began throwing stuff into musette bag, by dim candle-light. First made sure to load all of diary. Then some excellent canned rations that Lt. Milton Peterson gave me earlier in day. He used to be in 31st, left P.I. Oct. '41, now back with 148th Infantry. Got cigs, canned ham and eggs, pork sausage meat, sugar, salt from him. Wonderful treat! Threw in T-shirt, sox, khaki shirt, towel, address & autograph books, wallet, other toilet articles. Grabbed brief case; threw Khaki shorts and some odds and ends in there. Put musette on my back, grabbed crutches in one hand, brief case in other, sun helmet, took a look at the mess on and around bunk, leaving books, sheets, net, cups, cans mungo beans (forgot the "muffins"!), and with Jim Daly and Charley Wyatt, started for the gate. Sky a fiery red and fire seemed just outside Bilibid compound. Demolitions still at work. Frantic stir of excitement and a babble of chatter. All happy as hell about leaving Bilibid, but where'll we go? Stopped at Paynes, stuck service record and diary of his in my brief case. Thru dark building, guided by soldiers with flashlights out on to street where convoy of "Jeeps," well organized, was waiting with engines running. We piled into Jeep #4, Corporal Braves of Chillicothe, Ohio driving. First off he gives us a carton of Camels and fourteen packs of Luckies. Didn't know our destination

---

134 Gary, Indiana, which is located at the southern tip of Lake Michigan and southeast of Chicago, was home to many steel mills during the war.

but said trip would be safe — Nips all out of this area. At 9:30 p.m. convoy shoved off — just three of us and driver in #4. I had driver's guard rifle gripped, ready for trouble. Through Manila we drove, with blackout lites on. Pinos alongside curb cheering and clapping, shouting "Victory" and "*Mabuhay*."[135] Quite a thrill to be in a U.S. convoy and actually *out* of prison and heading for *freedom*! Was amazed at all the U.S. trucks, jeeps and various equipment we passed on the way. Driving lites were put on as we got further away. The extent of the fire area became visible — quite a spread; bright as daylite. Surprising just how calm I felt — driving along and smoking a Lucky and talking of the future. We wound up near Grace Park (Caloocan) at a former shoe factory. Graves gave us about ten cans of rations when we left the Jeep! Inside building some cots already set up. I got one luckily. Everyone greeted us gayly. No sooner got here than I had a snort of whisky and some beer!! Everything operating very efficiently. Preparations for breakfast underway. Civilians from Bilibid arrived here too! Total is 810 POWs, 450 Internees (1,260). Santo Tomas apparently not evacuated, or if so, not coming here.

Tuesday, Feb 6
Can't sleep. Now 5:00 a.m. We're to go to Tarlac or Clark Field from here. When, I don't know, but it's good to be free. Am so sleepy, can hardly see

words I write, as shown by type of writing! Everyone happy and looking forward to breakfast. Can smell bacon frying. That *does smell scrumptious!* Sent ten word message home today. Talked to Pino who has been killing Nips right and left. Told of cutting off a Nips ear and making him eat it, then killing him! He's to bring me a Nip pistol and watch and pen today. We'll see. I quit now.

Now getting good chow; "dry" and "wet" boxes of rations, in 2-box-units. For five men for one day, three meals. Includes 2 lbs. pork sausage meat, cans of tomatoes & ham and eggs, biscuits, cigs, matches, butter, candy, gum, beverage (lemon), cocoa, coffee, milk, jam, salt hand towels, toilet paper, water purification tablets. Tastes delicious, but Lord, it sure gives me a terrible amount of gas! Spent morning talking to various men and officers of fighting forces.

What the hell? We go back to Bilibid this afternoon! Conditions (sanitary) here are no good, and these front line troops are hard pressed for taking care of us and fighting *too*. Fire near Bilibid out, Japs under control there.

Back to Bilibid in late afternoon. Everyone angry. John and a few officers taken to Santo Tomas. Miss him. Part of our stuff here looted. Ward looks like dump. Water impure. Artillery duel on, no lites. All our old gear all ripped up. Helluva nite! Not much sleep — bed bugs, artillery and mos-

135 A Filipino greeting with various meanings, including "Long live," "May you live," and "Hurrah!"

quitoes. What's coming off here! How long do we remain here?

Wednesday, February 7
Those rations sure make good chow! General MacArthur and General Krueger here. Willoughby, General Moore came thru the ward this morning saying "hello" and stuff. Payne said he heard "Mac" state that we were to be flown down to Leyte. When, I don't know. There is a rumor that we're to go to Fort Stotsenburg.

I'm trying and hoping to get to Santo Tomas to see Miss Ernst, the nurses, Doc Waters, Bob Cecil and Johnnie. It's only about 1½ kilometers from here, but at the moment, there still seem to be some Nip snipers about and we can't go. Major Wilson said he'd let us know. Also said that when he was over there all the nurses mobbed him with questions about me! Why, my popularity overwhelms me!!! Hope I do get over. Lot of booming going on yet. Big fire seems short way off. Mortars firing away. Southern force to meet the 148th Inf. on Pasig [River] today. Met Polish lad yesterday, with incoming force. From Chicago, asked me to see (or write) his mother, tell her where and how he is. Looks good, nice chap; Pfc. Stan. F. Mazurkiewicz, 3408 So. Carpenter Street.

Just had [a conversation with] MP Zack. He was back in Chicago in November '44 for leave. Was good to talk to him. Sister will hear from me;

Miss Lorraine Zack, Bohemian 3808 W. 26th Street, Chicago.

Met a helluva nice chap today: Capt. Jack Carney, 11435 Prairie Avenue, Chicago. 572 Amph. Trac. Bn. He was glad as I was to see someone from Chicago. Lots of swapping of stories. I like him right off. Will keep in contact with him.

February 8
Another very rainy nite: lots of heavy artillery. Shells whistled over Bilibid all nite. Sounds like wailing of small siren. People chattering and worried some. Santo Tomas hit by several shells yesterday. Several Nip shells have landed outside Bilibid gate last nite and this morning. Some men from PCAU[136] killed; a number of wounded. Possibly Nip snipers with small mortars. Don't do much damage, but slow up operations and damned harassing nuisance.

PCAU took over serving chow today. Breakfast = bacon, stewed apricots, cereal, milk, sugar, coffee! Not much of it all, but good. Still trying to get to Santo Tomas. Water pressure very low. No showers. Toilets won't flush. Drinking water greatest problem, and H2O for washing gear. No news of

---

136   Thirteen Philippine Civil Affairs Units (PCAU) accompanied MacArthur's Sixth Army during the October 20 landing on Leyte (KING II). Many of the units were staffed by expatriate Filipinos from the United States. The units were responsible for assisting combat troops by caring for the civilian population. They supervised the distribution of relief supplies, reestablished schools and medical facilities, reconstituted local governments, and stimulated food production—all hastening the self-sufficiency of the people.

The billfold that Hinkle carried as a POW is filled with photos, handwritten prison check stubs, and other items. To the left is a photograph of "Toots." To the right is his treasured 1941 Pontiac Deluxe Torpedo V-Eight Metropolitan Sedan. *Hinkle Archive*

us leaving here or what's up. Met Mr. Chase of WLW, Cincinnati. Took my name and data to pass on to Don Starr of Chicago Tribune. Will tell Starr of me, maybe will get to see Starr. Chase says will be worthwhile of me to do something with my diary *soon* as get back. Tribune may want it, or Saturday Evening Post, or Colliers, etc.

Met Alberto Abinojar, PCAU, U of M student. Swell Filipino. Fixed me up with a Velvet (if only I had a good pipe!). Will bring me more. I hope. Artillery fire still going on. Our planes blissfully fly about real low. Snipers are biggest problem. Hear some Nips beginning surrender. Will surrender to U.S. but not to Pinos. George Roper and others rather shaken from the moving around we've had to do and the excitement. We're just not strong enuff. Resistance too low. U.S. troops and trucks steadily pouring into Manila. Bridges greatest problem. Nips blew them all. Thirty traffic bridges were out and engineers continually working on them. Traffic jam because

of this. More U.S. equipment in the compound than I ever knew we had. Everything new to me. Medical supplies in any quantity now available for us. Filipinos (Manila boys) all over camp. Most working for PCAU. Are very happy to be with us. Everything again is "Hello Joe!" Tell some horrible tales of what Nips have done to Pino people in past. Burned houses, took all their food, pigs, chickens; beat them up, tortured them, enslaved them. Pinos simply *itch* to get hands on Nip prisoners, and some *do* get said hands *on!*

Slightly rainy and overcast today, but cooler. Army and Navy camera men making pictures. I am in shot showing the famous Bilibid radio, built by the officers and men here of all kinds of junk, and built inside a small bench (rectangular stool). Earphone made of old Weston meter[137] and rubber tube from stethoscope. Top of stool hinged. Surface of stool cushioned. Presence of radio in stool not

---

137   Photographer's light meter.

Walter J. Hiinkle shows off his diaries in February 1945 to Pfc. Russ Simon, Buffalo, New York, a member of one of the US tank destroyer units that liberated Bilibid. The diaries were kept hidden inside a secret compartment built into Hinkle's "peg leg." Walter Hinkle's leg is now part of the permanent collection at the National Prisoner of War Museum at the Andersonville National Cemetery, Andersonville, Georgia. *National Archives photo #342-FH-3A30851- 83300ac*

discernible nor ever discovered by Nips. From this we got our "rumors." Most, almost all of camp ignorant of actual presence of this radio in our camp. This dope should *not* be released till all POWs recaptured, lest other camps suffer severe shakedown for similar contraband.

Don Starr of the Chicago Tribune came to see me, and he said the Tribune would be interested in printing [excerpts from my diary] and I would get a good rate per word. Decided to send it right off to Chicago tomorrow.[138] Hope the editors will not cuss me out too much when they try to decipher my writing! Didn't expect to have it done this way but Starr thinks it best, and this way it'll hit the press pronto.

Editor → Please let my folks know of your plans and date of first story. Mr. and Mrs. W.F. Hinkle, 8158 So. Green St. Chicago.

Jack Carney brought me some pipe tobacco, a gas stove and chocolate

---

138   The *Tribune* never published his diary.

bars. He certainly is a fine chap and I hope he pulls thru this so our friendships go on back in Chicago.

Lots of artillery last nite, Nips holed up in walled city I hear.

Got two letters from home today! Both from Chicago, dated November '44. First word since June '44. One from folks, other from Eleanor. Nice to get more than 25 words for a change, and best of all do know that they've been expecting our release. Wrote a letter home, too, explaining at last that I had my foot amputated.

Water pressure still low. Manila not yet cleaned up of Nips, but probably will be in day or so.

Friday, February 9th
Quite a bit of artillery fire last nite. Manila still in flames. Japs should be getting smoked out. Got my pieces of diary ready to give Simmons or Starr, whichever of two comes to get it. If I don't get contact from them, will at least get some written agreement.

To the editor, Chicago Tribune: A great deal of the writing in this diary will probably cause you headaches in deciphering. For this I apologize, since I had not expected to have this job shoved on to someone else's shoulders. Many sentences are just notes and I hope you'll be able to make sense out of them. Please overlook my swearing, caustic criticisms of other officers, and other personal items I have written down. I'm trusting you and your staff to pick out the "meat" from my writings, and hope you will not include anything that will be harmful to me in regards to my relations with the Army. The thing I wish to get over forcefully to the public is that the contents of my diary are *not* fictitious. Everything is *true*. Write it up so America and Chicago will *never* forget the hell her men went thru over here at the hands of the Japs.

Walter J. Hinkle
1st. Lieutenant
31st Infantry
U.S.A.

EPILOGUE

The Hinkle honeymoon. *Patricia Keiserman Archive (Eileen's cousin)*

Walter J. Hinkle and Eileen "Pete" Mathewson were married on July 30, 1945, sixteen years after they met as teenagers aboard SS *Île de France*. They honeymooned in the north woods of Minnesota around Jackfish Bay, in a cabin, with a big fireplace, furnished fairly well.

INDEX